UNSCHOOLING

Un estilo de vida lleno de aprendizaje

Sara McGrath

Traducción de Priscila Salazar

Con gratitud a
Maia, Ilana, y Kalea.
En palabras de Ilana. «Me alegro de que existan».

♡

En recuerdo cariñoso de
Trixie, Hannah, Sinopa, Kuruk, Ahote, Kaia, e Ivan
Pi-Chai «Bubba», mis otros niños.

Contenido:

Prólogo de la traductora

En 2011 leí este libro por primera vez. Mis hijos eran pequeñitos y yo me encontraba en un momento intenso de transformar viejas creencias en nuevos entendimientos. Acababa de leer varios libros de John Holt y mi mente seguía tratando de asimilar la profundidad de su filosofía. Aunque me parecía que sus ideas tenían mucho sentido, me costaba trabajo imaginarlas puestas en práctica en un hogar con niños pequeños.

Unschooling: un estilo de vida lleno de aprendizaje fue el puente que me permitió pasar de la elevación de la teoría a la sencillez de la práctica. A través de sus palabras, Sara McGrath me permitió asomarme por su ventana para ver su aplicación personal de los conceptos de John Holt a su día a día con sus tres hijas pequeñas.

Aunque ya han pasado más de diez años desde que se escribió, el contenido de estas páginas sigue siendo relevante, en especial ahora que las deficiencias del sistema educativo son más evidentes que nunca, y que cada día crece el número de padres dispuestos a asumir la responsabilidad de la educación integral de sus hijos.

Al comenzar con este proyecto me enfrenté con un dilema importante: ¿traducir la palabra *unschooling* o no?

La palabra *unschooling* es un término en inglés que se compone de dos partes: el prefijo *un* que quiere decir sin, y el sustantivo *schooling*, que quiere decir escolarización. *Unschooling* significa *sin escolarización* o *sin escuela*.

Lo que me llevó a considerar la posibilidad de traducirla fue, en primer lugar, mi resistencia a usar anglicismos cuando tenemos los vocablos equivalentes en nuestra lengua; y, en segundo lugar, la idea de aprovechar esta oportunidad para empezar a utilizar términos propios para estas modalidades.

Sin embargo, aunque es verdad que en español tenemos varias posibilidades para expresar el significado de *unschooling*, no me atreví a escoger palabras que pudieran diluir la esencia del pensamiento de Holt o que le dieran un matiz distinto a lo que él quería transmitir.

En el libro *Teach Your Own*[1], Patrick Farenga, amigo y coescritor de John Holt dice lo siguiente:

> En 1977, Holt fundó la revista *Growing Without Schooling* (Crecer sin escolarización) consolidando así su posición como el principal estratega para mostrar a la gente cómo pasar de la escolarización (*schooling*) al *unschooling*, un neologismo que creó en lugar de la palabra desescolarización que, en su opinión, «crea más confusión que comprensión». *Unschooling* no ha demostrado ser una palabra más clara, pero, como mencioné anteriormente, es un buen intento de describir el tipo de educación que Holt fomentaba: aprendizaje y enseñanza que no necesariamente suceden en el hogar. A principios de la década de 1980, el término *homeschooling* (escuela en casa) se había generalizado, e incluso Holt comenzó a usarlo indistintamente junto con *unschooling* (como lo hace a lo largo de este libro). Sin embargo, la mayoría de los educadores en casa, así como el público en general, sienten que los niños no aprenderán algo a menos que se les enseñe deliberadamente. El público en general no duda de la necesidad de educación: lo que le preocupa son los métodos y contenidos educativos y la financiación privada o pública. Aquí es donde entra la importante diferencia entre *unschooling* y *homeschooling*.

Por otro lado, desde hace varios años la palabra *unschooling* es cada vez más conocida, y, desafortunadamente, también malinterpretada.

«Hacer *unschooling*» o «ser *unschooler*» se ha vuelto sinónimo de tener licencia para desentenderse del estudio académico y para dedicarse a las ocupaciones propias prestando una atención mínima a las necesidades de los niños.

---

[1] Holt, J. & Farenga, P. (2003), *Teach Your Own*, Da Capo Lifelong Books.

Y hay padres que afirman «hacer *unschooling*» porque permiten que su niño elija qué hacer en los pequeños márgenes de tiempo que quedan entre las actividades que ellos han programado sistemáticamente.

La contracara de esta época llena de información y recursos es que también nos hemos inundado de interpretaciones subjetivas, citas sacadas de contexto y opiniones hechas a la ligera que han desvirtuado una perspectiva que originalmente no tenía esas implicaciones.

Considerando todo esto, decidí que era importante mantener la palabra en inglés para que quienes la han escuchado desliguen cualquier connotación errónea y asocien con ella su significado original.
La perspectiva de John Holt sobre la educación y el aprendizaje no tiene nada que ver con abandono o indiferencia; al contrario: es una filosofía llena de responsabilidad y confianza en el niño, y considero que Sara McGrath hizo un buen trabajo al ilustrar cómo se ve esta perspectiva puesta en acción en una familia con niños pequeños.

Hay dos aspectos de este libro que me parece importante comentar: las sugerencias para cumplir con los requisitos legales para la educación en el hogar y los recursos recomendados por la autora.

La información que la autora proporciona corresponde a la situación legal de Estados Unidos en el año 2009. Aunque ahora existe más información y más actualizada de la que contiene este libro, considero que las familias hispanohablantes que viven en EUA encontrarán consejos valiosos que pueden poner en práctica, o pautas para iniciar su propia investigación. Es importante recordar que antes de tomar cualquier decisión debemos darnos a la tarea de recabar datos rigurosos de los mecanismos específicos del país en el que vivimos. En el caso de nuestros países latinoamericanos, la situación es muy distinta a lo que la autora presenta en este libro.
En mi web puedes encontrar enlaces que te ayudarán a recopilar información actualizada y confiable: http://www.supraescolar.com/

En la versión original del libro, la autora incluyó muchas recomendaciones de los materiales y servicios que ella usaba en su momento. Al ir traduciendo me di a la tarea de revisar cada sitio web y solamente mantuve los que siguen vigentes. Si alguno de los recursos mencionados te llama la atención, búscalo en Internet. Vas a encontrar cosas muy interesantes. Es cierto que la mayoría de estas recomendaciones sólo tendrá utilidad para quienes vivan en EUA, pero lo que a mí me parece valioso no es tanto el recurso en sí mismo, sino lo mucho que podemos aprender de una actitud ingeniosa y proactiva para aprovechar y adaptar cualquier recurso a nuestro alrededor. Nuestros países latinos ofrecen acceso a una riqueza cultural inmensa. Despierta tu sensibilidad para percibir recursos donde nadie los ve, tu creatividad para aprovechar y adaptar cualquier circunstancia a las necesidades e intereses de tus hijos, y tu determinación para transformar o crear lo que sea necesario.

Por último, no olvides que el mensaje de la autora no deja de ser una apreciación personal. Considero que su análisis de los conceptos de John Holt es acertado y aportará claridad en nuestro proceso de aprender nuevas formas de criar y educar, pero no significa que sea la verdad absoluta o que debamos adoptar todo lo que ella hace. Reflexiona en sus palabras, aplica lo que consideres útil para tu familia, y continúa tomando tus propias decisiones.

A lo largo de mi vida he traducido muchos textos sobre diversos temas, pero esta es mi primera publicación completa sobre educación sin escuela. Para mí es un honor ser un medio por el que mis hermanos hispanos encuentren recursos de utilidad, y qué mejor forma de iniciar que con un libro por el que siento un cariño especial porque fue uno de los primeros peldaños en mi búsqueda y aprendizaje.
Deseo que la interpretación que he hecho de la experiencia de esta familia traiga nuevos recursos a tu proyecto familiar y un entendimiento fresco de lo que significa vivir sin escuela.

Priscila Salazar.

Introducción

Las personas que se sienten atraídas a los ideales filosóficos del *unschooling* a menudo me preguntan cómo llevarlo a cabo. Con este libro intento presentar un manual práctico para aprender sin escuela. Aunque admito que cada familia aborda el estilo de vida *unschooling* desde un punto de vista único, aquí ofrezco los detalles de la experiencia de mi familia junto con algunos consejos específicos para cumplir con los requisitos legales sin sacrificar nuestros ideales.

Decidí publicar mi libro yo misma e imprimir sólo las copias necesarias; de esta manera puedo hacer revisiones continuamente, lo cual aprovecho al máximo. Este libro actualmente existe en su cuarta encarnación más importante. Al igual que en mi vida, tengo muchas ideas que necesitan una continua re-*visión*.

Acerca del *unschooling*

Esta palabra a menudo confunde a la gente, ya que de alguna forma presenta un nombre poco apropiado. Por lo general, la palabra escolarización (*schooling*) se asocia con aprendizaje o educación, y, por consiguiente, se asume que *unschooling* significa *sin* aprendizaje o *sin* educación. Sin embargo, dejemos claro que el término *unschooling* no significa *sin* aprendizaje o *sin* educación. Simplemente describe el hecho de vivir *sin* las limitaciones de la escuela. Así que ¡imaginemos una vida de posibilidades *sin* límites!

En la ausencia de escuela, ¿qué hacen los niños? Juegan. Hacen lo que les produce gozo. Hacen lo que les atrae. Hacen lo que necesitan hacer para pasar del punto A al punto B, aprendiendo destrezas *útiles* a lo largo del camino.

Aunque *unschooling* literalmente significa «sin escolarización», esta traducción literal ofrece muy poco al querer explicar cómo es en realidad el *unschooling*, o cómo se siente vivir así. Tal vez, debido a que el término comienza con un prefijo negativo, muchas veces sus seguidores intentan definirlo a través de lo que excluye. La falta de una definición positiva contribuye a la concepción de ideas falsas acerca de la relación que existe entre los niños educados bajo esta filosofía y sus padres.

John Holt, el reformador de la escuela que se volvió partidario de la educación en el hogar y quien acuñó el término, lo hizo en oposición a la escuela (es decir: enseñanza coercitiva, premios y castigos, aprendizaje obligatorio, calificaciones, exámenes, división por materias, etc.) *Unschooling*, entonces, no se refería a ningún tipo de escolarización. Se refería a algo totalmente distinto. En los términos más simples, es quitar la escolarización de la vida y dejar todo lo demás. Suena bastante fácil, ¿verdad?

En realidad, unschooling significa mucho más que una forma de aprender a través de los sentidos, dirigida por el niño, basada en experiencias, etc. No describe una alternativa específica a la escolarización. Simplemente la quita del camino para que las formas únicas, dinámicas, personales y creativas de crecer, vivir, participar y contribuir con la comunidad, puedan desarrollarse.

Un término alternativo: *aprendizaje de la vida.*

Algunos *unschoolers*, incluyéndome a mí, preferimos usar el término «aprendices de la vida» en vez de *unschoolers*. Pero para propósitos de este libro, en gran parte he decidido usar este término original porque es mucho más común. Por otro lado, tenemos la opción de percibir el *unschooling* como posibilidades <u>sin</u> límites, lo que se siente como una celebración de la libertad.

El enfoque *unschooling* describe la manera en que aprendemos naturalmente cuando se nos deja seguir nuestros propios intereses personales. Como *unschoolers, poseemos* nuestros intereses –nuestras pasiones, sueños, metas– y también la *responsabilidad* de seguirlos y alcanzarlos. Respondemos a nuestros deseos y seguimos nuestros sueños con entusiasmo.

Como fundamento del enfoque *unschooling*, reconocemos que:
- Aprendemos todo el tiempo;
- Todo aprendizaje tiene valor; y
- Aprendemos mejor a través de nuestra propia motivación, a nuestra manera.

Las estrategias coercitivas de enseñanza pueden dañar e inhibir la curiosidad natural de un niño y su amor por aprender.

Los padres *unschoolers* confían en que sus hijos aprenderán lo que personalmente necesitan aprender. La coerción no tiene lugar en la práctica del *unschooling*. Por ejemplo, si una de mis hijas se resistiera a aprender una destreza como leer, yo no la forzaría con sobornos, amenazas u otras formas de coerción... lo cual no significa que no le ayudaré activamente a aprender a leer, sino que permaneceré dispuesta, disponible y alerta a lo que pueda estar provocando su resistencia.

Existe un sinnúmero de formas en las que los padres *unschoolers* pueden ayudar a que sus hijos aprendan, como introducir temas nuevos, compartir con y ayudar a los niños a buscar el conocimiento, iniciar y participar en actividades educativas, y proveer dirección e instrucción.

Los padres *unschoolers* tienen las mismas esperanzas y preocupaciones por sus hijos que cualquier otro padre. Las diferencias entre el *unschooling* y otros enfoques más convencionales para la educación en casa y crianza de los hijos radican en la filosofía más que en la práctica.

A simple vista, las actividades de una familia *unschooler* pueden parecerse o no a las de una familia educadora en casa más convencional. No obstante, lo más probable es que ambas se *sientan* diferente.

13

La vida *unschooling* se siente llena de alegría. Una vida automotivada, dirigida por la pasión y el propósito produce el sentimiento intrínseco de congruencia.

El estilo de vida *unschooling* nos lleva a cuestionar los verdaderos, sinceros y mejores intereses de nuestros hijos y de nosotros mismos, y a abrazar nuestra legítima naturaleza buscadora de alegría.

El estilo de vida *unschooling* nos anima a mantener una actitud respetuosa y consciente en nuestra interacción con otros y en todo lo que hacemos.

En el caso de mi familia, el sendero del *unschooling* nos ha guiado a establecer como prioridad la búsqueda activa de una vida satisfactoria y feliz, además de otras metas de crianza más convencionales.

«Vivir es aprender y cuando los niños están viviendo enteramente, con energía y felicidad, están aprendiendo mucho, aun cuando no siempre sepamos qué.»

– John Holt, *A Life Worth Living*, 1971.

14

Acerca de mí y de mi familia

Cuando cursaba el primer grado, mis maestros me etiquetaron como talentosa y dotada (TAG, por sus siglas en inglés). Junto con otros cuantos niños de seis años relativamente selectos, tuve que dejar mi salón normal para hacer experimentos prácticos en el salón TAG. Aunque me sentía «especial» (señalada), no entendía por qué no todos los niños de la escuela podían mezclar bicarbonato de sodio y vinagre o diseccionar almejas igual que yo. Yo no me sentía más lista que nadie. Mirando en retrospectiva, supongo que la limitación de fondos para materiales probablemente creó la necesidad de clasificar a los niños en castas académicas.

Gracias a mi perfeccionismo impulsado por la ansiedad de conservar mi elevado estatus, permanecí en los programas para niños talentosos o «de honor» durante mis años escolares. Sin embargo, resentía el tiempo que pasaba en la escuela, en el interior de un salón todo el día y bajo un estricto control. Para el primer año de bachillerato, difícilmente asistía a clases y prefería brincar en el trampolín de mi amiga, escalar rocas o andar en bicicleta en las montañas. No obstante, mantuve mis notas altas esquivando a los guardias de seguridad de la escuela, siguiendo el plan de estudios y entregando tareas y asignaciones extras. Cada trimestre me reunía con el consejero estudiantil para discutir mi creciente ausentismo. Notó mis perfectas calificaciones y me dijo que ya había visto este fenómeno antes. Me recomendó abandonar el bachillerato y entrar a la universidad; así que, con tal de cambiar de ambiente y con la esperanza de recibir un trato de adulto (respetuoso), seguí su consejo. Pasé sin dificultad las pruebas de ubicación sin haberme preparado, y comencé un camino carente de dirección o de un propósito mayor que alcanzar un estatus de adulto cuando por fin pudiera simplemente vivir.

Mi esposo disfrutó la escuela. Disfrutó todo el tiempo hasta el posgrado, cuando consideró hacer una carrera como profesor de investigación. Mientras que la filosofía *unschooling* inmediatamente encajó conmigo, él necesitó más tiempo para decidir qué pensaba al respecto.

Para cuando nuestra primera hija tuvo edad escolar, después de haberla observado aprender naturalmente por años, él se decidió firmemente a favor del *unschooling*. Ninguna de nuestras tres hijas ha asistido a la escuela. En las siguientes páginas encontrarás ejemplos de su vida diaria y de sus aventuras aprendiendo.

Una entrevista con mi hija Maia

Permíteme presentar a Maia, de casi ocho años, residente de Seattle, cuya familia practica el «*unschooling* radical» (también conocido como: «aprendizaje de toda la vida»).

Nada de tareas. Muchas actividades educativas.

–Maia nunca ha ido a la escuela. Esto significa que sus casi ocho años han estado llenos de nada más que juego (videojuegos y comida chatarra), ¿cierto? Por lo que probablemente no sepa leer o sumar (sin mencionar su inevitable inadaptabilidad social por su poca interacción), ¿cierto? –le pedí su opinión al respecto.

–Hmm, en realidad, no –dijo Maia–. Soy muy amigable. Algunas veces mi instructor de baile me pide que deje de hablar tanto, porque necesito concentrarme. Nuestro recital es el próximo sábado; éste es mi tercero. En el verano voy a hacer pulseras de amistad para todas las niñas de mi clase.

Maia ha tomado clases estructuradas como baile y arte desde que tenía cinco años. También participa en clubes y eventos con dos grupos locales de niños educados en casa. Uno de los grupos es abierto, y el otro es específicamente para *unschoolers*. En casa le gusta hacer «lo que yo quiera», lo cual significa hojas de trabajo, proyectos de ciencia, manualidades y una gran cantidad de actividades explícitamente educativas. Maia comenzó a leer cuando tenía cinco años.

—Estoy leyendo el segundo libro de la serie Avalon –comenta–. Terminé el primero cuando tenía seis años.

Son libros de 200 páginas dirigidos a niños de 9 a 12 años.

—Yo leo mucho –afirma Maia–. Algunas veces leo la Civilopedia por horas, porque me interesa saber de los gobernantes, de las civilizaciones antiguas y de mitología.

Su destreza favorita son las matemáticas.

—¿Videojuegos? Sí, también. Me encantan los videojuegos y los mundos virtuales en línea –expresa–. Acabo de comenzar a jugar *Planet Orange,* un juego interactivo para aprender sobre finanzas.

Los videojuegos y sitios de Internet le aportaron a Maia la motivación más significativa para aprender a leer. Algunos días pasa varias horas en Internet. Otros días le gusta trabajar en el jardín, cavar en el lodo, y observar el mundo natural.

¿Interacciones sociales? Maia juega con sus dos hermanas todos los días, con su vecina de ocho años muchas tardes (en cuanto termine su tarea), y con su grupo de juego que se reúne a la orilla del río todos los viernes después de la clase de arte. También conoce y es cortés con el personal de la oficina de correo, del supermercado, de la biblioteca y de otros lugares a los que su familia acude rutinariamente.

Cuando sea grande, Maia quiere trabajar como «bióloga marina la primera parte del día y como paleontóloga la segunda parte del día». Se está preparando para ese trabajo desde ahora. En un ensayo escribió: «Veo documentales y leo páginas en Internet relacionadas con mis intereses, para poder estar más preparada y saber más cuando crezca».

¿Y qué hay de la universidad?

Planea obtener un título en biología marina. Pero antes de eso, tiene la mira puesta en campamentos, entrenamientos y un trabajo de voluntaria en el Acuario de Seattle.

Nada de reglas. Mucha orientación.

He conocido a Maia toda su vida, porque soy su madre. Mi relación con ella es de colaboración y de amistad. Yo no le digo qué hacer y tampoco le demando que me respete o me obedezca. Yo me esfuerzo por ser una persona a quien ella respete. Le ofrezco experiencias y le ayudo a tomar decisiones. Ella me ve como una «autoridad natural», ya que tengo décadas de experiencia que pueden ayudarle a entender las cosas y a alcanzar sus metas.

Yo comparto con Maia (y con mis otras hijas) los principios detrás de las reglas comunes para que pueda pensar con mayor profundidad acerca de la vida. Tenemos una conversación continua sobre todos los aspectos de la vida, emociones, costumbres sociales, etc.
Veo a Maia como una persona completa ahora, en vez de verla como un adulto incompleto o un adulto en entrenamiento. Sus intereses y predilecciones actuales tienen un valor y un significado ahora, más allá de cómo puedan servirle en el futuro.

Acerca de la comunicación

En una familia *unschooler*, todos «viven sin escuela». Todos, incluyendo a los padres, buscan sus propios intereses. Cada miembro de la familia tiene intereses personales que expresan los aspectos únicos y en común de sus personalidades, y cada uno de ellos influye en la dinámica del grupo familiar.

Yo tiendo a escuchar más que a hablar, aunque me siento compelida a compartir lo que nos trae gozo a mí y a mi familia.

No me gusta discutir, así que no opongo el estilo de vida *unschooling* en contra de otras opciones. Disfruto compartir con personas receptivas que se sentirían atraídas a este enfoque si tuvieran más información. Me siento afortunada de haber escuchado acerca del *unschooling* antes de que mis hijas tuvieran edad escolar y me siento agradecida con las personas que se atrevieron a hablar y a compartir sus experiencias y sabiduría.

Tengo un fuerte interés en el lenguaje y la comunicación; particularmente, en *E-Prime* (inglés Prime, una forma de hablar inglés), en la comunicación no violenta y en la comunicación compasiva en general. He usado ampliamente *E-Prime* para escribir este libro. ¿Lo notaste? Espero que no. El lenguaje influye en la percepción.

Con la intención de mejorar la claridad, la franqueza y la honestidad, el lenguaje *E-Prime* simplifica el idioma (mayormente en inglés) al omitir los verbos ser y estar y todas sus conjugaciones (*to be* en inglés).
Los verbos ser y estar muchas veces promueven la pasividad y la ambigüedad en el lenguaje, lo que puede confundir o causar malentendidos en aquellos receptores sensibles a juicios sutiles o falsedades.

«¿Existir o no existir? he ahí el dilema».
– Hamlet *traducido*.

Por ejemplo, compara lo siguiente: «El lenguaje *E-Prime* <u>es</u> mejor».
Esta misma frase en lenguaje *E-Prime*, diría: «<u>Prefiero usar</u> el lenguaje *E-Prime*».

La herramienta del lenguaje *E-Prime* nos ayuda a tomar la responsabilidad de las acciones y de las ideas, ya que claramente se le atribuye a quien lo hizo, con qué o qué pensó o sintió, etc. Este lenguaje promueve la comunicación en voz activa, honesta, clara y no sentenciosa. El lenguaje *E-Prime* requiere que el hablante piense cuidadosamente antes de poner sus pensamientos en palabras.

Aun cuando podamos saber que un hablante se comunica desde una perspectiva personal y con base en su opinión, algunas personas responden a la defensiva cuando escuchan una opinión enunciada como un hecho, insinuado por un verbo ser o estar. El lenguaje *E-Prime* ayuda a la comunicación pacífica.

Para ilustrar mi punto:

«Soy *unschooler*» se traduciría como «aprendo a través de las experiencias de la vida».
«¡El *unschooling* es genial!» se traduciría como «el *unschooling* me funciona muy bien a mí», o «disfruto mucho del *unschooling*», o «yo prefiero el *unschooling*».
«Sé tú» se traduciría como «hazlo», «relájate», «existe», «Concéntrate en tu respiración», o «disfruta el momento».

En otras palabras: piensa más a fondo en lo que realmente quieres decir.

Algunas personas no notan la diferencia entre el lenguaje usando verbos ser y estar, y el lenguaje *E-Prime*. Yo sí, y por eso lo uso.
A veces me equivoco y uso un verbo ser o estar por costumbre, pero mis esfuerzos para mejorar continúan siempre hacia adelante, aprendiendo y desaprendiendo y volviendo a aprender. Justo cuando pienso que ya llegué a mi destino de total iluminación, me encuentro con un nuevo desafío y comienzo el ciclo otra vez, lo cual mantiene la vida interesante.

Acerca del comportamiento y el temperamento

He escuchado la sugerencia de que los padres atraídos por el *unschooling* seguramente deben de tener personalidades muy tranquilas y despreocupadas. Eso me hace reflexionar. Aunque yo pueda parecer paciente o relajada en comparación con otros padres, la verdad es que mis patrones de comportamiento han evolucionado de una personalidad controladora, ansiosa y perfeccionista, a una actitud que se siente mucho mejor y que continúa volviéndose más positiva y gozosa cada día.

Durante mi maternidad temprana, rápidamente me di cuenta de que tenía dos alternativas delante de mí: podía pelear para dominar la voluntad intensa de mi pequeña hija interponiéndome en su camino coaccionando y forzando mi voluntad sobre la suya hasta que cediera, o podía ser creativa y buscar la manera de suplir las necesidades de ambas y vivir una vida juntas mucho más feliz, más amorosa y respetuosa, que es lo que en realidad yo quería.

En esos días me cuestioné mucho «la manera en que se hacen las cosas» y a partir de entonces he experimentado muchos cambios que siguen trayendo gozo y contentamiento a mi vida y a las vidas de mis hijas, los cuales, mi personalidad pasada no habría concebido posibles.

Yo no gravité hacia el *unschooling* porque tuviera una naturaleza tranquila y despreocupada, sino que me aferré a ello porque quería esa paz y calma en mi vida.

Aprendizaje Natural

Para referirse al estilo de aprendizaje *unschooling,* sus partidarios a menudo usan adjetivos para calificarlo, como: aprendizaje autodirigido o autónomo, aprendizaje conducido por el interés, aprendizaje de la vida entera (holístico), o aprendizaje natural. Mahatma Gandhi una vez dijo algo en cuanto a que «no deberíamos confundir lo habitual con lo natural». Fácilmente podemos aplicar este pensamiento a la manera en que les ayudamos a los niños a aprender.

El *unschooling* ofrece un enfoque variado y flexible para experimentar y aprender, que es anterior al establecimiento de la metodología escolar convencional. Este enfoque suele destinar métodos convencionales a usos más amigables y adoptar nuevas tecnologías.

Este capítulo comprende las siguientes secciones:
La crianza con apego y el concepto del continuum
La importancia del juego
Unschooling y anarquía
Enseñanza
Instrucción académica temprana
Estilos de aprendizaje
Estilos de acción
Estilos de educación en el hogar
Televisión, Internet, videojuegos y comida chatarra
Una secuencia de estudios sobre Australia al estilo *unschooling*

No importa el nombre que le demos, el *unschooling* describe un enfoque de convivencia con niños en el que los miembros de una familia viven y aprenden juntos en una colaboración respetuosa. Muchas familias *unschoolers* vienen de un estilo de convivencia con niños natural, responsable, que practica la crianza con apego. Algunas personas se refieren al *unschooling* como aprendizaje natural, ya que por lo general se manifiesta como un conjunto de prácticas de aprendizaje más antiguas que la invención de los métodos escolares convencionales.

Estas prácticas naturales pueden comprender prueba, observación, invención, solicitud de instrucciones, o cualquier otra actividad que naturalmente se le ocurre al aprendiz como una manera de lograr sus metas personales. Aunque el término *natural* puede no evocar la imagen de un niño utilizando tecnología moderna como computadoras o televisión, estas herramientas también pueden encajar en un estilo de aprendizaje natural.

La crianza con apego y el concepto del continuum

En general, la filosofía de la crianza con apego consta de prácticas que demuestran conciencia y sensibilidad hacia las necesidades de un niño pequeño. Esta conciencia y sensibilidad para responder dependen de un fuerte vínculo fundamental entre la madre y su bebé, seguido de otras relaciones cercanas.

El Dr. William Sears, quien acuñó el término[2], registró siete prácticas fundamentales o «herramientas de apego» para desarrollar y sostener una relación de apego entre el niño y su cuidador:

- Establecimiento de vínculo en el nacimiento
- Lactancia materna
- Porteo (cargar al bebé la mayor parte del tiempo)

- Colecho (compartir la cama con el bebé)
- Creer en el llanto del bebé como comunicación
- Práctica de la disciplina positiva
- Búsqueda del equilibrio entre las necesidades personales y las del niño

---

[2] Sears, W. (2001). *The Attachment Parenting Book*, Little, Brown Spark.

En su libro,[3] Jean Liedloff describe una forma pacífica de convivencia con niños observada durante su tiempo con una tribu indígena de Sudamérica. Propone que todos los bebés tienen la expectativa innata de recibir un cuidado confiable y sensible que incluya un tiempo de porteo, lactancia a demanda, colecho, etc.

Más adelante, propone que cuando los cuidadores ignoran constantemente a los bebés, éstos aprenden a despreciar sus propias necesidades y sentido de valía, y que los berrinches, considerados normales en las culturas occidentales, son el resultado de la confusión y la frustración de no experimentar las expectativas naturales de amor y libertad.

La importancia del juego

Todos podemos sentir la energía gozosa y abundante que habita en el juego. Jugar crea un estado alterado en el que la mente se abre a nuevas posibilidades. Los niños instintivamente brincan y mueven su cuerpo, tocan y manipulan objetos, involucran a otros en simplezas y competencias amistosas, hacen ruido e imaginan historias. Jugar puede implicar fantasía, actuación, poesía, canto, drama, arte y más. Los niños usan dichas actividades para explorar y entender el mundo, para hacer descubrimientos útiles y significativos.

Cuando los niños pequeños se involucran en actividades automotivadas, aprenden un sinnúmero de conceptos de una forma natural, informal y placentera. Por ejemplo, con poca o ninguna instrucción explícita, los muy pequeños aprenden a caminar y a hablar, a contar y a identificar símbolos, a diferenciar entre luz y oscuridad y varios colores, a observar el mundo natural y las relaciones sociales, y a sentir los efectos del movimiento, de la gravedad, etc.

---

[3] Liedloff, J. (2015). *El concepto del continuum: en busca del bienestar perdido*. Editorial OB STARE

Los padres *unschoolers* toman el juego muy en serio, y mientras que los niños permanezcan libres de un ambiente de enseñanza coercitiva, continúan aprendiendo a través del juego, de divertirse, de experimentar. La presión coercitiva basada en el temor bloquea el aprendizaje exitoso, gozoso. Puede que hayas escuchado que aprender y divertirse no van juntos o que aprender no es sólo diversión y juegos, pero los *unschoolers* desafían este precepto. Nosotros afirmamos que: el juego ofrece un formato de aprendizaje perfectamente válido, y el aprendizaje efectivo no tiene por qué provocar dificultad o desagrado. Todos necesitamos jugar.

Unschooling y anarquía

Algunas personas temen que el *unschooling* promueva la anarquía, refiriéndose a «caos, ausencia de ley y desorden». Sin embargo, al igual que el prefijo *un* de *unschooling*, el prefijo an de anarquía simplemente significa no o sin, y la palabra griega *archós* significa dirigente o gobierno. *Sin dirigente.*

Al igual que con el *unschooling*, la gente a menudo malinterpreta el concepto de anarquía.

Un verdadero líder tiene autoridad natural. La palabra anarquía describe no la ausencia de orden, sino la ausencia de norma; es decir, una autoridad coercitiva y una estricta organización jerárquica de arriba hacia abajo. La palabra anarquía describe una comunidad de sociedades cooperativas, autogobierno responsable y relaciones voluntarias y respetuosas entre líderes y seguidores. En una comunidad anarquista los líderes ganan seguidores a través de su autoridad natural: de destrezas útiles y experiencia. Por otro lado, un dirigente –un padre autoritario, por ejemplo–, usa leyes, imposiciones y castigos para crear una relación involuntaria entre dirigente y seguidor. Por lo tanto, tal dirigente no está dirigiendo en realidad.

Los padres *unschoolers* utilizan su autoridad natural de adultos con experiencia para ayudar a sus hijos a alcanzar metas personales, pero siempre están dispuestos a seguir la dirección del niño cuando sea oportuno hacerlo. De esta forma, los niños y los padres viven cooperativamente en colaboración.

De acuerdo con la filosofía anarquista, los padres tienen la *responsabilidad* de y hacia sus hijos, pero no la posesión de ellos. Por ejemplo, mi capacidad de responder al llamado de mis hijas y satisfacer sus necesidades amorosa y confiablemente, crea el fundamento sobre el que ellas maduran como gente cooperativa y libre pensadora, sin las ataduras de necesidades insatisfechas. La cooperación respetuosa se aprende al experimentarla.

La filosofía anarquista ve la educación como inseparable de la vida misma, y la disciplina como el desarrollo de la autorregulación que sólo puede venir de una vida libre de inhibiciones, de amenazas y de coerción. Los padres *unschoolers* guían a sus hijos actuando de una manera considerada, responsable y cortés.

Si alguna de mis hijas actúa de manera que la ponga en riesgo a ella o a alguien más, yo respondo protegiendo a quien necesite protección. Puedo ofrecer empatía y acercarme al niño ofensor para tener una conversación acerca del incidente y ayudarle a entender los sentimientos involucrados, pero no intentaré agregar más dolor (donde ya hay dolor) a través de un castigo arbitrario.

Enseñanza

Normalmente, los *unschoolers* evitan la palabra *enseñar* para eludir la asociación que tiene con los métodos de enseñanza coercitiva y porque muchos no creen que el fenómeno de enseñar exista. Algunos idiomas no tienen una palabra para ello. En español, la palabra *enseñar* describe un hecho realizado por un maestro a un alumno, que hace que el alumno aprenda algo.

La filosofía *unschooling* sostiene que el aprendizaje sucede dentro del aprendiz a través de sus propios esfuerzos. Por ejemplo, cada una de mis hijas aprendió a usar los utensilios para comer, a caminar y a hablar a través de un deseo natural y una compulsión de dominar esas habilidades útiles. Mis acciones pudieron haberlas ayudado a aprender, pero yo no causé el aprendizaje. Yo no enseñé.
El aprendiz emprende el aprendizaje activamente en vez de recibir pasivamente información o instrucción de un maestro. Un padre *unschooler* no enseña, pero sí ayuda a que sus hijos aprendan.

A veces utilizo la palabra *enseñar* traducción: ayudar a aprender– con un sesgo no coercitivo en su significado. Tú puedes boicotear la palabra *enseñar*, o puedes reclamarla para tus propios usos; es tu decisión. Yo he decidido rehacer la palabra con una imagen propia.

Los padres *unschoolers* respetan y celebran la variedad de formas en que los niños aprenden naturalmente. Confiamos en que los niños quieren aprender. No tienen necesidad de coerción disfrazada de ánimo, incentivo o cualquier otra motivación externa.

Los niños se rebelan naturalmente contra la enseñanza coercitiva. La coerción es una falta de respeto hacia el niño y puede dañar su confianza en sí mismo. En otras palabras, la coerción desprecia los sentimientos y las necesidades del niño. Como criaturas sociales, nunca requerimos coerción (es decir, amenazas, presión, incentivos materiales) para inspirarnos a querer encajar.

Por naturaleza queremos conectarnos y ser parte de la comunidad. Queremos contribuir y tener un papel importante. Queremos aprender destrezas útiles (como lectura, escritura, matemáticas, observación y medición, etc.), debido a que necesitamos esas herramientas para abrirnos paso por el mundo.

Mi esposo usa matemáticas avanzadas y conceptos científicos diariamente. Yo no. Si yo necesitara esas destrezas, las aprendería. Si mis hijas necesitan esas destrezas, las aprenderán. Los padres *unschoolers* confían en que sus hijos buscarán esas destrezas cuando las necesiten. Sin embargo, no necesariamente esperan a que sus hijos soliciten información o dirección específica respecto a una destreza en particular. Un padre puede ofrecer ayuda o información nueva en cualquier momento. Todos aprendemos explorando, probando cosas, haciendo preguntas, y pidiendo ayuda cuando la necesitamos.

Los padres nuevos en el *unschooling* a veces dudan de iniciar conversaciones o actividades que parezcan enseñanza. Sin embargo, la filosofía *unschooling* apoya ampliamente cualquier interacción con niños interesados y receptivos, como demostración, instrucción, etc. A simple vista, podría parecer una clase o una tarea, pero la actividad desde el *unschooling* carecerá del elemento coercitivo u obligatorio. Siempre que nuestros hijos estén de acuerdo en participar, podemos compartir con ellos todo lo que sabemos y ayudarles a encontrar las respuestas a cualquier pregunta para la cual no tengamos una contestación preparada. Si ya supiéramos todas las respuestas, nos perderíamos de muchas aventuras al resolver misterios y buscar tesoros.

Como criaturas sociales, deseamos pertenecer y contribuir con nuestras comunidades; y lo logramos aprendiendo todo lo que podamos acerca de la gente y del mundo que nos rodea. Si permanecemos disponibles para nuestros hijos, si pasamos mucho tiempo con ellos y si nos divertimos juntos, ellos se sentirán seguros y con la suficiente confianza para salir al mundo y aprender todavía más.

Instrucción académica temprana

Los niños pequeños ansían y necesitan tener interacción directa con el mundo físico, lo cual significa cantidades generosas de libertad para tocar, saborear, oler, escuchar y ver. El juego libre introduce al niño en la observación científica (es decir, curiosidad y exploración).

Con el deseo de brindarle a su hijo una ventaja temprana, los padres pueden cometer el error de enfocarse en materias académicas abstractas antes de que el niño haya tenido suficiente experiencia explorando el mundo físico y concreto, y absorbiendo conceptos por inmersión.

En una sociedad alfabetizada, un niño no puede evitar observar las letras y los números. Los niños desean entenderlos. Aprenden matemáticas y lectura por etapas. Atraviesan una jerarquía de comprensión. Por ejemplo, un niño pequeño que está aprendiendo rápidamente a comunicarse, desarrollará una conciencia de los símbolos numéricos y alfabéticos. Puede que suceda mientras uno de los padres le lee, mientras ve la televisión o mientras juega con juguetes y libros, etc. Un niño debe aprender primero a reconocer las letras y los números antes de aprender a leer palabras, a calcular problemas matemáticos, a dominar la lectura de comprensión y a realizar cálculos más complicados con aplicación al mundo real.

Debido al énfasis que comúnmente se le da al aprendizaje académico por encima del juego imaginativo, los niños aprenden los números, las letras, a reconocer palabras y a contar, a edades cada vez más tempranas. Sin embargo, esto no significa que el niño realmente comprenderá el lenguaje escrito y los conceptos matemáticos más pronto que uno que no aprendió el ABC y el 123 siendo tan pequeño. A medida que los niños se acercan a la edad de jardín de niños y preescolar, los padres pueden sentir la presión de cumplir con el aprendizaje temprano oficial y los avances correspondientes a cada etapa de desarrollo; pero si respondemos a esta presión intentando coaccionar a nuestros pequeños para que logren esas metas, nos arriesgamos a transmitirles esa misma presión.

Much Too Early!
Artículo de David Elkind
http://besthomeschooling.org/articles/david_elkind.html

Al principio, nuestros niños se rebelan contra cualquier esfuerzo de coaccionarlos, pero con el tiempo, se darán por vencidos. Nuestra insistencia aplasta su curiosidad natural y su amor por aprender. Cuando nos mostramos desanimados ante su progreso, ellos también se ven a sí mismos como un fracaso. Si tenemos metas realistas para el aprendizaje de nuestros hijos (esto es, la adquisición de destrezas útiles y atractivas para ellos), no hay de qué preocuparnos. Pero si, por otro lado, nuestras agendas tienden hacia producir logros a nivel de prodigio o genio en intereses especializados, es posible que deseemos reenfocarnos en los intereses personales de nuestros hijos y meditar de nuevo en nuestra percepción de éxito.

Cuando me pregunto a mí misma qué es lo que más quiero para mis hijas, inmediatamente respondo: quiero que mis hijas vivan su propia idea de éxito. Cuando la preocupación, las dudas y el temor del futuro se introducen con sigilo en nuestro pensamiento, fácilmente podemos discernir que nuestras ambiciones para nuestros hijos se han descarrilado. Nuestros hijos tienen todo el tiempo del mundo para aprender cualquier cosa que necesiten aprender para lograr cualquier cosa que quieran lograr.

Generaciones de niños criados bajo la filosofía *unschooling* han probado que se puede aprender naturalmente a leer, a escribir, y a calcular de acuerdo con sus propios horarios, en su manera particular y por sus propias razones. Aprenden esas habilidades por medio de una continuación de los mismos métodos que usan los niños pequeños: jugando, explorando, probando cosas y pidiendo ayuda. Algunos niños buscan aprender a leer a los cinco o seis años. Otros aprenden después. Cualquiera que sea el caso, el niño crece y se convierte en una persona que puede leer y hacer cálculos, y tal vez incluso, ser una de las que disfrutan esas actividades.

Mi hija mayor, Maia, ve las matemáticas como una herramienta divertida y emocionante. Brinca y exclama de satisfacción con cada nuevo cálculo desafiante. A su edad, yo percibía las matemáticas como un trabajo que debía hacer para tener una buena calificación y así, ser una «alumna buena e inteligente». La presión y el miedo eran dolorosos.

Los intentos de coaccionar el aprendizaje temprano en un niño que todavía no tiene el interés o la habilidad se toparán con su resistencia y contribuirán a desarrollar una asociación negativa con la materia, lo que puede dificultar el aprendizaje futuro. Incluso cuando la coerción sí produzca un rendimiento académico temprano, los resultados podrían causarle un estrés innecesario al niño y un daño a su imagen de sí mismo. Los niños sí aprenden lo básico con el tiempo y a través de experiencias de la vida real, como escuchar a sus padres leerles historias, cocinar, cuidar el jardín, armar rompecabezas, construir, crear arte, experimentar, etc. Algunos niños eligen utilizar materiales educativos comunes como libros de texto y de ejercicios. Cualquiera que sea el caso, el progreso de las destrezas académicas básicas avanza naturalmente de acuerdo con las necesidades, las habilidades y los intereses naturales del niño.

Estilos de aprendizaje

La escolarización habitual no apoya –o quizá no puede apoyar– distintos estilos de aprendizaje. Los métodos educativos convencionales favorecen a los niños que tienen facilidad para aprender escuchando clases y leyendo libros de texto. Para los niños que aprenden más fácilmente de otras maneras, este prejuicio puede dar lugar a una percepción baja de la inteligencia general y a diagnósticos erróneos de discapacidades de aprendizaje.

En su libro[4], el investigador y profesor Howard Gardner propone que todos poseemos al menos siete inteligencias básicas con algunos tipos más prominentes que otros. En otras palabras, en lugar de tener un nivel general de inteligencia, para bien o para mal, el Dr. Gardner sugirió que todos tenemos una combinación única de inteligencias (también conocidas como formas de percibir y aprender). Las siete inteligencias de Gardner son:

- Lingüística,
- Lógica matemática,
- Espacial,
- Corporal cinética,
- Musical,
- Interpersonal, e
- Intrapersonal.

Después, el Dr. Gardner agregó una octava inteligencia: Naturalista, que muestra una memoria y una conciencia sensorial muy agudas.

---

[4] Gardner, H. (2009) *Estructuras de la Mente: la teoría de las inteligencias múltiples*. Fondo de Cultura Económica. México, D.F.

Esta inteligencia se compara con el temperamento «altamente sensitivo», que algunas personas confunden erróneamente con déficit de atención, pero que Richard Louv vio «curado» en un entorno natural[5].

Aunque evito limitar la percepción que tengo de mis hijas no etiquetándolas, sí valoro las *inteligencias múltiples* del Dr. Gardner por ampliar mi conciencia de las diferentes formas en que la gente piensa y aprende.

El estilo de vida *unschooling* les proporciona a los niños la libertad y la flexibilidad de aprender intuitivamente de las formas más fáciles y placenteras para ellos. Los padres *unschoolers* se mantienen conscientes de las fortalezas, habilidades e intereses de sus hijos para así poder abrir la puerta a actividades que mejor satisfagan las necesidades de cada niño.

Por ejemplo, en vez de etiquetar a Maia como una aprendiz espacial/cinética, o incluso como «mi pequeña científica» o «mi pequeña artista», yo reconozco que ella aprende mejor a través de presentaciones visuales junto con la libertad de moverse mucho. Habitualmente da pasos mientras resuelve problemas de matemáticas. De hecho, parece *necesitar* moverse mientras realiza actividades lógicas o cerebrales, como si el movimiento lubricara el engranaje de su cerebro para hacerlo funcionar.

Mi segunda hija, Ilana, canta muy bajito mientras dibuja y prefiere estar sola para bailar y jugar con su imaginación. Pide privacidad cuando está creando algo y es tímida en las actividades grupales estructuradas.

Yo soy consciente de que mis hijas expresan estas características en el presente, y de que ellas pueden cambiar sus hábitos y preferencias en cualquier momento.

---

[5] Aron, E. (2002) *The Highly Sensitive Child. Harmony*, New York. / Louv, R. (2008) *Last Child in the Woods*. Algonquin Books of Chapel Hill.

Lingüística. Los niños con una fuerte habilidad lingüística aprenden fácilmente de clases, discusiones, juegos de palabras, historias, lecturas, escritos, etc., siempre y cuando, por supuesto, tengan interés en el tema y actividad.

Lógica-matemática. Los niños con una fuerte habilidad lógica aprenden fácilmente de rompecabezas, experimentos de ciencia, juegos numéricos, pensamiento crítico, cuadernos de ejercicios, etc.

Espacial. Los niños con una fuerte habilidad espacial aprenden fácilmente de presentaciones visuales, actividades artísticas, metáforas, juegos imaginarios, etc.

Corporal-cinética. Los niños con una fuerte habilidad cinética aprenden fácilmente de actividades físicas prácticas, experiencias táctiles, dramas, bailes, ejercicios de relajación, etc.

Musical. Los niños con una fuerte habilidad musical aprenden fácilmente de canciones, ritmos, etc., (la música involucra conceptos matemáticos).

Interpersonal. Los niños con una fuerte habilidad interpersonal aprenden fácilmente de actividades grupales, clases entre compañeros, reuniones sociales, conversaciones uno a uno, etc.

Intrapersonal. Los niños con una fuerte habilidad intrapersonal aprenden fácilmente de una instrucción individualizada, del estudio independiente, etc.

Naturalista. Los niños con fuertes habilidades naturalistas muestran interés en la conciencia sensorial aguda, atención a detalles sutiles, y una gran cantidad de conexiones de memoria.

Estilos de acción

Así como cada uno de nosotros tiene su propio estilo óptimo de aprendizaje, también tenemos estrategias personales para comenzar y proseguir con proyectos, para resolver problemas y para otros esfuerzos de aprendizaje. En un artículo publicado en *O Magazine*[6], Martha Beck propuso cuatro estilos instintivos de acción:

- Inicio rápido (entrar de inmediato y descubrirlo mediante prueba y error);
- Buscador de hechos (buscar información e instrucciones antes de comenzar);
- Práctico (crear modelos, manipular el problema físicamente);
- Sistemático (crear sistemas, métodos, formularios a seguir).

Beck señala que las escuelas tradicionales fueron diseñadas principalmente por los estilos del tipo sistemático, lo cual puede causar problemas a los niños que aprenden de forma diferente. Maia y yo tendemos a entrar de lleno a un nuevo proyecto y aprender sobre la marcha.

Nos entendemos una a la otra: «¡Vamos, hagámoslo!», y comenzamos enseguida.

Ilana, en cambio, toma una actitud más cautelosa de observar y esperar ante nuevas actividades. Primero quiere leer las instrucciones, observar a otros hacer la actividad, y visualizarse a sí misma haciéndola antes de dar el primer paso.

A pesar de tener diferentes maneras de hacer las cosas, mis hijas se complementan entre sí y trabajan muy bien juntas. Por ejemplo, Maia por lo general comienza el proyecto mientras que Ilana observa, reúne más información y se prepara para ver el proceso hasta su culminación.

---

[6] Beck, M. (2006, enero). How to Be Wildly Successful. *O Magazine*. Recuperado de https://www.oprah.com/spirit/martha-beck-how-to-be-wildly-successful/all

Estilos de educación en el hogar

Los cálculos actuales estiman que en los Estados Unidos hay 1.9 millón de estudiantes en el hogar. Existe toda una gama de enfoques educativos: desde los más estructurados que literalmente llevan la escuela a la casa, hasta los menos estructurados que llevan el *unschooling* a un estilo de vida radical. La mayoría de las familias educadoras en casa se ubica en algún punto entre esos dos extremos y con el tiempo pueden ir cambiando para ajustarse a los intereses y necesidades de cada niño en particular y a los de toda la familia, como un todo estrechamente relacionado.

Cuando la gente me pregunta, yo generalmente utilizo la etiqueta *unschooling* para describir el enfoque educativo de nuestra familia. Esta definición limitada les dice que no seguimos ningún currículo, pero podemos *usar* materiales curriculares para nuestros propósitos. Yo rara vez consulto guías para maestros o padres, pero algunos intereses nos inspiran a emprender proyectos más estructurados mientras que otros inspiran esfuerzos más creativos.

Escuela en casa. La gran mayoría de educadores en el hogar sigue un currículo estructurado o programa de estudios que imita la escuela tradicional con materias, tareas, exámenes, calificaciones, etc. Existen muchos currículos diferentes en el mercado y varían en su contenido, pero básicamente incluyen una guía para los padres, libros de texto, tareas y evaluaciones para los niños.

Este enfoque de escuela en casa puede ser el concepto más fácil de asimilar para los padres porque se asemeja a la experiencia que muchos de nosotros tuvimos en la escuela, y además porque la cultura occidental promueve el apego a un programa.

Estudio por unidades. Algunos programas curriculares enfatizan el estudio por unidades, el cual cubre varias materias bajo un tema, como, por ejemplo, un periodo de tiempo específico o un lugar.

El enfoque de estudio por unidades o por temas, puede ofrecer una presentación más interesante para los niños que el enfoque de materia por materia; ya que integrar las materias bajo un tema se asemeja más a la vida real que, por ejemplo, extraer las matemáticas, la ciencia, la literatura, el civismo, etc., de un evento y enseñar cada materia por separado.

Relajado, ecléctico. Algunas familias educadoras en el hogar practican una forma híbrida entre escuela en casa y *unschooling*. Por ejemplo, pueden asignar un currículo para matemáticas, pero dejar que los niños dirijan su propio aprendizaje en otras áreas.

Unschooling. Las familias *unschoolers* confían en que el aprendizaje ocurre espontáneamente durante el curso diario de la vida. De esta forma, puede parecer que un niño *unschooler* «no hace nada» gran parte del tiempo. Otras veces, con metas de aprendizaje específicas en mente, un niño *unschooler* puede utilizar materiales educativos junto con otras herramientas o recursos disponibles, incluyendo instrucción y dirección (enseñanza), lo cual puede generar una actividad idéntica en apariencia a la de un niño que trabaja siguiendo un currículo. Sin embargo, el *unschooler* hace el trabajo por su propia motivación. Su deseo de ir a la universidad, por ejemplo, se manifiesta en su empeño enfocado y autodirigido para cumplir con los requisitos de admisión.

A mis hijas les gusta usar materiales curriculares. Les gustan las hojas de ejercicios, los videos y juegos de computadora educativos. Toman estos materiales educativos y los usan a su manera. Hacen muchos o pocos ejercicios, según lo deseen. Ven tanto de un video o juegan tanto de un juego como sientan la necesidad o la inclinación de hacerlo.
Cuando necesitan un descanso, lo toman. Sin embargo, un niño *unschooler* puede nunca utilizar materiales educativos explícitamente ni involucrarse en actividades del tipo escolar.

Unschooling radical. Mientras que el término *unschooling* se refiere al aprendizaje, el *unschooling radical* se refiere al estilo de vida.

Las personas que siguen la filosofía del *unschooling radical*, también llamados *aprendices de la vida entera* aplican los ideales del *unschooling* como la libertad y el respeto mutuo, al resto de su vida. No perciben el aprendizaje como separado de ninguna otra actividad de la vida, y tampoco perciben su labor de padres como separada de ningún otro acto de la vida.

La palabra *radical* significa tanto raíz como revolución. El *unschooling radical* se refiere tanto al estilo de vida raíz, que necesariamente carece de una separación arbitraria de las diversas actividades de la vida, como a una revolución, vista como un marcado desvío del modo de vida convencional en la cultura institucional.

Los conceptos *unschooling* y *unschooling radical* pueden ser más difíciles de asimilar para los padres, ya que divergen bastante de la forma en que la mayoría de nosotros ha vivido. A medida que aprendemos a vivir de una nueva manera, puede que pasemos por un proceso conocido como *desescolarización* o *desprogramación,* durante el cual desaprendemos los conceptos que antes sosteníamos acerca del aprendizaje y la crianza de los hijos. Muchas familias se encuentran en diferentes puntos de la gama de enfoques educativos durante distintas etapas de su vida. Incluso dentro de una sola familia, los niños pueden preferir niveles variados de estructura y dirección. La filosofía *unschooling* anima a los padres a encontrar el mejor ajuste para su familia, honrando las necesidades de cada uno de sus miembros.

Televisión, internet, videojuegos y comida chatarra

Es muy común que el tema de la televisión y otros medios como Internet y los videojuegos, al igual que el de la comida chatarra, provoquen sentimientos encontrados. La filosofía popular del *unschooling* sostiene que la televisión y el Internet acercan el mundo a nuestros hijos y que ellos naturalmente aprenderán a autorregular su uso si se les da la libertad de hacerlo. Lo mismo sucede con la comida chatarra.

En gran parte estoy de acuerdo: los niños sí se autorregulan *de la mejor manera que pueden*. Sin embargo, yo creo que mi responsabilidad como madre de nutrir a mis hijas incluye crear y mantener una atmósfera segura en el hogar y proveer alimentos nutritivos.

Sospecho que a las familias *unschoolers*, al igual que a mucha gente en nuestra cultura, les gusta ver televisión, navegar en Internet, jugar videojuegos y comer deliciosa comida chatarra. Desde este punto de vista personal, defendemos lo que nos gusta.

Mi esposo juega videojuegos y trabaja como programador profesional de videojuegos. Yo sabía que los videojuegos formarían parte de la vida de mis hijas. ¿Qué mensaje les estaría enviando acerca de su papá si les prohibiera jugar videojuegos?

En el tema de los medios y la comida, yo observo a mis hijas. Mientras que ellas disfruten y se sientan bien con sus actividades y decisiones, yo también me siento bien. Cuando veo que no se sienten bien, como cuando comen de más o cuando tienen reacciones negativas (mis hijas sufren de alergias a la comida), entonces les digo lo que estoy viendo. Hablamos sobre ello y les ayudo a que vean la conexión, de modo que puedan usar esa información para futuras decisiones.

Yo quiero que mis hijas disfruten lo que hacen, lo que comen. Quiero que se sientan felices y saludables. Escucho mi intuición y me dejo guiar no por el temor, sino por el gozo.

Una secuencia de estudios sobre Australia, al estilo *unschooling*

La siguiente secuencia de eventos ilustra cómo mis hijas y yo estuvimos rodeadas por muchas circunstancias y temas relacionados con Australia. Yo no tenía planeado estudiar Australia ni tampoco sentía nada por aquel remoto continente más que una leve curiosidad. Sin embargo, comencé a ver Australia por todas partes.

- Llega a mi escritorio el kit *Case # 12455 "The Dilemma Down Under"* de la serie *Top Secret Adventures*[7], que trata el tema de Australia.
- Terminé de leer *Steve and Me*[8] de Terri Irwin, la viuda del Cazador de cocodrilos. Mi hermana puso ese libro en mis manos porque Terri es originaria de nuestro pueblo.
- Cuando leía *Steve and Me*, nunca tuve que consultar el diccionario australiano, porque ya había aprendido varias palabras locales en el material de *Top Secret Adventures*. A menudo detenía la lectura para compartirles algunas anécdotas a mis hijas, usando varias de esas palabras regionales.
- Después de leer las memorias de Terri Irwin, vi todos los documentales del Cazador de cocodrilos en Netflix.
- Las niñas y yo vimos un mapa de Australia y señalamos el ecuador. Hablamos acerca de cómo la tierra gira con relación al sol y cómo las estaciones son diferentes en los hemisferios norte y sur. Descubrimos que el centro del continente australiano es un gran desierto y que la mayoría de las personas vive en las costas.
- Mis hijas han visto la serie de televisión australiana *H2O: Sirenas del Mar*, la cual inspiró en ellas un interés por las fórmulas químicas.
- Descargué la versión gratis de prueba de dos juegos relacionados con Australia: *The Wild Thornberrys Australian Wildlife Rescue* y *Australia Zoo Quest*.
- Ahora tenemos el deseo de tomar unas vacaciones familiares en Australia. Mi abuela ha visitado Australia y tiene amigos que viven allá. Uno de ellos llamó durante nuestra nochebuena en EE. UU., que en Australia era la mañana de navidad, lo que provocó una conversación sobre la línea horaria internacional.

---

[7] *N. de la T.*: Es una serie de paquetes de la marca Highlights con materiales para que los niños resuelvan misterios mientras que descubren información acerca de gente, cultura, ubicación geográfica e historia de países específicos.

[8] Irwin, T. (2008) *Steve and Me*, Gallery Books, New York.

- Cuando le regresé el libro *Steve and Me* a mi hermana, me prestó otro libro titulado *Las voces del desierto,* de Marlo Morgan[9]. Me gustó tanto, que conseguí el siguiente libro: *Mutant Message From Forever*[10], de la misma autora. En ambos libros encontré mucha sabiduría aborigen que después compartí con mis hijas.

Y esto continúa…

---

[9] Morgan, M. (2018) *Las voces del desierto*. Editorial Vergara.
[10] Morgan, M. (1999) *Mutant Message from Forever*. Harper Perennial, New York.

La filosofía *unschooling*

Más allá del aprendizaje infantil, la filosofía *unschooling* se extiende a la crianza de los hijos y a todos los aspectos de la vida. Consiste en percibir el aprendizaje como una parte integral de vivir en el mundo. Este capítulo comprende las siguientes secciones:

¿Recibir educación?,
Definiciones de *unschooling,*
Unschooling en la vida diaria,
Una nota sobre las labores domésticas, y
Partidarios del *unschooling.*

El estado de ánimo no escolarizado proporciona una forma de ver y vivir en el mundo. Este estilo de vida nos impulsa a mantener un nivel de conciencia suficiente para honrar y respetar las verdaderas necesidades de nuestros hijos y las nuestras.

Cuando apoyamos a nuestros hijos para que asuman la responsabilidad de su propio aprendizaje, *para poseer su propio aprendizaje,* les damos más de lo que jamás podríamos darles al dirigir su educación. Les damos confianza, control de sus vidas, libertad y posibilidades ilimitadas para el éxito personal y placer en la vida.

¿Recibir educación?

Así como podemos decidir usar las palabras *ayudar a aprender* en vez de *enseñar,* es posible que también deseemos comprender mejor el uso común de la palabra *educación.*
Cuando las personas hablan de educación, por lo general usan frases como: «recibir educación» u «obtener una educación». Ambas formas de expresarlo sugieren una resignación pasiva a, o una búsqueda activa, pero a regañadientes, de este asunto de la educación: el paquete del conocimiento estándar.

Crear definiciones bien delineadas de las diversas terminologías de aprendizaje y desarrollo puede ayudarnos a describir con mayor claridad el enfoque *unschooling* a los demás, así como a comprenderlo más plenamente nosotros mismos. Todos tenemos intereses únicos y metas para el presente y el futuro (pasiones, sueños, llamados).

Nuestras comunidades requieren una amplia variedad de habilidades, y ningún cuerpo común de conocimientos ni ninguna educación estandarizada puede suplir las necesidades tan diversas de una comunidad. Sin embargo, la mayoría de los niños invierte una cantidad considerable de tiempo y esfuerzo en programas educativos para los que muchas veces no tiene el interés ni el uso. En vez de eso, los niños junto con los adultos en sus vidas podrían usar ese tiempo nutriendo sus talentos únicos y trabajando para alcanzar sus sueños.

Los niños, al igual que los adultos, aprenden con facilidad y entusiasmo cuando pueden decidir qué aprender a través del mundo real, a partir de los intereses y necesidades que tengan sentido para ellos; a diferencia de lo que sucede cuando se sienten coaccionados o amenazados para aprender porque alguien le ha designado valor a la información. Cuando se les da la libertad de actuar de acuerdo con sus propias motivaciones, los niños aprenden intuitivamente y de las formas que les parecen más fáciles. De esta manera, fortalecen la confianza en su habilidad para desarrollar nuevas destrezas, resolver problemas y encontrar la información deseada. No es necesario pensar conscientemente en el proceso de aprendizaje, ya que sucede naturalmente. Cuando nos encontramos con un obstáculo para llevar a cabo una actividad, aprendemos lo que necesitamos saber para superar el reto.

A menudo la gente les pregunta a mis hijas: «¿Qué aprendiste hoy?», lo cual las confunde. Ellas no perciben sus experiencias diarias en términos de materias académicas. Simplemente viven cada día como viene, siguiendo temas de interés deliberadamente, haciendo descubrimientos espontáneamente, descifrando cómo hacer cosas nuevas, y perfeccionando sus habilidades.

Juegan con libros de ejercicios, arte y materiales para construir. Hacen descubrimientos cuando ven documentales y viven aventuras cuando leen.

Los niños *unschoolers* aprenden las «materias», los conceptos básicos, de una manera lógica a través de sus experiencias diarias motivadas individualmente. Por ejemplo, puede que aprendan conceptos matemáticos horneando, construyendo, programando en la computadora, tomando una clase de matemáticas o viendo un video, dependiendo de sus intereses personales o estilos de aprendizaje.

Un niño con un interés en programación seguirá ese interés, por necesidad, hasta llegar a matemáticas avanzadas. Un interés en diseño de modas o arquitectura conducirá a conceptos de geometría. Hornear puede requerir conversiones de un sistema de medida a otro, e incluso puede requerir algo de álgebra. Estos conceptos y herramientas existen en el mundo real. De otra manera, ¿para qué los necesitaríamos? Pregúntate a ti mismo: ¿usas raíces cuadradas? Si no es así, ¿quién sí lo hace y para qué?

Los niños *unschoolers* se hacen expertos en encontrar formas de aprender lo que necesitan para alcanzar sus sueños. Cuando los padres no tienen el conocimiento que sus hijos requieren, les ayudan a encontrarlo a través de diversos recursos (capacitaciones, credencial de la biblioteca, páginas amarillas, Internet, cursos, expertos, tutores, maestros, profesionales, empresarios, etc.)

Definiciones de *unschooling*

1. *Unschooling*: Aprender haciendo, cuestionando y encontrando soluciones. Es el aprendizaje natural, autodirigido e impulsado por el interés, que obedece a la agenda del propio aprendiz, quien avanza naturalmente de interés en interés, a lo largo de un trayecto de por vida en busca de conocimiento y experiencias que contribuyen a su propósito significativo.

Mi hija Maia se siente especialmente atraída a la vida marina y a las culturas antiguas. Quiere estudiar, ayudar a proteger, entrenar o trabajar con mamíferos marinos, además de trabajar en el campo de la paleontología. A menudo visitamos las costas cercanas y el acuario local, a cuyo programa de voluntariado juvenil Maia planea inscribirse. Mientras que eso sucede, tiene previsto asistir a las clases del acuario y a los campamentos de niños, además de seguir buscando otras oportunidades encaminadas hacia su meta.

Cuando viajamos, visitamos costas y acuarios. El interés de Maia por la vida marina y las culturas antiguas la ha conducido a ver documentales sobre dinosaurios, paleontólogos, biólogos, buzos, cineastas, acuarios del mundo, ballenas y delfines, vida antigua del océano, la problemática de los arrecifes de coral, etc. Estudia la vida marina y las culturas antiguas en enciclopedias y colecciona figuras de mamíferos marinos, anfibios, dinosaurios y dragones.

Sus intereses, que comenzaron con los mamíferos marinos y dinosaurios, han ido creciendo para incluir hábitats, vida vegetal, peces y tiburones, aves de la costa, entrenamiento de animales, buceo, marismas, islas, clima, magnetismo, y más.

Durante este proceso, mis hijas han visto varias series de televisión sobre mamíferos y reptiles antiguos, al igual que una serie de sirenas en la que la curiosidad científica de la bióloga marina antagonista le hace perder de vista los derechos naturales de la vida del océano. Incluso el título de la serie: *H2O: Sirenas del mar* inspiró el interés de mis hijas hacia las fórmulas químicas, lo que luego las llevó a realizar numerosos experimentos de ciencias con el equipo *Pop Bottle Science*.

Estos intereses han introducido a mis hijas en muchas áreas académicas (biología, ecología, química, ciencias terrestres y climatológicas, matemáticas, conservación ambiental, etc.), de una forma integrada, en el mundo real.

Su búsqueda de información consta de actividades que ellas escogen y en las que se involucran libremente, como leer libros, ver videos, visitar zoológicos, museos y playas, hablar con profesionales, y asistir a clases y campamentos. De esta manera, *su* manera, ellas aprenden mucho más fácil y rápidamente, impulsadas por su propia curiosidad y emoción por descubrir.

2. *Unschooling*: Aprender sin escolarización. *Unschooling* describe el aprendizaje a través de las experiencias de la vida. El aprendizaje no requiere escolaridad ni enseñanza. El acto de enseñar implica, en el mejor de los casos, ofrecer información; y, en el peor, presión o amenaza para aprender. En vez de enseñar en este sentido negativo, los padres *unschoolers* les ayudan a sus hijos a aprender incluyéndolos en las actividades diarias, permaneciendo disponibles, contestando preguntas, y asesorándolos en su búsqueda de respuestas y de nuevas destrezas. Además, estos padres montan el escenario para el aprendizaje proveyéndoles a sus hijos de un entorno rico, con libre acceso a recursos variados.

Unschooling en la vida diaria

Las dinámicas familiares varían de una familia *unschooler* a otra. Puede que uno o ambos padres trabajen desde el hogar. Puede que los niños tengan distintas edades, desde muy pequeños hasta adolescentes.

Algunas familias siguen rutinas diarias para las comidas, los recados fuera o la administración de un negocio familiar. Los niños pueden pasar algún tiempo a solas leyendo, jugando, creando o experimentando, y también puede que pasen tiempo con sus hermanos, padres, tutores o cuidadores. Puede que los niños participen en los recados o en el trabajo con sus padres, o tomen clases de música, asistan a los *scouts*, a clubes con otros niños educados en el hogar, o trabajen como voluntarios fuera de casa.

Todos necesitamos periodos de actividad y de descanso.

Algunos días los niños parecen aprender productivamente mientras que otros días parece que no aprenden nada. Las apariencias pueden engañar. Gran parte del procesamiento ocurre durante los días de descanso. Necesitamos días para enfocarnos en el interior y días de descanso. Asimismo, los días llenos de juego e imaginación pueden brindarle al niño la oportunidad de explorar nuevas ideas y desarrollar nuevos intereses que lo guiarán a un aprendizaje más enfocado en el futuro.

Los intereses de los niños y las formas en que los buscan cambian a través del tiempo. Un niño pequeño activo y juguetón puede convertirse en un jovencito serio y centrado, o un niño que antes era muy independiente podría comenzar a requerir más ayuda. El padre *unschooler* responde manteniendo la confianza, la sensibilidad y la disposición para brindar apoyo y guía en cualquier forma que el niño necesite.

Para mi familia, todos los días de la semana son diferentes. Trabajo desde casa y tengo un horario flexible. Mi hija menor todavía es lactante y mis otras dos hijas mayores han alcanzado diferentes etapas de dependencia.

Mis hijas mayores pasan algunas porciones del día ellas solas y juntas. Usan sus computadoras para navegar en Internet, jugar videojuegos y trabajar en programas de arte. También juegan con muñecas y animales de juguete. Construyen máquinas sencillas con piezas de LEGO, con pajillas y crema de afeitar, o con otros materiales. Dibujan, pintan, recortan y pegan para confeccionar todo tipo de obras de arte. Ven videos de todo tipo. Leen libros. Inventan cosas cuando ven una necesidad o simplemente cuando se sienten aventureras.
Juntas hacemos experimentos de ciencia, jugamos en el jardín, pintamos, hacemos proyectos de arte y manualidades, leemos revistas, hacemos labores domésticas, y cualquier otra cosa. Regularmente ponemos a la mano una pila de libros y revistas acerca del tema de interés del momento, y los leemos a lo largo del día, cuando sentimos ganas de hacerlo.

Mi bebé por lo general observa todas estas actividades desde su cómodo portador que llevo en la espalda. La práctica del porteo me permite realizar muchas de mis responsabilidades, al mismo tiempo que le doy a ella la oportunidad de tener una vista elevada desde la cual participa en nuestros proyectos.

Mi familia no sigue un horario regularmente, pero con el tiempo hemos creado algunas rutinas cómodas. Nos levantamos alrededor de la misma hora todos los días y comenzamos a bajar el ritmo y nos acostamos alrededor de la misma hora todos los días. Mi esposo y yo nos turnamos para leerles cuentos a las niñas antes de dormir. Yo les leo una serie y él les lee otra. Preparo un par de comidas durante el día más o menos a la misma hora; o bien, mantengo una bandeja bien surtida de diferentes bocadillos que pueden tomarse con los dedos y mojarse en aderezos (similar a nuestro concepto de ofrecer un bufé variado de libros, nuevas experiencias e información).

Casi todos los días salimos a hacer el mismo recorrido de recados: al correo, al supermercado, quizá a la farmacia y a la ferretería. Mis hijas vienen conmigo a todas partes y aprenden a hacer lo que yo hago. Hacen listas de compras y pagan en la tienda. A mi segunda hija, Ilana, le encanta empujar el carrito y poner las cosas en la caja para que las cobren. En la oficina de correo depositan sus cartas y recogen paquetes. Los empleados de la zona las conocen por nombre.

Tenemos algunas citas programadas a las que debemos llegar a tiempo. Recogemos una caja de vegetales de una granja local cada semana durante la temporada de cosecha. Nos reunimos en el parque con otras familias una vez a la semana. Las niñas tienen actividades regulares con nuestro grupo local de educadores en casa, y toman clases en el estudio de danza local, en el centro de arte, en el centro de artes marciales, u otras clases que la comunidad ofrece y que captan su interés. Adaptamos nuestra rutina a cada estación del año, a los intereses de mis hijas y a mi horario de trabajo. Creemos que nuestro estilo de vida es un proyecto creativo.

Una nota sobre las labores domésticas

Cuando menciono labores domésticas no me refiero a labores asignadas a las niñas. Me refiero al mantenimiento del hogar que cualquiera de nosotros puede realizar.

En mi familia nunca hemos asignado labores, y, sin embargo, cada niña se ofrece espontáneamente a hacerlas cuando ve la necesidad. Vivimos en una colaboración y hablamos del hogar y su mantenimiento como algo que es de todos. Algunas veces yo limpio su recámara porque prefiero una casa ordenada o quiero mejorar la atmósfera emocional. Otras veces ellas la limpian porque necesitan espacio en el piso o quieren mejorar la sensación de su cuarto.

Mi hija mayor, Maia, se refiere a sí misma como «la mamá chica», y activamente busca maneras de ayudarme a cuidar a sus hermanas menores. A Ilana *le encanta* lavar los platos. Mis hijas quieren ayudar y aprender las destrezas que se requieren para el mantenimiento de la casa y el cuidado de los niños. Yo espero que ellas ayuden en la casa tal como espero que aprendan todo lo que necesitan aprender para funcionar bien en la vida. Lo espero porque sucede naturalmente cuando las personas viven juntas en una colaboración.

He escuchado a algunas personas sugerir que se sentirían resentidas si hicieran la mayor parte de la limpieza. Puedo identificarme con eso, ya que mis pensamientos muchas veces se desvían hacia una perspectiva negativa, especialmente si me siento demasiado cansada o estresada. Sin embargo, no tengo por qué sentirme así. Yo puedo escoger sentirme bien por crear una atmósfera pacífica y hermosa para mi familia o puedo escoger no limpiar cuando me siento sin energías. Admito que prefiero vivir en una casa arreglada porque me hace sentir mejor. Por lo tanto, reconozco que limpio para mí misma.

Partidarios del *unschooling*

He leído mucho sobre educación, especialmente de educación en la primera infancia y desescolarización. Cada uno de esos autores aportó algo nuevo a mi filosofía personal.

«Adán era el único hombre que, cuando decía algo bueno,
sabía que nadie lo había dicho antes que él.»

– Mark Twain, *Notebook*, 1867.

Aunque he trabajado en varias instituciones de cuidado infantil donde los niños me llamaban maestra, nunca he trabajado como maestra certificada en una escuela. Mis hijas nunca han ido a la escuela. Mi conocimiento principal de la escolarización proviene de muchos años de mis propias experiencias de la infancia en la escuela pública. Varios de los siguientes defensores destacados del *unschooling* fueron maestros de escuela y tienen una amplia experiencia trabajando en el sistema educativo. En esta sección elegí destacar específicamente a los maestros que se convirtieron en partidarios. En el capítulo Estantería, al final del libro, encontrarás a más defensores.

John Holt & GWS
https://www.johnholtgws.com/

John Caldwell Holt fue quien acuñó el término *unschooling*. Fue maestro de escuelas privadas por muchos años antes de escribir sus primeros libros: *How Children Fail*[11], y *How Children Learn*[12].
Fue partidario de la reforma escolar hablando y escribiendo libros que exploran la teoría de la educación y su práctica, los derechos de los niños, las escuelas alternativas, y muchos otros asuntos sociales relacionados con la escolarización. Con el tiempo, el enfoque de Holt mudó de la reforma escolar a alternativas para la escolarización.

---

[11] Holt, J. (1995). *How Children Fail*, Da Capo Lifelong Books, New York.
[12] Holt, J. (2017) *How Children Learn,* Da Capo Lifelong Books, New York.

En 1977, comenzó la primera revista sobre educación en el hogar, *Growing Without Schooling*. Sus últimos dos libros, los únicos dos que hablan específicamente sobre educación en el hogar, son *Teach Your Own*[13] y *Learning All The Time*.[14]

Patrick Farenga, autor de *The Beginner's Guide To Homeschooling*,[15] revisó y volvió a publicar el libro original de Holt *Teach Your Own* y continúa el trabajo de promoción de John Holt.

Actualmente ocupa el puesto de presidente de Holt Associates, Inc., y publicó la revista *Growing Without Schooling* desde 1985, después de la muerte de John Holt, hasta que dejó de publicarse, en noviembre de 2001.

Susannah Sheffer escribió varios libros[16] y también editó la revista *Growing Without Schooling*.

Matt Hern también es autor de varios libros.[17] Dirigió una escuela alternativa para niños pequeños y trabajó con una escuela pública libre muy grande y con un centro alternativo para adolescentes.

Sandra Dodd

http://sandradodd.com

Sandra Dodd escribió *Sandra Dodd's Big Book of Unschooling*.[18]Fue maestra de secundaria antes de convertirse en partidaria del *unschooling*.

---

[13] Holt, J. & Farenga, P. (2003) *Teach Your Own*, Da Capo Lifelong Books.

[14] Holt, J. (1990) *Learning All the Time*, Da Capo Lifelong Books.

[15] Farenga, P. (2000) *The Beginners Guide to Homeschooling*, Holt Associates

[16] Sheffer, S. (1991) *A Life Worth Living: Selected Letters of John Holt*, Ohio State University Press. / Sheffer, S. (1992) *Writing Because We Love To*, Boynton/Cook. / Sheffer, S. (1997) *A Sense of Self*, Boynton/Cook.

[17] Hern, M. (1998) *Deschooling Our Lives*, New Society. / Hern, M. (2003) *Field Day*, New Star Books. / Hern, M. (2008) *Everywhere All the Time*, AK Press.

[18] Dodd, S. (2009) *Sandra Dodd's Big Book of Unschooling*, Lulu.

Desde 1998, editó la revista en línea *Home Education Magazine* y condujo una charla semanal sobre *unschooling*. Su sitio web proporciona artículos sobre muchos aspectos del estilo de vida del *unschooling radical*. s

Not Back to School Camp

http://nbtsc.org

Grace Llewellyn es autora de *The Teenage Liberation Handbook*[19] y *Guerilla Learning.*[20] Fue maestra de inglés de secundaria. Dirige un campamento anual llamado «Not Back to School Camp», en Oregon y Vermont.

John Taylor Gatto

http://johntaylorgatto.com

John Taylor Gatto escribió *Dumbing Us Down*[21] y *Weapons of Mass Instruction.*[22] Ganó el premio del maestro del año en Nueva York.

---

[19] Llewellyn, G. (1998) *The Teenage Liberation Handbook*, Lowry House.

[20] Llewellyn, G. (2001) *Guerilla Learning*, Wiley.

[21] Taylor Gatto, J. (1992) *Dumbing Us Down*, New Society Publishers.

[22] Taylor Gatto, J. (2008) *Weapons of Mass Instruction,* New Society Publishers.

Desescolarización

La naturaleza no coercitiva del estilo de vida *unschooling* puede hacer que algunos padres, especialmente quienes asistieron a la escuela convencional, experimenten sentimientos pasajeros de inseguridad y pérdida de control, sobre todo cuando se enfrentan a la preocupación o críticas de amigos y familiares.

Este capítulo comprende las siguientes secciones:
Dudas y temores,
Desprogramación,
Vida escolar,
Vida entera,
Conversaciones con familiares, y
Requisitos legales de aprendizaje.

Aun ya establecidos más naturalmente en el mundo del *unschooling*, es posible que todavía sintamos preocupación cuando comparamos el aprendizaje automotivado y creciente de nuestros hijos con el del promedio de los niños escolarizados convencionalmente. Sin calificaciones ni exámenes, no tenemos una medida para satisfacer fácilmente a nuestros temerosos amigos y parientes.
Ya que muchos de nosotros fuimos a la escuela convencional y no escogimos nuestras propias experiencias educativas, a veces tenemos dificultad para deshacernos del patrón de control y expectativas al que estamos acostumbrados. Antes de llegar a un estado de confianza es posible que atravesemos por un proceso llamado desescolarización en el que sobrescribimos años de programación cultural.

Dudas y temores

Quizás el aspecto más difícil del *unschooling* es renunciar a la ilusión de control y, en su lugar, confiar y permitir que nuestros hijos aprendan lo que ellos personalmente necesitan aprender. Muchos padres no lo creemos hasta que lo vemos, y cuando dejamos que nuestros niños aprendan así, no nos decepcionan. Puede que no midamos el aprendizaje de nuestros niños por unidades, pero vemos que continuamente están aprendiendo. Mis hijas me comparten con entusiasmo cualquier nuevo tema que hayan descubierto. Soy testigo de que continúan progresando y desarrollándose a un ritmo rápido, tal como lo hacían cuando eran bebés. No obstante, algunos padres temen que sus hijos criados bajo esta perspectiva no aprendan todas las materias estipuladas por el currículo oficial, y que, por lo tanto, no se forjarán una base adecuada para la universidad o para su vida laboral. La escolarización convencional proporciona una educación estandarizada a través de un plan de estudios dividido por edades y más adelante, por materias. Los niños educados así digieren los temas siguiendo una misma agenda.

Por el contrario, los niños *unschoolers* crean sus propias agendas de aprendizaje personalizadas, que pueden diferir mucho de las usadas en la escuela. Sin embargo, los niños que aprenden libremente han demostrado que sí aprenden materias académicas tradicionales a través de la búsqueda de actividades motivadas personalmente.

Por ejemplo, mis hijas han cumplido con los estándares obligatorios de aprendizaje académico general de nuestro estado en las áreas de estudios sociales, ciencias, lenguaje, salud y seguridad, y matemáticas a través de actividades de su propia elección. Sé que han aprendido estas cosas de la misma forma en que sé que pueden leer, componer canciones y poemas, saltar la cuerda, hacer movimientos de baile hip hop, reconocer decenas de dinosaurios e identificar plantas y animales en nuestro jardín. Vivimos juntas. Hablamos. Hacemos cosas juntas.

Maia compuso su primer poema durante una caminata al supermercado. En un día frío a finales de otoño comenzó a repetir frases al ritmo de sus pasos: «No más hojas coloridas. Sólo árboles pelones. No más hojas coloridas. Sólo árboles pelones.» Para cuando terminamos nuestras compras y casi habíamos llegado a casa, completó su poema:

54

No más hojas coloridas,
sólo árboles pelones.
El invierno viene pronto
así que esconde tus hojitas,
que el invierno viene pronto.
– Maia McGrath, 6 años.

Al cabo de dieciocho años, no solo confío, sino que tengo la certeza de que mis hijas habrán adquirido al menos el mismo conocimiento básico que cualquier otra persona de esta cultura.

De acuerdo con los objetivos oficiales de aprendizaje de mi estado, un niño educado debería ser capaz de:

Leer, escribir, comunicarse efectivamente;
Pensar creativa y lógicamente para resolver problemas, y
Establecer metas y trabajar para lograrlas.

Desde esta perspectiva más amplia, veo sin dudas, que mis hijas continúan progresando maravillosamente.

Desprogramación

Años de programación institucional hacen que muchos padres vean el aprendizaje automática y habitualmente en función de categorías de materias establecidas oficialmente, tales como estudios sociales, ciencias, lenguaje, salud y matemáticas.

Los niños que aprenden en libertad abordan estos temas desde una variedad de perspectivas. Por ejemplo, mis hijas estudian los animales desde las perspectivas de un biólogo, de un naturalista, de un artista, de un granjero, de un zoólogo, de un veterinario, de un entrenador, de un criador, de un trabajador social, de un conservacionista, etc. Deliberadamente buscamos gente que esté viviendo los intereses que a ellas les apasionan.

De esta manera, las categorías se traslapan, se mezclan y se hacen imperceptibles.

Las divisiones por materias que se conocen en el ámbito escolar no necesariamente existen en la vida. El lenguaje, las ciencias sociales y naturales, el arte, las matemáticas, la educación física, etc., todo se relaciona y se integra en el mundo real. La música requiere matemáticas, y la ciencia ocurrió en la historia. ¿Puedes definir la ciencia? Biología, botánica, química, física. En realidad, estos temas y herramientas de estudio divergen y a la vez se relacionan, dependiendo de las circunstancias en que se usen.

El primer semestre de bachillerato reprobé la materia de biología. Después de esa decepción, no tenía muchas esperanzas de obtener mejores notas en química o física, puesto que en mi mente esas materias estaban vinculadas como ciencias. También reprobé la última clase de matemáticas que tomé. Para mí, esa calificación fue una prueba de que yo no era buena en matemáticas.

Afortunadamente, los niños no escolarizados rara vez, si no es que nunca, llegan a pensar así. Ellos diseñan sus propias vidas y encuentran su lugar haciendo lo que aman hacer y siguiendo lo que les llama. Pese a recibir una educación estandarizada diseñada para crear miembros productivos de la sociedad, cada persona tiene sus propias fortalezas, talentos e intereses. El mundo necesita miembros de la comunidad con una amplia variedad de destrezas y pasiones.

Cuando Maia sugirió que quería dedicarse a bailar o tocar música rock como profesión, yo le dije: «¡qué genial!», mientras que una respuesta más convencional la habría desalentado de un sueño poco práctico.

Cuando le dije a mi maestro favorito que quería dedicarme a pintar o escribir novelas, ¡o ambas!, me respondió con una palabra que logró extinguir mis sueños: «impráctico».

Lo que yo escuché fue «estúpido», «sin sentido», y «no tienes el talento». Me tomó años y años, hasta bien entrada la edad adulta, antes de reanudar la búsqueda de esos sueños.

Mientras que mi hija quiera perseguir el sueño de tocar en una banda de rock o de descubrir pruebas de plesiosauros vivos, yo la apoyaré por completo y la ayudaré en todo sentido.

Vida escolar

Los niños *unschoolers* experimentan el aprendizaje como la satisfacción de su curiosidad natural y la adquisición de herramientas útiles.

Aquellos de nosotros que obtuvimos la mayor parte de nuestro aprendizaje enfocado en un entorno escolar, experimentamos el aprendizaje de una forma notablemente distinta; es decir, no por el bien de aprender algo en particular, sino como una disciplina requerida para tener una calificación en una boleta, quizás para complacer a los padres o para ganarnos la admisión a una universidad, y en última instancia, por la idea de éxito de esta cultura: un puesto de trabajo importante, bien remunerado y fama como un beneficio adicional.

El proceso de aprendizaje en la escuela dirige a los niños hacia una recompensa futura vagamente definida. Dicho aprendizaje puede no derivar en verdadero aprendizaje, sino en una memorización temporal o una deducción en el acto suficiente para pasar un examen.

Los niños escolarizados aprenden a perseverar durante años en actividades desagradables con la esperanza de una libertad final y descanso, además de un empleo. Sin una presión hacia lo contrario, nuestros niños *unschoolers* viven sus vidas momento a momento. Buscan el gozo en todo lo que hacen. De lo contrario, no sentirían ningún propósito para hacer algo.

En la infancia, mi vida giraba alrededor de la escuela. Recuerdo cómo me lamentaba, especialmente en el invierno, por pasar casi todas las horas de luz solar en el interior de un salón de clases iluminado artificialmente, en un edificio de piedra sin ventanas.

Cuando finalmente llegaba a casa por las tardes, pasaba horas haciendo tareas, a menudo hasta la hora de dormir. Incluso la práctica de clarinete, que había disfrutado en un principio, se sentía como un ejercicio tedioso. Bajo otras circunstancias, tal vez habría disfrutado aprender sobre los temas que los maestros tocaban en la escuela. Pero en vez de eso, sentía la presión de las fechas límite y las calificaciones, lo que provocó que mis compañeros y yo estuviéramos en continuo pique, además de que amenazó mi promedio y mis futuras oportunidades universitarias. Mis compañeros y yo también competíamos por estar en el cuadro de honor.

Durante dos años logré mantenerme en el programa de honores del bachillerato, con un promedio general dentro del tres por ciento más alto de toda la escuela; y, sin embargo, mi vida se sentía como una jornada sin fin. Me discipliné para seguir trabajando con los ojos puestos en la recompensa prometida: mi graduación, la universidad, una carrera bien remunerada, y finalmente, paz y felicidad.

Mientras más me acercaba al final del bachillerato, más ansiosa me sentía de pensar en la universidad y en mi futura carrera. En secreto lo que más anhelaba eran las mismas ambiciones de mi infancia: tener hijos y cuidarlos. Pero nadie hablaba de la maternidad como una ambición, así que hice a un lado mi verdadero deseo y me mantuve en la senda educativa prescrita y vagamente dirigida que había dominado la mayor parte de mi vida.

A la edad de 16 años dejé la escuela y aprobé fácilmente el examen de desarrollo de educación general (GED, por sus siglas en inglés) equivalente al nivel de bachillerato que ofrece la universidad de la comunidad local. Mis tres hermanos menores pronto hicieron lo mismo.

Haber dejado la escuela dos años antes de terminar fue el primer paso hacia tomar la responsabilidad y ser consciente de las posibilidades para mi propio futuro. Ahora veo mi escape de la preparatoria como la liberación de mi mente y mi corazón.

Durante los siguientes años redescubrí el gozo de aprender. Procedí a aprender todo lo que quise a través de una combinación de formas. Tomé clases y talleres de arte y escritura. Leí libros. Y lo hice, ya no con el propósito de obtener un empleo ni por demostrarle nada a nadie, sino por puro enriquecimiento personal.

Vida entera

Algunos padres educadores en casa intentan separar las actividades de aprendizaje del resto de la vida familiar. De igual manera, algunos padres convencionales intentan separar sus responsabilidades de crianza del resto de la vida. Una familia que practica la escuela en casa (*homeschooling*) puede crear separación al reservar bloques de tiempo para el aprendizaje obligatorio, tal vez en áreas designadas para eso.

Por su parte, los miembros de familias *unschoolers* viven juntos como socios de vidas completas e integradas, libres de divisiones ilusorias. Sabemos que no podemos vivir sin aprender y no necesitamos designar un tiempo especial para hacerlo, por lo que estos niños rara vez perciben una separación clara entre lo que hacen y lo que aprenden. El aprendizaje simplemente sucede, a menudo, sin que el aprendiz sea consciente de ello. Los niños de estas familias se sienten a gusto en su mundo. Sus padres actúan como modelos a seguir en el mundo real y los invitan a participar en actividades de adultos, por lo que los niños desarrollan un nivel de confianza y conciencia propia que rara vez vemos en la gente escolarizada.

Los *unschoolers* tienen el tiempo y la libertad para conocerse a sí mismos y a las demás personas en su vida. Tienden a interactuar con adultos más cómodamente que los niños escolarizados, quienes deben ver a sus mayores como superiores. Tienen la libertad para valorar y respetar la aptitud de los adultos que pueden proporcionar experiencias y oportunidades de aprendizaje. Mis hijas expresan gratitud espontáneamente a mí, a su papá y a todos sus maestros de la comunidad.

Puede ser que los niños que sí fueron a la escuela en el pasado necesiten algún tiempo para desescolarizarse: para borrar las divisiones arbitrarias en sus vidas. No obstante, debido a la flexibilidad y adaptabilidad naturales de los niños, es posible que su proceso sea más fácil que el de un adulto completamente escolarizado. Para los niños, gran parte de la vida se percibe como algo nuevo. Con nuevas experiencias, continuamente se encuentran formando y cambiando grandes ideas. Continúan explorando y descubriendo sus pensamientos y sentimientos sobre cómo viven o les gustaría vivir de manera diferente.

Cuando los niños que fueron escolarizados dejan atrás la escuela, de repente sus vidas se vuelven más ligeras y libres. Puede que al principio se resistan a las actividades que ellos interpretan como educativas (al menos aquellas en las que conscientemente reconocen la enseñanza), pero con el tiempo bajan la guardia, se relajan y recuperan su curiosidad natural y el simple gozo de aprender y hacer cosas nuevas. Tú también puedes hacerlo.

Conversaciones con familiares

Muchas veces me asombro de cuánto interés y preocupación expresa la gente por los niños que no van a la escuela.

Amigos y parientes preocupados sin experiencia personal en la educación sin escuela se imaginan que los niños tendrán oportunidades de aprendizaje limitadas, que carecerán de experiencias sociales, que tendrán problemas para entrar a la universidad o para adaptarse a la vida laboral.

Puedes intentar disipar esos temores hablando de la amplia variedad de oportunidades de aprendizaje que hay para educadores en casa, las experiencias sociales y de aprendizaje de la vida real disponibles a través de tu comunidad, y el hecho de que generaciones de niños educados en casa no sólo llegan a la universidad, sino que tienen carreras exitosas. Sin embargo, si tus respuestas no convencen a otros, trata de no preocuparte. Así como no puedes enseñar a un niño poco receptivo, tampoco puedes llegar a adultos poco receptivos.

No necesitas defender tus decisiones ni demostrarle nada a nadie. No necesitas enredarte en polémica simplemente porque alguien desafía tus preferencias. Si lo deseas, puedes responder las preguntas desafiantes con tus propias preguntas. Pregunta por qué.

El temor nace de lo que no entendemos, de lo que conocemos poco o de lo que no hemos experimentado. La mayoría de la gente en la cultura occidental fue a la escuela y muchos creen que los niños necesitan ir a la escuela para convertirse en adultos competentes. Nunca han imaginado algo distinto.

Requisitos legales de aprendizaje

Los requisitos educativos para los niños dependen del lugar donde vivas. En los Estados Unidos el gobierno de cada estado regula la certificación de niños educados en casa a través de documentación requerida o de una prueba anual o evaluación.
Por lo general, las asociaciones o grupos locales de educación en el hogar son la mejor fuente de interpretaciones prácticas y requisitos legales para educar sin escuela.

Algunas localidades tienen requisitos para los padres educadores, como:

- Aprobar un curso de capacitación;
- Haber completado un número mínimo de créditos universitarios;
- Reunirse periódicamente con un maestro certificado; o
- Recibir aprobación del gobierno local.

Los estándares académicos o requisitos de aprendizaje no suelen dictar el estilo o método de aprendizaje, sino que simplemente disponen expectativas de rendimiento para cada grado.
Bajo las leyes de mi gobierno local para la educación en el hogar, mi familia no ha tenido problemas para cumplir con los requisitos legales de aprendizaje (estándares académicos, objetivos por grados o expectativas de rendimiento).

Documentación. Con un poco de creatividad, puedes traducir las actividades de aprendizaje *unschooling* de tus hijos al lenguaje institucional y al formato que los funcionarios escolares y gubernamentales entienden y prefieren. Por ejemplo, pasar un rato en la playa se traduce como «salir de excursión», «actividades prácticas», o «clase de ciencias de la tierra, magnetismo, química, biología», etc.

Algunas veces, a medida que aumenta su conocimiento de las expectativas institucionales, los niños *unschoolers* son víctimas de la preocupación de cómo sus logros académicos se comparan con los de los niños escolarizados de su misma edad. Puede que sientan presión por parte de sus compañeros o parientes. Si esto les ocurre a tus hijos, puedes proponerles que revisen una lista de estándares académicos generales para que se evalúen ellos mismos.

La enciclopedia World Book prepara un programa de estudio generalizado para los Estados Unidos, desde preescolar hasta bachillerato. Tú y tus hijos pueden usarlo como una guía o como una fuente de ideas de temas y habilidades por seguir.
Muchas veces, consultar esta lista da tranquilidad, pues lo que parece una larga lista de requisitos, en realidad contiene mucha repetición y sentido común.
En todo el mundo hay familias que siguen la filosofía *unschooling*. Encuéntralos, reúnete con ellos, formen comunidades, y ayúdense unos a otros a investigar las leyes sobre educación en casa, así como a desafiar la legislación y proteger libertades cuando sea necesario.

World Book
https://www.worldbook.com/

Un ambiente de aprendizaje

Los padres *unschoolers* apoyan a sus hijos proveyéndoles una rica atmósfera de aprendizaje llena de posibilidades y libre de presión.

Este capítulo comprende las siguientes secciones:

Materiales,
Enriquecimiento,
Vida familiar, y
Actividades diarias.

Aunque el tiempo que las familias no escolarizadas pasan en casa varía mucho, la casa normalmente sirve como base de operaciones. Mis hijas realizan muchas de sus actividades de aprendizaje en casa y emprenden la mayoría de sus aventuras desde casa. Crear el espacio en el que vivimos supone mucha actividad que toda la familia disfruta. Descubrirás un sinfín de posibilidades en los objetos cotidianos y en la multitud de personas de tu vida. Tener acceso a gente y cosas interesantes contribuye a una rica atmósfera de aprendizaje.

Cada familia trabaja de manera diferente y cada niño tiene diferentes necesidades e intereses, por lo que el espacio que cada familia crea tiene un toque único. Puedes comenzar a observar tu hogar y el de otros a través del lente de una curiosidad fresca. Enriquecer tu hogar no necesariamente debe ser costoso. Las familias educadoras en casa tienen diferentes presupuestos y usan su creatividad para explorar sus intereses con poca inversión económica.
Piensa en bibliotecas, intercambios de saberes y de libros, etc. El que una familia llene su casa de materiales educativos en abundancia o que use más los recursos externos, depende mucho del lugar donde viva, de su proximidad con recursos comunitarios y de sus finanzas.

Materiales

Se vale de todo. Artículos del hogar, materiales para manualidades, libros, textos, enciclopedias, cuadernos de ejercicios, videos, computadoras, Internet, videojuegos, objetos de la naturaleza, herramientas de jardinería, utensilios de cocina, etc. Los niños pueden usar todo ello en su búsqueda de información y experiencia.

Puedes comprar materiales educativos y otras cosas, tomar prestados libros y películas de la biblioteca local, conseguir materiales usados en ventas de cochera o tiendas de segunda mano, y compartir materiales entre otras familias educadoras.

Los grupos locales de familias educadoras en casa a menudo organizan intercambios de materiales. Existen otras fuentes de donaciones comunitarias, intercambios y ventas de bienes usados, como las siguientes:

Freecycle, *http://freecycle.org*
Paperback Swap, *http://paperbackswap.com*
eBay, *http://ebay.com*

Educar en casa no tiene por qué ser gravoso para el presupuesto familiar. De hecho, de acuerdo con un estudio reciente[23] en el que se comparan familias que educan en casa y familias con estudiantes en escuelas públicas, las familias en casa gastan dramáticamente menos dinero por año por estudiante ($600 USD en promedio), que las escuelas públicas ($10,000 USD en promedio), con resultados significativamente mejores.

Libros. Los libros proveen información de fácil acceso. Algunas de las editoriales favoritas de mis hijas son Usborne, Scholastic, Random House, y Klutz.

---

[23] Ray, B. (2009) Progress Report: Homeschool Academic Achievement and Demographics. National Home Education Research Institute (NHERI).

En vez de tener el clásico cuarto de televisión, la recámara principal de nuestra casa es la biblioteca familiar. Tenemos libreros alineados con las paredes y comparten el espacio con un sofá, una silla cómoda, una mesita pegada a la pared, y libros por todas partes.

A mis hijas les gusta crear colecciones de libros de sus temas favoritos (dinosaurios, caballos y ponis, vida marina, mitología, etc.) Nos han regalado muchos, muchos libros de familias cuyos hijos ya no los necesitan. Disfrutamos llenar nuestro carrito con los libros que ya no necesitamos e ir a intercambiarlos en la biblioteca local de libros usados. A menudo busco en eBay colecciones económicas como la serie *El autobús mágico*, que a mis hijas les encanta. *Wright on Time* es una serie de aventuras escrita por Lisa Cottrell-Bentley, acerca de una familia *unschooler*.

Arte y manualidades. Generalmente se pueden encontrar materiales para arte y manualidades de muy buena calidad en librerías escolares, tiendas de arte y de manualidades, tiendas de maestros o tiendas de arquitectura y diseño. Mis hijas también disfrutan el beneficio de todos los materiales que usé en la universidad, cuando estudiaba la carrera de artes plásticas.

Si el estilo artístico de tus hijos tiende hacia la abundancia, entonces un rollo de papel para dibujar en un dispensador o un caballete pueden ser una solución económica para mantenerlos siempre abastecidos. Las tizas, los lápices, acuarelas, esponjas, crayones, marcadores no son muy costosos.

Música. Hagan música. Toquen música. Escuchen música. Intenten no aprender música. No dejes que practicar música se convierta en tarea escolar. Dales instrumentos a tus hijos y déjalos tocar. Desde que eran muy pequeñas mis hijas han compuesto piezas musicales sorprendentemente hermosas y creativas con guitarras, teclados, armónicas, tambores, cascabeles, panderos, sus voces y sus cuerpos. Veo un video de Ilana de tres años tocando su guitarra y cantando una canción que ella misma compuso, y me asombra lo naturalmente melodiosa, rítmica y hermosa se oye su música.

Encontré una tabla de acordes para manos pequeñas y la puse en la pared cerca de las guitarras. Mis hijas no han tenido ninguna instrucción musical formal, pero a la edad de seis años, Maia leía las notas y tocaba los acordes. De manera similar, dijo que tocaría *Mary tenía un borreguito* con su flauta dulce. Y lo hizo, a pesar de que nunca había recibido ninguna instrucción de solfeo ni de flauta.

Había conseguido un libro y ella sola descubrió cómo hacer lo que quería. No fue hasta que estableció su capacidad por sí misma que se mostró receptiva para recibir más instrucciones de mi parte.

Los tambores son, instintivamente, los primeros instrumentos. Mi hija menor, Kalea, ha tocado el tambor desde que tenía cuatro meses. Cuando vi que le gustaba aplaudir y palmear su cuerpo para hacer música, le di un tambor. Repite ritmos que escuchamos en un disco y luego inventa los propios. Lo hemos hecho desde que tomamos clases juntas en Musikgarten.

Remo Percussion fabrica tambores para niños de calidad profesional. Mi familia tiene varios tambores Remo, así como varios tambores de juguete que suenan muy lindo, comprados en tiendas departamentales.

Remo Percussion
(*Instrumentos de calidad profesional para niños*)
http://www.remo.com

Mis hijas tienen la antigua casetera de su papá en su cuarto junto con mi colección de música de adolescente y otros casetes de parientes que hemos coleccionado.

Cada verano asistimos a conciertos gratis que se llevan a cabo en el parque, disfrutamos de una variedad de música local y bailamos junto con nuestros vecinos.

Materiales educativos. A mis hijas les gustan los libros de ejercicios, de acertijos, las enciclopedias, los equipos de ciencias, y otros productos abiertamente educativos. En las exposiciones de currículos para educación en el hogar se encuentra una gran variedad de paquetes curriculares, libros, materiales de arte y manualidades, clases y programas, etc. Nos encantan los estands de LEGO y Usborne.

En especial, a mis hijas les encantan las series de libros informativos, como:

El autobús mágico, (Scholastic), para ciencias;
Magic Tree House (Random House), para historia y geografía;
Max Axiom (Capstone Press), para ciencia gráfica.
Chester Comix (Bentley Boyd), para historia gráfica.

Quienes educan en casa pueden aprovechar las rebajas de muchos productos durante el año escolar, al igual que los precios de oferta de fin de año y los descuentos para los grupos de educación en casa.

Homeschool Buyers Co-op
(*Cooperativa de compras para educadores en casa*)
https://homeschoolbuyersco-op.org/?source=21877
(El número al final del enlace es mi código de afiliados)

Enriquecimiento

Sandra Dodd, partidaria de la filosofía *unschooling*, promueve una práctica a la que ella ha llamado siembra[24]. Consiste en dejar cosas interesantes por toda la casa donde los niños puedan descubrirlas. Mis hijas me inspiraron a que nombráramos nuestra propia versión de esta práctica *espolvorear*, teniendo en mente la imagen de un hada con una varita mágica que esparce o espolvorea nuestra casa con regalos y sorpresas. A esta práctica yo también le llamo enriquecimiento del hogar.

Polvo de hada tomarás,
la pluma de un ángel,
y un poquito de ternura y amor.
Todo junto lo mezclarás,
sin olvidar un sentimiento o dos,
un deseo sincero, un puño de encanto,
y un rayo de sol...
Es la receta para una niña excepcional.

– Autor desconocido.

Enriquecer tu hogar puede significar poner un nuevo pliego de papel sobre el caballete, dejar lápices de colores al alcance, acomodar libros o revistas en un estante bajo o poner a la vista libros de acertijos, juegos, videos, equipos deportivos, instrumentos musicales, etc.

Yo *espolvoreo* la bandeja de bocadillos de mis hijas con nuevos alimentos. Cuando conseguimos un vegetal nuevo en nuestra caja semanal de la granja, abro nuestro catálogo de productos frescos en la página correspondiente y lo pongo en la mesa. Cuando veo algo interesante en el departamento de frutas y verduras del supermercado, como brócoli romanesco, o coliflor naranja, lo compro.

---

[24]*N. de la T.:* La palabra inglesa es *strewing* (esparcir, desparramar), pero en español algunas mamás se han referido a este mismo concepto como siembra.

Luego quizá mencione algo de las figuras fractales o la familia de las crucíferas, para ver si las niñas quieren saber más.

Muchos papás suelen rotar los juguetes de las áreas de juego de sus hijos. Esta práctica hace que los juguetes viejos recuperen su frescura y atractivo, y reduce el gasto de comprar juguetes nuevos continuamente. Cuando noto que mis hijas no han jugado mucho con algo, lo guardo y lo cambio por otra cosa que no han visto en algún tiempo. Algunos espacios de nuestra casa se saturan tanto, que, con agradecimiento, ellas ayudan a empacar las cosas para reducir el desorden. Los espacios abiertos nos refrescan y nos abren a la creatividad. Una mesa vacía y materiales bien ordenados como papel, plumas, lápices nos ruegan ser usados. Tomamos prestadas cosas interesantes de la biblioteca, o de amigos y familiares, y compramos otras usadas o con descuentos a precios muy bajos.

Los artículos no necesariamente deben tener un propósito educativo para despertar interés. Por ejemplo, algunas piedras de río podrían encauzar muchas aventuras emocionantes (geología, geografía, energía, fósiles, minería, arqueología, etc.) A mis hijas les encantan las exposiciones de rocas y gemas, al igual que nuestras expediciones para recolectar piedras. Los juguetes viejos que los abuelos guardan pueden inspirar proyectos de genealogía, historia, fabricación de juguetes, tecnología. Cuando mi suegra nos regaló un antiguo juego de té de plata que requería pulirse, Maia se embarcó en un estudio de metales.

Con deleite, mi esposo le contó todo lo que sabía sobre el tema, desde elementos básicos hasta armas medievales y herrería.
Ilana constantemente me sorprende al expresar su interés por algunas de mis posesiones, las cuales nunca pensé que le atrajeran. Cuando tenía dos años, me pidió una baraja de tarot que estaba lejos de su alcance. Después de observarla, me pidió el libro que la acompañaba. Luego hablamos de las imágenes arquetípicas con las que estaba familiarizada por algunos cuentos populares.

Sandra Dodd amplía la siembra llevando a sus hijos a lugares donde puedan descubrir cosas que de otra forma no habrían descubierto: ventas de cochera, tiendas de antigüedades, centros comerciales, mercados, lotes baldíos, áreas naturales.

Recientemente, mis hijas y yo nos desviamos de nuestro camino para llegar a una tienda de antigüedades atiborrada de objetos, pero fascinante. Me hizo recordar el departamento de mi abuela, así que platicamos de ella, de sus adornos, de sus muñecas de porcelana de los años 50, sus discos de vinilo, sus acordeones...

Las niñas se sintieron atraídas por unos señuelos de pesca antiguos y también platicamos de ellos. Eso condujo a un viaje para pescar, a prácticas de lanzamiento en nuestra piscina, al estudio de una guía de pesca para niños, a una serie de libros para niños sobre pesca con mosca, a charlas de cuando a su papá le encantaba pescar, y a un interés continuo en todo lo relacionado con la pesca.

Ellas muestran el mismo entusiasmo para ir a una nueva tienda departamental, que para ir al zoológico o a cualquier otro destino recreativo. Recuerdo el sentimiento de exploración y descubrimiento que nos producía mirar escaparates a mis hermanos y a mí cuando éramos niños. Sospecho que mis hijas experimentan sentimientos similares incluso cuando vamos de paseo y tomamos una ruta diferente a la de la vez anterior.

Cuando se entretienen justo en el momento que yo quisiera apurarme y terminar rápido algún recado en la calle, entonces me recuerdo a mí misma que para los niños el mundo es nuevo e interesante. Ellas me lo recuerdan cuando me muestran botones de flores y orugas que, de otra forma, yo habría pasado por alto.

Vida Familiar

Durante sus primeros dos años, noté la forma en que Ilana y Kalea observaban a su hermana mayor con asombro e imitaban mucho de lo que ella hacía. Al parecer, ella misma les proporcionó lo más interesante durante algún tiempo, tal vez porque representaba su potencial en un futuro cercano. Tener personas de quiénes aprender quizá cumpla un propósito más importante que los propios materiales. Las personas dentro del hogar y quienes nos rodean son los primeros modelos de los niños. Cuando ellos nos ven leer, escribir o usar el dinero, muestran interés en hacer lo mismo, o al menos, en entender por qué hacemos esas cosas.

Los niños se convierten en adultos, por lo que buscan aprender sobre los adultos: nos observan a nosotros y a los demás adultos en sus vidas. Podemos brindarles la oportunidad de que participen en nuestras actividades regulares, como las labores domésticas, los mandados, nuestros pasatiempos. Por más que algunas veces lo único que quiero es terminar con alguna tarea, reduzco la velocidad cuando Kalea quiere sacar la ropa de la secadora o jugar con agua en el fregadero.

De igual manera, Maia e Ilana regularmente quieren intentar cocinar, ayudarme a cuidar a la bebé, y muchas otras de las actividades de mi rutina. Ambas crean sus propios libros y también se sientan ante el ordenador un rato todos los días. No es de sorprender que se sientan atraídas a las computadoras, viéndome a mí tecleando y a su papá programando videojuegos. Las dos tienen una propia y las han usado sin ayuda desde que tenían tres años. El deseo de Maia de navegar en los menús la inspiró a aprender a leer.

Los padres, hermanos y demás miembros de una familia *unschooler* pasan tiempo participando en juegos y en proyectos, y otras veces, simplemente se mantienen disponibles para responder preguntas o ayudar en la búsqueda de los intereses del niño o en la solución de problemas.

Por lo general, los niños más pequeños hacen más preguntas, ya que todavía no saben cómo encontrar las respuestas por ellos mismos. Cuando no sepas la respuesta a una pregunta, muéstrale a tu hijo cómo encontrarla y pronto estará encontrando más y más respuestas él solito.

Por ejemplo, Maia solía acudir a mí cada vez que no entendía una palabra. Le enseñé a usar el diccionario y entonces comenzó a venir, entusiasmada, a mostrarme definiciones. Luego descubrió las enciclopedias, seguidas de otros libros de referencia, como diccionarios de sinónimos y antónimos, atlas, etc. Veo manuales de gramática en su futuro.

Mis hijas tienen la colección de enciclopedias *Childcraft* publicada por World Book, que pertenecía a su papá cuando era niño, y que ellas valoran mucho debido a esa historia. También tienen un par de libros infantiles que nos pertenecieron a su papá y a mí cuando éramos niños.

A veces los niños preferirán actividades grupales o individuales, estructuradas o libres, de aprendizaje enfocado o de juego imaginativo. A veces tus hijos preferirán seguir sus propios intereses y otras veces expresarán curiosidad por los tuyos. Permite que ellos te den la pauta. Ciertamente puedes ofrecer información o sugerir una actividad, pero si se resisten, no insistas por el momento: déjalo para otra ocasión.

Yo me enfoco en mi papel de mamá. Mis hijas quieren que yo haga lo que hago para que puedan aprender de mí. Cuando tienen intereses de los que yo sé muy poco o nada, les ayudo a encontrar personas que sí saben acerca de esos intereses; no necesariamente maestros, sino gente real que realiza ese trabajo, pasatiempo o lo que sea, porque le encanta hacerlo. Amigos, parientes y miembros de grupos de educadores en casa pueden poner en común sus habilidades y ofrecerlas a todos los niños de la familia o del grupo.

Todos somos expertos en alguna área, desde programación de computadoras hasta reparación de autos, carpintería o trabajo doméstico.

Mis hijas tienen una bisabuela que confecciona patrones para ropa; otra abuela que hace colchas y era dueña de una tienda donde los vendía; un papá que programa videojuegos y una mamá que hace trabajo de madre, el cual ellas aspiran realizar, y que tiene una pasión por habilidades naturalistas, música folclórica y narración. Entre nuestros vecinos hay un músico y un constructor de barcos. Nuestra localidad tiene muy buenos instructores de danza, maestros de arte y un bibliotecario infantil que siempre recuerda los nombres de mis hijas y les pregunta cómo están, al igual que los cajeros del supermercado y los empleados de la oficina de correos. Hemos realizado algunas excursiones al departamento de policía local, a la oficina de correos y a la tienda de mascotas.

Durante mi infancia temprana, mi abuela me enseñó a coser, a seguir una receta, a cultivar y cosechar hortalizas y a hacer conservas. El asilo de ancianos de nuestra localidad ofrece clases a familias que demuestran esas habilidades también. Las oportunidades abundan.

Actividades diarias

El orden en un hogar *unschooler* generalmente funciona por rutinas más que por horarios. En casa tenemos rutinas familiares que incluyen un tiempo de actividades que mis hijas realizan por su cuenta, y un tiempo de interacción conmigo, entre ellas, o con personas fuera de casa.

Por ejemplo, en un día normal, Ilana puede jugar un rato a solas, dibujar, bailar, cantar, armar rompecabezas, jugar con muñecas, o algún otro juego de fantasía. Más tarde, puede ser que quiera acompañarme a preparar la comida o a hacer alguna labor doméstica, o tal vez quiera ver un video o escuchar música. Muchas veces me pide que le prenda la computadora, que juegue con ella o que le lea. Maia también pasa algún tiempo a solas resolviendo libros de actividades y tomando clases en línea, jugando videojuegos, viendo videos, o algún otro proyecto. Más tarde, puede que pase algún tiempo en el jardín o en la casa de la vecina.

Todas mis hijas toman clases en la comunidad y asisten a actividades regulares con nuestros grupos de apoyo de educadores en el hogar. Pertenecemos a una asociación estatal, a un grupo local de educadores en casa, y a un grupo local de *unschooling*. También comenzamos un club de juegos en nuestra ciudad.

Mis hijas tienden a enfocarse en intereses particulares por ciclos. Por ejemplo, Maia ha pedido tomar un período sabático de las clases de arte. Mientras tanto, ha trasladado su atención creativa a las manualidades, diseño de modas y danza. También tomó un descanso similar del *ballet*, durante el cual bailaba por su cuenta en casa, antes de regresar a la instrucción formal de nuevo.

Muchas veces, mis hijas utilizan diversas formas de tecnología, como videos y suscripciones en línea (Netflix, JumpStart, BrainPOP, Discovery Streaming), y una variedad de sitios de Internet y programas para la computadora.

Algunos padres *unschoolers* aceptan fácilmente las posibilidades que ofrecen la televisión, los videos, los juegos de computadora, el Internet, las cintas de audio, etc., mientras que otros expresan miedo. Entre los argumentos para limitar o excluir actividades «de pantalla», en general se encuentran los siguientes:

- La televisión y los videojuegos dañan, o al menos, no benefician a los niños;
- La televisión y los videojuegos consumen tiempo que los niños podrían pasar haciendo otras actividades más benéficas;
- La televisión y los videojuegos proporcionan una visión poco realista del mundo que enfatiza las peores características de nuestra sociedad (violencia, comercio, sexismo, etc.)

Entre los argumentos para usar la televisión y los medios asociados (videos, videojuegos), en general se encuentran los siguientes:

- La televisión y los videojuegos ofrecen entretenimiento;
- La televisión y los videojuegos brindan experiencias de aprendizaje o disparan aprendizajes futuros a través de una variedad de caricaturas, programación regular, televisión pública, documentales y canales de interés especial.

Es común que los niños que recién dejaron la escuela se den atracones de televisión y videojuegos durante el proceso de desescolarización o después de que los padres hayan levantado una restricción. Sin embargo, innumerables familias han contado historias similares en las que las respuestas de desenfreno de los niños se van equilibrando con el tiempo. (El mismo concepto se aplica a las restricciones alimentarias y los atracones).

Yo nunca he limitado el tiempo de pantalla de mis hijas. A veces pasan toda una semana sin prender la televisión o la computadora. Nunca hemos tenido servicio de televisión. La han visto en casa de otras personas, pero nunca la han pedido.

Entre los argumentos en contra del uso de la computadora por lo general prevalece el miedo a que los niños pequeños que usan Internet queden expuestos a contenido inapropiado, a acosadores cibernéticos o a citas peligrosas. Sin embargo, se puede evitar contenido perturbador usando navegadores con protección infantil, servicios como una interfaz de video segura para niños y motores de búsqueda para niños.

Yo he preferido que mis hijas tengan acceso a Internet de una manera relativamente ilimitada al mismo tiempo que protejo su seguridad: en vez de usar un navegador con protección infantil, tengo un blog para ellas con todos sus enlaces favoritos y nuevas publicaciones diarias, lo que les ayuda a mantenerse en la esfera de su comodidad e intereses. Hablamos sobre los peligros potenciales en el ciberespacio, cuál información mantener privada, y algunas otras prácticas de seguridad en línea.

Experiencias de Aprendizaje

A medida que una familia se instala en el estilo de vida *unschooling*, cada vez más va reconociendo el aprendizaje que cada uno de sus miembros adquiere a través de las actividades diarias. Los padres van desarrollando sensibilidad para saber en qué momento sus hijos están receptivos a la guía e instrucción de nuevos temas, y aprenden a confiar en ellos para buscar qué quieren o qué necesitan saber.

Este capítulo comprende las siguientes secciones:

Aprendizaje en casa,
Útiles escolares y planes de estudio,
Aprendizaje fuera del hogar, y
Clases estructuradas.

Los niños aprenden algo de todas sus actividades y períodos de descanso, sin importar qué tan obvio o no, o qué tan valioso o no pueda parecer ese algo para los demás. Con el tiempo, los papás aprenden a reconocer el aprendizaje diario, a ver el valor de la actividad y del descanso, y a respetar el valor particular de todo aprendizaje.

Cuando una de mis hijas me dice que no quiere continuar con un proyecto, yo aprecio el hecho de que ha aprendido a respetar sus propios límites y que se dé un descanso cuando lo necesita. No quiero verla ir en contra de su deseo saludable de tomar un descanso. Continúo desescolarizando mi propia inclinación entrenada para luchar en contra de mi necesidad natural de descanso.

Dependiendo de las diferencias de estilo de vida, los niños que viven la filosofía del *unschooling* pueden tener más aprendizaje dentro o fuera de la casa, a través de experiencias naturales de la vida o a través de medios educativos más convencionales. En cualquier caso, cuando los niños disfrutan de lo que hacen con su tiempo, existen abundantes posibilidades de crecimiento.

Aprendizaje en casa

Aprendemos *haciendo*, y mucho de lo que hacemos se lleva a cabo en la casa, cerca de ella, o desde ella, como punto de partida. Para nuestra familia, la casa incluye nuestro jardín, el bosque detrás de la casa, el arroyo, el parque más cercano, el río en la colina, el lago después de la colina, y el vecindario y negocios cercanos.

En casa, un niño puede realizar actividades como leer, escribir, dibujar, hacer manualidades, cocinar, hornear, limpiar y reparar la casa, cuidar mascotas, trabajar en el jardín, observar el cielo, tener conversaciones sobre cualquier tema, hacer negocios, nadar, andar en bicicleta, imaginar... Las actividades explícitamente educativas suelen ofrecer objetivos de aprendizaje claros. Entre las actividades educativas que un niño puede realizar en casa se encuentran: tomar cursos en línea, cursos en video o por correspondencia, ver videos, escuchar casetes, leer libros y manuales, trabajar en libros de texto, hacer experimentos, explorar y observar, etc.

Libros de no ficción. Podemos escoger libros de no ficción, comprados o prestados, para ayudar a nuestros hijos a alimentar sus intereses específicos y encontrar respuestas a sus preguntas. Dependiendo de su edad, puede que prefieran que nos involucremos activamente en el proceso o que sólo les ayudemos a conseguir los libros. Los libros narrativos escritos por personas apasionadas por un tema pueden captar la atención de los lectores e inspirarlos. Los libros de texto, de referencia y narraciones como autobiografías y memorias, pueden servirnos como fuentes de consulta.

Carpetas interactivas (Lapbooks). Básicamente, una carpeta interactiva es un fólder que contiene una colección de libritos, sobres, páginas, gráficas, historias, dibujos y cualquier cosa que el niño quiera añadir. Es una manera muy vistosa de presentar una recopilación de lo aprendido en un tiempo determinado. Pueden ser usadas de maneras muy variadas para propósitos variados.

Las carpetas interactivas involucran a los niños activamente y les brindan la oportunidad de usar sus habilidades manuales y su creatividad.

Mis hijas han confeccionado carpetas interactivas sobre temas como el dinero, los delfines, nuestra historia genealógica, los primates, la conservación ambiental, las manzanas, efemérides y la historia de nuestra ciudad. Las guardamos en una caja de archivos y les gusta mucho verlas y añadirles cosas cuando aprenden algo nuevo.

Matemáticas. Muchos de nosotros aprendimos las matemáticas de forma abstracta y confusa, como se enseñan en la escuela: a través de explicaciones, leyendo libros de texto, haciendo muchos ejercicios y presentando exámenes. De este modo, dependíamos casi totalmente de la memorización de tablas y fórmulas, y casi nada del entendimiento conceptual, que a menudo les resulta difícil a los niños adquirir en el entorno escolar.

Si bien es fácil que los padres comprendan cómo sus hijos pueden aprender las habilidades de matemáticas básicas y cálculo simplemente a través de las actividades cotidianas, puede que los temas más avanzados y especializados de las matemáticas sean los que les preocupan más, ya que probablemente nunca las dominaron ellos mismos.
Los chicos *unschoolers* aprenden los temas avanzados de las matemáticas a medida que surge la necesidad. Todos usamos las matemáticas como una herramienta para muchos propósitos, como cocinar, construir, cultivar, distribuir porciones y usar dinero. Un chico *unschooler* puede desarrollar matemáticas más avanzadas para averiguar cómo programar una computadora o para usar algún *software* complicado.

La aplicación de las matemáticas engloba reconocer patrones, clasificar, medir, pensar con lógica, resolver problemas, usar probabilidades, crear estadísticas. La destreza matemática nos ayuda a doblar el tanto de una receta, a construir una casita de juguete, a dividir parcelas en el jardín, a jugar un juego de mesa, a comprar juguetes.

Cuando nuestros hijos desean aprender un concepto avanzado de matemáticas que nosotros mismos no entendemos, no hay de qué preocuparse. Lo único que necesitamos es ayudarlos a encontrar la información de donde puedan aprenderlo (libros, juegos de computadora, videos, clases, tutoriales, tutores, profesionales, etc.)

Lectura y Escritura. Según publicaciones en la web, los niños de Norteamérica, por lo general, reciben instrucción y comienzan a leer solos en algún momento durante el primer grado, alrededor de los seis o siete años. Sin embargo, ello no quiere decir que estos niños comprendan lo que leen y que puedan redactar trabajos con buena caligrafía.

Conforme a los valores de confianza y respeto de esta filosofía, los chicos *unschoolers* aprenden a leer y a escribir cuando ellos así lo deciden. El proceso de aprendizaje para leer puede tomar meses o años, y puede comenzar a cualquier edad. Si se les da el tiempo y el espacio para hacerlo, y la libertad para que cada uno encuentre su método preferido, aprender a leer puede ser un proceso sin estrés.

En mi familia, por ejemplo, observé cómo mis hijas ponían atención a las letras cuando tenían alrededor de dos o tres años, fingiendo que leían (jugaban a leer). Aprendieron los sonidos como a los tres o cuatro años, y pronunciaron y reconocieron palabras enteras a partir de los cinco.

Mis hijas aprendieron a leer usando muchos recursos. Su papá y yo siempre nos hemos turnado para leerles todas las noches antes de acostarse, y también en otros momentos durante el día. Han usado fragmentos del programa *Hooked on Phonics,* el sitio web Starfall, las series de televisión de Plaza Sésamo, y las lecciones del libro *Teach Your Child to Read in 100 Easy Lessons*[25].

---

[25] Engelmann, S. (1986) *Teach Your Child to Read in 100 Easy Lessons*, Touchstone, New York.

Ilana aprendió a leer a una edad más temprana que Maia, quien es mayor. Tal vez porque ya había materiales para aprender en nuestra casa y muchas actividades por doquier. Para cuando se me ocurrió ofrecerle una lección a Ilana, ella ya sabía leer, aunque no se había memorizado la canción del alfabeto.

Los libros constituyen sólo una forma de material de lectura. A un niño que no se sienta atraído a los libros de cuentos, ofrécele revistas, cómics o videojuegos. Si un niño no expresa interés en leer a la edad de seis o siete, léele tú, o lee para ti misma, esparce material de lectura por toda tu casa y no te preocupes innecesariamente. Los niños van a querer leer por su cuenta en algún momento.

Ciencias. Al igual que las matemáticas, las ciencias nos rodean. La ciencia en general involucra observación, medición, y razonamiento acerca de qué pasaría si las circunstancias cambiaran. Tus hijos muestran interés en conceptos científicos cuando juegan en el lodo, cuando ayudan a cocinar, o cuando preguntan cómo funcionan las cosas.

Antes de usar un vocabulario especializado, ofréceles herramientas como microscopios, portaobjetos previamente preparados, lupas, vasos de precipitación, pinzas, reglas, colorante comestible, y muchas oportunidades para explorar. Muéstrales a tus hijos tu propia curiosidad por el mundo. Respóndeles sus preguntas y ayúdalos a encontrar las respuestas que no sabes (en libros, clases, videos, experimentos.) No te preocupes por las disciplinas científicas o por la terminología. Tus hijos aprenderán esos nombres cuando persistan en algún tema. Concéntrense en divertirse explorando y experimentando.

Recuerdo que cuando Maia tenía unos tres años, me decía que quería aprender sobre «peceología». Quizá era una señal temprana de su fascinación por el mundo acuático.

Con el tiempo, mi familia ha creado su propia forma de aprendizaje por niveles, en la que primero aprendemos de la forma más casual y experimental, y después nos damos la oportunidad de profundizar en las complejidades del tema conectando conceptos, usando recursos tecnológicos y algunas veces, realizando trabajos escritos.

Historia y Ciencias Sociales. Las disciplinas de humanidades, historia y ciencias sociales nos cuentan historias. La historia que yo recuerdo de mis días en la escuela enfatizaba hechos, eventos cronológicos, fechas, nombres... que se encontraban en un libro de texto. Mis hijas tienen acceso a biografías, narraciones, documentales, docudramas, obras de teatro históricas, y en algunas ocasiones, hasta personas que recuerdan eventos históricos. Cuando viajamos, tomamos nota de monumentos y lugares históricos.

No te preocupes por el orden cronológico. Los niños se sienten atraídos en diferentes momentos a personas, áreas geográficas o periodos de la historia específicos. El contexto cronológico para esos tiempos y lugares se desarrolla a medida que tu hijo aprende sobre diferentes periodos. Puede que a tus hijos les guste usar líneas de tiempo y mapas para marcar eventos.

Mis hijas tienen una línea de tiempo de la prehistoria que se extiende a lo largo de la pared, al lado de su litera, y un gran mapa del mundo en el pasillo afuera de su puerta. También han disfrutado aprender sobre lugares y gente a través de una suscripción mensual de aventuras en las que se resuelven misterios: cada una de ellas se desarrolla en una parte diferente del mundo. Además de series de historias de aventura que se desarrollan en los 50 estados de EUA, como también de las series de *La Casa del Árbol* por Mary Pope Osborne. Cada vez que recibimos una nueva entrega o libro, creamos una pila nueva de libros relacionados en nuestra biblioteca, y observamos cuando el tema llega a nuestras vidas de otras formas.

Puede que el interés histórico de tu hijo se desarrolle a partir de otras áreas de interés como las artes, los carros, construcciones, aparatos, lugares históricos, etc. La historia, al igual que otras «materias», se conecta con todo lo demás. No necesitamos centrarnos ni limitarnos a una sola materia o programa de estudios en particular.

Útiles escolares y planes de estudio

La clave para usar materiales escolares o educativos diseñados especialmente para aprender reside en el uso que tus hijos le den a lo que ellos mismos elijan y bajo sus propios objetivos. Mis hijas han usado programas de estudio como el de *Hooked on Phonic*s, pero ellas lo usan a su manera. No necesariamente siguen los pasos ni completan todas las repeticiones.

Selección de programas educativos. De la misma forma, yo disfruto buscando currículos y programas en catálogos educativos o sitios web sobre educación en casa, como Homeschool.com. Uso estos recursos como fuentes de ideas que puedo ofrecerles a mis hijas cuando presiento que podrían gustarles.

Un currículo generalmente consta de planes de clase para el maestro y libros de texto, libros de trabajo y materiales complementarios para los estudiantes. El programa puede incluir el servicio de un maestro certificado para asesorías y exámenes. Algunos programas expiden un certificado escolar si los niños completan el programa de acuerdo con sus normas, lo que podría ser de utilidad para los jóvenes *unschoolers* mayores, si, por ejemplo, quieren obtener un diploma de preparatoria.

Otros recursos educativos:
- Libros de referencia (como atlas, diccionarios y enciclopedias)
- Guías de campo
- Periódicos
- Revistas

- Artículos de la biblioteca (libros, videos, audios)
- Juegos educativos para la computadora
- Equipo y materiales de ciencias
- Material para arte y manualidades
- Herramientas y equipo de construcción
- Instrucción e instrumentos musicales

Materiales compatibles con el unschooling. Existen compañías, como Fun Books, a través de la cual se pueden ordenar currículos compatibles con el *unschooling* y materiales educativos sobre muchos temas, así como números de la revista *Growing without Schooling*, de John Holt.

Fun Books
http://fun-books.com

Con montones de materiales educativos por toda la casa, uno puede sentir que ya ha cubierto todo, pero también busca en recursos comunitarios como librerías, museos, sitios históricos, palacios de gobierno, museos de historia natural, al igual que personas que conozcas que puedan compartir habilidades, responder preguntas y permitirles a tus hijos observar o incluso participar en su trabajo.

Aprendizaje fuera del hogar

Muchas de las experiencias de aprendizaje se realizan fuera de casa en lugares obvios como bibliotecas, museos y escuelas, pero también durante visitas a amigos, diligencias diarias, viajes a lugares favoritos o nuevos, y mucho más.

Maia tiene un lugar secreto al aire libre donde se sienta, piensa, se relaja, observa el vecindario y solo ella sabe qué más. Tiempo y espacio para ella. A menudo llega a casa con mucho que contarme.

Mis hijas toman clases, asisten a eventos de la biblioteca y van a representaciones musicales y teatrales gratuitas durante el verano. Participan en clubes, actividades y ferias de ciencia con nuestro grupo de educación en casa. Hacemos viajes a parques nacionales y otros destinos de los alrededores. Aprovechamos las charlas gratuitas impartidas por guardabosques, ambientalistas marinos y en acuarios. Visitamos jardines comunitarios, centros naturales, parques, reservas de vida silvestre, zoológicos, tiendas de mascotas, pequeños museos, galerías de arte, eventos sociales históricos, eventos sociales de astronomía, recorridos por los juzgados, etc.

Algunos niños se ofrecen como voluntarios a cambio de lecciones o la admisión a museos o eventos artísticos. Otros participan en programas para aprendices, trabajos voluntarios, viajes en grupo y otras oportunidades. Vecinos, amigos, familiares y otros miembros de la comunidad representan una miríada de fuentes potenciales de conocimiento y experiencia.

Los padres de grupos de educación en el hogar pueden poner en común su experiencia en beneficio de todos los niños. Aprender de los profesionales de tu comunidad puede concretarse a través de entrevistas, observación, participación, lecciones, cursos prácticos, o asesorías.

Los grupos locales de educación en casa organizan clubes y actividades, y comparten recursos de aprendizaje. Mi familia pertenece a varios grupos. Cada uno ofrece actividades atractivas y la oportunidad de conocer muchas personas interesantes con quienes pasar el tiempo. Los papás y los niños fácilmente pueden iniciar un grupo sobre algún interés en especial, como un grupo de estudio, un círculo de lectura, o un club de actividades como astronomía, geología, técnicas de supervivencia, escritura, libros, manualidades, música pop, inglés, *geocaching* (esconder y encontrar «tesoros» en cualquier lugar, con la ayuda de un GPS), correspondencia en correo convencional, y mucho más.

Los clubes de escuelas públicas, las escuelas autónomas, las escuelas alternativas y los colegios comunitarios a menudo admiten a chicos que estudian en casa para tomar clases individuales. Sin embargo, es importante prestar atención a los requisitos para asistir a estas escuelas. En algunos casos, incluso el asistir de medio tiempo puede significar la pérdida de algunas libertades asociadas con la educación en el hogar.

Clases estructuradas

Las clases pueden cubrir intereses como teatro, música, danza, gimnasia, arte, deportes, artes marciales, idiomas, programación, etc.

Las tácticas y actitud del instructor pueden marcar toda la diferencia en la experiencia del niño. Cuando estés buscando una clase, considera el estilo de aprendizaje de tu hijo y su temperamento. Las clases privadas conllevan los mismos riesgos que la escolarización para la espontaneidad, creatividad y amor al aprendizaje de un niño.

Cuando Maia tenía cinco años, quiso tomar clases de *ballet* en el centro de artes local. A mí me preocupaba que no le fueran a gustar las clases estructuradas. Durante su primera sesión hubo ratos en que estuvo inquieta y no seguía las instrucciones, pero su rígida instructora simplemente la ignoró. Quise sacarla, pero ella quería quedarse. Al final de la clase llegó otra instructora que daba una pequeña sesión de claqué. Tenía un estilo muy alegre y relajado que atraía la atención de los niños. Cuando llegó el momento de inscribirla para la siguiente sesión, me aseguré de que estuviera con esa maestra. El cambio de instructora tuvo un efecto positivo e inmediato en la conducta de Maia. Sospecho que en la primera sesión actuó de esa forma como un intento de traer alegría a esa atmósfera tan solemne.

Las clases en video son otra opción. Ilana también quería aprender *ballet*, pero no quería quedarse en las clases sin mí, así que le compré un DVD llamado *Baby Ballet*, de Kultur Video, y aprendió tanto como su hermana, o tal vez más.

Existen distintos tipos de clases. Hay muchas organizaciones que ofrecen clases, como, por ejemplo:

- Parques y centros recreativos
- Universidades
- Tiendas de manualidades
- Galerías de arte
- Teatros
- Tiendas de música
- Museos
- Centros de ciencias
- Centros naturistas

Entre otros recursos figuran maestros privados, tutores, programas de mentores, cursos correspondencia, clases en línea y demás. Mis hijas han tomado clases para montar poni y clases de fútbol a través del programa de parques y recreación de mi ciudad, que también ofrece clases de arte, educación física, jardinería, fotografía, geología, *rafting*, historia local, idiomas y mucho más.

Si tu hijo desea obtener créditos académicos, las clases que se imparten en colegios comunitarios[26], escuelas cooperativas, escuelas autónomas y escuelas privadas acreditadas pueden ofrecer dichos créditos a los estudiantes en casa por los cursos que hayan completado.

Sin embargo, considera el impacto que podría tener en su estatus legal como estudiante en el hogar el hecho de incorporarse a tiempo parcial en una escuela acreditada.

---

[26] *N. de la T.:* En los Estados Unidos, los *community colleges* son instituciones que ofrecen en dos años una educación para estudiantes que desean obtener un título vocacional o transferirse a una universidad con cursos profesionales de cuatro años.

Al apuntarte a una clase o curso, puede que te den a elegir entre distintos formatos de clase, como clases grupales o privadas, clases para grupos de una edad específica o de todas las edades, clases para adultos que permitan adolescentes, etc., por lo que podrías solicitar un periodo de prueba para determinar si la clase ofrece o no lo que tu hijo tiene en mente.

Es común que los grupos locales de educación en el hogar ofrezcan listados de clases en la comunidad que admiten a chicos educados en casa. El sitio web de mi grupo local tiene un directorio de negocios que dan descuentos a los educadores en casa, al igual que una larga lista de clases y actividades de interés para los chicos que estudian en casa. Esta lista incluye oportunidades de voluntariado, programas de enriquecimiento curricular, recreación y deportes, artes, danza, teatro, etc.

Nuestra biblioteca pública local ofrece una clase específicamente para que los estudiantes en casa aprendan a usar los recursos de la biblioteca para la investigación, así como grupos de estudio, clubes de lectura y otras oportunidades.

También puedes explorar las páginas amarillas de tu localidad en busca de negocios que podrían ofrecer oportunidades de aprendizaje para tu hijo. Además de las muchas empresas que ofrecen clases específicas, hay profesionales que podrían aceptar ser entrevistados por estudiantes y algunos incluso estarían interesados en dar mentorías. Si tu hijo se siente atraído a una carrera en particular, o a un área de alguna carrera, podría entrevistar a un profesional que le brinde información realista sobre la carrera o carreras relacionadas.

Por ejemplo, muchos niños saben que quisieran trabajar con animales, pero no conocen la gran variedad de posibilidades de carreras que existen en esa área. Tener una asesoría o trabajar como aprendices, les brinda a los chicos una experiencia realista.

Cuando escogemos con cuidado, las clases nos sirven como recursos útiles de información y de experiencias que se relacionan con los intereses del niño, y proveen una introducción al formato institucional de muchos lugares de trabajo y de la sociedad.

Registro académico y requisitos legales

Cumplir con los requisitos legales depende en gran medida de cómo llevemos nuestro registro académico. Los padres *unschoolers* pueden decidir llevar un registro de las actividades académicas de sus hijos por razones personales o legales, según los requisitos normativos de su localidad.

Este capítulo comprende las siguientes secciones:

Medición del aprendizaje,
Cumplimiento de los requisitos legales,
Métodos de registro académico, y
Preparación para exámenes y evaluaciones.

A algunos padres les gusta llevar un registro académico. A otros no, y otros solamente lo hacen para cumplir con requisitos legales. Llevar un registro no solamente puede servir como recuerdo personal, sino como referencia para futuras solicitudes de ingreso a la universidad o de empleo.

El registro académico se puede llevar de muchas maneras, como en forma de diario, de portafolio de evidencias, de gráfica o de formulario para completar. Cada estrategia de registro tiene puntos fuertes y débiles y se puede usar para diferentes propósitos. Algunos papás compran sistemas ya hechos para llevar su registro, y otros prefieren hacerlo ellos mismos.

Cualquiera que sea el método que elijas, te recomiendo mantener el registro principalmente para ti, en especial con niños pequeños, para que no se sientan evaluados.

Medición del aprendizaje

Los padres *unschoolers* muestran un interés activo en las actividades de sus hijos, por lo que no necesitan calificaciones o exámenes que les demuestren cuáles habilidades han adquirido. Sin embargo, algunos papás sí documentan las actividades de aprendizaje de sus niños.

En algunas localidades se exige cumplir con los requisitos legales de evaluaciones y presentación de formularios oficiales, mientras que en otras se les permite a los padres escoger entre realizar exámenes, presentar un portafolio de evidencias o redactar informes.

Los estilos más convencionales de educación en el hogar se prestan más fácilmente para llevar un registro, en contraste con el *unschooling*, que por lo general requiere más creatividad para adaptar las experiencias de aprendizaje a las categorías de las materias. Sin embargo, familias de todos los estilos han encontrado formas de satisfacer los requisitos del registro académico. Quizás la forma más sencilla de registrar las actividades de aprendizaje de un niño *unschooler* implique hacer una lista periódicamente de las actividades a las que ha dedicado su tiempo, como lo que ha leído, lo que ha creado, lo que ha visto, lo que ha escuchado, lo que ha visitado, de lo que ha hablado, etc.

Mi forma de llevar un registro ha cambiado a lo largo de los años. El gobierno de mi estado pide como requisito que cuando el niño cumpla los ocho años y cada año a partir de entonces, se le dé de alta como educado en casa, se lleve un registro académico y presente evaluaciones anuales que correspondan con el año escolar.

Durante los primeros años de mis hijas, yo mantenía una lista mensual de las actividades que habían realizado o de los temas que habíamos hablado. Guardo dibujos y otros proyectos en mi caja de tesoros. (Todavía lo hago). Cuando Maia tenía 3 años, yo sabía muy bien que se sentía atraída a los animales, especialmente a los dinosaurios, y que podía nombrarlos e imitar a cientos de ellos.

Sabía que ella aprendía de libros, de videos, de paseos a tiendas de mascotas, al zoológico o a ferias. La práctica de registrar las actividades de Maia me hizo ser consciente de lo mucho que ella aprendía, cosa que tal vez no habría notado de otro modo y que, además, reforzó mi confianza en el *unschooling*.

A medida que los niños van creciendo y haciéndose más independientes en sus ocupaciones, también pueden asumir una parte de la responsabilidad de llevar el registro de sus intereses y actividades.
Algunos papás les piden a sus hijos mayores que lleven un diario de los libros que han leído, de las actividades que realizan y de cualquier otra cosa que quieran registrar.

Cumplimiento de los requisitos legales

Casi en todas las ciudades de Estados Unidos hay leyes que regulan la escolarización obligatoria, por lo que las nuevas familias *unschoolers* querrán aprender cómo es que la educación en casa en general se adapta a esas leyes y cuáles son los requisitos legales específicos para su localidad. Ten en cuenta que los objetivos académicos para los niños educados en casa pueden ser diferentes a los de los niños escolarizados. Yo recomiendo que no te identifiques con el término *unschooling* ante las autoridades. Para no provocar temor o críticas, es mejor decir que tus hijos son educados en casa y siguen un plan de estudios personalizado.

Las regulaciones para la educación en el hogar, tales como requisitos de aprendizaje o evaluaciones, no armonizan con la filosofía del *unschooling*, por lo que los padres podrían tener dificultades para conciliar los sentimientos de molestia o injusticia con el convencimiento de que deben cumplir con los requisitos legales para poder seguir educando en casa. Seguir nuestros principios e ideales es maravilloso, pero también debemos considerar seriamente las consecuencias de honrarlos, como lo sería la anulación de la libertad que se nos ha concedido para educar en casa.

Busca información legal en diversas fuentes, en vez de confiar en funcionarios escolares, quienes probablemente sepan poco o nada sobre educación en casa y te den respuestas desalentadoras, puesto que las escuelas dependen de la asistencia estudiantil para obtener recursos económicos. En algunos lugares, las leyes locales no autorizan abiertamente la educación en casa, pero se puede llevar a cabo si las familias registran una casa, iglesia, u otro grupo como escuela privada o por medio de algún otro mecanismo.

Los grupos de apoyo de familias educadoras en casa son, tal vez, la fuente más confiable de información acerca de asuntos legales.

Los padres educadores en casa experimentados pueden explicarte no sólo lo que dice la ley, sino cuáles son los procedimientos prácticos en que se lleva a cabo. Por ejemplo, mi estado exige que un maestro certificado aplique un examen anual y debemos mantener un registro de ello, pero no es necesario informar los resultados del examen. Además, algunos maestros certificados ofrecen aplicar un «examen» (que en realidad no lo es) compatible con el *unschooling*.

Home School Legal Defense Association
(*Asociación de Defensa Legal de la Educación en el Hogar*)
http://www.hslda.org
Información sobre leyes y litigios.
(Nota: Organización Cristiana).

Entre los requisitos legales de tu localidad, puede que se te solicite lo siguiente:

- Llenar y presentar formularios tales como una declaración de intención de educar en casa.
- Dar de alta tu hogar como una escuela privada.
- Presentar un plan de estudios o currículo, o
- Llevar un registro de asistencia (días escolares) y completar un número específico de días por año.

Haciendo uso de tu creatividad, puedes adaptar las experiencias de aprendizaje de tu hijo en los formularios estandarizados. Carol Narigon, una mamá *unschooler*, creó una muestra de un currículo *unschooling* que puede servir como modelo.

El currículo *unschooling* de Carol Narigon
http://www.sandradodd.com/unschoolingcurriculum.html

Un currículo *unschooling* incluye los temas que tú y tu hijo esperan cubrir. En otras palabras, explica lo que a grandes rasgos tú y tu hijo estarán realizando durante el ciclo escolar, usando los objetivos académicos de tu gobierno y algún programa de estudio como guía, por ejemplo, el de la enciclopedia World Book. Yo conozco los intereses de mis hijas y asumo que seguiremos buscando actividades relacionadas.

Sin buscarlo intencionalmente, mis hijas han cumplido los objetivos oficiales básicos a través de suscripciones a juegos y programas en línea que se basan en objetivos oficiales:

BrainPOP
http://www.brainpop.com

JumpStart
http://www.jumpstart.com

KidzClix
http://ww7.kidzclix.net

Si mi gobierno local sí requiriera que presentase un plan educativo, llevaría el currículo *unschooling* un paso más allá, y clasificaría las actividades previstas bajo materias estandarizadas:

- Ciencias Sociales,
- Ciencias,
- Idiomas,
- Salud,
- Matemáticas, y
- Educación artística.

93

Tal vez colocaría el club LEGO en la materia de Matemáticas. Jardinería y repostería en Ciencias, y el club de inglés en las materias de Estudios Sociales e Idiomas. Usa tu creatividad.

Si algunas de las regulaciones para la educación en casa parecen injustas, reúnete con otros padres educadores y trabajen para cambiar las leyes. Yo creo que llegará el día cuando el mérito del *unschooling* sea reconocido y aceptado por la mayoría. El sistema escolar no siempre ha existido en la historia del ser humano. Las cosas pueden cambiar.

Métodos de registro académico

Existen distintos métodos para llevar un registro de las actividades académicas de tu hijo, tales como:

- Llevar un diario,
- Escribir en un blog,
- Armar un portafolio,
- Crear gráficas, o
- Llenar formularios.

Diarios. Tradicionalmente se escribe una narración al final de cada día. Por eso se llama diario. Pero también se pueden tomar notas semanales, mensuales, o cuatrimestrales. Tú o tu hijo, o ambos, pueden llevar un diario. Se pueden registrar listas de actividades, descripciones de viajes realizados, aprendizajes específicos observados y demás. Posteriormente se puede tomar la información del diario y vaciarla a un portafolio o formularios, según sea necesario. Algunos papás escriben su diario al final de cada día, anotando todas las actividades que observaron. Otros papás escriben con menos frecuencia, tomando nota de actividades e intereses destacados. Yo tomaba notas más frecuentemente durante los primeros años de mis hijas, cuando cada día dominaban habilidades significativas, pero ahora sus proyectos abarcan periodos más largos de tiempo.

Blogs. La palabra blog es una combinación abreviada de las palabras inglesas *web* (red) y *log* (bitácora). Un blog puede usarse como un diario virtual. Puede configurarse para que sea privado o para que todo el mundo lo lea.

Nosotros tenemos un blog familiar que funciona como un recurso de *espolvoreo*[27] para mis hijas. Es decir, una ruta que pueden seguir si ellas así lo desean. Pero también, es un método de registro para mí.

Cada entrada del blog está fechada y clasificada en alguna de las categorías que yo nombré con las materias oficiales; de esta forma, fácilmente puedo seleccionar una categoría y ver todo aquello a lo que mis hijas han estado expuestas durante periodos de tiempo específicos. Además, escribo en el blog para compartir nuestros acontecimientos con familiares y amigos a distancia.

Portafolio de evidencias. Puedes recopilar muestras del trabajo de tus hijos para armar un portafolio (obras de arte, hojas con sus cálculos matemáticos en sucio, páginas de su diario, etc.)

Un portafolio se puede presentar en forma de álbum de fotos, de fichero, de caja o de alguna combinación que te permita exhibir el conocimiento de tu hijo sobre los requisitos académicos, así como otros intereses. El portafolio puede contener informes escritos, páginas de ejercicios, listas de libros leídos, notas de diario sobre diversas actividades, obras de arte, cintas de video, fotos, o cualquier otro objeto. Para preparar el portafolio de tu hijo para su revisión, elige piezas que muestren logros de aprendizaje específicos tal como se hace referencia en los requisitos de tu localidad para la educación en el hogar.

---

[27] *N. de la T.: Sprinkling* en inglés (espolvorear, esparcir). Es la palabra que la autora decidió usar para referirse a su práctica particular de *siembra* o enriquecimiento familiar.

Gráficas. Puedes crear una gráfica o una cuadrícula dividida en categorías de materias con listas de actividades de aprendizaje. La gráfica puede tener una lista de materias académicas en un eje y los días de la semana en el otro. Escribe las actividades en todas las categorías que les correspondan. Por ejemplo, construir con legos puede ir en la casilla de matemáticas, arte o estudios sociales; y aprender inglés puede ir en la casilla de idiomas y estudios sociales. El inglés se puede considerar como una unidad de estudio que abarca muchas categorías.

Formularios. Algunos distritos escolares proveen formularios oficiales que recogen información de los objetivos educativos que han sido cubiertos. En algunos lugares se acepta el uso de un lenguaje común para describir las actividades de aprendizaje, mientras que otros prefieren el uso de jerga educativa. Por ejemplo: leer un libro por horas puede llamarse «lectura ininterrumpida, silenciosa y sostenida».
Las actividades dirigidas por el interés del niño que cubren múltiples categorías podrían traducirse como «estudios de unidades interdisciplinarias utilizando actividades iniciadas por el alumno», o «aprendizaje por proyectos» o «aprendizaje en bloque».

Años de registro de actividades de aprendizaje pueden ser muy útiles al preparar un expediente académico junto con la solicitud de ingreso a una escuela, a la milicia o a un empleo. Al igual que con otros formularios tradicionales, tendrás que usar tu creatividad para presentar la educación de un *unschooler* en dicha forma.

Mary Griffith nos da un ejemplo del expediente académico de un chico *unschooler* en su libro, *The Unschooler's Handbook*[28].

Mary Griffith
http://marygriffith.net

---

[28] Griffith, M., (1998), *The Unschooling Handbook*, Prima Publishing, Roseville, California.

Otra alternativa es presentar un portafolio en vez del expediente académico.

Preparación para exámenes y evaluaciones

Entre los requisitos académicos, tu localidad podría solicitar:
* Evaluaciones estandarizadas,
* Revisión de portafolio,
* Evaluación del desempeño, o
* Reportes de progreso.

Consulta cuáles son los requisitos específicos con tu grupo de apoyo de educación en el hogar o con tu distrito escolar local. Puedes encontrar un resumen de los requisitos legales de tu área en los sitios web de la Asociación de Defensa Legal de Educación en el Hogar (HSLDA) o del departamento o ministerio de educación de tu gobierno local.

HSLDA
http://hslda.org

Depto. de Educación de E.U.
http://www.ed.gov

Evaluaciones Estandarizadas. Si tu localidad requiere evaluaciones estandarizadas, puedes solicitar una copia de una edición anterior de la prueba para que tú y tus hijos puedan revisarla y practicarla. Puedes intentar negociar un nuevo examen u otro tipo de evaluación si sientes que la prueba muestra un sesgo en contra de tu filosofía educativa.

El gobierno local puede requerir evaluaciones con una frecuencia anual o menor. Algunos gobiernos requieren que las pruebas se realicen sólo cerca del final de años escolares específicos, como tercero y quinto de primaria, y segundo de secundaria y de bachillerato.

Los distritos escolares suelen proporcionar, administrar y pagar las pruebas, aunque los padres pueden tener la opción de contratar a un evaluador independiente. Pide a grupos y asociaciones de educación en el hogar que te recomienden evaluadores independientes que simpaticen con el *unschooling*. Incluso puedes encontrar algún examen por correspondencia que tú y tu hijo puedan contestar juntos en casa.

Los alumnos educados en casa generalmente obtienen una calificación del 85% o superior en las evaluaciones. Los alumnos educados en casa suelen superar a los niños escolarizados en las pruebas estandarizadas. En el momento de esta publicación, los alumnos educados en casa de mi país superaban a sus compañeros escolarizados en un 37%[29].

Revisión de portafolio. Como una alternativa a las evaluaciones estandarizadas, algunos gobiernos locales aceptan que se presente un portafolio. En este caso, tú y tu hijo presentarían una selección de muestras de trabajo que exhiba los logros de aprendizaje de tu hijo. El portafolio puede incluir reportes escritos por personas que han trabajado con tu hijo, cintas de video o audios, fotografías, recortes de periódicos relevantes, folletos de lugares que han visitado, lista de libros leídos, etc.

Evaluación del desempeño. En este caso, tu hijo se sometería a una entrevista o a realizar tareas que muestren dominio de las materias requeridas. Estas tareas podrían incluir presentaciones de actividades o proyectos como obras teatrales, informes escritos o proyectos de ciencias.

Reportes de progreso. En lugar de las pruebas, tu localidad puede requerir que se presenten informes de progreso periódicos que describan las actividades de aprendizaje de tu hijo durante un período de tiempo específico, como un trimestre, un semestre o un año escolar. La información de tu diario puede ser muy útil para crear este tipo de reporte.

---

[29] Dr. Brian Ray. Progress Report 2009: *Homeschool Academic Achievement and Demographics*. National Home Education Research Institute (NHERI).

Ejemplo de un registro académico para *unschoolers*
Maia, diciembre - febrero

Práctica: Experimentos de ciencias con el equipo Pop Bottle Science, actividades en las páginas *faunasphere.com* y *jumpstart.com*, misiones en *poptropica.com*, clases de *ballet*, club de español, gimnasia.

Creaciones: Rompecabezas de madera de T-Rex en 3D, construcción de máquinas simples con equipo de física, construcción con equipo de LEGO Crazy Action Contraptions y LEGO robotics, confección de muñecas de papel, dibujo.

Lecturas: *Wright on Time*, *La Casa del Árbol #29*, *Avalon* libro 2, las series de *Harry Potter*, *Eragon*; chistes y acertijos, *Alicia en el país de las maravillas*.

Escritura: Cuento de una princesa, poemas, canciones, caligrafía en cursiva, mecanografía, *kanji*.

Material visto: *Doctor Who*, *Invasores Primitivos*, películas de navidad, *Johnny Test*, *Animated Hero Classics*, *El autobús mágico*.

Material escuchado: Audiolibros de cuentos de hadas, música pop, *reggae*, música navideña, clases de francés en CD.

Temas de conversación: Megalodón, mitología de hombres tiburones, delfines, Barbie entrenadora de mascotas, maquillaje, ropa estilo punk, peinados, California y Arizona.

Planes: Viaje nocturno en tren, próximo eclipse lunar, telescopio, video de Galileo.

Visitas: Parque temático marino para ver delfines.

Ejemplo de un plan de estudios para *unschoolers*
Tercer grado

Estudios Sociales: Planeamos explorar días festivos, costumbres populares y culturas de todo el mundo, la historia de los nativos americanos y de los Estados Unidos. *La historia de las cosas* (*http://storyofstuff.org*), geografía local y mundial, mapas y orientación.

Ciencia: Planeamos estudiar la vida salvaje animal y vegetal, la vida prehistórica, los ciclos de la vida, los hábitats, conservación, el cambio climático, electricidad y magnetismo, el espacio exterior y naves espaciales, ciclos solares y lunares, máquinas, y el método científico.

Lengua: Planeamos leer ficción y no ficción, prosa y poesía, usar el diccionario, practicar letras y ortografía, escribir composiciones, practicar escritura en letra de molde y cursiva, mecanografía y puntuación.

Salud: Planeamos observar una buena higiene, aprender sobre seguridad en Internet, comer alimentos saludables, estudiar sistemas anatómicos, realizar actividad física, vestirnos de acuerdo con el clima y saber dar primeros auxilios cuando sea necesario.

Matemáticas: Planeamos construir, medir, experimentar, hornear, coser, dividir, sumar y restar, estimar, resolver acertijos matemáticos, hacer gráficas y tablas, discutir el concepto de los números negativos, comparar medidas y sistemas numéricos, y realizar un seguimiento del tiempo.

Arte: Planeamos asistir a clases de danza y arte, hacer obras de arte y manualidades en casa, escribir composiciones, representar obras de teatro y tomar fotografías.

Una secuencia de estudios *unschooler* sobre Día de Muertos

La siguiente secuencia de eventos ilustra cómo disfrutamos mis hijas y yo el tema de Halloween y Día de Muertos.

«Mictecacihuatl, reina de Mictlán, el inframundo, vigila los huesos de los muertos. La Señora de la muerte preside el Día de Muertos, el festival para honrar a nuestros antepasados. Algunas personas creen que esta época del año, el noveno mes del calendario azteca, facilita el acceso de las almas para visitar a los vivos. Algunas familias ponen altares con objetos conmemorativos y ofrendas para sus amados ancestros». – El día azteca de los muertos. (Entrada escrita en nuestro blog familiar).

- Llegó por correo un ejemplar de *Top Secret Adventures: Case #32751, The Mystery South of the Border.*
- Cada mañana, mi hija mayor consulta el calendario y cuenta los días que faltan para que llegue Halloween.
- Mis hijas y yo asistimos al club de español, una actividad de nuestro grupo de apoyo local de familias educadoras en casa, donde aprendimos un poco sobre Día de Muertos, e hicimos calaveras de azúcar, papel picado y máscaras de calaveras
- Sacamos una pila de libros de la biblioteca sobre Halloween, Día de Muertos, los aztecas, el origen de dulce o truco, etc.
- Fuimos a una hortaliza de calabazas, y vimos *Es la gran calabaza, Charlie Brown.*
- Busqué en internet más actividades sobre Halloween y el Día de Muertos y mis hijas y yo decoramos la casa con esas ideas.
- Sacamos las decoraciones del año pasado de Halloween y las pusimos.
- Escribí una entrada sobre el Día de Muertos en el blog de aprendizaje de mis hijas, que también es su página de inicio para navegar en Internet.
- Vimos un video de Brain Pop sobre el español y México, en el que se menciona el Día de Muertos.

- Leímos un libro sobre esqueletos y Halloween (*The Search for the Missing Bones*) del autobús mágico y también comenzamos a jugar con el equipo de anatomía *Un viaje al cuerpo humano*, de la misma marca.
- Colocamos un póster grande de un esqueleto, pusimos etiquetas con los nombres de los huesos, y luego los localizamos en nuestro cuerpo.
- Escuchamos música de miedo y discutimos las diferencias entre el escalofriante Halloween y el alegre Día de Muertos.

Y apenas era el comienzo…

Ejemplo de narración de un tema de aprendizaje

Mi hija Maia se siente muy atraída a la vida marina y al mundo acuático. Quiere estudiar, ayudar a proteger, entrenar o trabajar de algún modo con mamíferos marinos. Hemos visitado numerosas veces el acuario local, a cuyo programa de voluntariado juvenil Maia planea inscribirse. Mientras tanto, asiste a las clases del acuario y a campamentos para niños, además de buscar otras oportunidades que la acerquen a su meta.

Pasa tiempo a la orilla del mar. Con suavidad toca estrellas de mar, erizos y anémonas. Toma cangrejos y caracoles con las manos y una vez se quedó asombrada ante los restos erosionados de un tiburón. Visitamos acuarios y parques marinos cuando viajamos.

El interés de Maia por la vida marina la ha llevado a ver documentales sobre biólogos, buzos, cineastas, acuarios de todo el mundo, ballenas y delfines, vida prehistórica en el océano, el problema de los arrecifes de coral, etc. Estudia sobre la vida marina en enciclopedias y colecciona figuras de mamíferos acuáticos y anfibios. Su interés, que comenzó con los mamíferos marinos, ha crecido para incluir hábitats del océano, vida vegetal, peces y tiburones, aves costeras, entrenamiento de animales, buceo, pozas de marea, islas, clima, magnetismo, y mucho más.

A lo largo de este periodo, Maia y su hermana han visto una serie de televisión sobre sirenas, donde la curiosidad científica de la antagonista bióloga marina, le ha causado perder de vista los derechos naturales de la vida marina. Incluso el título del programa *H2O: Sirenas del mar*, inspiró el interés de Maia en las fórmulas químicas, lo que la llevó a hacer muchos experimentos con el equipo de ciencias Pop Bottle Science.

Universidad y carrera

Los jóvenes educados en casa que planean ingresar a la universidad suelen hacer su solicitud de ingreso presentando su expediente académico o portafolio, o a través de un proceso de admisión oficial modificado.

Este capítulo comprende las siguientes secciones:
Los años de adolescencia,
Perspectivas universitarias y profesionales,
Adaptación a los entornos institucionales, y
Alternativas para la universidad.

Los jóvenes *unschoolers* no cuentan con boletas de calificaciones ni certificados que puedan presentar para ser admitidos en la universidad. Sin embargo, muchas escuelas, si no es que la mayoría, aceptan expedientes académicos de educación en casa y facilitan un proceso de admisión modificado para los estudiantes que tienen un antecedente educativo no tradicional. No obstante, algunos padres se preocupan por la transición de su hijo *unschooler* al pasar de experiencias de aprendizaje libres de presión a tareas universitarias, fechas de entrega, calificaciones, y exámenes. Puede que los chicos *unschoolers* no tengan experiencia en el modelo de enseñanza tradicional, o tal vez sí; pero lo que sí tienen es la inventiva y la habilidad para asumir la responsabilidad de su propio aprendizaje, lo que les será de mucha utilidad en el ámbito universitario y profesional.

Los años de adolescencia

Un chico *unschooler* puede pasar sus años de adolescencia de manera muy similar a sus primeros años: realizando actividades dirigidas y motivadas por él mismo que luego podrían ampliarse para incluir prácticas enfocadas a su carrera, programas de aprendizaje, voluntariados o cursos universitarios.

104

La idea o el recuerdo que muchos padres tenemos del bachillerato puede que nos haga pensar en materias «avanzadas» como cálculo, física, química, y temer que no podremos ayudar a nuestros hijos a aprenderlas.

En primer lugar, un adolescente que quiere aprender estas materias puede encontrar la manera de hacerlo. En segundo lugar, las materias avanzadas tienen su aplicación específica, la cual puede encajar o no con la idea que tu adolescente tiene de una vida laboral significativa. Además, no todos los estudiantes de preparatoria toman clases avanzadas.

Durante mis primeros años de adolescencia pensaba que quería ser contadora. Con esa idea en mente, tomé todas las clases de matemáticas que pude... hasta el día en que mi abuela me llevó a conocer a su contador. Me fui preparada con una lista de preguntas sobre su trabajo, y regresé con una imagen muy diferente a la que me había formado. Si no hubiera conocido a un contador real, muy probablemente habría seguido tomando clases de matemáticas y contaduría durante toda la universidad.

Lo que me dejaron esos años de bachillerato, más que los temas tratados, fue la intranquilidad y la ansiedad por «ocuparme en algo», hasta que fui completamente libre en el mundo adulto. El ajetreo de la preparatoria inhibió mi búsqueda de un trabajo significativo, y mi impaciencia ganó cuando dejé la escuela antes de tiempo.

Por otro lado, los jóvenes *unschoolers* tienen la libertad de avanzar en línea recta hacia sus metas. Si un adolescente todavía no ha encontrado un trabajo significativo para su vida, puede centrar sus actividades de aprendizaje en explorar carreras, conversar con personas acerca de su trabajo, desarrollar relaciones con mentores, relacionarse con personas dentro del medio que le interesa, trabajar como voluntario, etc.

Perspectivas universitarias y profesionales

Los chicos que planean asistir a la universidad querrán familiarizarse anticipadamente con las políticas de admisión específicas para jóvenes educados en casa, las opciones de becas, subvenciones y los procesos de solicitud de apoyo económico. Por lo general, el proceso de inscripción consiste en presentar un examen de ubicación, entregar el expediente académico o portafolio, y quizás, cartas de recomendación, ensayos y estados financieros.

Pruebas. Algunas universidades solicitan que los aspirantes acrediten algunas pruebas estandarizadas de admisión, como SAT, PSAT, y ACT, además del examen de ubicación de la escuela. Los chicos *unschoolers* pueden prepararse para estas pruebas usando alguno de los muchos libros de preparación disponibles en el mercado, o algún curso en línea. Algunas bibliotecas públicas ofrecen talleres de preparación o asesorías. Para obtener una muestra del expediente académico, puedes hacer una búsqueda en Internet con las frases *«high school transcript simple»* o *«homeschool transcript template»*.

Expediente Académico. Además de las pruebas, es posible que las universidades requieran que los jóvenes educados en casa presenten un expediente académico, o que resuman todo lo que han aprendido y que demuestra su preparación para tomar cursos a nivel universitario. El expediente académico debe incluir las materias oficiales de bachillerato requeridas para los aspirantes a universidad (en otras palabras, una lista de actividades de aprendizaje y experiencias traducidas a los nombres estándares de los cursos), junto con el equivalente de los grados y las horas en créditos para cada materia.

Colegios comunitarios. Algunos jóvenes *unschoolers* toman cursos en colegios comunitarios o en escuelas técnicas a través de un programa de doble matriculación, antes de entrar a la universidad.

Algunos colegios comunitarios y escuelas técnicas ofrecen programas de transferencia, como artes liberales, en los que los alumnos pueden cubrir muchos de sus créditos universitarios a un costo menor que en una universidad más grande. Esta opción puede facilitar la entrada a la universidad a los jóvenes *unschoolers*.

Los cursos de los colegios comunitarios también pueden ofrecer la experiencia, si los chicos no la han tenido, de estar en un salón de clases, de cumplir con horarios y asignaciones, y de interactuar con compañeros que no necesariamente buscan aprender por gusto.

Adaptación a los ambientes institucionales

Los chicos *unschoolers* tienen años de experiencia asumiendo la responsabilidad de su propio aprendizaje, al igual que otras decisiones importantes en su vida. Cuando ingresan a instituciones como universidades o lugares de trabajo, llevan con ellos el beneficio de esta experiencia.

A menudo, los jóvenes *unschoolers* comienzan a tomar cursos universitarios a edades más tempranas que los jóvenes que asistieron a la escuela pública, por lo que cuando llegan a la universidad ya saben qué esperar. Quienes comienzan la universidad en sus primeros años de adolescencia sienten menos urgencia de terminar y se toman su tiempo para adaptarse a las nuevas rutinas.

En general, a los *unschoolers* les gusta aprender y por esta razón, puede que se les dificulte comprender a sus compañeros que buscan atajos y alternativas para simplemente pasar exámenes y acreditar cursos. La curiosidad natural y el amor por aprender de un chico no escolarizado influyen en su experiencia de la vida universitaria y laboral.

Los *unschoolers:*

- Usan su creatividad para encontrar formas agradables de aprender el material requerido.
- Saben cómo encontrar fuentes alternativas de información y experiencia, además de las fuentes asignadas por los instructores.
- Se sienten cómodos asumiendo su responsabilidad y tomando decisiones importantes.

Independientemente de que un emprendedor o un empleado tenga un título, tendrá que aprender para hacer su trabajo. Los empleadores saben esto, cosa que puede convertirse en una ventaja para los jóvenes *unschoolers* ingeniosos, ya que ellos están acostumbrados a asumir la responsabilidad de su propio aprendizaje, saben cómo resolver problemas por sí mismos, saben cuándo pedir ayuda y dónde encontrarla. Su amor por aprender y la falta de un disgusto aprendido por el trabajo asignado, les favorece en la universidad y en su éxito profesional.

Alternativas para la universidad

John Holt dijo: «Si sabes qué tipo de trabajo quieres hacer, avanza hacia él de la manera más directa posible. Si algún día quieres construir barcos, dirígete a donde haya gente construyéndolos, averigua todo lo que puedas.»

La universidad brinda un camino, no necesariamente el mejor, para que tu hijo se prepare para una vida laboral significativa. El aprendizaje práctico y las pasantías pueden ofrecer una ruta más fácil y potencialmente óptima hacia una carrera gratificante. Participar en una relación de mentoría podría convertirse en el primer paso que tu hijo dé hacia la exploración de una futura carrera. Programas de estudio independientes, cursos por correspondencia, capacitaciones, prácticas, voluntariados: todo puede convertirse en senderos para encontrar un trabajo significativo.

Abundan oportunidades para aprender sobre lo que a uno le interesa y todos aprendemos más efectivamente cuando tenemos la oportunidad de hacer.

Al presentarse en entrevistas de trabajo, los jóvenes *unschoolers* que se han abierto paso en el mundo laboral de los adultos pueden presentar un *currículum vitae* con su experiencia laboral en vez de un título universitario. Un historial de voluntariados, relaciones con mentores y capacitaciones prácticas destacará entre los de los recién graduados de la universidad.

Algunos egresados de la universidad descubren, después de haber invertido años de su tiempo y miles de dólares, que pudieron haber seguido un camino más fácil para llegar adonde se encuentran; o peor: se sienten insatisfechos al descubrir la realidad de la carrera que eligieron. Por el contrario, los jóvenes educados en casa que tienen la oportunidad de probar diferentes ocupaciones ofreciéndose como voluntarios, pueden evitar tal decepción. Las experiencias en el trabajo real les permiten encontrar la mejor ocupación para ellos y dedicarse a ella.

Un sinfín de recursos

Existen abundantes recursos para aprender fuera de la escuela, y siguen aumentando a medida que crece el número de familias educadoras en el hogar. Este capítulo final incluye una lista de:

Sitios web sobre *unschooling*,
Sitios web sobre educación en el hogar,
Sitios web educativos para niños,
Sitios web educativos de código abierto,

Recursos gratuitos,
Servicios y artículos educativos,
Grupos y asociaciones de familias educadoras en el hogar,
Conferencias sobre *unschooling*, y
Fuentes de información sobre legalidad.

Sitios web sobre *unschooling*

Sandra Dodd
http://www.sandradodd.com
Siempre aprendiendo.

Joyfully Rejoycing
http://joyfullyrejoycing.com
Unschooling, crianza pacífica y vida en familia llena de alegría.

John Holt y su revista Growing Without Schooling
http://www.johnholtgws.com/
La obra de John Holt y su continuación.

The Natural Child Project
http://www.naturalchild.org/articles/learning.html
Artículos sobre aprendizaje y vida con niños.

Life Without School
http://lifewithoutschool.typepad.com
Publicación en línea y comunidad de blogs.

Life Learning Magazine
http://www.lifelearningmagazine.com
«Un aprendizaje de la vida personalizado, no coercitivo y dirigido por el interés.»

Sitios web sobre educación en el hogar

Learn in Freedom
http://learninfreedom.org
«Asume la responsabilidad de tu propio aprendizaje.»

Homeschool.com
http://www.homeschool.com
Muchos artículos y recursos.

A to Z Home's Cool
http://a2zhomeschooling.com/
Ideas para lecciones, recursos y artículos.

Best Homeschooling
http://www.besthomeschooling.org
«El mejor consejo de padres con experiencia y otros educadores».

National Home Education Research Institute
http://www.nheri.org
Investigación e información.

Sitios web educativos para niños

CBeebies
http://www.bbc.co.uk/cbeebies
Juegos, cuentos y actividades para niños producido por la BBC.

Cyberchase
http://pbskids.org/cyberchase
Juegos y actividades de matemáticas.

PBS Island
http://pbskids.org/read
«Cultivar lectores»
PBS Kids Go!
http://pbskids.org/go
Juegos en línea.

PBS Kids Sprout
http://www.sproutonline.com
Juegos y actividades para niños de preescolar.

Poptropica
http://www.poptropica.com
Juego de aventuras a través de completar tareas.

Poisson Rouge
http://www.poissonrouge.com
Juegos para niños de preescolar.

Sesame Street
http://www.sesamestreet.org
Juegos y videos de preescolar y educación temprana.

Starfall
http://www.starfall.com

Sitios web educativos de código abierto

Los siguientes sitios web ofrecen cursos en línea gratuitos:

OpenStax
http://cnx.org
Libros de texto online.

Khan Academy
http://www.khanacademy.org
Brinda una educación de primera a cualquier persona, en cualquier lugar.

Wikiversity
http://en.wikiversity.org
Libera el aprendizaje, desde el preescolar hasta la universidad.

MIT Open Courseware
http://ocw.mit.edu/index.htm
Cursos, apuntes, exámenes y videos gratuitos del Instituto de Tecnología de Massachusetts.

Homeschool Share
http://www.homeschoolshare.com
Comparte plantillas para carpetas interactivas, unidades de estudio, planes de estudio, etc.

Homeschool Helper
http://www.homeschoolhelperonline.com
Comparte ideas para unidades y planes de estudio, para carpetas interactivas, hojas de trabajo, hojas para colorear, etc.

Recursos gratuitos

Los *unschoolers* son especialistas en aprovechar los recursos gratuitos. ¿Por qué comprar lo que se puede obtener gratis y además conocer gente en el proceso?

Cuando participaba regularmente en Freecycle, conocí a otras personas con intereses similares a los míos.
Cuando mi familia y yo nos preparábamos para mudarnos, la gente de Freecycle vino, y con mucha gratitud se llevó los muebles grandes y pesados que yo ya no quería. ¿Necesitas algo? Publica un anuncio.

Freecycle
http://www.freecycle.org
Ofrece y busca artículos de cualquier tipo, sin cargo, entre los miembros de tu comunidad.

Paperback Swap
http://www.paperbackswap.com
Intercambia tus libros pagando solamente en costo del envío.

Couch Surfing
http://www.couchsurfing.org
Para los aventureros, recibe viajeros en tu sofá a cambio de quedarte en el sofá de alguien cuando viajes.

Servicios y artículos educativos

Las siguientes son algunas de mis compañías favoritas de servicios y artículos educativos.

FUN Books
http://fun-books.com
Libros orientados hacia el *unschooling*, juegos y otros materiales.

114

Homeschool Buyer's Co-op
http://www.homeschoolbuyersco-op.org
Participa en compras en grupo y ahorra dinero.

eBay
http://www.ebay.com/
Compra y vende en línea.

Useborne
http://www.usbornebooksandmore.com
Libros infantiles de todo tipo.

Timberdoodle
http://www.timberdoodle.com
Empresa familiar que ofrece artículos para la educación en el hogar.

Discount Dance Supply
http://discountdance.com
Excelente ropa de danza a excelentes precios.

Remo Percussion
http://www.remo.com
Instrumentos de calidad profesional para niños.

LEGO Education
http://education.lego.com/
Prácticas de matemáticas, ciencias y tecnología.

Grupos y asociaciones de familias educadoras en el hogar

Un grupo de apoyo, particularmente uno con énfasis en *unschooling*, puede proporcionar una fuente de apoyo valiosa, especialmente para una familia que de otra forma no tendría contacto con otras familias educadoras en el hogar o que no recibe suficiente apoyo por parte de su familia. Si el grupo de apoyo de tu localidad no satisface tus necesidades, considera iniciar uno propio.

Los grupos de apoyo organizan excursiones, actividades, clubes y grupos de discusión para niños educados en el hogar y también para sus padres. Existen grupos nacionales, regionales y locales que proveen diferentes servicios. Algunos grupos solamente operan en línea, y otros se reúnen presencialmente para formar comunidades locales de familias educadoras en el hogar. Las asociaciones más grandes por lo general tienen listados de los grupos regionales.

Family Unschoolers Network
http://www.unschooling.org
Orientación sobre educación en el hogar, *unschooling* y aprendizaje autodirigido.

Home School Legal Defense Association (HSLDA)
http://www.hslda.org
Orientación, información legal y noticias sobre legislación y casos legales.

Conferencias sobre *unschooling*

Hay conferencias que suelen ofrecer pláticas de oradores, talleres y actividades atractivas para toda la familia.

LIFE is Good, *unschooling* conference
http://www.lifeisgoodconference.com
«Aprendizaje en libertad todos los días».

Not Back to School Camp
http://nbtsc.org
Una reunión para jóvenes *unschoolers*.

Fuentes de información sobre legalidad

La mayoría de los gobiernos permiten la educación en el hogar. Las asociaciones de educación en el hogar suelen proporcionar las fuentes de información más confiables sobre las leyes locales de educación en el hogar. Para localizar fuentes gubernamentales, busca *«Department of Education in the U.S.»*, o *«Ministry of Education in Canada»*.

Home School Legal Defense Association (HSLDA)
http://www.hslda.org
Orientación, información legal y noticias sobre legislación y casos legales.

U.S. Department of Education
http://www.ed.gov

Libros

Recomiendo los siguientes libros sobre:

Unschooling,
Crianza, y
Aprendizaje en la naturaleza.

Unschooling

Aquí unos cuantos de los muchos libros que hay sobre *unschooling* y aprendizaje autodirigido:

Dodd, Sandra. *Sandra Dodd's Big Book of Unschooling.* Lulu, 2009.

Dodd, Sandra. *Moving a Puddle, and other essays.* Lulu, 2005.

Fitzenreiter, Valerie. *The Unprocessed Child: Living Without School.* Unbounded Publications, 2003.

Gatto, John Taylor. *Dumbing Us Down.* New Society, 1992.

Griffith, Mary. *The Unschooling Handbook: How to Use the Whole World as Your Child's Classroom.* Prima, 1998.

Hern, Matt. *Deschooling Our Lives.* New Society, 1998.

Holt, John Caldwell; Farenga, Patrick. *Teach Your Own.* Perseus Books, 2003.

Holt, John Caldwell. *Learning All the Time.* Da Capo Press, 1989.

Jensen, Derrick. *Walking on Water: Reading, Writing, and Revolution.* Chelsea Green Publishing, 2005.

Kream, Rue. *Parenting a Free Child: An Unschooled Life*. Rue Kream, 2005.

Llewellyn, Grace. *The Teenage Liberation Handbook*. Lowry House, 1998.

Martin, Dayna. *Radical Unschooling: A Revolution Has Begun*. Tasora Books, 2009.

Prieznitz, Wendy; Aldort, Naomi; Martin, Dayna; et al. *Life Learning: Lessons from the Educational Frontier*. The Alternate Press, 2009.

Sheffer, Susannah. *A Life Worth Living: Selected Letters of John Holt*. Ohio State University Press, 1991.

Takahashi, Tammy. *Deschooling Gently*. Hunt Press, 2008.

Van Gestal, Nanda; Hunt, Jan; Quinn, Daniel; et al. *The Unschooling Unmanual*. The Natural Child Project, 2008.

Crianza

Aron, Elaine, Ph.D., *The Highly Sensitive Child*. Random House, 2002.

Cook, Julie, *Unvaccinated, Homeschooled, and TV-Free: It's Not Just for Fanatics and Zealots*. No Regrets Publishing, 2010.

Faber, Adele; Mazlish, Elaine. *Siblings Without Rivalry*. Avon Books, 1998.

Kohn, Alfie. *Unconditional Parenting: Moving from Rewards and Punishments to Love and Reason*. Atria Books, 2005.

Kurcinka, Mary Sheedy. *Raising Your Spirited Child: A Guide for Parents Whose Child is More Intense, Sensitive, Perceptive, Persistent, and Energetic*. Harper, 2006.

Liedloff, Jean. *The Continuum Concept: In Search of Happiness Lost.* Perseus Books, 1977.

Neufeld, Gordon; Mate, Gabor. *Hold On to Your Kids: Why Parents Need to Matter More Than Peers.* Ballantine Books, 2005.

Noelle, Scott. *The Daily Groove: A Creative Parents' Guide to the Art of Attraction Parenting.* Scott Noelle, 2009.

Pearce, Joseph Chilton. *Magical Child.* Plume, 1977.

Sears, William; Sears, Martha. *The Attachment Parenting Book.* Little, Brown and Company, 2001.

Small, Meredith. *Kids: How Biology and Culture Shape the Way We Raise Young Children.* Anchor Books, 2001.

Aprendizaje en la naturaleza

Louv, Richard. *Last Child in the Woods: Saving Our Children from Nature-Deficit Disorder.* Algonquin Books, 2005.

Young, Jon; Haas, Ellen; and McGown, Evan. *Coyote's Guide to Connecting with Nature.* OWLink Media, 2008.

Aquí finaliza tu introducción a una vida sin escuela. Sigue tus sueños y conviértelos en lo que anhelas. Deseo para ti la mejor vida en familia, llena de felicidad y profundamente satisfactoria.

Hasta luego, y feliz *No* regreso a la escuela,

Sara McGrath
Duvall, Washington
Septiembre 2010

120

The Miller's Daughter

Born in Gainsborough, Lincolnshire, Margaret Dickinson moved to the coast at the age of seven and so began her love for the sea and the Lincolnshire landscape. Her ambition to be a writer began early and she had her first novel published at the age of twenty-five. This was followed by many further titles including *Plough the Furrow*, *Sow the Seed* and *Reap the Harvest*, which make up her Lincolnshire Fleethaven Trilogy. She is also the author of *Welcome Home*, *The Buffer Girls* and *Daughters of Courage*. Margaret is a *Sunday Times* Top Ten bestseller.

Margaret Dickinson

The Miller's Daughter

PAN BOOKS

First published 1997 by Pan Books

This edition published 2017 by Pan Books
an imprint of Pan Macmillan
20 New Wharf Road, London N1 9RR
Associated companies throughout the world
www.panmacmillan.com

ISBN 978-1-5098-3918-6

A CIP catalogue record for this book is available from the British Library.

Typeset by SetSystems Ltd, Saffron Walden, Essex
Printed and bound by CPI Group (UK) Ltd, Croydon, CR0 4YY

For Robena and Fred

Acknowledgements

'Forrest's Mill' has been inspired by Lincolnshire County Council's Burgh-le-Marsh Windmill. My sincere thanks to the volunteer members of the Burgh-le-Marsh Mill Group, who staff and work the mill on open days, for their interest and help in providing technical information.

My very special thanks to Mrs Marjorie McClory for the loan of family papers written by her father, Frank Dobson, whose family owned the mill from 1930 until 1965.

I am also very grateful to Phillip and Joyce Garrad for sharing their memories with me.

As always my love and thanks to my husband and daughters, Dennis, Mandy and Zoë, for their constant support and encouragement, never forgetting those who read and comment on the novel in the early stages: Linda and Terry Allaway and Pauline Griggs.

And to Darley Anderson – the very best of agents – I am so glad I found you!

Part One

One

LINCOLNSHIRE 1918

'I'll tell you something, Emma Forrest. The only way you'll ever find a husband is 'cos they'll be trying to get their hands on my mill.'

Deliberately, Emma kept her face expressionless. The remark, made so often, had long ago ceased to hurt.

'Yes, Father,' she murmured softly, so accustomed to pandering to this man's demands that agreement came automatically to her lips. But then, for once, a spark of defiance glittered in her violet eyes, making her add, 'But you never know, perhaps someone will be glad of a hardworking housekeeper.'

Frowning, Harry Forrest glared at her. 'You answering me back, girl?' There was surprise in his tone, as if he had never thought the day would come when his eighteen-year-old daughter would show insolence, and to him of all people. For a moment she stood facing him.

If only he had cared to look properly at his daughter, Harry Forrest would have seen that she had her own special kind of beauty. A broad, smooth forehead, a nose that was straight and high cheekbones above a full-shaped mouth that, despite the hardship of her life, smiled far more readily than it ever pouted. But her eyes were her best and most unusual feature. Large and black-fringed, they were the deepest blue, almost violet. True, her build was a little too tall, her figure a little too buxom for the word 'dainty' ever to be applied to Emma Forrest. 'Handsome' or 'a fine figure

3

of a young woman' might be, and was, said of her, but only by others for Harry Forrest never looked – never really looked – at his daughter.

Hiding a mischievous smile, she turned away and in answer to his sharp reprimand, murmured, 'As if I would.'

'Aye well, just mind you don't. And another thing, ya can forget ya mooning over young Metcalfe. Don't think I don't know about it, 'cos I do.' Harry Forrest wagged his forefinger at her. 'I know what he's after and let me tell you, girl, there'll never be a Metcalfe in my mill. Not while there's breath in my body.'

As Emma bent forward to pick up another sack of grain, her long, black plait swung forward. Impatiently, she flicked it back over her shoulder, gritting her teeth as her strong arms heaved the sack on to the running barrow. The metal wheels rattled on the hard surface of the yard as she pushed it from the granary towards the mill, the noise shutting out any more of his ranting. Out of the corner of her eye she saw her father turn away with a disgruntled shake of his head and walk round to where the brake rope and the striking chain hung down the side of the mill. As she watched him, Emma noticed how rounded his shoulders had become so that he appeared almost hump-backed and today his legs looked even more bowed than usual. Yet Emma knew that the appearance of frailty was deceptive. Harry Forrest was a strong man physically and in character too.

But one of these days, Emma promised herself silently as she tipped the sack from the barrow, he'll have to be told the truth about Jamie Metcalfe and me.

She carried the heavy sack of wheat up the four steps and dumped it inside the open double doors of the mill just as her father came back.

'I hope you're keeping a tally of what you're bringing across, girl?'

'Yes, Father,' she said evenly and moved towards the battered wooden desk set against the wall and turned the page of the open ledger. 'It's Farmer Leighton's wheat.'

Harry Forrest gave a satisfied grunt. 'Good. We'll get some good flour today then.' He began to heave himself up the wooden ladder to the meal floor above to begin his day's work. Without pausing in his climb, he went on, 'And there's going to be a good wind. We should manage two pairs today. Bring Leighton's barley across next.'

Outside again, Emma pushed the empty barrow back towards the granary once more. In the middle of the yard she paused to glance up at the huge sails as they began to turn just above her head. Her heart lifted at the sight and she stood a moment, her gaze roaming over the tall black shape of the mill and the white-painted sails against the scudding grey clouds. Shrewdly she studied the sky. Today the cold November wind was constant, blowing across the flat land from the sea with enough strength to keep the sails turning steadily and enabling the miller to run two pairs of millstones at once. One pair, the French burr stones, would grind the wheat into fine flour for their own bakehouse and the second pair, fashioned from Derbyshire Peak stone, would grind barley and oats for animal feed for the farmer. It was perfect milling weather and her father would be working all day and possibly far into the night if the wind stayed constant.

It was their way of life; from dawn to dusk Emma Forrest's days were filled with work, beginning in the bakehouse kneading the dough and finishing late at night wiping down the shelves in the bakery in readiness for the following morning's fresh bread. In between there were meals to cook, clothes to wash and the house to clean, to say nothing of helping in the mill, as she was supposed to be doing at this minute, she reminded herself, instead of standing here idling in the middle of the yard.

As she climbed the granary steps again, the fear that shadowed every moment of her day and disturbed her sleep at night pushed its way into Emma's thoughts. Once more she found herself repeating the fervent, silent prayer for Jamie's safe return inside her head. The war was really over, after four long, terrible years. There would be no more killing, no more maiming. At last, the boys were coming home. Already, one or two soldiers had returned to the village. Then why, Emma worried, had there been no news from Jamie?

It was all she had ever wanted, to be Mrs Jamie Metcalfe. Whatever her father said, she knew Jamie loved her and, besides, she didn't think Jamie wanted her father's mill. He was a proud man, proud of his own skills and of the blacksmith's and wheelwright's business that had been in the Metcalfe family for generations. She sighed, wondering if the news of the recent death of both his parents had even reached Jamie in the mud and squalor of the trenches. It was bad enough that he was out there in a foreign country, but to think of him hearing such awful news from home with no family or friends close at such a time made Emma shudder. There had been no word from him, not even to his brother, William, in reply to the letter bearing the sad news. Poor William, Emma thought. Too young to go to war, he had been plunged suddenly into manhood, struggling to cope with the work single-handed until Jamie came home.

Closing her eyes, she could see Jamie as clearly as if he were standing in front of her as he had on the day, three years ago, when he had marched away from the village, the sound of his neighbours' cheering ringing in his ears, the band playing as more volunteers left for the Front.

'But you can't go,' Emma had tried to argue with him. 'You're only seventeen.'

'Shan't tell 'em I'm not eighteen for six months.' He had grinned, his dark brown eyes teasing her.

Resisting the urge to fling herself against him, she had stared at Jamie, willing him not to go, fearful for him and yet proud of him all at the same time. He was so tall and broad and strong; he could pass for twenty, never mind eighteen. His smile had creased the lines around his mouth and sparkled in his eyes that were gentle for her alone.

'Now you be a good girl while I'm gone,' he had said softly, reaching out with strong, toughened fingers to touch her cheek with surprising tenderness; the hand of a man that could soothe a temperamental mare as easily as it could swing the heavy forge hammer. 'Remember, you're *my* girl.'

It was the very first time he had said the words.

Friends through childhood, the three of them – the two Metcalfe boys and Emma Forrest – had grown up together in the small community of Marsh Thorpe. They had gone to the village school, to the chapel and they had played together. As they had grown older, they met on Sunday afternoons for a few precious hours of freedom from work. Sometimes in summer, Harry Forrest would grudgingly allow them to use the small cart in which he delivered bread and collected grain from the farmers to be ground in his mill. On those rare occasions Jamie would drive them along the straight road leading to the coastal town of Calceworth, the pony's silky mane rippling in the sea breeze as he trotted. The three friends would stroll along the promenade, watching the sun glistening on the sea and sniffing the salt air. Walking between the two brothers, dressed in her best Sunday dress and bonnet, Emma would feel such a happiness well up inside her that she thought she would burst. William was her dearest friend, but it was Jamie she loved and it seemed as if she had loved him for ever.

On the day Jamie had gone to war, through the unshed tears she had tried valiantly to keep hidden, Emma had watched him march away. His broad shoulders swinging easily, his black curly hair glistening in the sunlight, his wide grin and a cheery wave were the last things she remembered.

He had written regularly at first and she had replied, sending news of all that was happening in their village. But about a year ago his letters had become spasmodic, the words stilted as if he could no longer write to her in the spirit of their old, easy friendship. Then the letters to her had stopped, although she knew from William that he was safe. Lately, even William had heard nothing. She could not stop the tremor of fear running through her afresh, even though she tried to tell herself that, soon, everything would be all right. The war was over and he would be coming back. He must come back, she told herself, as if by the strength of her willing it to be so, she could make it happen.

Resolutely, she made herself dwell on happier thoughts and plans for their future together. Maybe he would be home in time for Christmas and perhaps, in the spring, they could be married and those happy, sunlit days would come again. Thinking of him, she smiled, remembering his laughter, the look in his eyes as he had touched her cheek. What would Jamie think of *her* now, after three years?

When he had gone to war, she had been a young girl of fifteen and, although she had grown no taller, she had now filled out into womanhood. As she ran her hands down her sides, feeling the curves of her own body and imagining herself in his arms, her pulse quickened. Oh no, Emma was sure Jamie wouldn't be marrying her just to get his hands on Harry Forrest's mill.

But oh, please, please, let him come home soon.

Two

'I do wish ya'd let me do that, Emma lass.'

Emma glanced up to see Luke Robson emerging from the doorway of the mill and coming down the steps. She smiled at the elderly man. Although his wispy white hair seemed to be disappearing at an alarming rate so that his pate was smooth and shining, Luke always seemed to have a broad smile on his wrinkled face. Once, he had been as strong as the man who employed him, but now the cough that racked him was robbing him of his strength. Luke would not have thanked her, though, if he had guessed that Emma tried to do much of the heavy work to help him.

'I'm fine, Luke,' she reassured him, her clear tones carrying above the constant sound of the whirling sails. 'Hard work never hurt anyone.'

But as she tipped the sack off the running barrow to land at his feet, the older man shook his head disapprovingly. 'He shouldn't expect a pretty lass like you to work like a lad. Housework and looking after the bakery, mebbe, but you shouldn't be working out here in the yard and the mill. T'ain't right. These sacks are too heavy for some lads, ne'er mind a lass. And I've told him so time and again, but he won't listen. One of these days we'll come to blows over it.'

'Oh, Luke,' she said softly and touched his gnarled hand. 'There's nothing dainty and pretty about me, now is there?'

10

For once there was a wistfulness in her tone. 'I was born and bred for work.'

'Ya shouldn't put yarsen down so.' He wagged his finger in her face in mock admonishment. 'Ya're a bonnie lass. Dun't you ever let anyone tell ya different.'

Emma smiled and said once more, 'Oh, Luke!' An impish grin drove away some of the longing from her voice as she added, 'I'm a fine strapping lass. Isn't that what they say about me in the village? That I'll be a good catch for some lucky feller, eh?' Now she could not prevent the bitterness creeping back into her tone. 'Me *and* my father's mill!'

Knowingly, old Luke shook his head. 'So, he's been on about that again, has he? And I've no doubt young Jamie Metcalfe's name just happened to crop up in the conversation, eh?'

Emma bit her lip and turned away, but her silence gave Luke his answer. 'Aye, I thought as much,' Emma heard him mutter.

Not much gets past Luke Robson, Emma thought, but then he had been at Forrest's mill all his working life.

'He was a grand old man, ya grandpa,' Luke never tired of telling Emma. 'A real character, old Charlie Forrest was. Eh, I could tell you some tales, lass. That I could. Me an' ya dad started working at the mill about the same time and I'll give ya grandpa his due, he nivver showed his own son any favours over me.' At this point in his well-worn tale, the faded blue eyes would twinkle. 'We had some high old times together, me an' ya dad, when we was young 'uns.' His eyes would mist over as if he were seeing back down the years. Then he would turn away abruptly, murmuring, 'Shame things turned out the way they did . . .'

She was walking away now, trundling the sack barrow before her, calling back cheerfully over her shoulder. 'We'd

11

best get this grain up top for 'im, else we'll both be in trouble.'

Behind her she heard Luke's wheezing laughter. 'If I know 'im,' he jerked his thumb towards the floors above, 'he'll have t'other pair of stones working 'afore the day's out, if this weather holds. And he'll not handle all *three* pairs on his own. So, what would Harry Forrest do without either of us two, lass? Ask yarsen that!'

As she heaved the next sack of barley on to the barrow and turned once more towards the mill, Emma thought to herself, what indeed?

She drew the back of her hand across her smooth, tanned brow that shone with sweat even in the cold wind of a winter's day.

As she came close again, Luke said, 'You going to Bilsford market with him next week, then?'

Her violet eyes were full of mischief as she glanced at him. 'I shouldn't think I'll be let loose there again for a while yet, Luke. Not after last time!'

The old man snorted. 'Huh, such a lot of fuss over a bit of frippery. Why shouldn't you have a pretty new bonnet, lass? I ask you?'

Yes, Emma thought, as the smile faded from her mouth. Why indeed had it been such a sin for her to buy the straw hat decorated with pink ribbons that had caught her eye on a market stall? The way her father had ranted all the way home in the pony and trap, she might have broken one of the ten commandments. Luke was still muttering. 'I could've understood it if ya mam had been, well, a plain sort o' woman. But she weren't. She were the prettiest little thing you ever did see. Allus dressed up, she were, never a curl out o' place. Ya dad bought plenty of hats for *her*.'

'Maybe that's just it, Luke,' Emma murmured, longing for her mother sweeping through her afresh.

'Eh?' She felt his glance as her words interrupted his line of thought. 'What d'ya mean?'

Hesitantly, with a trace of the wistfulness once more in her tone, she said quietly, 'I'm nothing like my mother, am I? If only I was, then perhaps . . .'

The words lay unspoken between them and she lifted her violet eyes to meet his gaze, the hurt showing plainly in their depths.

His wrinkled hand reached out to her. 'Aw lass, don't tek on so. Ya not like ya mam, no. Ya like – ya like – ' he hesitated as if unwilling to speak the words but he had gone too far to draw back now. 'Ya like old Charlie Forrest – the female version, o' course,' he added swiftly, conscious that perhaps he was adding to Emma's already injured pride.

She thought of the portrait of Charles Forrest that hung above the mantel in the best parlour upstairs. The subject had adopted a stiff-backed, formidable pose with a stern frown drawing his bushy eyebrows together. Yet on close inspection, the artist had captured a spark of mischief in the dark blue eyes; eyes that were all-seeing, all-knowing, staring straight out into the room as if still watching the goings-on in his mill. The man in the painting had a broad forehead, a straight nose and high cheekbones and beneath the moustache was a full and generous mouth with the tiniest hint of a puckish smile twitching at the corner.

'Ya could do a lot worse than be like ya grandpa, Emma. He was an old rogue, but a lovable old rogue, if you know what I mean.'

Emma laughed, a low infectious sound. 'Oh, Luke, you say the nicest things to a girl. If only you were twenty years younger.'

The old man grinned, showing black gaps between his yellowing teeth. 'More like forty, lass.' Then he winked broadly. 'I were a bit of a lad in me time, an' all. Me an' ya dad got into a few scrapes together as young uns.'

'Oh do tell, Luke,' she teased him, knowing that not for one moment would he let out the secrets of their youth.

He shook his head. 'Nay, lass, 'tis more 'n me job's worth.'

Emma wagged her finger at him playfully. 'Don't you worry, Luke Robson. I'll ask your Sarah next time I see her.'

'Ya can ask, but she'll not tell you, 'cos she don't know.'

'Oh, *you.*' In mock anger, Emma shook her fist at him as he turned away to heave the sack of grain up the steps and into the mill. He was still chuckling to himself, safe in the belief that Emma could not learn anything about his youth, or about her father's early years, save what he, Luke Robson, chose to tell her.

'I'll see you tomorrow morning,' she called.

'Aye, bright and early, lass.'

She stood watching him for a moment as he disappeared into the mill and she heard the jingle of the sack hoist chain as he hauled the last sack up to the bin floor. Then he would climb the three flights of narrow ladders to unload and tip the sack into its right container. Her gaze wandered lovingly over the black tapering shape towering above her. She listened to the gentle rattle of the revolving sails. To Emma, the sound was the heartbeat of the working mill. She lifted her head and felt the wind on her face. She loved it when it was good milling weather, even if it did mean her working day was even longer. To her it was an affront when her father was forced to start the engine in the nearby building and run the long, wide belt across the space between the shed and the mill. With the belt looped around the pulley wheel on the outside of the mill, the engine drove the pair of auxiliary stones. It was the only way they could keep the mill working when there was no wind strong enough to turn the sails, yet Emma hated it. But there was no need for it on a day like this when the wind blustered from the sea and sent the sails spinning sails faster and faster.

Her work here done for the moment, Emma walked across the yard away from the mill. To her right was the granary and on her left, the tip of its roof only just beneath the sweep of the sails, was the engine house. Behind it and through a gap in the hedge was their orchard and beyond that, a small cottage belonging to Harry Forrest but occupied by Luke and Sarah Robson who both worked for him. Before her was their own house. On the ground floor was the bakery at the front, facing onto the village street. At the back was the bakehouse and in between the two was their kitchen, with bedrooms and the best parlour on the first floor.

Three generations of Forrests had lived here in this house. The first Forrest, old Charlie, had seen his two sons, Charles and Harry, born in the front bedroom above the shop and had rejoiced in the knowledge that he had heirs to follow him. To old Charlie's disappointment, his eldest son had no interest in the mill and had run away to sea at the age of thirteen or so. The ebullient man had shrugged his huge shoulders and forgiven his wayward offspring, for there was still Harry to give him grandsons.

But that had not happened, for the only child to survive had been a girl, and now Emma Forrest was the only heir to old Charlie's mill.

Three

It was the time of day she loved the best. Very early on a winter's morning with the yard outside still in darkness, it was warm and cosy in the bakehouse. With her father across at the mill, and before Sarah came to open the shop, there was just Luke lighting and stoking the fire in the firebox at the side of the brick oven and Emma mixing the first batch of dough for fifty farmhouse loaves.

'Tell me again,' she coaxed. 'Tell me about Grandpa Charlie?'

And Luke needed no more persuasion.

'Eighteen-fifty-two, your grandpa built this mill, Emma. With his own bare hands.' Luke would spread his own hands, pitted with the long years of work. 'He'd been apprenticed as a boy to a millwright and by the time he was in his twenties, what Charlie Forrest didn't know about mills and milling weren't worth knowing. It was his dream to have his own mill. Aye, and everybody laughed at him, an' all.'

'Why? Why did they laugh at him?'

'Because they said it'd not catch the wind where he was building it, here, under the lee of the hill. It's even lower than the church up yonder.' Luke jerked his thumb over his shoulder in the direction of the church towering on the highest point in the village that clustered on a gently sloping hill which the history books said had been constructed by the Romans as a lookout across the North Sea. 'They told

16

him he should have built it on top of the rise, but Ben Morgan had already built his mill there years before.' Luke laughed again. 'And old Ben wasn't too pleased about this young feller and his plans for another mill in the village, so they say.'

'Or out on the marsh,' Emma murmured, joining in the tale she knew by heart.

'Aye,' Luke agreed, 'it'd have caught the wind out there all right.'

Beyond Marsh Thorpe the flat, fertile land stretched right to the sea.

'So why . . .?'

Luke tapped the side of his nose knowingly. 'Ya grandpa might have been young, lass, but he was as sharp as a cartload o' monkeys. He bought this bit of waste ground here for a song,' Luke pointed down to the ground. 'Nearly an acre, there is, but he knew what he could do with it *and* with the derelict house on it.' The old man's smile widened. 'And isn't that what we're standing in right now, Emma? Oh, Charlie Forrest knew what he was doing, all right. He knew it'd make not only a home, but a bakehouse and bakery too.'

'And so, he built his mill,' Emma said, plunging her hands into the flour.

'Brick by brick, timber by timber, it rose towards the sky.' Luke raised his arms, becoming quite poetic as he warmed to his theme. 'He put all the heavy machinery in on each floor as he went and he even built the sails himself. Fancy that, Emma. I remember me dad telling me that the whole village turned out to watch the day the sails were hoisted.'

'But why,' Emma asked, knowing the answer full well, but humouring Luke in his enjoyment of telling her the story yet again, 'did the villagers call it "Forrest's Folly"?'

17

'Because he was a young feller, only in his twenties, reckoning he could build and run a mill all on his own, and because of where he was building it.' Luke adjusted the damper at the side of the oven and laughed wheezily. 'Allus an awk'ard old beggar, ya grandpa were. Liked to do what people least expected him to do.' Luke's eyes would mist over. 'But he were a grand chap. He knew what he were doin' all right and there weren't a finer craftsman for miles around. "This mill will last generations," he used to say. "It'll pass to my son and my son's son and on and on down the generations. There'll always be a Forrest at Forrest's Mill."' Here Luke would stop suddenly, realizing he had got carried away in his tale-telling and was touching on a subject that was like an open wound in the present generation of the Forrest family.

'It's all right,' Emma smiled gently and touched the old man's arm. 'Even Grandpa Charlie couldn't play God.'

'And when he'd finished building his mill, do you know what they say old Charlie did, Emma? He climbed up on to the gallery – there was one in them days, running all the way round the outside of the mill just above the windows of the meal floor – and he caught hold of the end of one of the sails and he went full circle round on the end of it.' Luke swept his arm in a wide arc to demonstrate. 'By, he were a daredevil, was old Charlie.' He gave a rasping bark of laughter. 'He tried to get me an' ya dad to do the same thing when we finished our apprenticeship, but we weren't 'aving none of it. I've never 'ad much of a head for heights. But old Charlie . . .' Luke was shaking his head again.

Emma frowned. 'You know I can vaguely remember there being a gallery.' Her memories were hazy, clouded by that awful day when she had seen her grandpa fall from the mill. Even when she deliberately tried to recall it, there was always something just out of reach of her consciousness.

18

'Oh aye, it was taken down after your grandpa got killed. That's how he got on to the sails, y'know? Off the gallery. That's what it was there for, for doing repairs to the sails an' that, but afterwards, well, ya dad had it removed.'

'Why – why was Grandpa up there that day? At his age?' Her eyes widened. 'You don't mean he was trying to go round on the end of a sail *then*?'

'No, no. He'd gone up to do some repairs,' Luke said quickly. 'Old Charlie never did accept that he was getting on a bit. Silly old fool thought he could carry on just like when he was young.'

Emma shuddered, trying to blot out the dreadful pictures in her mind, but they persisted. Her grandfather had his arm about her and was saying something to her, pointing up towards the mill. Then he had moved away from her. The picture blurred and her next memory was of him climbing up one of the sails. He had turned to look down at her standing in the yard, far below him and then ... Emma swept her hand across her eyes trying to erase the terrible sight of old Charlie Forrest falling, arms flailing the air, down, down to the yard below. Still she could hear the awful thud as his body hit the ground. Then she could remember no more.

'I'll tell you summat, though,' Luke was saying dragging her mercifully back to the present. 'Whatever ya dad ses, I reckon old Charlie would have been proud of you. You're a handsome lass.'

Emma made no reply. It was not quite the compliment she would have liked, yet she knew Luke intended it to be one.

'And you've a lot of his spirit in you, Emma. I often see flashes of it.'

'Me? Spirit? Oh, Luke, come on.' Now she did laugh. 'I'm the most obedient of daughters.'

19

Luke shook his head. 'That's nothing to do with being spirited. Ya can still "honour thy father" and yet have a will of ya own.'

'Just so long as it's the same as dad's will, eh?' Emma murmured, though more to herself than to Luke. She was thoughtful now, surprised to hear that Luke, shrewd and wise as he was, had already seen something in her that she was only just beginning to recognize for herself. That in her was a spark of rebellion, a growing determination to lead her own life, to make things happen the way she wanted.

'Ya still young, lass,' Luke was saying, 'but your time will come, Emma. I can see it in those lovely eyes of yours. Ya might be tied to this mill by tradition and by your father's wishes at the moment, but ya'll never be a slave to any man.' Luke laughed wheezily. 'There's too much of old Charlie's blood running in your veins for that to happen.'

The door opened and the icy cold of the November morning blew into the bakehouse.

'Time to stand yapping all day, 'ave yer?' Harry Forrest demanded of Luke. 'I need you across at the mill.' His glance swivelled towards Emma. 'And where's me breakfast?'

Unhurriedly, Luke started setting the bread tins out. 'You go, lass, I'll finish here.'

'Thank you, Luke,' she smiled at him. 'Breakfast will be ten minutes, Father.' She turned and went through into the kitchen, ignoring Harry Forrest's grunt of annoyance.

Later in the day, when she had finished her work in the bakehouse and went through to the shop at the front, her mind was still filled with thoughts of the past which Luke's words had evoked. Of course, she had her grandfather's blood coursing through her veins and maybe she was more like him than she had realized. But Charlie Forrest was a legend. Could she really live up to the tales Luke told about him?

I just hope old Luke *is* right, Emma thought, because if I'm going to marry Jamie Metcalfe then there is going to be a real battle ahead.

'There you are,' Sarah Robson's cheerful voice greeted her. 'Are you free to tek over now, Emma? I'll have to go and get Luke's tea ready in a few minutes. By the way, we've no cottage loaves left and I must remember to bring some more honey across tomorrow.'

Emma yawned and drew the back of her hand across her forehead. 'I'll do extra in tomorrow morning's second batch.'

'We need more scones an' all,' Sarah said.

'I'll do them along with the cakes after the first two batches of loaves,' Emma nodded. 'As the oven cools.'

She glanced up at the ceiling as they both heard the sound of Harry Forrest moving about in the living quarters above. 'I'd better make a start on Father's tea, too,' she murmured. 'I expect he'll be working late tonight if this wind holds.'

She heard Sarah's sniff. 'Shouldn't bother. I reckon he's on his way out.'

Emma's eyes widened. 'Out? Out where?' Her father rarely left the mill and then perhaps only on a market day. It was unheard of, at this time on a Wednesday evening, that he should be upstairs changing from his working clothes to go out *and* on a day when the wind still blew strongly in the late afternoon. It was the lot of the miller that he worked at any time of the day or night when the wind demanded.

'Search me,' Sarah shrugged. Emma eyed her keenly. The woman turned away, but not before Emma had seen the smile twitching at the corner of Sarah's mouth.

'Sarah?' she began warningly, 'You know something.' At that moment Harry Forrest's heavy boots sounded on the stairs and Sarah bustled away to busy herself wiping the crumbs from the shelves behind the counter ready for the fresh bread to be placed there the next morning.

The door at the bottom of the stairs opened and shut and Emma heard him cross the kitchen to leave by the door leading into the yard. Intrigued, she left the shop and went to look out of the kitchen window. Now she could see that the mill's five sails were motionless, parked in the position the miller always left them at the end of his working day. Leaning against the deep white sink beneath the window, Emma saw her father standing outside the back door. He was dressed in his brown Sunday suit, the toecaps of his boots shone and he was pulling on his best cap.

'He's even shaved,' she murmured. Normally, Harry Forrest shaved once a week on a Sunday morning in readiness for attending chapel, the rest of the week his face bore a peppered stubble. His features were thin. His nose had a slight bump in the middle that gave it a hooked appearance and his grey eyes were sharp. Too sharp sometimes, Emma thought, for they seemed to miss nothing.

She saw him cross the yard and step into the road, pulling the gate shut behind him. Overcome with curiosity, Emma went out of the back door and towards the gate too. From across the road came the clatter of buckets as workmen swilled down the cobblestones of the cattle market after a busy day. Their voices echoed through the gathering dusk and the pungent, sweet–sour farmyard smells drifted across to her. But, leaning on the gate, Emma's attention was on Harry Forrest.

'Now just where are you going, Father?' she asked aloud as she watched him walk up the incline of the main road which curved past the mill and through the village. He passed the market place without even glancing to his right and disappeared round the corner towards the church and out of her sight.

From behind her came Luke's wheezing laughter. 'Off to see the Merry Widow, lass. That's where ya dad's off.'

Emma turned swiftly, but Luke was walking away, his hobnailed boots echoing on the yard. She could hear him chuckling to himself. 'There's still a bit of old Charlie in Harry after all.'

'Luke . . .?' she began, but Luke only waved his hand in the air without turning round and continued his way towards the gap in the hedge that led through the orchard, past the three bee hives and towards his own cottage. 'Harry Forrest can go gallivanting if he likes,' she heard him chuckle. 'But I'm off 'ome to put me feet up.'

Her father did not return until after midnight.

Lying awake in the darkness, hearing the wind rattling the slates on the roof and rustling the tree outside her window, Emma waited, every muscle tensed, listening for the sound of his return. It was so totally unlike him. She could not remember a time when her father had acted like this. He should be here, working the mill, she thought crossly. The granary was bulging with sacks of grain waiting to be ground and Harry Forrest was wasting precious hours of a good milling wind.

She heard the back door slam, the sound of his boots on the stairs and the creak of his bedroom door. She heard him moving about his room. Then the door opened once more and he stepped out on to the landing again. Throwing back the bed covers, Emma swung her feet to the cold floor and pattered across the room. Peering round the door, she saw her father going back down the stairs, a candle in his right hand to light the way.

'Father? Are you all right? Where have you been till this hour?'

Without pausing in his descent, he rasped, 'That's no concern of yours, m'girl. Go back to yar bed.'

'But—'

'Don't argue.' The gruff command had become an ill-tempered roar. Emma flinched and shut her door at once. Moments later, she twitched back the curtain to see the dim shape of her father crossing the yard towards the mill, determined not to miss any more of the good milling weather.

But where, she thought with an insatiable curiosity, had he been?

Four

'Sarah, do you know where my father went last night?'

'Now, Emma, how would I know a thing like that? 'Sides, it isn't any of my business.'

Emma glanced at her archly. She felt like saying 'Since when has anything to do with a member of the Forrest family *not* been your business?' Instead she said quietly, 'But you do know, Sarah, don't you?' The woman avoided meeting Emma's eyes and still said nothing.

Into the silence, Emma asked, 'Who is "the Merry Widow"?'

Her steady, violet gaze was on Sarah, whose cheeks flamed as she darted a fleeting, uncomfortable glance at Emma. Turning away, Sarah bit her lip. 'Don't ask me, Emma love, please don't ask me.'

Emma felt a twinge of unease. She could not remember Sarah ever being so evasive nor so agitated. What *was* all the mystery?

I know, she thought suddenly, I know who I can ask.

By midmorning, when the mill sails were spinning and Sarah was being kept busy with customers in the bakery, Emma slipped away. She marched up the road, past the turning leading to the chapel and on towards the market place, purpose in every stride. Past the butcher's on the corner, the cobbler's and the long, low whitewashed pub, she came to the far end of the square where the smithy and the wheelwright's workshop stood next door to each other, joined by a semicircular brick archway. Attached to the archway was a sign declaring in bold, black lettering, METCALFE.

Standing in the open doorway of the forge, she raised her voice above the clang-clang of the hammer. 'William, have you any news of Jamie? Is he safe? When's he coming home?'

The gaunt young man straightened his back from where he had been stooping over the anvil. With one hand he dropped the horseshoe, glowing red hot, from the end of the tongs into the butt of water where it spat and sizzled. He turned to face her, the smile creasing his thin face and banishing for a moment the haunted look that always seemed to be in his eyes these days, making him seem so much older than his seventeen years. 'What a lot of questions all at once, Em.'

'Well, *have* you heard anything, William? Anything at all?'

Sadly, he shook his head and the anxious look came back into his blue-green eyes. His voice was scarcely above a whisper, 'No, no, I haven't—' He seemed about to say more but stopped abruptly in mid-sentence and ran the back of his hand across his forehead, wiping away the beads of sweat.

A sudden tremor of fear ran through her. Her heart quickened its beat and she caught her breath. 'William, you don't mean – you're not afraid something's happened to him, are you? Oh, it couldn't. Not now, right at the end of the war. It would be too cruel.'

'No, no, Em,' he said swiftly, putting out his hand towards her. 'I don't mean that. It's just that – it seems a dreadful thing to say, but for some things, I'm dreading him coming back.'

Emma's violet eyes darkened with sympathy. 'I know, I know,' she said gently and reached out to touch his arm, bronzed and sinewy from his work.

William Metcalfe shrugged. 'I don't even know if my letter about our parents' death ever reached him. I've heard nothing from him. Not a word.'

'Oh. Oh dear.' She scarcely knew what to say. She was silent now, in sympathy for the young man who awaited his elder brother's return with such a mixture of emotions. She was remembering the time only three months earlier when the whole village had turned out for the funeral of Josiah Metcalfe. The procession had wound its way from the Metcalfes' home behind the blacksmith's and the wheelwright's premises in the market square to the chapel. The memory caused Emma not only sadness for Jamie and William, but acute embarrassment. Whenever she thought of that day, she almost squirmed with humiliation. Of all the village folk, only her father had stayed away from the funeral. She had been aware of the whispers and, although she had tried to hold her head high as she joined the congregation in the chapel, she had felt angry and uncomfortable that her father was so conspicuous by his absence. The whole village knew that the two men, Josiah Metcalfe and Harry Forrest, had little time for each other, but even Emma had not realized that their quarrel went so deep that Harry Forrest would callously snub the family in such a deliberate and public manner. And to make matters worse, when, only one week later William's mother had died, Harry Forrest had stayed away from her funeral too.

'Least he's not a hypocrite,' Luke had tried to comfort Emma. 'No one can say that of him, lass.'

William's voice broke into her thoughts. 'I can still hardly believe they both went like that. So quick. A great, strapping chap like me dad . . .' His voice fell away and his gaze, suspiciously bright, met Emma's troubled eyes. 'Nowt but skin and bone by the time he died. Jamie – ' his voice broke, 'wouldn't have recognized him.'

Emma felt tears prickling the back of her throat. 'I know. And your mam wore herself out caring for him, didn't she?'

He nodded. 'Her heart just gave out. But at least she was spared all that pain and suffering me dad went through. He used to grab hold of her arm and beg her to give him summat for the pain. Great bruises, she had on her arm, where he'd gripped her.'

Emma swallowed painfully. 'Luke said he heard your dad yelling out sometimes when he came to the smithy. Even from inside the cottage at the back there.'

'It must have been bad, Emma, 'cos me dad was no coward when it came to bearing pain. Why, I've seen him when a horse has given him a nasty kick, just shrug it off as if it were nowt. He suffered badly. I know he did.'

He glanced about him and sighed heavily. 'And what my big brother's going to say to all this, I don't know.'

The smithy's yard was littered with old horseshoes and bits of metal and ashes blew about the cobbles in little flurries. Emma glanced around the brick walls where usually the blacksmith's tools hung in well-ordered rows. Now they hung higgledy-piggledy. Several hooks were empty and, when Emma looked about the floor, she saw why. Tools lay everywhere, as if William had been too busy to replace them in their rightful position between jobs. A pile of horseshoes had been slung in one corner and out in the yard, three ploughs awaited repair. As William turned away towards the glowing forge, Emma saw he was limping.

'Have you hurt yourself?'

William grimaced. 'Ben Popple's shire kicked me day 'afore yesterday.'

Emma pulled a face in sympathy and said, 'Ouch,' as if she too could feel his pain.

William nodded and said with feeling, 'Yeah, "ouch" indeed. I'm no good with 'osses, Em. Jamie's got that special touch, y'know.'

Emma almost blushed and was thankful William could not read her thoughts. Swiftly, she quelled her romantic daydreams and brought her wandering mind back to William.

'I'm better working wi' wood,' he nodded to his left towards the wide passageway that ran between the smithy and the wheelwright's workshop. 'But I've had to close that for the time bein'. I just haven't been able to cope with both businesses. There's still one of Farmer Leighton's wagons waiting for a broken wheel to be repaired. But I can't get anyone to give me a hand with the tyre. It needs both smith and wheelwright.'

She had watched Jamie and his father working in partnership to shape the huge round of the metal tyre. They heated it in a bonfire and then, lifting it with long-handled tongs, they carried it between them, to fit it over the wooden cartwheel. Finally they poured cold water on it to cool it quickly so that the metal contracted to fit tightly on to the wheel. William was right. It was a two man job.

He was picking up a piece of metal and examining its usefulness as a horseshoe with a half-hearted interest. 'I'm losing business here an' all, now. Just what Jamie'll say when he does get home, I daren't think.'

As William thrust the metal into the fire, Emma wandered out of the forge and peered over the closed gate leading into the wheelwright's yard. Broken wheels stood leaning drunkenly against one wall. In the centre, a wagon with a broken shaft and its blue paint peeling off in flakes waited forlornly for attention. Everywhere were piles of wood waiting to be made into wagons and in one corner a neglected heap of elm butts, still with the bark on, were already collecting mildew.

She went back and stood watching, feeling the heat from the fire, smelling the aroma of singeing hoof that clung to the walls of the smithy. William brought another shoe out of the fire to the anvil and picked up his hammer to beat the white hot metal into shape.

William was a year younger than Emma and no taller, with light brown hair and greeny-blue eyes. He had always been thin, but now that slimness had a gauntness to it, as if the burdens he had been obliged to shoulder alone threatened to weigh him down and break his slender frame and gentle soul.

When the noise of his hammer ceased, she said, 'He'll understand, William. Jamie will understand what you've been through, what you've had to cope with all on your own.' She did not add, though the thought was in her mind, that Jamie would not have expected his young brother to cope at all. William had been only fourteen when Jamie had gone away. It would be how he was still picturing him – as a boy. Now Jamie was returning to find a man, but a young man who had borne the heavy weight of losing both his parents so suddenly and struggling alone to keep the family concerns going. 'Would you like me to come and help you?' she asked.

He glanced up, his warm smile creasing the lines around

his eyes. 'Would you? Just to tidy the house up a bit.' He pulled a comical face. 'It's as bad in there as out here.'

She chuckled. 'Well, I meant out here, with Farmer Leighton's wheel, but if you'd rather . . .'

William was shaking his head. 'I wouldn't want you to help me with that. I wouldn't let you. It's not the sort of work a lass ought to do.'

Now Emma threw back her head and laughed, 'Oh, William. I love you when you get all protective. It's me, remember, Harry Forrest's great carthorse of a daughter.'

'Don't talk like that, Emma,' he said and at the use of her full name, Emma's laughter died.

William only ever called her 'Emma' when he was annoyed, which was so unusual that she could not remember the last time he had called her by her full name. Since childhood, to William, she had always been 'Em'.

'I'm sorry,' she said swiftly. 'But I could help you out here, really I could.'

William shook his head emphatically. 'No, Em, but I'd be really grateful for some help in the house.' He was smiling again, his easy, good nature restored at once.

'Right then, I'll come Sunday afternoon complete with bucket and mop. And as for all this,' she swept her hand in a wide arc to encompass the smithy and the neighbouring yard too, 'Jamie will soon be home now to help you. Why,' she tried to smile brightly at him, to lift the young man's spirits, 'it'll be just what your father always wanted, two Metcalfe brothers running the business with Jamie as the blacksmith and you as the wheelwright. Isn't that so?'

'Oh, Em,' the young man sighed. 'What would I have done without you these last few months? You always seem to make things better.' He glanced away, back towards the

31

fire and muttered gruffly, 'I hope our Jamie knows what a lucky feller he is with a girl like you waiting for him.'

Emma laughed, the sound echoing around the walls of the smithy. 'I hope he does too.'

'But you're right,' he went on. 'Our dad inherited the two businesses from his father and his Uncle George, who had no family, and he always planned that one day Jamie and me would work side by side again like the old days.' He grinned at her. 'Lucky he had two sons, wasn't it, and not daughters?'

The smile faded from Emma's mouth and her glance fell away. 'Yes,' she said quietly. 'That's what my father has always said.'

The young man was at once contrite. He dropped the long tongs on the floor with a ringing clatter and came swiftly towards her. 'I'm sorry. I wasn't thinking. Me an' my big mouth. You know I wouldn't say anything to hurt your feelings.'

She put up her hand to him and forced a smile to her mouth. 'I know you wouldn't.'

William was one of the most compassionate, kindly men Emma knew. Her violet eyes softened as she looked at him now. She was so glad he was going to be her brother-in-law. She couldn't wait for the day when she would come to live in the little cottage behind the smithy and the wheel-wright's and care for both her husband and his brother, at least until William found himself a bride too. But it wouldn't do to say so, not now. She bit her lip, holding back the words, not daring to tempt a Fate that had not yet brought her Jamie safely back from the war.

'William,' she began, deliberately changing the subject, 'there's something I want to ask you . . .'

'What's that, Em?'

'Do you know who "the Merry Widow" is?'

Five

'Where've you been gallivanting off to when there's work to be done?'

Harry Forrest was standing in the doorway of the mill, looking out across the yard, his thumbs hooked in his braces, his collarless shirt sleeves rolled up above his elbows. Even in winter, he wore only a waistcoat over his shirt, but underneath, he wore a thick woollen vest and long johns, garments that were the devil's own job to get dry on a wet wash day, Emma thought. Corduroy trousers, heavy boots and a cap completed the miller's working clothes. Indeed, they were almost a uniform, for not only Luke, but all the farm workers, even William and Jamie too, wore similar workaday attire.

Emma closed the gate and walked across the yard towards him. 'I've been to take old Grannie Bartlett's bread, Father,' she answered, outwardly placid, but inwardly seething. It was a truthful answer, if not the whole truth. She could have said, 'And finding out things about you. Things I'd rather not have known.' But she kept silent about calling to see William Metcalfe. It did not do to arouse Harry Forrest's wrath too often.

Her father grunted. 'We're not a delivery service for the locals, girl. Old Mrs Bartlett should get a neighbour to fetch 'er bread.'

Emma said nothing, knowing he was spoiling for an argument if she gave him the opportunity. 'Anyway,' he muttered, 'ya took yar time, didn't ya? I've been waiting for a hand. Get up top and unhook these sacks as I send 'em up. They want to go in Ben Popple's bin.'

Emma nodded and set down her basket on the floor. Hitching up her skirt, she began to climb the narrow ladder up to the bin floor of the mill. 'Mind ya gets the right bin,' came her father's irritable voice. 'I don't want Ben on me back 'cos we've mixed up his grain wi' summat else. You know how fussy he is about his own special mix for his pig feed.'

'No, Father,' Emma called, without pausing in her climb. She stepped on to the meal floor where the ground flour or meal came down the spouts from the millstones on the floor above into the waiting sacks. It was where the miller stood for most of his working day. Between the fingers and thumb of one hand he felt the texture of the ground grain as it poured down the wooden chute. With the other hand, he adjusted the tentering gear to raise or lower the stones above to produce the exact fineness of flour or meal he wanted. It was a skilled and exacting job and the slightest change in the strength of the wind meant a tiny, precise adjustment to the gearing.

On this floor too, was the pair of auxiliary stones driven by the engine.

Out of her father's sight, Emma gave a quick, exasperated shake of her head. She hardly needed to be given such an elementary instruction. They all knew, had known for years, that Ben Popple liked his own grain, and no one else's, used to make up the feed for his own animals.

'After all the trouble I tek to produce a good crop, I dun't want it mixed in with the likes of old man Tollison's, full o' weeds an' muck,' Ben Popple would boom in his loud, carrying voice every time he brought grain to the mill. 'And don't you go letting anyone else have my special mix either, Harry Forrest.' He would tap the side of his nose. 'It's my secret how I gets my pigs fatter than anyone else's. See to it, Harry.'

And Harry saw to it, handing out the instruction every time, even to Luke, who knew the foibles of the farmers around here as well as, if not better than, anyone. But Harry Forrest liked to let everyone know just who was master of the mill.

Her father's voice still floated up to her. 'And it wouldn't do to upset Ben Popple, now would it, me girl?' A sly innuendo had crept into his tone.

Emma climbed on, deliberately scraping her feet on each rung as she climbed to make as much noise as possible so that she could not hear any more. She passed the stone floor where the huge cast iron spur wheel in the ceiling drove the three smaller stone nuts, each one connected to an upright spindle in the centre of each pair of stones. Above each set of millstones, a wooden spout brought the grain down from the bin floor above and fed it into hoppers and then, via the vibrating feed shoe, into the centre of the grinding stones.

Arriving on the next level, the bin floor, Emma sighed. Ben Popple was at least twice her age if not more; fat, pompous, with bad teeth and breath to match. He had never married, yet he acted as if he thought himself irresistible to women.

'Now then, Emma,' he would greet her every time he came to the mill, hanging about the yard until she appeared. 'My, but ya're a bonny lass. When are you going to let me speak to ya dad 'bout us being wed, eh? I could do with a good strong wench about me farm and to warm me bed at night.'

'When the sun shines both sides o' the hedge, Mester Popple,' she would tease him.

Ben Popple would roar with laughter. 'I like a bit of spirit in a wench, an' all. Harry can keep his lah-di-dah fancy women but you'll do fer me, Emma Forrest. You'll do fer me.'

At first she had taken his words as the kind of innocent joking between an older man and a young girl, without any offence being meant nor taken. But then one day Harry Forrest had overheard Ben and he had chosen to view the wealthy farmer's banter very differently. 'You could do a lot worse, m'girl, and with your looks, probably not a lot better.'

On the bin floor she unhooked each sack from the hoist as it came rattling through the trap doors, lugged it over to the small bin in the far corner and heaved in the grain. There was scarcely room to move between the wooden bins and soon the confined space was thick with dust. It clung to her black hair, tickled her throat and made her blink, but for Emma it was her way of life, and if not exactly oblivious to the discomfort then she thought nothing of it. Besides, today her mind was filled with what William Metcalfe had told her.

'The Merry Widow' was a woman called Bridget Smith who had recently come to live in a tiny cottage on the other side of the village. But just how, Emma pondered the problem, as she heaved and grunted and pushed another sack load into the bin, am I going to get to see her for myself?

'That's the lot,' Harry's voice drifted up from three floors below. 'You finish off here, I'm off to the house. I shan't be wanting any tea.' A pause, then he bellowed again, 'You hear me, Emma?'

'Oh I hear you, Harry Forrest,' she muttered and then raised her voice to shout down, 'Yes, Father.'

She bent and looked out of the small window overlooking the yard to see him walking towards the house. She was tempted to shout, 'May I come with you, Father?' The thought of doing so made her clap her hand to her mouth as if to stop the mischievous words escaping her lips of their own accord.

Once more, she ate her tea alone and went to bed long before Harry Forrest returned home.

The following morning as Emma carried a tray of warm cottage loaves from the bakery into the shop, the door bell clanged and Emma, with a ready smile on her lips, looked up to greet her customer. The woman standing on the other side of the polished wooden counter was a stranger to the village and immediately Emma realized who she must be and the smile on her generous mouth faltered. But the woman was smiling and holding out her gloved hand across the counter.

'I thought it was high time we met. My name is Bridget Smith. And you . . .' her voice was high-pitched but pleasant and she paused as if to give emphasis to her next words, 'must be Emma?'

Slowly Emma held out her hand and found it clasped gently in the soft fabric of the woman's lilac coloured gloves. Emma knew she was staring at the face before her, but she could not tear her mesmerized gaze away. This was the woman the villagers called 'the Merry Widow', the woman her father was keeping company with and in turn making himself at best, the idle talk of the pub bar, at worst, a laughing stock.

Bridget Smith was small and slim. Her bright, blonde hair was drawn neatly back from her face into a stylish chignon at the nape of her neck. Little tendrils curled on to her forehead and framed her delicate, pink cheeks. Her coat, a vibrant red on this cold November day and with a luxurious fur collar, fell in straight lines to her neat ankles and her button boots encased tiny, dainty feet. A delicate, flowery perfume wafted across the counter towards Emma as she gazed into the woman's face. She wore face powder so skilfully applied that her skin looked soft and velvety. Her lips were darker than their natural colour, toning perfectly with her scarlet coat and her eyes were the blue of a summer sky, twinkling as she smiled, her cheeks dimpling.

'I'm *so* pleased to meet you,' Mrs Smith said and, releasing Emma's hand, she hitched herself elegantly on to the high stool that always stood on the customer's side of the counter. She crossed her slim ankles in an action that was almost coquettish.

Taking a deep breath, Emma tried to force out the responding words, but she could utter no sound. Her mind was reeling. All she could think about was what William had told her. 'Arrived out the blue, she has. No one knows who she is, or where she's come from, nor anything about her.' He had glanced at Emma awkwardly and then added, a little hesitantly, 'But she – er – seems to have set her cap at ya dad. At least,' he added quickly, 'that's what everyone reckons. Mind you, ya know what village gossip is. And I'm sure your dad has more sense than to get caught up with the likes of her.'

Emma had stepped closer to William. 'What do you mean "the likes of her"?'

He had wriggled his shoulders uncomfortably as if wishing he had not said so much. 'Well, er, she seems a flashy piece. Y'know?'

'No,' Emma had murmured, 'I don't know.' But William could not be persuaded to say any more.

Facing Bridget Smith now across the counter, Emma was seeing for herself the woman whom the village gossip

38

described as 'a flashy piece'. Now, trying valiantly to be fair and unbiased, Emma thought the name a little uncharitable, in fact, now she saw the woman for herself, very uncharitable. Certainly Bridget Smith was elegantly dressed, extravagantly so if compared to the village women, yet it was not in the bold, brassy manner she had anticipated from William's description. What Emma felt as she took in the whole of the woman's appearance, was not disgust but envy. How she would have loved the chance to dress in such clothes, to have her hair prettily styled and to wear cosmetics. And the woman's expression was warm and friendly and though Emma had determined to be on the defensive when she met 'the Merry Widow', instead she found any planned resentment melting under Bridget Smith's smile.

'Oh, your father is so *lucky* to have a daughter,' Bridget gave an exaggerated sigh. 'How I do *envy* him. I have only one son, the absolute *bane* of my life.' She held up her hands, palms outwards as if in despair, but the tinkling laugh that accompanied her statement belied her words.

In spite of herself, Emma felt her own smile widening. 'I don't think,' she murmured, speaking for the first time since the woman had entered the shop, 'that my father would agree with you.'

'Oh, go on with you,' Bridget flapped her hand playfully towards Emma. 'I've heard all about that, don't you worry. Him and his silly mill. Besides, from what *I've* heard,' she leant forward, sympathy in her voice, 'he has you working every bit as hard as any son.'

Emma nodded. 'But it's the name, you see. Even when I marry . . .' she paused, almost tempted to spill out the hurt of years, but she took a deep breath and corrected herself, 'even *if* I were to marry, it wouldn't be a *Forrest* at the mill.'

Bridget shrugged her elegant shoulders. 'Does that really

matter so much? You and your children would still be Forrest *descendants*, now wouldn't you?'

Emma sighed. 'Yes, but that's still not enough. Not for my father.'

At that moment, the subject of their conversation came into the shop from the door leading into the kitchen. Seeing Bridget sitting there, he gaped in surprise for a moment and then, as she watched, Emma saw the most astounding transformation come over her father.

'Why, Bridget, my dear.' He was moving round the counter, holding out his hand and smiling such a sycophantic smile that Emma stared in astonishment. Bridget was looking up into his face, fluttering her eyelashes, putting her dainty gloved hands into his dusty paws and allowing him to help her down from her perch on the high stool. Standing beside him – she only came up to his shoulder – she looked like a delicate china doll beside the tall, slightly stooping frame of the miller.

'We've been having *such* a nice chat,' Bridget trilled and Emma stifled her amusement. The woman seemed to speak with an emphasis on nearly every other word. '*What* a dear girl. I can't *wait* for her to meet my Leonard.' She leaned towards Emma again with a conspiratorial air. 'You're not engaged or promised to anyone, are you, my dear?'

'Well—' Emma began but her father's loud guffaw swept away any such ridiculous notion.

'Suitors for my daughter aren't exactly queuing at the door.'

'Now, now, Harry,' Bridget scolded and tapped his arm playfully. 'She's a lovely girl and if you were to allow her to buy some pretty dresses – with my help, of course – ' Bridget turned her head slightly and gave Emma a broad wink, an action that could not have been missed by the girl's father, 'you'd soon see.'

Emma held her breath but then her mouth dropped open as Harry Forrest, a stupid, besotted grin on his face and his gaze never leaving Bridget's, said, 'Whatever you say, my dear.'

Six

'I wouldn't have believed it possible if I hadn't seen it with me own eyes,' Emma confided in Sarah, though her hands never paused in kneading the dough beneath her strong supple fingers. 'He's like a lovesick lad. Mind you, she seems very nice.'

Sarah's reply was a snort, her round little body shaking with indignation. She pushed the long handled, wooden spade-like peel into the depths of the bread oven and brought out a cottage loaf. Six more followed swiftly, all round and brown and perfect, their smell permeating the bakehouse and drifting appetizingly through the kitchen and into the shop. Sarah, her face flushed from the heat of the oven, shot a tight-lipped look at Emma. 'You bin taken in an' all by her pretty ways and her fancy clothes? Aw, Emma, I'd have thought better of you.'

'Eh?' Emma's eyes widened. 'Why, is there something more? I know the village folk reckon she's a flashy piece,' she smiled as she repeated William Metcalfe's words, 'but then, any stranger who dares to set foot in the village is eyed with suspicion until they've been here about fifty years.'

Sarah wagged her finger at Emma. 'Now then, dun't you mock. Mebbe we're slow to accept new faces, but once we do, then they're friends for life.'

Emma nodded, 'Yes, that's true.'

Indeed it was. The small community of Marsh Thorpe

protected its own and as Sarah said, although they were suspicious of newcomers for a time, almost requiring that the stranger should prove themselves worthy of living in their midst, once they had accepted them, then they welcomed them wholeheartedly.

'I suppose it's the same in most villages,' Emma murmured.

'Aye, well, mebbe it is. I wouldn't know about that,' Sarah said and her tone was almost smug. Sarah had lived all her life in Marsh Thorpe, hardly venturing beyond its boundaries. She had visited Lincoln, but London might as well have been on another planet for all Sarah knew about it.

Emma set the dough in the proving hole below the firebox and followed Sarah through to the shop, carrying a tray of the steaming, freshly baked cottage loaves.

'So, come on, Sarah, tell. What is it you've heard about Mrs Smith?'

Sarah wriggled her plump shoulders and her cheeks grew even pinker. She was a homely soul, content with her lot. A country woman, born and bred, who never seemed to question the need for her to work from morning until night, Sarah had not married until the age of twenty-eight when, only five years ago, she had wed the much older Luke Robson.

She had come to live at the millhouse as a young girl of seventeen to help the delicate Frances Forrest and to care for the two-year-old Emma. The affection between Luke and Sarah had grown slowly, but now their love glowed in their eyes every time they looked at each other.

'He needed someone to care for him,' Sarah always laughed if anyone dared to remark on the difference in their ages. 'He'd been on his own ever since his first wife died. Must have been twenty years or more, and that's too

long for any man. And I weren't no great shakes as a catch.'
The laughter would grow louder. 'Not many young fellers
like us big lasses, but my Luke he says there's plenty to get
'old of.' At this point she would grab the folds of flesh
around her waist and roar with laughter and wink saucily.
'Love handles, he ses I've got.'

But now she seemed curiously reticent. ''Tain't my place
to say owt, Emma lass.'

Deftly, Emma placed the loaves in a line along the shelf.
'Oh, now come on, Sarah. You've been like a mam to me
since me own died.'

Sarah's voice was soft now and there was a suspicion of
tears in her eyes. 'And you've been like a daughter to me
and Luke.' Her voice dropped almost to a whisper. 'The
daughter we'll never have now.'

It was the only disappointment in her otherwise happy
and contented life: she and Luke could not have children.

'So,' Emma prompted, 'what is it you know that I
don't?'

'I really don't think I ought . . .'

'Sarah . . .' Emma began warningly.

'Oh, very well then, but only because I don't like to see
you taken in an' all. It's bad enough with '*im*.'

'For heaven's sakes! *What* is?'

Sarah leant forwards, sharing a secret. 'They reckon
she's not a widow at all. That she's never been married.'

Emma's mouth dropped open. 'That can't be right. She
said she had a son . . .' Then as realization dawned, her
eyes widened and comically she said, 'Oh heck!'

Sarah nodded. 'Exactly!' There was a pause before she
added, a little mysteriously, 'But there's more to it than
that now, ain't there?'

'Is there? What?'

Sarah's shoulders lifted again, but she would not meet

Emma's questioning gaze. 'Well, they reckon she's still young enough to have bairns.'

The words fell like stones into the silence. 'Oh,' Emma said flatly. 'Oh, I see. So that's what they're saying, are they? That my father's still after a son.'

There was another silence and then Emma said slowly, 'Well, soon it won't worry me.' She lifted her eyes to meet Sarah's concerned gaze. 'Because once Jamie comes home—'

'Aw lass, he'll never let you wed a Metcalfe. You know that.'

'Sarah, if Jamie Metcalfe comes home safely from this war, then nothing and no one will stop me marrying him.'

Sarah shook her head and her double chin wobbled. 'Ya stacking up a lot of disappointment for ya'sen.'

'No, I'm not. If Father wants to marry Mrs Smith, then it'll make it all the easier for me to leave.' She put her arms about the woman's ample waist and hugged her. 'Oh, Sarah, please try to understand. I've always loved Jamie. Didn't you know?'

'Well,' the fat arms came around Emma and held her lovingly. 'I know you're fond of the lad, fond of 'em both if it comes to that, but I thought it were only a girl's first romantic nonsense. You're a woman now, Emma, and you ought—'

The shop bell clanged and the two women drew apart and turned to face their customer. Whatever Sarah had been going to say was to remain unsaid.

William was standing in the bakery shop doorway, blurting out the news even before the sound of the doorbell had died away. 'He's coming home! Jamie's safe and he's coming home. I've just heard.'

Emma eyes shone. 'Oh, William. That's wonderful. When? When will he be here?'

Beside her, Sarah's inner struggle with her emotions could be seen plainly on her round face. Jamie Metcalfe was coming home and all Sarah could see was trouble ahead for her beloved Emma. Yet the woman rejoiced in the safe return of the young man.

Gently, she said, 'Now that is good news, William. You must be so thankful.'

'It's a big relief all round, I don't mind admitting.' William sighed and shook his head. 'I'm so glad he's safe.' He ran his hand through his soft brown hair and glanced at Emma. Dropping his voice, he muttered. 'But it isn't the sort of homecoming I'd have wished for him.'

Emma moved swiftly round the counter towards him. 'If your mam and dad had still been here, they'd have wanted him welcomed home with a brass band playing and all the flags out. At least, your dad would. You know he would have, William.'

William's smile was wistful, as if thinking of the big man who had always been at the forefront in organizing village events or sorting out problems for the village folk.

'He fancies hissen as the Mayor of Marsh Thorpe,' had been Harry Forrest's resentful comment years earlier, but the rest of the villagers had been content to leave such matters to Josiah Metcalfe. 'Ask Mester Metcalfe, the blacksmith, he'll sort it out.' And even, 'Ask the Mayor.' The title had stuck so that when Josiah later became Chairman of the Parish Council many of the villagers believed that the title was official and even addressed him as Mester Mayor. Josiah, basking in the importance, had said nothing to disillusion them and secretly Emma had been amused that the name her father had bestowed so scathingly on the man he disliked had then been accepted as a reality. Harry had become even more bitter seeing Josiah Metcalfe accorded all the deference that such a position demanded.

46

As they stood in the shop together Emma could see that William was remembering the final weeks and months of his father's life, how the big man had wasted away so swiftly, so painfully that he could not even hang on to life until the day his hero son returned from the war. Now there was only William to welcome his brother.

'Aye, you're right, of course, Em. But I don't know, well, if it would be quite the right thing to do. Not now. You know what I mean. We're not really out of mourning for me mam and dad.'

Emma's violet eyes softened. 'I know how you feel.' Then she brightened and turned to Sarah. 'But let's ask around the rest of the village. See what everyone else feels. What do you think, Sarah?'

The older woman's face was unusually serious as she flicked her duster absentmindedly at nothing in particular on the already spotless counter top. 'Mm, well, I suppose we could. I'll have to think about it.' She seemed ill at ease, and Emma, guessing what was coming next, fought valiantly to keep the smile from her face and waited for Sarah's next words. 'Er, would it be all right if I just nip home for a moment, Emma?'

Airily, Emma said, 'Of course. We're not exactly rushed off our feet just now.'

Sarah untied her apron and bustled through to the kitchen to fetch her hat and coat from the peg behind the door. Jamming her hat on her thick hair, she popped her head back round the door and said, 'I won't be long, I promise, only I must go . . .' As she turned away again to leave by the back door to hurry across the yard towards the orchard, they heard her mutter. 'I must tell the bees about this.'

Emma clapped her hand to her mouth, her eyes brimming with laughter and as soon as Sarah's bustling little body was well away from the shop, her merriment bubbled over and she leant weakly against the counter. She looked up at William and was relieved to see that he was grinning, the anxiety for the moment wiped from his young face. He shook his head and said fondly, without a trace of ridicule in his tone. 'Oh dear, Sarah and her bees.'

To Sarah Robson, the old superstition of 'telling the bees' of important events in the lives of the family who owned them must never be ignored, but she seemed to carry it further than that. Everything that happened in the village of Marsh Thorpe, good or bad, was faithfully reported to the hives in the orchard which lay between the mill yard and the cottage where she and Luke lived.

'I reckon,' Emma told William, 'she doesn't just tell them things, she actually asks their advice, you know.'

Far from mocking the ways and beliefs of the woman, William asked, in all seriousness, 'How does she know what they say?'

'By their buzzing, I think. Whether they approve or disapprove.'

William shrugged and grinned. 'Well, I wouldn't like to argue. I don't fancy a swarm of 'em after me 'cos I'd upset them. Won't they be asleep, though, as it's winter?'

Emma shrugged. 'Bees don't hibernate as such, just sort of – ' she searched for an appropriate word and then laughed, 'doze.'

'What does she do, then? Wake them up?'

Her chuckle was deep, infectious. 'I really don't know. I know she taps the hives though. And if it's about our family – the Forrest family – she takes the back door key and taps the hives with that.'

'Really?' He paused and then added, 'You've always had bees in the orchard, haven't you?'

Emma nodded. 'Yes. Grandpa Charlie brought them the

same time he built the mill. The tale goes that he baited a skep and a swarm just arrived. He always said that as long as there was a Forrest at the mill, the bees would stay and the mill would prosper. If the Forrest family always had bread and honey, he said, then they'd never go hungry. Luke says the bees swarmed on the side of the mill the day Grandpa was killed.' Emma shook herself as vague, disturbing memories flickered somewhere in the deep recesses of her mind, memories she did not want to think about today. 'But I don't remember that.' More briskly, she said, 'Never mind Sarah and her bees just now, you still haven't told me exactly when Jamie will be home.'

'Saturday afternoon. On the train that gets in about three o'clock.'

'That doesn't give us much time to get the bunting out,' Emma laughed.

'Aye, an' it dun't give me much time to get the workshops straightened up a bit before he gets here.' The anxious look was back in William's face. 'By the way, thanks for coming last Sunday. The house looks great now. I only wish the rest was as tidy.'

Emma touched his arm. 'Don't worry,' she said confidently. 'Once he's home, everything will be all right.' Her own heart lifted with the thought.

Jamie, her beloved Jamie, was coming home. In three days' time, he would be here. She could picture him now, striding along the platform towards her, his kitbag resting lightly on his broad, strong shoulders, a warm smile lighting up his dark brown eyes. His curly black hair might have been cut short by army regulations, she pondered, but it would soon grow again. And there he would be, putting his arms about her, swinging her round as if she were as light as a feather. A small smile played on her lips. Oh, Jamie, she murmured inside her mind, you're the only man who makes me feel small and feminine and not like some great carthorse.

Jamie was a big man, like his father had been before his illness, taller, broader and stronger than his younger brother, even though during the past three years the heavy work of the smithy had made the boy fill out. But, at this moment, with anxiety clouding his eyes, William looked very young and vulnerable.

'I just hope you're right, Em,' he was saying, the worried frown creasing his forehead. 'I just hope everything *is* going to be all right.'

Seven

'Such a lot of fuss and carry on,' Harry muttered morosely. 'I suppose you reckon you're going to tek the afternoon off and go gallivanting off to the station to meet young Metcalfe?'

'The whole village will be there, Father. We can't possibly not go.'

He sniffed. 'Oh yes, we can.'

Emma was silent for a moment watching her father as he carved the joint of beef. If Harry Forrest could stay away from a funeral, then he could certainly stay away from Jamie's homecoming. For once, Emma thought, she would have to be a little devious. As he passed each plate to her, she added mashed potatoes and salted green beans and poured gravy over it all. Placing one plate in front of her father, she took her own seat on the opposite side of the table, the spread of the snow-white tablecloth between them. Without a word of thanks, Harry picked up his knife and fork and began to eat.

With deliberate casualness, Emma said, 'Mrs Smith is hoping her son will be on the same train.' She paused, letting the piece of information sink in and take root. Slyly, she added, 'It would be a nice welcome to his new home if Leonard Smith was included in the celebrations for Jamie.' Again she waited just a moment. 'Don't you think, Father?'

Keeping her eyes lowered, she concentrated deliberately on shaking salt and pepper on to her dinner and then picked up her knife and fork. Risking a glance, she found her father's eyes upon her, boring into her. 'Ya scheming little baggage!' he said, but to her surprise there was a hint of admiration in his tone. 'Think I won't refuse to go if Bridget Smith's going to be there, eh?'

He paused a moment as if thinking, then to her amazement Harry gave a bark of wry laughter. 'Well, ya right. I wouldn't miss that. We will be there, but mark me, me girl,' he pointed his fork at her, stabbing the air and showering droplets of gravy on to the clean tablecloth. 'It'll be Bridget's lad ya'll be welcoming home, alongside o' me. *Not* young Metcalfe.'

Emma's eyes widened as she stared at him. 'But Father, Jamie and me—'

'I know all about James Metcalfe making a play for you, girl. It was always Josiah's scheme to wed his son to you so that he could get his greedy hands on Forrest's Mill.'

Tears of humiliation stung her eyelids. She blinked rapidly, determined that he should not see how much his accusation hurt her.

'And it'll not mek any difference even though the old man's gone. Young Jamie is just as grasping.' At his next words she knew that his bitterness had clouded his judgement. 'I'd sooner see the mill flattened to the ground when I go,' he thundered, 'than see anyone other than a Forrest own it. You hear me – *girl*?'

Every moment of his years of bitter disappointment was in that final insult, yet her father's deep hatred of the Metcalfe family only served to strengthen Emma's resolve to marry Jamie. For what was Forrest's Mill to her without the love of the man she adored?

*

It seemed as if the whole village turned out to greet Jamie Metcalfe and to give him a true hero's welcome. Five soldiers had already returned to the village and eight more would never come home, leaving their saddened families without even a grave to mourn over. Jamie was the last to come back and the kindly villagers wanted to help ease the sadness he must feel knowing his parents were no longer there to greet him. They wanted to let him know they sympathized and yet were proud of him and overjoyed to see him safely returned. They wanted to give him the welcome his mother and father would have done.

Only Sarah Robson was uneasy. She joined the throng, but there was a worried look in her eyes and she bit her lip in a tense, nervous manner.

Emma, wearing the new bonnet she had bought from the market stall as a deliberate gesture of defiance towards her father, linked her arm through Sarah's. 'What is it, Sarah? Are you worried about William? He seems happier today.' She laughed. 'I think he's been giving the workshops a regular spring clean.'

Absently, Sarah nodded. 'I know. And you've been up to give the lad a hand, ain't you?'

Emma squeezed the plump arm. 'Shh, don't let Father hear you. He thought I was cleaning the chapel.'

Still, the worried expression did not leave the woman's face. Emma watched her for a moment and then asked again, 'So, what is bothering you? 'Cos there's something.'

Sarah glanced at her and tried to smile, though the anxiety never left her eyes. 'You're a mite too sharp, Emma Forrest, at times.' She bit her lip again and then said slowly, 'I know you'll mebbe laugh, but – but it's the bees.' She shook her head. 'They're – they're not happy about . . .' she waved her hand towards the gathering of people waving homemade paper flags, at the village's silver band lining up along the edge of the platform and waiting for the signal that the train was approaching. The conductor was standing on the very edge of the platform leaning precariously out over the tracks, craning his neck to look down the line. Then suddenly he gave a shout and hurried back to stand in front of the four neat rows of bandsmen. 'She's coming. Train's coming,' he said and raised his hands in the air. Trumpets, bugles, euphonium; all were raised to moustached lips and at the very back the man with the huge drum resting on his stomach twirled his sticks in readiness.

Emma saw Sarah open her mouth but her words were drowned in the sudden blast of noise. Putting her mouth close to Sarah's ear, Emma said, 'What did you say?'

The woman's gaze was fastened on the approaching train. 'They don't like it,' she mouthed and Emma bending nearer caught the words. 'The bees, they don't think all this fuss is the right thing to do. Something's going to go wrong I know it is.'

Emma squeezed her arm and began to say, 'Oh, Sarah . . ' but her attention was caught by the huge bulk of the engine drawing into the tiny station, its smoke drifting over the waiting crowd. With a great deal of hissing and puffing the train came to a halt. 'He's here. He's really home. Whatever can go wrong now?'

She let go of Sarah's arm and, drawn towards the edge of the platform, her gaze scanned the carriages, watching for Jamie to appear. The crowds surged forward and Emma was carried along until she felt a firm grasp on her arm and heard her father's gruff voice 'And where do you think you're going, girl? I told you to stay by me.'

'Oh, Father, please—'

'Do as I tell you,' he snapped and his fingers tightened on her arm. He pulled her away from the crowd and along the platform to where the diminutive figure of Bridget Smith stood on tiptoe, stretching her neck to see above the heads of the throng, a small paper flag clasped in her gloved hands. As they reached her, Emma, casting anxious glances back towards the front of the train, so afraid of missing the moment when Jamie appeared, heard Bridget say, 'Oh, Harry, I can't see him. You don't suppose . . .? Oh Harry, what if . . .?' She clung to Harry Forrest's free arm, looking up into his face, her blue eyes brimming with sudden tears.

Emma felt her father release her arm and listened as, in a surprisingly gentle voice, Harry said, 'Now, now Bridget, my dear. He'll be here, I'm sure. Just wait a moment.'

His back was half-turned away from Emma as he bent over Bridget, trying to console her. Emma inched away from his side and at the split second he turned back to her, she picked up her long skirt and skipped out of his reach.

'Emma!' he bellowed, but, although she knew she would be in dreadful trouble later, she pretended not to hear above the clamour and dodged in amongst the crowd, ducking low so that he could not see her tall figure above the other heads. Relying on Bridget's need of her father, Emma searched amongst the crowd for William. Surely, he must be here.

Then she saw him, standing disconsolately at the back of the crowd, looking very agitated and unsure. She pushed her way through to him and said, 'Come on, William. You must be the first to meet him.' She linked her arm through his and tried to urge him forward.

Uncomfortable in his Sunday suit with its starched collar, William stood twisting his cap round and round between his fingers.

There was a sudden burst of noise, of shouting and cheering. Turning, Emma saw a man standing in the doorway of a carriage. He was tall, but thin and gaunt, and on his forehead was a deep frown. Her glance flickered away from him, searching down the length of the train but then her gaze came back to him. The crowd were surging forward, reaching up towards him with outstretched arms. The band struck up a rousing march.

'Jamie. Jamie Metcalfe,' the cry went up.

Emma gasped and her fingers fastened on William's arm. 'Oh no, that's not – it can't be – *Jamie*?'

Transfixed, they both stared at the man, who picked up his kitbag and stepped down from the train. Ignoring the villagers clustering around him, he shouldered his way roughly through them towards the exit. So close that if they had reached out, they could have touched him, he seemed about to pass them by, but then something made him glance directly at them. He stopped, his dark glare going from one to the other.

Emma could not speak and William's voice was hoarse as he said, hesitantly, 'Jamie?'

'Did you arrange this – this *fiasco*?'

Stunned, Emma gasped and beneath her fingers she felt William tremble. 'I – I—' he began, but Jamie gave a grunt of annoyance and turned, striding away from them, from everyone and speaking to no one.

The crowd, robbed of their expression of pride, of joy, fell silent, save for a low, disgruntled murmur spreading amongst them. The band too fell silent, the notes dying away in a disorderly, tuneless petering out as Jamie disappeared from their view.

Then suddenly from the far end of the platform there came a delighted shriek and heads turned to see the newcomer in their midst, Bridget Smith, stretching out her arms towards a young man in uniform standing in the doorway of a carriage further down the train.

'Leonard! Oh, my Leonard, my darling boy.'

The young man threw his kitbag onto the platform and raised his arms high in the air, a wide grin stretched across his face. 'Mother!'

He jumped down and threw his arms about her, lifting her up and swinging her round and round, whilst Bridget shrieked with laughter.

The crowd, surprised to find that, after all, there was another soldier on the train, were determined not to be cheated of welcoming someone, anyone, home from the war. They surged forward, milling around Bridget and her son, clapping and cheering. Emma saw that her father was pushed to the back of the throng, for the moment, forgotten.

'Play, let's play,' the bandmaster hissed and glancing over his shoulder, raised his arms. Once more, the musicians lifted their instruments to their lips.

William put his mouth close to Emma's ear and above the noise, said, 'I'd better go and find him.'

Emma nodded and, as she felt him move away from her, stared enviously down the platform at the joyous scene. The young man was being patted on the back by a dozen hands and then two of the village lads hoisted him on to their shoulders and carried him along the platform, followed by Bridget and the crowd, laughing, clapping and cheering.

If only, Emma thought, that had been Jamie.

Someone touched her arm and she turned to see Sarah's troubled face watching her.

'We should have listened to the bees, Emma lass,' Sarah said sadly. 'I knew summat weren't right. We should have listened to the bees.'

Eight

'I thought I told you to stay with me instead of mekin' a fool of yasen running after young Metcalfe?'

Her father was angry, as she had known he would be. Emma kept her glance downcast as she placed his supper in front of him, deliberately feigning meek apology and keeping hidden the fire of anger she knew flashed in her brilliant eyes. In a tight voice she said, 'Jamie didn't want us there anyway.'

Her father grunted. 'Serves ya right for mekin' such a to-do-ment. I'll give the lad that, he's not like his show-off of a father, our so-called Mayor!' He picked up his knife and fork and added gruffly, as if afraid his daughter might think he was relenting. 'But I've no time for any of them Metcalfes. None of 'em and you just remember that, me girl.'

Now she raised her eyes and said craftily, 'Perhaps it was a good job we did put on a bit of a show. Mrs Smith and her son seemed pleased.'

Mollified a little, as she had hoped, Harry said, 'Aye, aye, they were.' There was a pause and his keen, steely gaze was upon her. 'Now there's a grand lad, 'er son. He got a medal in the war. Mind you're nice to him, girl. You hear me?'

'Yes, Father,' came the automatic reply, though her mind was still on Jamie. Emma had been trying to slip away all evening to go to the forge and see the Metcalfe brothers. She was sure that once Jamie was home and had a chance to talk to William, everything would be all right. But she needed to know, needed to see for herself. It was too late now. She would have to wait until the following morning. Perhaps, she comforted herself as she went upstairs to her bedroom, carrying the candle in its holder carefully so that the shivering light did not blow out, it would be better to leave the two brothers to settle down together first. After all, there was a lot for them to talk about; unhappy things that she should perhaps have no part in just now.

Emma closed her bedroom door, set down the candle and sank on to the small stool. Leaning her elbows on the surface of the dressing-table and cupping her chin in her hands, she stared at her shadowy reflection. In the flickering light, she could fancy herself beautiful though her violet eyes were dark pools. The soft glow caught her high cheek bones, accentuating the fine structure and the strength of her face, defining the curve of her cheek and the firm jawline that was just short of being square. She slipped off her blouse; her shoulders were smooth, like silk in the gentle light. Loosening her undergarments, she ran her hands over her full, firm breasts and down to her surprisingly slim waist, then out again over generous hips. A small smile played on her mouth. She was a woman now; a woman for Jamie. Unwinding her plait and loosening the long black hair from its twists until it fell, covering her breasts, to below her waist, she brushed it until it gleamed in the candlelight.

Emma took one last look at herself and, sighing, rose from the stool and turned away from the mirror, disheartened by her reflection. At school she had seen a picture in a book of a famous painting by Rubens showing voluptuous women. Then, she thought, if I had lived then, I might have been thought beautiful. But not now, when the fashion was for slim, almost shapeless women, with skirts above their ankles and hair cut short to frame sweet, delicate faces. Maybe that was the sort of woman Jamie wanted now. It was certainly the kind her father admired and, unbidden, the vision of Bridget Smith came into her mind.

Emma slept fitfully, disturbed by uneasy dreams of bands playing, people shouting, soldiers spilling from the train on to the platform. She was being swept away by the excited crowd before she could reach him. She was stretching out her hand, struggling through the throng, but she couldn't get to him, couldn't touch him . . . She awoke sweating, her legs tangled in the sheet and her long hair strewn wildly across her face. His name was upon her lips, 'Jamie'. She heard a noise outside her door and then the sound of her father's footsteps descending the stairs and knew it was time she rose. She gave a groan, pushed back the covers and swung her feet to touch the cold floor, feeling more tired now than when she had gone to bed the previous night. But there was no shirking the day's work ahead.

As she was dressing and splashing her face with cold water from the ewer and jug on the marble wash-stand in the corner of her room, she heard the rattle of wagon wheels in the yard. Buttoning her blouse, Emma bent and looked out of the low window overlooking the mill and found herself staring down into the upturned face of Ben Popple standing in the yard below beside a cart laden with sacks of grain. Even in the pale, early morning light she knew he had seen her and she straightened and stepped back quickly from the window.

Tensing every muscle in her body, she waited for what would surely come next; her father's voice calling from the foot of the stairs. 'You there, girl? Ben Popple's here. Get yarsen down here and help unload.'

She groaned aloud. Now there would be no escape until all the bulging sacks were stored in the granary and Ben Popple's wagon empty. Then the odious man would invite himself into the kitchen to share their breakfast. He would sit in the wooden rocking chair at the side of the hearth – the chair that had been Grandpa Charlie's – watching her as she moved about the kitchen, a smirk on his mouth and suggestive remarks coming from his lips.

Leaving her bed unmade, Emma banged her bedroom door. Downstairs, she strode through the kitchen and into the yard to begin heaving the sacks from the cart without even a civil word of greeting to Farmer Popple.

Now it would be the middle of the day before she could even think of seeing Jamie.

It was late afternoon and growing dusk before Emma managed to slip away unnoticed. The bakery was closed for the day and Sarah had gone home. Her father's tea was prepared and the table laid, but there was every possibility he would be late in for his meal this evening, for the mill's sails whirled in a strong easterly gale and Harry Forrest knew that with the coming of darkness, the wind might drop suddenly. He could not waste a precious moment of a good milling wind, not if he wanted to keep on the right side of Ben Popple.

Praying that the wind would not drop for at least half an hour, Emma hurried up the incline, past the end of the road leading to the chapel and on towards the market square.

The forge and the wheelwright's shop were in darkness. Pulling her shawl over her head, Emma stepped beneath the brick archway bearing the sign P HWFDOIH and passed between the smithy and the workshop towards the cottage standing behind them. She found she was holding her breath as she lifted her hand to knock on the door. And then, from inside, came the sound of raised voices, arguing heatedly.

'You've done nothing but complain since you came home. Give it a rest, can't you?'

Emma drew breath sharply. That was William's voice. Gentle, placid William and talking to Jamie in such a way. She could hardly believe what she was hearing. Her hand fell away and she leant a little closer to the door, unashamedly eavesdropping.

'There's plenty to complain about. The wheelwright's business is all but gone and I daren't think how many customers you've lost us from the smithy. You never were much of a hand with the hammer.'

'Well, I've had plenty of time to learn these last three years, 'cos poor old dad couldn't do much for the last part of it.'

There was a heavy, uncomfortable silence and then Jamie's voice, bitter and belligerent, came again. 'You'd have done better to keep the wheelwright's side going. You're a bit better at the joinery, but not a deal.' The praise, if praise it could be called, was given grudgingly.

William's voice, softer now and with an infinite sadness in it, said, 'Whatever I'd done, it wouldn't have been right, would it, Jamie?'

Again there was a silence, as if Jamie could not find an answer.

Suddenly the door was flung open. Emma, bending close, had not heard any movement from beyond and so was caught unawares. Embarrassed at being found obviously listening to their conversation, she straightened up and stammered, 'I – er – came to see how you were.'

The frown on Jamie's face deepened. 'Oh, it's you. Come in, why don't you?' He pulled the door open wider. Stepping across the threshold, she came close and looked up at him, her gaze taking in every contour of that well-beloved face. It was the vision she had carried in her mind's eye and in her heart for three years from childhood into womanhood. She was so close, she could have reached up and touched his face, a face that was so much thinner now, the hollow cheeks and grey skin giving it a haggard look. She ached to caress his brow, to smooth back the unruly lock of dark hair that fell on to his forehead, to trace the strong jawline with her fingertips. But she kept her hand firmly by her side. The man who stood so close that she could feel the waft of his breath on her face, was almost a stranger to her. There was angry, bitter resentment in his tone. 'Why not invite the whole village round to view the hovel this place has become? If me mother could see it now . . .'

Emma glanced towards William and her tender heart went out to the young man. He looked crushed, defeated. The longed-for return of the brother he had so loved and admired and, yes, revered and idolized, had turned into his worst nightmare.

William did not deserve such treatment and Emma's violet eyes flashed. Turning back to Jamie she faced him squarely. 'If your mother were here now,' she said, speaking with deliberate emphasis, 'she'd be thanking the Good Lord for your safe return. But she would *not*,' she flung her arm out towards William, 'be blaming William for something that is not his doing, not his fault.'

'Oh, so that's how the land lies, is it?' A sneer twisted

Jamie's mouth. 'William's the blue-eyed boy with you now, is he, young Emma? I'm forgotten, I suppose.'

Emma gasped and shook her head slowly in disbelief. 'What's got in to you, Jamie Metcalfe? You're not the same—'

Harshly, he said, 'Of course I'm not the same. The things I've seen . . .' Suddenly she saw the pain of remembered horrors in his eyes before he turned his head away from her saying roughly, 'And nothing's the same here either, is it? It's all I thought of – out there. All I clung to, the thought that home was always here, just the same as it always had been. And now . . .' He gave an angry sweep of his arm encompassing not only the house, but the smithy and the wheelwright's workshop too. 'Oh, what's the use . . .' Roughly he pushed past her and went out of the door banging it behind him with such force that the whole cottage seemed to shake.

Emma stared at William in disbelief. The young man ran his hand through his hair in a hopeless, distracted gesture. 'Oh, Em, I'm sorry you saw all that. You came at just the wrong moment.'

'What is it? What's the matter with him?'

William shrugged. 'I suppose it must be hard for him, coming back to all this,' he gestured with his hand. 'And – and – ' his glance went to the mantelpiece where a matching pair of framed photographs of their parents stood, 'and them not being here.' He moved to the fireside chair that had always been Josiah's place and sat down wearily in the worn, comfortable seat. A fire burned in the grate, the only light in the room. William leant forward, resting his elbows on his knees. The flickering firelight illuminated his gentle, youthful face that was, at times, still vulnerable and yet, at this moment, Emma saw a strength in his features, a mature understanding of the harsh realities of life. Quietly she moved forward and knelt on the peg rug on the hearth.

'I suppose,' William went on, thinking aloud. 'Like he ses, he carried the picture of us all still here, the home as he had always known it, the forge, everything. Imagining it all to be still just as he'd left it. It was what kept him going. I mean—' He lifted his face to look at Emma. Though his eyes were in shadow and she could not read the sorrow in their depths, she knew it was there; she could hear it in his voice. 'I mean, there have been some dreadful tales about what it was like out there, in the trenches. He must have been through an awful lot, you know. Mebbe all the while, he was carrying this mental picture of his home with him, clinging to it. It must be a dreadful shock for him to come back and find – this.'

She was quiet too for a moment, staring into the flickering flames. Slowly, she said, 'Maybe you're right.' Then she was scrambling up. 'I'm going to find him. I'll talk to him.'

'Oh no, Em, don't. I don't think it will do any good.'

But Emma, intent on putting matters right, was not listening to William's words of caution and did not see, as she hurried from the room, his gentle, troubled gaze following her.

Outside, she stood listening. Through the deepening dusk of the winter's evening, she could hear sounds coming from the forge. Pulling her coat closely round her, she bent her head against the wind, thinking briefly that at least her father would still be in the mill, and made her way into the blacksmith's yard.

Jamie was standing in the middle of the cluttered yard, picking up pieces of metal, bits of wood and hurling them with frustrated anger into the farthest corner.

'It's like a rubbish tip,' she heard him mutter. 'Gone to wrack and ruin.'

'Jamie.'

Startled, he swung round.

'What are you doing? Creeping about like that?'

Stung, she retorted heatedly, 'I'm not "creeping about".' She moved closer and asked more gently, 'Jamie, what is it? What's the matter?'

'The matter? You ask what's the matter? This – ' he flung his left arm in a wide arc to encompass the littered yard, '*this* is the matter. Three years in the trenches with thick slimy mud as my bed and rats as sleeping companions, to come back to *this*.'

'William's done his best, Jamie. It hasn't been easy for him either. He's only young. He was only a boy when you left and he's had to cope with – with losing both your parents and trying, single-handed, to keep everything going. Don't be so hard on him.'

'William, William, *William*. That's all I seem to hear from you.' He came and stood close to her, glaring down at her through the dusk, his eyes dark pools of accusation. His strong, blacksmith's hands grasped her shoulders with the grip of a vice, 'What about me? Does no one think of me?' He pulled her to him roughly, crushing her against him. He bent his head and pressed his mouth hard against hers, so hard that she felt his teeth grinding against hers. There was no love in the embrace, not even a passion arising out of desire. It was a brutal, bitter attack. His fingers grasped roughly at the high neck of her blouse and tore at the fabric. She felt the neckline strain against the back of her neck and then a tearing sound and the cotton tore, the top button flying off. His hand was groping inside the top of her blouse, seeking . . .

'No, Jamie, no! Please . . .' She was shocked and

repulsed by his violence. This was not the Jamie Metcalfe she had known, not the man she had loved.

'Ya still a child,' he said scornfully. 'Ya not woman enough to understand a man's needs.' He gave her a violent push as if to hurl her away from him as, minutes before, he had been throwing the rubbish about the yard. Had she not been so robust and strong, Emma would have fallen to the ground. Physically, she was unharmed, but emotionally she was heartsore and wounded.

Through the gloom she stared at him, trying desperately to understand him. He was like a wild man. With a woman's intuition, Emma knew he had to be tamed. Somehow the young man Jamie had once been had to be reached. And she was the only one who could do it.

Nine

'We've company coming tonight. Mind you mek a nice meal, girl.'

Emma continued kneading the dough without looking up, her mind on Jamie.

'Yes, Father,' she replied automatically. Then, as the meaning of his words penetrated her wandering mind, she lifted her head and stared at him. He was turning away, opening the door of the bakehouse to go across the yard to the mill. The winter sky was lightening in the east and the black shape of the mill and its sails rose majestically against the pale light, but dawn had not yet come into the enclosed yard below. Outside the back door, the miller lifted his face and sniffed the clean air of a new day. A light breeze ruffled his wispy hair as he pulled on his cap, hunched his shoulders and made to pull the door closed behind him.

'Who, Father?' Emma's voice stilled his action. 'Who's coming?'

He paused and looked at her, his hand resting on the door knob. 'Bridget and her boy.'

Then, with a slam of the door, he was gone, his footsteps echoing in the sharp early morning air, leaving his daughter staring with wide eyes at the woodwork of the door between them.

*

'He's invited Mrs Smith and her son to come to supper tonight,' she told Sarah later that morning.

'Has he now?' Sarah nodded knowingly.

'Whatever am I to make for them? I can't do the fancy dishes they'll be used to.'

Sarah laughed. 'A nice bit of home-cured ham, Emma, and your plum bread and a bit o' cheese for afters. I bet that young feller won't have tasted grub like that for a while.'

Emma smiled and the worried frown cleared a little from her smooth forehead. 'Perhaps you're right. What about a pudding? Do you think it's too late for that? What do the gentry eat for supper?'

Sarah laughed out loud now. As a young girl, she had been in service for a year at a big house on the outskirts of Marsh Thorpe, but she had never risen above a kitchen maid and when Emma's mother had asked her to come to the mill to help her in the house, Sarah had been thankful to give in her notice and move into the tiny attic room above the bakehouse.

'The gentry, as you call 'em,' she said, teasing Emma gently, 'have dinner in the evening with four, mebbe five or more, courses.'

'Oh, heck,' Emma said with such a flustered expression on her face that Sarah chuckled afresh.

'The Smiths won't be expecting owt like that, I can promise you.'

'But Father said "a nice meal". I think he's expecting me to take a bit more trouble than just a bit of ham and bread and cheese.'

Sarah shrugged. 'Aye well, mebbe so. We'd best get our thinking caps on then. How about vegetable soup to start with, a nice cut of pork and all the trimmings as the main course, followed by a nice pudding? What about a steamed ginger or current sponge? You could still finish the meal off with plum bread an' cheese if anyone's got a corner left to fill after all that.'

'Are you sure?' Emma still looked doubtful but when Sarah reassured her firmly, 'It's better than that flashy piece deserves,' Emma giggled and said, 'Don't say things like that, Sarah. And besides, I rather like her, though I do wish . . .' There was silence between them as they worked, lifting the bread from the oven with the peel, their faces red from the heat of the long brick oven.

'What do you wish?' Sarah prompted.

'That it was Jamie and William he'd invited to supper.'

Sarah glanced at her and gave a snort of laughter. 'That'll never happen. A Metcalfe and a Forrest sitting down to eat at the same table? Never, lass, never. You should know that, Emma.'

Emma stopped what she was doing, resting the long-handled peel on the edge of the oven and staring at Sarah, but the older woman merely said, 'Come on, get this bread out else it'll burn.'

Automatically, Emma obeyed, but her mind was in turmoil. 'Yes, I do know,' she said as, together, they set the loaves out on cooling trays. 'I could hardly fail to know that Father's always been at loggerheads with old Mr Metcalfe – Jamie's father – but what I don't know,' a slight note of resentment crept into her tone, 'what I've *never* been told, presumably because I've been thought too young, is exactly what this silly feud is all about and why he's carrying it on to the next generation, to Jamie and William. I mean, he used to let us play together when we were little, so why—?'

'That was when ya grandpa Charlie was alive,' Sarah put in, as if that explained everything. Yet, for Emma, it did not.

'Do you know what it's all about, Sarah?'

'Oh, it goes back a long way. I don't know the truth of it all mesen.'

Emma was getting a little annoyed now by all the mystery. Over the years she'd heard village gossip, yet no one had ever really explained it all to her. 'What goes way back, Sarah?'

The woman glanced at her and then looked away. 'The reason for this 'ere feud. It's not the sort of thing to be talked about in front of a child. And ya dad's not exactly a one for a lot of chitchat'

That was true, Emma thought wryly. Harry Forrest was no conversationalist, at least, not with his daughter. The only time he spoke to her seemed to be to issue orders. 'Get up, go to bed, get my tea,' or, more often, 'Come on, there's work to be done.'

'I don't know the whole story,' Sarah was saying, 'only that it started between your grandfather, old Charlie Forrest, and Josiah Metcalfe's father and brother.'

'You mean the two who started the blacksmith's and wheelwright's? But that's years ago.'

'Aye, I know. At first it was only like a teasing, a friendly rivalry with the Metcalfe brothers saying they'd have old Charlie's mill one day, and 'im saying they'd never get their hands on it, that there'd allus be a Forrest at the mill.' The kindly woman paused, knowing she was in danger of touching on a painful subject for Emma. Sarah cleared her throat and went on. 'But then well things got a bit more serious.'

'Why? What happened?'

Suddenly, Sarah was evasive. 'I – er – I'm not sure. Some rivalry over his wife, I think.'

Emma laughed aloud. 'Not over Grandmother Forrest. Surely not.' Emma had never known her grandmother. All she knew of her was the picture of the sour-faced old battleaxe adorning, if that could be the right word, the wall in the best parlour upstairs. It was a companion picture to that of her husband, Charlie Forrest, and showed a formidable woman with her hair pulled severely back from her face. She had a thin, hard mouth and piercing eyes that seemed to follow everyone around the room, as if she was still watching all that went on in the family down the generations. Emma had often marvelled that huge, laughing, jovial Grandpa Charlie could have ever married such a woman.

'Eh?' Sarah glanced at her, a puzzled expression on her face and then she said, 'Oh no, not her. Not ya *grand*-mother.' She chuckled. 'No, ya can't imagine any young fellers fighting over that owd beezum, can ya?'

'Then who? Sarah, just who *are* you talking about?'

Sarah looked away, uncomfortable now, as if she was already regretting having said so much. She faced Emma and took a deep breath. 'It was between ya dad and Josiah that things got – well – worse. Over – ya mam.'

Emma stared at her. 'My mother? But how, I mean, what happened?'

But now Sarah shrugged her plump shoulders. 'I dunno the details.'

'Oh, really, Sarah, fancy telling me all that and then leaving me high and dry. Who does know? Luke?'

Sarah whirled round, surprisingly quickly for her size. 'Now don't you go asking him. He'll give me a good hiding for opening me big mouth.'

Now Emma laughed. The very idea of Luke even raising his hand to his dear Sarah was just a joke. Sarah, reassured, turned away but Emma stared after her thoughtfully. Somehow she had to find out the truth because instinctively she felt it had something to do with Jamie and herself.

Maybe this so-called family feud really might affect their future happiness together.

That evening Emma laid the table with care. A smooth white cloth, the best dinner service and the silver cutlery that had been a wedding present to her parents from Grandpa Charlie. A small frown of concentration furrowed her forehead as she tried to drag from the recesses of her memory, the vision of her mother teaching her, a ten-year-old girl, the niceties of a formal dinner party.

'Now, my darling, watch carefully. Knives, forks, dessert spoons and forks, soup spoons – just so,' her mother's low, cultured voice had instructed as the young Emma had watched her long slender fingers with their well-shaped and manicured nails lay out the cutlery. Now, glancing down at her hands with their short nails and skin that was chapped and calloused by work, Emma was reminded sharply of the difference between the delicate, pianist's hands of her mother and her own.

'I suppose I've probably inherited old Charlie's mill-building hands,' she murmured aloud to the empty room and sighed. But her mother had scarcely lifted a finger about the house. She had done no housework, had not even cooked or baked. Sarah, as the live-in maid, had done everything whilst the lady of the house had reclined on a sofa, cosseting herself with her current pregnancy. It had seemed to the young Emma as if her mother had always been in a 'delicate condition'. Pampered and fussed over by her husband who talked constantly about 'This time everything will be all right. This time we shall have a son. The next Charles Forrest.'

But each time, often in the middle of the night, there had been the cries from her mother's room and then the pounding feet scurrying to fetch the doctor. The long, pacing wait in the rooms downstairs and then the blood-soaked sheets bundled out to the wash-house by Sarah. Then the silence, the awful silence that had always followed, when Emma was not allowed to see her mama and wondered if indeed she were still alive. And finally, listening solemnly whilst Sarah explained gently, but with the kindly bluntness of a matter-of-fact country woman, that yet again there would be no baby.

There followed the long, lonely days when her father was sunk into gloom. If the foetus had been recognizable as a male child, she had seen the bitter resentment in his eyes every time she was in his presence. At those times she had avoided having to be with him until her mother was well enough to emerge from her room and fill the house with laughter once more, hugging her daughter and reminding Emma that she was her own precious darling and that she must not mind Papa.

'Men always want sons, my dearest girl,' Frances Forrest had explained gently. 'And none more so than your father. Maybe next time, we shall be blessed.'

But there had been one 'next time' too many and the life of the pretty, vivacious woman had been taken too, along with the son whom she had managed, with cruel irony, to carry to seven months. Emma could never forget that the last sound she had heard her mother utter had been a piercing cry of agony. It had sent a shudder of fear through the young girl and she had known, even before anyone told her, that the worst had happened.

Harry Forrest's grief had been monstrous and Emma truly believed that he would never forgive her for being his only surviving child: a girl.

From that moment, Sarah Robson had been the mainstay of Emma's young life and had filled, as much as possible, the yawning chasm left in her life by the death of her mother and by the subsequent unforgiving attitude of her father.

As Emma had grown and taken on the reins of mistress of the house, she had watched the growing fondness between Sarah and the older Luke Robson, who, for many years, had lived alone in the cottage just beyond the orchard. But Luke had none of Harry Forrest's bitter rage in his heart against the blows life had inflicted upon him and now Emma could see every day the happiness in his eyes, as if he never ceased to marvel that Sarah had agreed to become his wife. So Sarah was still here, an important part of the Forrest household, even if her work was now in the bakery rather than in the house itself.

Idly, Emma's thoughts wandered as she laid a round spoon at the side of a knife. Maybe, she thought, Bridget Smith would be the one to put the light of love back into her father's eyes. Then, as the spoon slipped from her fingers, a sudden thought struck her and dragged her back to the present. 'Soup! Oh heck! I haven't made the soup.' She stood a moment, biting her lower lip in agitation. Then she sprang towards the door. 'I wonder if Sarah . . .'

Leaving by the back door, she ran towards the gap in the hedge, through the orchard and beyond to the low cottage where Luke and Sarah lived. Sarah Robson usually had a big cauldron of soup bubbling away on her range.

'I haven't, Emma lass,' Sarah answered her urgent knocking. 'We've just eaten the last drop. I'll be making a fresh lot tomorrow, but . . .'

Tomorrow was not tonight and not soon enough. Emma sighed. 'Never mind, I'll have to think of something else.'

'Well, give 'em Yorkshire pudding and raspberry vinegar to begin with.'

'But I was doing strawberry syrup with the steamed pudding. I can't do both.'

'Well, have custard with the pudding,' Sarah said reasonably.

Emma looked at her doubtfully. 'Is Yorkshire pudding quite the sort of thing for a dinner party?'

'If it's good enough for folks in our part of the world, then it's good enough for them,' Sarah bristled, then she laughed. 'Don't try to be something you're not, lass. Let 'em see how you live. All right, go to an extra bit of trouble – ' she shrugged her plump shoulders, 'like we do at Christmas. But don't try to do things and fancy dishes ya not comfortable with.'

'You're right, of course. But – but I have this feeling that Father wants to make a good impression.'

'Does he now?' Sarah said softly.

That evening, Emma, in her best Sunday dress, found herself opening the back door to a huge bunch of flowers. She gasped in surprise and the flowers quivered as if the person holding them was laughing. The bouquet was lowered and in the soft light thrown by the lamp in the kitchen behind her, Emma found herself looking into the laughing eyes of the soldier at the railway station. Behind him, in the dusk of early evening, Emma saw her father helping Bridget Smith down from the pony and trap which he had used to fetch his guests to the millhouse.

Emma opened the door wider and stood back to one side, gesturing with her hand to the young man to step inside. 'Please – please come in.'

'These are for you,' he said and held the flowers out towards her.

She felt an unaccustomed blush creeping up her face. 'For – me?' she stammered and took the proffered bouquet.

'No one has ever brought me flowers before.' The truthful remark was innocently beguiling.

'Then it's high time someone did,' the young man remarked and held out his hand. 'We haven't been introduced properly, but I have seen you before. I noticed you at the station.'

'Really?'

'Yes, really,' he smiled, giving an exaggerated wink. 'How could any man fail to notice you, Miss Forrest?'

A warm glow spread through her and yet a small voice prompted her to be wary. Was he laughing at her, insinuating that, with her height, she stood head and shoulders above any other woman? She returned his gaze steadily but could detect no ridicule in the clear blue-grey eyes.

He was still holding out his hand towards her as he said, 'My name is Leonard Smith.' And as she put her hand into his warm, firm clasp, he added, 'How do you do, Emma Forrest? I am delighted to make your acquaintance.'

He was no longer dressed in uniform. Tonight he wore a well-cut black suit in an expensive fabric over a stiffly starched white collared shirt and a neatly knotted, bright red, tie. Looped across his waistcoat was a watch chain, from the centre of which hung a small gold cross. His sleek, dark hair was cut short and greased to shining neatness. Although his nose was perhaps a little large, he had a firm jawline and white, even teeth.

Leonard was lifting his nose in the air and sniffing appreciatively. 'My word, that smells good. I can't tell you how much a chap misses home cooking. Army rations aren't quite the same you know.' He gave a low chuckle and his eyes twinkled with merriment.

'It's nothing special . . .' she began but at that moment Bridget Smith stepped into the house in a flurry of laughter.

The evening was a great success. Emma could not remember ever having seen her father so relaxed or so jovial. Certainly not since her mother had died. He was openly flirting with Bridget Smith who, with her tinkling laughter, her bright blue eyes and the coquettish way she tossed her head, fascinated Emma. Was this, the young girl mused, the way a woman was supposed to behave to catch her man? Her mouth twitched at the corner as she wondered if this was the way she ought to behave. Would such skittish behaviour win Jamie Metcalfe?

'A penny for them,' Leonard Smith's spoke softly at her side. She was so deep in her own thoughts that the sound of his voice startled her, making her jump. 'Oh, I'm sorry.' Flustered, she began to babble, 'I was just watching – I mean – admiring your mother. She's very beautiful.'

It was not quite the truth. Bridget Smith was not beautiful. She was pretty and although that word didn't seem quite the right description for a woman of her age, but it was what she was: pretty. And vivacious, charming – oh, certainly charming – captivating and flirtatious. But to her son, Emma could only say that his mother was beautiful.

It had been the right thing to say. 'Yes, she is, isn't she?' he said, his fond glance upon his mother. 'She's an amazing woman.'

Emma's glance followed the line of his gaze. Bridget's face in the soft light from the fire and the low lamplight, appeared younger than ever, she could be taken for only a few years older than Emma herself. She was leaning towards Harry Forrest, tapping his arm playfully with her fingers and then leaving her hand resting upon his arm. Her father, Emma noticed, had the look of a mesmerized rabbit in front of a stoat.

She felt Leonard touch her hand and his voice came

softly. 'There's a fair on the common at Lincoln. Would you do me the honour of spending a day with me?'

Emma turned wide eyes towards him. 'A fair. Oh, how lovely. No one's ever taken me to a fair before.'

He pretended to be scandalized at such an omission in her education. 'Then it's high time . . .' he began and, laughing, Emma joined in the final words of his sentence, '. . . someone did.'

Ten

'Ya father's mekin' a right fool of himself, then?' Jamie said bluntly as they walked down the lane from the chapel after evening service. It was the only time she saw Jamie, the only time he seemed willing to talk to her. She had gone, often, to the forge, but he always seemed so busy, cleaning the place up, flinging things about, an angry frown furrowing his brow. He worked long hours into the night trying to build the blacksmith's business up again to what it had once been. He had no time to talk. Only William, next door in the wheelwright's shop, stopped whatever he was doing and sat on an upturned box to talk to her. Jamie was always too busy to pay any attention to her.

And now here he was spoiling the few precious moments they had together.

'I don't know what you mean,' she began defensively. 'Mrs Smith and him are just friends.'

Jamie's mouth twisted with sarcasm. 'Oh, so you do know what I'm talking about.'

Emma stopped walking and turned to face him in the middle of the road. Hotly, she said, 'How dare you say such a thing?'

Miss Wilhelmina Tomkinson and her sister, Miss Tilly, passed by and Emma heard their 'Tut-tut. Such behaviour in the street!'

'And just after chapel too . . .'

She ignored the two spinsters, though normally Emma

80

would have passed a pleasant, dutiful word or two with them.

It was only Jamie's deepening frown that made Emma lower her voice, lean towards him and hiss. 'What harm can it do?' She was about to add, 'He's missed my mother dreadfully all these years,' but she bit her lip, holding back the words. The loss of Jamie's own parents was so recent that such words must open the raw wound.

'Jamie won't even talk about them,' William had told her. 'He won't listen to what I want to tell him. He doesn't want to know what happened even. He shuts his mind to it all. I don't think he's even been to their graves in the churchyard since he got back.'

'Perhaps,' Emma said slowly, 'that's the only way he can deal with it. He's burying himself in his work, isn't he? Maybe, in time, he'll feel better and be able to talk about it.'

William's soulful face had looked doubtful. The young boy, who had been thrust so suddenly into manhood, needed to talk. He wanted to talk to his brother, but Jamie shut him out. So William talked to Emma. Emma listened and comforted. Emma – the girl who longed to become his sister-in-law – was there for him whenever he needed a friend.

Now, she was standing in the middle of the lane, shaking her head sadly as all these thoughts flitted through her mind. 'Oh, Jamie,' she said softly, gently. 'What is the matter with you?'

He gave a snort. 'The matter with me? There's nothing wrong with me. It's ya dad. And you, if it comes to that. Can't see what's under ya nose?'

'I don't know what you mean.' Now she really was mystified.

He looked at her hard, and then, seeing the genuine

puzzlement in her eyes, said harshly. 'Ya being taken in by a couple of gold-diggers, that's what. Empty promises, that's all you'll get from the likes of Bridget Smith – and her son.'

She opened her mouth, but then the denial was stilled on her lips as she realized that perhaps there was some truth in what Jamie was saying. It had been three weeks since the Smiths had been to their house for the evening meal she had taken such pains over and, despite his promises, since that time she had not seen Leonard Smith again. 'He's gone away on business,' Bridget had told her, vaguely waving her hand in the air. 'Lincoln, I think.' Leonard had promised to take her to the fair in Lincoln, Emma thought now, but he'd gone away without another word.

Jamie moved closer to her, looking down at her as she stared up at him, not wanting to believe his taunts, yet she could not prevent a niggling doubt from creeping into her mind. Slowly he shook his head and the habitual look of bitterness softened for a fleeting moment. Suddenly, she saw a glimpse of the old Jamie, the man she had loved and still did, if only . . .

'Emma, oh, Emma. There's no chance for us. Not now.' He reached up and with a sudden gesture of tenderness, smoothed an escaping tendril of hair back from her forehead. She caught at his hand, holding it, pressing it to her cheek, oblivious to the fact that they were standing in the middle of the road in full view of all the worshippers still coming out of the chapel. Fear flooded through her. 'Why? Why not? I – I love you, Jamie. I always have. You must know that. I've been waiting, praying, for you to come back safely from the war. There's only ever been you. And I . . .' she hesitated, then plunged in rashly, 'I thought you loved me. You said I was your girl. Don't you remember?'

His huge hand still rested in her clinging grasp and he made no effort to free himself. 'Oh, I remember.' His deep voice was husky with emotion. 'It was only the thought of you. Of coming home to you, that kept me going. In the trenches, in the night, in the cold and the wet and the mud. Oh, the mud!' His eyes darkened as he remembered. 'And even when the bullets were flying and my comrades were dropping dead at the side of me, even then, I thought only of you . . .' Then he seemed to shake himself, drag himself back to the present.

Her hold on his hand tightened. 'Then why,' she whispered, 'why are you being so cold with me, so angry? What's changed? I'm no different. I still—'

Suddenly, she wondered if he thought, mistakenly, that she was involved with Leonard Smith? No doubt the whole village knew about the dinner party. Maybe . . . She opened her mouth but before she could speak she heard an angry shout from behind her and they both turned to see her father hurrying towards them, shaking his fist in the air.

'You leave 'er be, James Metcalfe. Don't think I don't know what you're after. My mill, that's what. That's all your family's ever wanted. To get their thieving hands on Forrest's Mill.'

At once Jamie wrenched his hand from Emma's grasp, twisting her wrist painfully.

She gave a little cry, more from shock and bewilderment than from the pain. 'Father, what are you saying?'

He had reached them and was standing before them, breathing hard, his face glowering and red with rage. Stepping between them, he took hold of her arm and pushed her along the road, away from Jamie. Emma struggled, but although she was stronger than most women, even she was helpless against the strong grip of the miller.

'Father, please—'

'You're going home with me, girl. This minute.'

Emma twisted around, looking back over her shoulder at Jamie but she was being forced to walk forward. 'Jamie . . .?' she cried, appealing to him to help her, but he merely stood in the road and watched her being dragged away from him.

Once in the house, Emma's anger at being so humiliated exploded and she rounded on her father and faced up to him in a way she never had before in her young life. 'How could you do that in front of everyone?'

'You were mekin' a fool of yasen.'

Anger made her reckless. 'It's not me they're saying that about in the village – it's *you*.'

'What are you talking about, girl?' he thundered.

Rashly she blurted it out, 'They're all saying you're making a fool of yourself over Mrs Smith. That she's nothing but a – a . . .' She hesitated, but only momentarily. She had gone too far already to hold back now. 'A gold-digger.'

She saw his fist clench, saw his arm come up and thought for a moment that he was going to strike her. Quick tempered though her father was, he had never hit her. His word had always been enough to chastise her. But now, she was defying him in a way she had never done before. He held his arm rigidly half-raised, as if he were fighting the urge within himself. 'Is that what he told you? Young Metcalfe?'

She hesitated a fraction too long. She was tempted to lie, wanted to, but she had always been a truthful girl and lying did not come glibly. Before she could say anything, her father said, 'Aye, you've no need to answer. I can see by ya face that he did.'

He stepped close to her and Emma pulled in a deep breath, every muscle in her body tensed waiting for the blow. He did not strike her. Instead he thrust his face close to hers and said slowly, with deliberate emphasis on every word, 'I forbid you to see young Metcalfe again. Do you hear me, girl?'

She stared into his face. Inside she was quaking but she faced him with an outward boldness. 'We are going to be married. I'm his girl—'

Now, with unexpected suddenness, his arm came up and his hand struck the side of her face with such force that she stumbled sideways and caught the edge of the table to steady herself. She gave a cry and put her hand to her cheek, the skin stinging from the blow.

'Father!'

Now he was wagging his forefinger in her face. 'Over my dead body, girl.' It was a clichéd phrase, but Harry Forrest was not using it as such; he meant every word. 'Ya'll do as I tell you, else I'll – I'll throw you out!'

He turned away with a jerky, angry movement, pulled open the back door and slammed it behind him, leaving Emma standing in the middle of the kitchen, staring at the closed door, her hand still to her cheek.

'Luke,' she called up the winding steps of the mill. 'Luke, you up there?'

Her father was out. He had gone to visit a farmer to haggle over the price of his grain and Emma needed to talk to Luke.

There was no answer and she guessed that he was on the bin floor emptying another sack of grain into one of the bins and above the noise of the huge millstones grinding, he could not hear her. She climbed up to the meal floor and then up again to the stone floor where the hopper chattered, feeding the grain down the chute to the stones.

He was coming down the ladder from the floor above. 'Hello, Emma lass. D'ya want me?'

She moved towards him and as she did so Luke, his face streaked with the pale creamy dust, squinted at her. 'What's up with ya face, lass. You fell and bumped yasen?'

'Oh no, it's . . .' She hesitated, reluctant to tell the truth even to Luke, especially to Luke. 'It's nothing really. Luke, I need to talk to you. Privately. There's – there's something, well, odd, that I don't understand.'

'Oh aye.' He paused a moment and then said, 'Well, we'd best go down below. We can talk whilst I work.' He smiled at her then nodded towards the busy machinery.

Back on the meal floor, Luke took up the miller's position between the spout from the stones above and the tentering gear. He opened the flap of the spout and the flour flooded into the sack below. Though one pair of stones still rumbled above them, they could talk to each other without raising their voices.

'That's about fine enough,' Luke murmured, letting the flour run over his hand. Then his attention came back to Emma. 'Out with it then, lass.'

'You know that Jamie Metcalfe and me – well, what I mean is – I thought that when he came back from the war, we'd be planning to get married.'

She saw Luke's keen glance at her, but he said nothing. 'But my father is against it.' That was an understatement if ever there was one, she thought wryly, but went on aloud, 'And now he's forbidden me to see Jamie but he won't tell me *why*.' Her eyes were dark with anxiety. 'Luke, do – do *you* know why? I know about their stupid feud, but . . .' She spread her hands in a despairing gesture and fell silent.

The older man gave a sigh and looked at her for a long moment. Then he gestured towards the bruise on the side of her face. 'Did he do that? Ya dad? Tell me the truth now, 'cos I need to know.'

When she nodded, he muttered a low oath and then said brusquely, 'Is he out?'

'Yes. He's gone to Farmer Popple's.' She pulled a face. She was very much afraid her father did not view Ben Popple's flirting with her as merely fun.

A smile twitched the corner of Luke's mouth but the anger never left his eyes. 'Oh, he'll be a while then, argy-bargying with that a'kward owd cuss.' He stood listening for a moment to the sound of the stones, then he glanced across at the bulbous orbs of the governor which protected the mill from tearing itself to pieces if a sudden gust of wind sent the sails spinning faster than was safe.

Emma waited patiently. While the mill sails whirled, the stones grated and the flour poured out in a steady creamy-white stream, Luke began to talk.

'It all started years ago, in old Charlie's day when he first built this mill, but then it *was* just a joke between him and the Metcalfe brothers. They say old Nathaniel and his brother George used to come and stand watching Charlie when he was building this mill. "Fine mill you're building for us, Charlie Forrest," they'd shout up. "That's what you think," Charlie would shout back. "This is a Forrest mill and it always will be". The old Metcalfe brothers would laugh and say, "Ya'll have to get yasen wed then and sire a son or two." George weren't married but Nathaniel was and he'd already got a son, Josiah, your boy's father, him that died not long back.'

Emma nodded, saying nothing that might stop Luke in his storytelling, even though at the moment he was telling her things she already knew.

'It was a standing joke between 'em in them days,' Luke

went on. 'Y'know how it is in a village, lass? There was nothing nasty in it.' He paused a moment and Emma bit her lip to prevent herself urging him on.

'So Charlie got married and had a son, ya uncle Charles, and then of course, ya dad came along.'

'Uncle Charles ran away to sea, didn't he?'

'That's right, when he was about thirteen.' There was a wry note in Luke's tone. 'He was the black sheep of the family. Didn't want owt to do with the mill. Nearly broke old Charlie's heart at first, he was so set on their always being a *Charles* Forrest at the mill, y'see.'

'What happened to my uncle Charles then? I can't ever remember anyone talking about him.'

'No, ya wouldn't, nor will ya, not now. Yar Grandpa got over his disappointment and after a while, he'd just shrug his shoulders, laugh and say, "Oh well, there's always young Harry to give me a – a—"' Luke paused and glanced at her but there was no turning back from what he had been going to say.

Emma finished the sentence for him, 'A grandson.'

'Aye, lass, a grandson. That was what old Charlie had set his heart on. A grandson called Charles Forrest. But funnily enough it's ya dad who's always been so very bitter about the fact that he only inherited the mill by – by – now what's the word . . .' Luke wrinkled his forehead. 'Oh aye – by default. That's it – by default. I could never understand why he felt that way mesen.'

'I suppose,' Emma murmured slowly, 'when he didn't get a son, he felt he'd failed in giving Grandpa Charlie what he wanted most.'

'That's about the size of it, lass.'

She was quiet for a moment and then said haltingly, 'But I still don't understand what all this has to do with the Metcalfes.' She knew she was treading on dangerous ground now. Sarah had warned her not to question Luke too closely, yet she felt that right at this moment, old Luke just might be persuaded to give away a little more than he normally would do. Right now, he was angry with Harry and that wrath might very well loosen his tongue. Emma held her breath.

Luke sighed and shifted himself a little. 'After the two old fellers. Nathaniel and George, died the rivalry ceased to be a joke. It got more serious. Josiah Metcalfe was a greedy, grasping old beggar. He would have given anything to have got his hands on this mill. You know all the stories about him being the so-called Mayor of Marsh Thorpe, well, it weren't a joke to him. That's just what he did imagine himself to be. He wanted to rule the village and get his hands on whatever business he could in the district. And then, of course . . .' Luke stopped and glanced at her. 'There was all the rumpus over ya mam.'

Here it came; this was what she wanted to know. Deliberately keeping a note of innocence in her tone, Emma said, 'My mother?'

Luke nodded. 'Aye, that's when the trouble really started. She first came to Marsh Thorpe to keep house for her uncle after his wife died. He had the saddler's shop in the market place.'

'The saddler's?' Emma was puzzled.

'Oh aye, of course, you won't remember it. It's gone now. It was where the cobbler's is now. When her uncle died it was left to his son, ya mam's cousin, but he lived in a city somewhere. I don't think I ever knew where exactly, but that dun't matter. Anyway, he sold it.'

This was all new to Emma; she couldn't remember ever having been told much about her mother's family.

Luke went on. 'Anyway, I'm over-running me tale. Where was I?'

'When my mother first came here,' she prompted. 'And about some trouble?'

'Oh aye.' He paused a moment and his eyes misted over as if he were seeing pictures from the past. 'She were a pretty little thing, flirting with all the young fellers. Oh, no offence, Emma,' he said swiftly, 'She was only young and just out for a bit of fun. There was nothing wrong in her. She was a lovely-looking lass and all the young fellers were round her like bees round a honey-pot.'

Emma was silent. Her own memories of her mother were of a beautiful, sweet face always laughing, always full of fun, despite the devastating disappointments of her frequent miscarriages and she knew Luke was speaking the truth.

'Ya dad started courting ya mam. He really fell hard for her and her for him even though he was about twelve years older than her. Josiah Metcalfe . . .' He paused a moment as if still reluctant to speak of it, but he took another breath and continued. 'Josiah was already married, but the family hadn't come along then.'

Again he paused and sighed heavily. 'Josiah became besotted by Frances. It was the scandal of the village at the time. If ever a man made a fool of hissen over a woman, then it were Josiah Metcalfe. He used to stand under her window – she lived above the shop with her uncle – and shout up to her. Ya dad and Josiah had a fight one night about it, right there in the middle of the market place. There was doors opening and curtains twitching, I can tell you. And everyone in the pub turned out to cheer 'em on.'

She was trying to imagine her father being so passionate about anything that he would get into a brawl like that. 'What about Josiah's wife. Did she know?'

Luke gave a snort of wry laughter. 'Oh aye, she knew

all right. Ya can't keep that sort of thing quiet in a village. Besides, Josiah made no secret of it. Rumour had it, but I don't know if it was true, that he wanted her to divorce him so he would be free to marry Frances. But his wife said she'd never divorce him nor give him the grounds to divorce her. And of course, she blamed ya mam. Said she'd led Josiah on.'

Divorce! Even the mention of it was a big scandal.

'But – but did my mother *want* to marry Josiah then? I mean, he must have been even older than my father.'

Through the floating dust of the meal floor she saw Luke shake his head. 'That's the daft part about it all. She loved ya father. She wouldn't have nowt to do with Josiah. It was all in his mind. He was always such a self-opinionated old beggar he thought that whatever he wanted, he could get. Even after ya mam and dad got married, he used to taunt your father. "I'll get her one day, Harry Forrest," he used to say. "Her *and* ya mill." Then when Jamie and William Metcalfe were born and ya poor mam kept losing her boys, the taunts became even crueller. "Ya can't sire sons, can ye, Harry Forrest? There'll be a Metcalfe at your mill one day. You just wait and see." I've seen Josiah stand at that gate out there,' Luke jerked his thumb towards the gate leading from the yard into the road, 'and heard him say it mesen. Ya dad would shake his fist at him, but old Josiah would just stand there laughing. By, he were a vicious old beggar.'

No wonder, Emma thought, her father had refused to attend the funerals of both Josiah and his wife. Now she understood why.

There was silence between them now, the only sound the throbbing heart of the working mill. Forrest's Mill. Emma was thoughtful. What had started as friendly banter between her grandfather and the old Metcalfe brothers had become a bitter feud between her father and Josiah. But it was no longer about a man's desire for another man's wife; not now, not in this generation.

Now it was all about Forrest's Mill.

Eleven

'Jamie, did you know about this feud between our families?'

Her eyes, soft and dark as the midnight sky, tried to hold his gaze, but Jamie Metcalfe refused to look at her and turned away, muttering something that even Emma's sharp ears could not quite catch.

'What? What did you say?' She caught hold of his arm, feeling his firm muscles beneath her fingers. During the weeks since his return from the war, his body had filled out and his superb strength was returning as he daily wielded the hammer, working long hours from early morning into the night to rebuild the blacksmith's, the business that was now his. As she had stepped into the smithy, she had seen the improvement at once. Now all the tools hung in neat rows. Tongs, pincers, pliers, the hammers with their differently shaped heads, from a small leaf hammer right up to the heavy sledge hammer, all were cleaned and oiled. The floor was no longer littered with scraps of discarded metal and in the yard two ploughs she had not seen on earlier visits stood waiting to be repaired. So, she thought briefly, new work was coming in now. The fire blazed so that even standing in the doorway, Emma could feel its heat and Jamie's bare arms glistened with sweat.

But Emma noticed all this with only half a mind, for today there was something far more important she wanted to talk to Jamie about. Under her hand she felt his muscles tense and he snatched his arm away as if her touch offended him. She gasped and her eyes widened. Maybe his outward appearance was returning to normal, but his attitude, his treatment of her, was nothing like it had been before he went away.

He turned to face her, the angry frown, which seemed to be permanently on his forehead, a deepening crease. 'I've always known there's been a bit of rivalry between your father and mine, but I never realized, never knew, it went so deep. Not until a few months ago.'

Once more, Emma was surprised. 'But you weren't here a few months ago.'

Jamie nodded. Now his dark gaze met hers. 'Me father wrote me a letter. A long one. He knew then just how ill he was and he wanted me to know a few things before – ' Jamie's voice sank deeper, 'before he died.'

'What *things*?'

'He wanted me to promise to marry you when I came back from the war. *If* I came back.'

There was a strange note of bitter reluctance in Jamie's tone that frightened Emma. She ran her tongue over her lips that were suddenly dry. In a voice that was little more than a husky whisper, she said, 'But that's what we'd planned, wasn't it? I've waited for you, Jamie. I've thought of nothing else but the time you would come back and – and . . .' Her voice trailed away in uncertainty.

Harshly, Jamie said, 'He wanted me to marry you to unite our two families. It was only so that eventually our family would own Forrest's Mill. Even from beyond the grave, he wanted to carry on the feud. He wanted to die thinking that at least his son would one day own your father's mill. Oh, he really spelt it all out to me. He put it in his letter. "I want the whole village to know that at long last a Metcalfe will be the owner of Harry Forrest's mill." '

Emma gasped. 'But that's not why *you* want to marry me, is it?'

Her heart began to thud painfully as Jamie spoke again, words that were a death knell to all her hopes, all the girlish dreams she had cherished and nurtured through the long years of waiting.

'I won't marry you, Emma Forrest. Not now. Not if that's what people are going to say about me. That I've married you to get the mill. The whole village must have known about this feud and that's what they'll say. A man's got his pride. *I've got* my pride. I won't be a party to my old man's scheming.'

She stared at him, unable to believe what she was hearing. 'But – but I don't understand.' Then realization came to her and with it, a great sadness that was a physical pain in her chest. 'You don't love me, Jamie. All that's just an excuse.' She fought to keep the tears from welling up in her eyes, determined not to let him see how his words were like a knife through her heart. Slowly she shook her head and the lower lip of her generous mouth trembled suddenly. 'You can't love me.'

'Of course I do,' he argued angrily, 'but it wouldn't work Emma. Not now. Not knowing what people were thinking, saying about us. About me. It would eat away at us. It would destroy us.'

She shook her head again, this time more vehemently. 'Only if you let it, Jamie. Don't include me in that statement because I love you enough to rise above any village tittle-tattle, enough even to go against my own father's wishes.' She stopped but her unspoken words hung between them like an accusation. You don't love me enough, Jamie Metcalfe, her silence said.

As if unable to defend himself Jamie averted his glance from her steady gaze. 'It wouldn't work,' he muttered again and turned away.

Emma watched him walk back towards the glowing coals in the fire of his forge. With savage ferocity, he worked the long handle of the bellows until the red glow became white hot. She stepped back, feeling the heat growing too much for her to bear. But Jamie, close to the furnace, seemed oblivious to any discomfort. Emma waited a moment longer, watching him, but when he did not turn round, did not even glance over his shoulder at her, she turned away and left the forge. As she passed beneath the brick archway into the market place, she heard the sound of his hammer striking the anvil as he worked on a horse's shoe, a slow, rhythmic clang, clang, like the tones of the passing bell.

It sounded to Emma like the death knell of their love and she covered her ears against it.

'You know, Sarah, I really did think Jamie loved me.'

Sarah shrugged. 'I've no patience with the lad. Y'know, I've always liked the Metcalfe boys, 'specially young William. But Jamie, well, I can't believe how he's changed.' She was quiet a moment and then, as if kindly trying to find excuses for him, added, 'I 'spect it's the war and coming back and his mam and dad not being here any-more . . .' Her voice trailed away, but then she wagged her finger in the air and said more strongly, 'but it dun't give him the right to treat you like this. Mekin' promises to a young lass and then not keepin' them. Oh, dear me, no.'

Emma was silent, slowly wiping down the counter with a damp cloth, so lost in her own thoughts that when loud knocking sounded suddenly on the shop door, she jumped.

'We're closed,' Sarah shouted. 'Can't you read the sign?' But the knocking came again.

Emma sighed and went round the counter. 'Evidently they either can't read or won't take no for an answer.'

She unbolted the door and opened it to find herself staring once more at a huge bunch of flowers and behind it was the merry, smiling face of Leonard Smith. Emma stepped back in surprise and, as if taking that for an invitation, Leonard stepped across the threshold. He gave an exaggerated bow and held out the flowers towards her.

'Beautiful flowers for a beautiful lady. Would you do me the great honour, Miss Forrest, of allowing me to take you to the fair?'

For a moment she thought he was teasing her, making sport of her plainness, of her workaday clothes, her rough, work-worn hands. She opened her mouth to make a sharp retort, but when she looked into his handsome face she saw that although he was adopting the pose of a courtly gent, acting a part almost, the question in his blue-grey eyes was genuine.

'I – I – ' she stammered, 'I thought you'd forgotten.'

'I'm sorry it's been a while,' he said at once. 'I've been away – er – working, you know.' His voice dropped. 'But no, I'd not forgotten.'

She felt a flush creep up her cheeks and she buried her face in the flowers, hiding her growing confusion from him. When she was once more in control of her senses she said, 'Won't you come in, please? We've almost finished here. Please go upstairs, I won't be a moment.'

'You go with the young gentleman, lass,' Sarah said. 'I can finish here.'

'Are you sure?' Emma asked and then turning back to Leonard she said, suddenly strangely shy, 'Please, come this way.'

As she led the way up the dark stairway and into the front parlour above the shop, the windows of which also looked out on to the village street, Emma was conscious of him following her closely. In his fine city clothes, the white shirt and neatly knotted silk tie, a flower in his lapel, the gold watch chain looped across his waistcoat, she was surprised to find he seemed entirely at ease. Placing his black hat and ebony cane on a small table, Leonard strode across the room, nimbly avoiding the conglomeration of old-fashioned furniture that crowded the parlour and held out his hand towards her father, who sat in his easy chair before the fire.

Harry made as if to rise, but at once Leonard said, 'Please don't disturb yourself, sir. I only came to ask you if I may take Emma to the fair tomorrow afternoon?'

Emma held her breath, knowing what would happen next. There would be grumbles and mutterings about her wanting to go gallivanting when there was work to be done and then her father would shake his head and say she could not be spared. Two farmers were due to bring their grain in tomorrow, she knew. There would be no visits to the fair for her.

To her amazement, Harry Forrest was smiling, 'Well, I don't see why not, young feller. Where is this fair then?'

'On the sea front at Calceworth.'

Her father grunted. 'Well, mind she's back here by ten o'clock.'

Emma glanced at her father shrewdly. Oh, so that's your game, is it, Father? Leonard Smith, son of Bridget, is an acceptable escort, is he? But then, she thought grimly, perhaps anyone was acceptable as long as he wasn't a Metcalfe.

The young man turned towards her and, with his back to her father and unseen by him, Leonard gave her a deliberately saucy wink. 'Two o'clock tomorrow. And wear your best bonnet.'

Emma forced a smile to her mouth. Whatever her father's schemes were, they were not of Leonard's making. 'Oh, I will,' she said brightly and, with a hint of rebellion, she cast a glance towards her father and added, 'I have a lovely new straw bonnet I bought on a market stall a little while back.'

As Leonard said politely, 'Goodnight, sir, and thank you,' Harry Forrest nodded and smiled and Emma followed Leonard out of the door to the top of the stairs to see him down once more. Resting his hand lightly on the banister he said, 'I'll let myself out, Emma.' He pointed towards the flowers. 'You'd better get those in water.' She glanced down to see that she was still clutching the bouquet in her arms.

He leant forward suddenly and his lips touched her cheek, 'See you tomorrow.' Then he was running lightly down the stairs, leaving her standing at the top staring after him.

'Where are you off to, Em, all dressed up?'

Emma whirled around. She had not heard him approach and the sound of his voice startled her. She was standing by the gate, her gaze fixed on the curve in the road around which she expected Leonard to appear. Nervously she smoothed her gloved hands down the skirt of her costume. It was her best outfit, indeed her only smart outfit. Royal blue that accentuated the colour of her eyes, the jacket fitted snugly to her waist and the skirt fell in straight well-cut lines to her ankles. A white blouse with ruffles at the throat and the straw hat completed her outfit. It was not in the height of fashion, she knew. Indeed, it was the style of dress that had been worn before the war, but it was all she had. Her father allowed her no money to spend on new clothes and these were second-hand, altered to fit Emma by the village dressmaker.

'William! You made me jump.' Then she smiled at him, knowing full well what effect her next words would have on him. 'I'm going to the fair in Calceworth.'

His reaction did not disappoint her. 'The fair? In Calceworth? And ya dad's letting ya go?' His tone was incredulous. 'Why, I reckon the last time we all went to the fair, your grandpa took us in his pony and trap. The three of us, do you remember? You, Jamie and me.'

'Oh, yes,' she murmured. 'Do you know, I'd forgotten that.'

'He was a lovely man with children. By heck, that were a day.' William shook his head remembering. 'But d'you mean you're going on your own, Em? If you'd said, then I . . .'

At that moment, the rattle of wheels and the clip-clop of a horse's hooves sounded and a smart trap rounded the corner, the pony's white mane rippling in the breeze. In the back, the reins held lightly in his hands, sat Leonard Smith. He drew the trap to a halt beside Emma and jumped down. Ignoring William as if he wasn't even there, Leonard gave a low bow and said, 'Your carriage awaits, m'lady.'

Emma held out her hand to him, which he took and raised to his lips in a courtly gesture. Then, still holding her hand, he helped her up into the back of the trap.

He climbed in, sat beside her and took up the reins. 'Ready?'

'Yes, oh yes,' Emma said, her brilliant eyes shining, 'I'm ready.'

Leonard flapped the reins and the trap jerked forward. She turned to look back at William, raising her hand to wave to him but the smile on her mouth faded and her hand fell back into her lap. He was staring up at her with a strange look upon his face. Anger, hurt, even despair – all were mingled in his gentle eyes. As the trap drew away, all Emma could do, was to watch the diminishing figure of William as he stood, motionless, staring after them.

Twelve

Resolutely, Emma pushed away the memories of a trip to the fair with her grandpa Charlie and the two Metcalfe brothers. Today, she would not even think about them, she told herself. The carefree days of her girlhood seemed so far behind her now, even though it was less than four years since she had last gone to the beach with Jamie and William. So much had happened since, so much had changed and those idyllic days were now like a long-lost memory. And the sedate walks along the sea front with the Metcalfe brothers, when she had believed herself to be so happy, even they seemed staid beside the fun that Leonard Smith showed her.

At first, as the trap bowled along the straight road towards the coast, she had felt very far from being able to enjoy the outing. The memory of the reproachful look on William's face haunted her, but as they approached the town and clip-clopped along the main street, Emma found herself fascinated by the bustle, drawn by the fashionable ladies and the shops. And all the time, Leonard's cheery conversation gradually made the picture of William's angry face fade from her mind and Emma began to enjoy herself.

The fair was a revelation. The hazy childhood memories, which William had evoked, were only of a coconut shy and a big swingboat which had held all three children at once. Now, Leonard took her hand and said, 'I'll take you on everything. What do you want to do first? The Great Wheel or the Figure Eight? You choose.'

Emma looked about her, holding on to her straw hat as the breeze from the sea threatened to whip it from her head and toss it into the air. She was overwhelmed by the crowds and the laughter and the music. She tilted her head back to look at the big wheel turning slowly above them 'It – it looks awfully high,' she murmured.

Leonard squeezed her hand. 'You'll be with me. You'll be quite safe.'

And she was. With his arms around her in the swinging seat and a bar in front of them, she did feel safe and, as they reached the top of the wheel, Emma gave a cry of delighted surprise. 'Oh, it's wonderful. Just look at the sea and all the boats.' In the distance, tiny white-sailed boats bobbed on the glittering, undulating surface of the water. Then the wheel turned and they went down towards the ground again.

Emma laughed. 'It must be like going round on our mill's sails.'

Clutching her hat, she waved to the folks below, strangers to her, but holiday-makers and day-trippers, like her, out to enjoy themselves.

Next, Leonard took her on the Figure Eight where she clung to him as they whizzed up and down and round until she was quite breathless.

'Now I'll win you a coconut,' he said confidently and to her surprise with his second shot, he knocked a coconut from its holder and the stallholder handed it to her, teasing, 'Tek him away, Miss. He's a mite too good. I'll not mek a penny profit on the day.'

Laughing, Leonard guided her towards the helter-skelter and insisted that they ride down on the same mat, his arms tightly around her.

Emma fanned her hot face. 'Oh, no more for a minute, Leonard,' she panted. He put his arm about her shoulders and said, 'All right, let's have a go on the ducking pond.'

'The what?'

'Come on, I'll show you.'

They stood at the back of a small crowd and watched a man throwing wooden balls at a bullseye beneath which a man sat on a board dressed in a striped bathing suit. 'What happens?' Emma asked.

'The man in the bathing suit, he's part of the show. If a ball hits the centre of the bullseye, the board he's sitting on will tip up and he'll get a ducking.'

The crowd groaned as the man having a try, threw the last ball and missed the bullseye completely.

Come on, let's show them how it's done,' Leonard said, grabbing her hand and weaving his way through the crowd to hand his money to the stallholder and be given three small wooden balls in return.

'Right, darling, stand back.' Gently Leonard put her a small distance from him so that he could raise his arm and take aim. The ball flew from his hand, straight and true and hit the bullseye with a crack and the man on board pretended surprise as he felt the wood beneath him tip forward. Throwing his arms in the air, he gave a bloodcurdling yell and fell into the tank of water beneath him. The crowd cheered as the man in the water played up to his audience by pretending to struggle as if he was drowning, floundering and splashing and sending a shower of droplets over those standing too near. Joining in the merriment, the crowd shrieked with laughter. Leonard stood watching, smiling and waiting with two more wooden balls still in his grasp. After a few moments the man climbed out of the water and back on to the board above the tank. Again, Leonard took aim and hit the bullseye smack in the centre.

This time, the surprise on the man's face as he felt himself falling once more, was genuine.

The crowd were loving the show and were clapping and attracting more to join in. They jeered and whistled as the dripping man climbed wearily back on to his perch. Playfully, he shook his fist at Leonard who just laughed, took aim and let loose the third and final ball. Again the man splashed down into the water and the cheering rang all around them.

Emma clapped in delight. 'Oh, Leonard, how clever you are.'

He took her arm, and as they threaded their way through the throng, several people patted Leonard's back. 'Well done, lad. Never seen that done before. Here, come on, Tom, let us have a try.' Several men were clustering round the stallholder and handing over coins. As they walked away, they heard a shout behind them and the stallholder came running after them. 'Wait a minute, mate!' He reached them and pressed some coins into Leonard's hand. ''Ere, mate. 'Ave this one on me. You've done me a good turn, you 'ave, attracting a crowd like that. Never 'ad so much interest.'

Leonard accepted the coins and doffed his hat to the stallholder who was already hurrying back shouting, 'Roll up, roll up, you've seen how it's done. Now you have a go.'

Laughing together, Emma linked her arm through his and said, 'I think you've made that little man's day.'

Leonard looked into her eyes and said softly, 'But it's your day I wanted to make, Emma Forrest.'

'Oh, you have, indeed you have.'

It was dark when they drew into the yard. Leonard sprang from the trap and held out his hand to help Emma alight.

As she stepped down, she raised her eyes to the black shape of the mill looming out of the night. 'I wonder why the mill isn't working,' she murmured. The sails were motionless and parked despite the fact that a stiff breeze, sufficient to turn them, was blowing.

Leonard's deep laughter came out of the blackness. 'Your father needs some fun too sometimes, you know.' He paused and then said, 'He'll be visiting my mother no doubt.'

'Oh. Oh, yes,' she murmured. 'I hadn't thought of that.'

Again she heard his low chuckle.

As they moved towards the back door, Emma said, 'Won't you come in for a moment?' She hesitated and then, greatly daring, added, 'Perhaps you would like a glass of homemade wine?'

Mentally she crossed her fingers hoping that he would decline, but he did not and she was obliged to lead him up the stairs and into the parlour. She turned up the lamp and went towards the cut glass decanter on the sideboard which she was forbidden to touch.

Perhaps, she prayed as she poured the clear yellow liquid into a glass, her father would not notice.

'Please sit down,' she invited as she held out the glass to him but as he made to do so, she added in alarm, 'Oh, not there. That's Father's chair.' But Leonard's only reply was to raise his left eyebrow rather sardonically and sit in the very chair that she had asked him not to use. For a moment Emma stood uncertainly, then suddenly she laughed at her own foolishness. 'I'm sorry,' she said. 'Old habits die hard.'

'You're a young woman now, Emma Forrest,' he said softly. 'No longer a child.'

Under his intense gaze, Emma felt a moment's confusion and when his glance dropped away from her face to her ample bosom, down to her slim waist and generous hips, she felt a warm blush creeping up her face.

'You know,' he said, 'you have the most perfect Edwardian woman's shape I think I've ever seen.'

Emma stared at him, and forgetting her politeness said bluntly, 'Eh?'

He laughed. 'An hourglass figure. Do you wear one of those tightly laced corset things to get that shape?'

'Well, really!'

'Oh, come on, Emma. Don't play the coy, naive girl with me. You're a country lass – a buxom wench with plenty to offer a virile man. A man like me. We could do very nicely together. What do you say?'

A shocked gasp escaped her lips, but whatever she might have said was stilled as she heard her father's footsteps on the stairs and a moment later the door opened and he entered the room.

Emma jumped to her feet but Leonard, completely at ease rose, almost languidly, from the chair and held out his hand towards Harry Forrest. Emma found she was holding her breath, waiting for her father's swift temper to erupt, but although for a moment he seemed rather surprised to see them there, he grasped Leonard's outstretched hand and said, 'Sit down, sit down, lad.' Then he glanced towards her and said, 'Well, girl, you had a good day with this young feller, then?'

Amazed, Emma sank back into her chair and stammered, 'Yes, yes, thank you, Father.'

'Good, good.' Harry Forrest rubbed his hands together and, his glance now taking in the glass of wine that Leonard still held, said, 'I think I'll join you.'

Having poured a glass for himself, her father came and sat on the sofa. Turning to Leonard, he said, 'Your mother tells me you have to go back to Lincoln tomorrow.'

'I'm afraid so, sir. Matters of business.' There was an expectant silence, but Leonard made no offer to explain what his 'business' in the city was exactly. 'But I'll be home again by the weekend,' he added.

Emma stood up again. 'If you'll excuse me. I – I have to be up early in the morning.'

'I'll see to the bakehouse in the morning,' Harry Forrest offered.

Emma gaped at him in astonishment. Allowing her a day out in the company of Bridget Smith's son was one thing, but agreeing that she could lie abed the following morning, when there was work to be done, was quite another.

Leonard set down his empty glass and got up too. 'It's all right, sir. I must be off home now, anyway. I've an early start as well.'

Harry grunted and then said, 'Well, see the young man down the stairs, Emma girl.'

'Yes, Father,' was the only reply she could muster.

'I can hardly believe it,' she said to Sarah the next morning as they stood side by side in the bakehouse, plunging their hands into the soft dough, kneading, pounding, rolling and patting it into shape. 'Father is quite obviously encouraging him. I suppose . . .' she sighed wistfully, 'it's as much to keep me from seeing Jamie as to keep himself in Leonard's mother's good books.'

Emma had lain awake half the night, though whether through excitement after her trip to the fair, or because a handsome young man seemed to be paying court to her, she could not herself be sure. She had to admit, though, that after the hurt of Jamie's surly and cruel rejection of her, Leonard's easy charm was a balm to her wounded pride.

'He seems a very nice young man, but – ' Sarah began and then stopped. Emma glanced at her.

'But what?'

'Oh, I'm being silly.'

Emma hid her smile. 'The bees? You've been talking to the bees.'

Sarah looked sheepish. 'Mm.'

'And?'

The older woman lifted her shoulders in a shrug. 'Nothing. No response at all.'

Emma's smile broadened. 'Oh *dear*,' she said teasingly.

Sarah laughed. 'Now then, Miss, none of your sarcasm.'

'As if I would, Sarah. As if I'd *dare*.'

Their laughter rang through the bakehouse, but never once did their busy hands slow in their work.

'You must be hard up for a feller if you have to take up with the likes of him. I thought better of you, Emma.'

'And what has it got to do with you, Jamie Metcalfe?' she retorted hotly, and added pointedly, '*Now*?'

They were standing in the middle of the busy cattle market, the noise of the animals and the murmur of voices all around them, punctuated now and again by the auctioneer as he moved from pen to pen.

Jamie's only reply was a scowl and a grunt as he turned away.

She knew he always came to the cattle market. It was an opportunity for him to meet and talk to the local farmers which was not to be missed. 'Someone's got to build the business back up again, now William's let it go to wrack and ruin,' he had said more than once in Emma's hearing, so how often poor William had it flung at him in bitter resentment, she did not like to imagine.

This morning, from the mill yard opposite, she had seen him moving amongst the crowd, nodding to acquaintances, stopping to talk to people he knew well. Before she had stopped to think, she had crossed the road and slipped amongst the pens to reach him. Her heart raced at the sight of his dark head and broad shoulders above all the rest. As she weaved her way through the throng, she still expected him to turn and see her moving towards him, his eyes lighting up at the sight of her and the old smile she remembered curving his mouth. But he did not see her approach and when she touched his arm and he turned his head around to look at her, his mouth twisted in a sneer and his first words were, 'Where's ya fancy man this morning then?'

'If you mean Leonard,' Emma retorted, 'he's in Lincoln. He had business to attend to yesterday.'

Jamie's mouth twisted even more. 'Huh! That's what they're calling it these days, a' they?'

'Calling what? I don't know what you're talking about.'

'Well, if you don't know what he gets up to on his visits to the big city, I aren't going to be the one to tell you.' It was then that he had added the final insult and now, having delivered her own parting shot, she whirled away and pushed her way back through the crowd, tears smarting her eyes and blurring her vision, so that she blundered through cattle droppings and stumbled against a pen, bruising her hip. As she grasped the rail and leant against it for a moment, Emma heard a voice calling her name. 'Em. Emma!'

It was a familiar voice, but it was not Jamie's and she did not look back. She didn't want anyone to see her like this. She could face no more insults, no more rejection from the man who had held her heart since childhood, the man for whom she had waited through girlhood and into womanhood, wanting no other, saving herself for her returning war hero. It was over, she knew it now. Jamie had changed. Maybe the war had altered him, or maybe the different circumstances of his home life had embittered him. Whatever it was, over these weeks and months since his homecoming, his resentment had grown deeper. He did not love her and the reality of the man with his dark moods obliterated her fond memory of the boy with the laughing eyes. His words 'you're my girl' were now only a mocking, hollow memory.

She pulled her shawl more closely around her shoulders, wrapped her arms around herself and, bending her head, hurried out of the cattle market and ran across the road straight into the waiting, outstretched arms of Leonard Smith.

Thirteen

They were married in the September of 1919 and Emma could not remember having seen such a grin stretched across her father's face. She had hoped to keep the ceremony quiet with only her father, Leonard's mother, and of course, Luke and Sarah Robson, present. But the villagers of Marsh Thorpe were not to be cheated of a pretty wedding, the first with proper wedding finery since before the terrible war.

Emma had dared to argue with her father. 'We don't want a lot of fuss. I don't need fancy clothes that I can never wear again.'

Harry wagged his finger at her. 'I'll not have folks say I can't give my daughter a proper wedding. You'll only get married once, girl.' He coughed awkwardly and then added quickly, 'Bridget will see to everything.'

Emma sighed with resignation. 'Do you mind very much?' she asked Leonard worriedly. 'I can't understand it. I've never known my father to be like this. Wanting to make a fuss over *me*.'

Leonard laughed and put his arms about her, kissing her forehead. 'My dear girl, your father and I understand each other. Of course I don't mind. You'll make a beautiful bride.'

Emma eyed him doubtfully. Was he teasing her? As for the remark about her father, that at least was undoubtedly true. During the past week since Leonard had proposed to her and then gone dutifully to ask Harry Forrest for his permission, she had seen her father and Leonard deep in conversation on more than one occasion, but as soon as she approached them, their earnest discussions ceased. Once or twice she had felt a little uneasy as if there were secrets between the two men, but because they both seemed so happy, she pushed any doubts to the back of her mind.

'Besides,' Leonard was saying, laughter in his voice, 'think of my mother. She's going to have the time of her life helping you plan everything.' And then he echoed the words her father had used. 'She'll see to it all.'

Bridget had certainly 'seen to everything', and, after her initial reluctance, Emma had to admit that she found herself swept along by Bridget's obvious enjoyment and infectious enthusiasm.

'My dear girl, why ever do you want a *quiet* wedding? It's the most important day in any girl's life. The day when *every* girl makes a beautiful bride.' Bridget clasped her hands together, more like an excited schoolgirl than the mother of the bridegroom.

Emma smiled faintly, but said nothing. How could she tell Leonard's mother, of all people – indeed, how could she tell anyone – that although for years she had secretly planned her wedding, had trembled with hope and longing at the mere thought of that day, in those dreams her bridegroom had not been Leonard, but Jamie?

'I just thought that father . . .' she began hesitantly, scrabbling around in her mind for any excuse.

'Oh, your father,' Bridget flapped her hand dismissively. 'Just you leave your father to me. In fact,' she added, linking her arm through Emma's, 'we'll go and speak to him right this minute.'

Moments later, Bridget was standing before Harry Forrest, placing her hand on his dust-covered arm and gazing

113

up at him, whilst Emma watched in astonishment and not without a little admiration.

'Now, Harry,' Bridget said, fluttering her eyelashes beguilingly, 'I'm going to take Emma to this wonderful little dressmaker I've found. She makes all my clothes and she only lives in the next village, Thirsby. And together, she and I will help Emma choose all her wedding finery.'

'Oh, Mrs Smith, really, I—' Emma began, but the woman flashed her a winning smile and wagged her forefinger in playful admonishment, 'Now, Emma, I've told you, it's "Bridget" from now on. All this "Mrs Smith" indeed. You're about to become my daughter-in-law.' She came to Emma's side and slipped her arm through hers, hugging the young woman to her. 'Oh, Emma, I always wanted a daughter. My dear, dear girl, we'll have *such* fun.'

Emma glanced at her father but his besotted gaze was on the pretty, vivacious woman at her side.

Miss Jefferson knelt on the floor surrounded by paper patterns, scraps of fabric and, with her mouth full of pins, tried valiantly to raise the hem of the dress to the middle of Emma's shapely calf. Bridget stood watching, tapping her forefinger against her lips thoughtfully. 'You know, Miss Jefferson,' she said slowly, 'I'm sorry to say it, but that dress really doesn't suit Emma. What do you think?' The little dressmaker stood up and took a step back to survey her customer. Her lips pursed, her head on one side, she ran her gaze over Emma, who felt like curling up with embarrassment under their scrutiny.

'Now be honest, Miss Jefferson,' Bridget said, as if Emma had no say in the matter at all.

'We-ell,' the middle-aged spinster glanced apologetically at Emma, 'if I'm really honest, no, it doesn't.'

'I'm not built for pretty clothes, Mrs Sm – Bridget,' Emma sighed, but the dressmaker put up her hands to contradict.

'My dear, you have a magnificent figure. So – so . . .' she stumbled as if struggling for an adjective to describe Emma's build in the kindest way possible.

'Huge,' Emma murmured wryly.

'Majestic,' Bridget suggested triumphantly.

'Yes, yes, that's it exactly. So tall and such a shapely figure, just like the perfect Edwardian figure . . . Oh!' Miss Jefferson cried, and at the same moment Bridget clapped her hands and the two women looked at each other.

'That's it, Miss Jefferson. An *Edwardian* wedding dress. Oh, how clever of you. Emma, you will look *magnificent* in an Edwardian dress.'

'But won't it be dreadfully expensive?' Emma began, only to have her doubts waved aside by Bridget whilst already Miss Jefferson was scrabbling amongst drawings and patterns. Triumphantly she held one up. 'Here it is. The dress I made for Lady Stoneham's daughter.'

Three heads bent over the picture of a dress of rich, white satin extravagantly trimmed with lace around the neckline, the close-fitting bodice curved over a full bosom and hugged the tiny waist. The straight skirt had a long brocade train falling from the waist and a long, tulle veil was held in place by a coronet of orange blossom. Miss Jefferson pointed with her long, clever fingers to the picture. 'We use whatever flowers are in season, of course,' she explained.

'And I'll do your hair for you on the day, Emma, all piled up on top of your head. Oh, you'll look a picture, my dear.'

'It's beautiful,' Emma murmured wistfully, 'but – but it's not exactly me, is it?'

'Of *course* it is, Emma.' Bridget was adamant. 'You have just the figure for it.'

That's what Leonard had said, Emma thought and wondered if, for once, she dare let herself believe their compliments. Later, when she told Leonard of their visit to the dressmaker, though without revealing the secret of her wedding dress, she said, 'Your mother has been so sweet.'

Leonard laughed, 'I don't know when she last enjoyed herself so much. I think she's really looking forward to having a daughter to spoil.'

Emma gazed at him. He was a handsome man and she was very lucky, she told herself, that someone like Leonard Smith should want to marry her, and that, already, she liked her future mother-in-law.

If only . . . Resolutely she pushed the thoughts away even before they could enter her mind. Forget him, she told herself sharply. Forget Jamie Metcalfe. He doesn't love you.

She forced a bright smile to her face and brought her wayward thoughts back to the man in front of her, the man who was soon to be her husband. 'I bet your mother looked lovely at her own wedding. What did she wear?'

Leonard shot her a strange look and then said airily, 'I really couldn't tell you. I wasn't there.'

Emma laughed. 'No, of course you weren't, but I thought you might have seen photographs.'

'No, no photographs,' he said shortly. 'Look, I really must go. I'll see you next week when I'm home again.' Swiftly he planted a kiss on her forehead and was gone.

The choice of bridesmaids seemed to be the only thing which caused Bridget consternation. 'Emma, you really *can't* have Sarah Robson as Matron of Honour. She's too old and besides . . .' she seemed about to say more, but then decided against it and finished lamely, 'Well, she *is* too old. Have you no little girl relatives, or friends with little girls?'

Emma shook her head. 'There's no one.'

'Well, then, we'll just have to do without. It's a little unusual, but if there's really no one you can ask. Come along, my dear, Miss Jefferson needs you today for a fitting. *Do* come along.'

Half an hour later Emma was standing once more in the little dressmaker's workroom.

'Oh, Emma,' Bridget breathed. 'You look absolutely splendid. Don't you think so, Miss Jefferson?'

The dressmaker stood back, beamed and nodded. 'Yes, she does. Even if I say it myself. My, my, it's taken me back making one of these beautiful gowns again. The fashions today are so plain.' She waved her hand dismissively in disgust and then the little spinster's eyes blinked more rapidly than usual. 'A proper village wedding, even if it is to an outsider. Oh!' Her eyes widened and she cast an apologetic glance towards her valued customer, fearful of offending. 'Begging your pardon, ma'am, but you know what villages are like.'

Bridget only laughed her tinkling, merry laugh, flapped her hand and said gaily, 'Of course I understand. We *are* outsiders, we're "furriners". Of course we are. But I must say the village folk have been most kind to us since we came to live here, especially to me when my dear boy came back from the war. And even now, when he's away so often on – er – business. And I do get so lonely. Why, Emma, I don't know what I'd have done without your father and his little visits.' She glanced coyly at Emma, then laughed again and came back to the business in hand, the fitting of her future daughter-in-law's wedding gown.

117

Bridget clasped her hands together. 'It's beautiful, my dear. *You* look beautiful. Your father will be so proud of you.'

A small smile lightened Emma's thoughtful expression. It was strange, but apart from Bridget, her father seemed to be the only other person who was pleased about her forthcoming marriage to Leonard. Whilst she had not expected the Metcalfes to wish her well, she had been totally unprepared for William's reaction. The gentle friend whom she had always looked upon as the brother she had never had and whom she had hoped would one day be her brother-in-law, had burst into the bakehouse early one morning. He looked as if he had thrown on his clothes and rushed to see her as soon as daybreak arrived. His eyes were wide and red-rimmed as if he had hardly slept the previous night and his hair was wild and unbrushed. He was breathing hard, panting almost, as he stood in the doorway leading into the bakehouse from the yard. That he – a Metcalfe – should even venture into the yard of Forrest's Mill proved the urgency of his mission.

'Is it true? Oh, Em, say it isn't true.'

Emma closed the heavy metal door on the batch of dough she had just put into the oven. She adjusted the damper slightly at the side of the oven and then turned slowly to face him. She stared at him for a moment and then nodded, saying quietly, 'It's true.'

William ran his hand through his hair, making it stand on end even more. He looked like a startled scarecrow. If the atmosphere had not been so charged, his appearance would have amused Emma. As it was, the frantic look in his eyes killed any merriment.

'Why? In Heaven's name, *why*?'

'Because he asked me to marry him,' she said simply.

'But, Emma, are you sure about it – about him? I mean – well – do you know what he does for a living?'

With a start, she became painfully aware that William had called her 'Emma'. He really was angry with her. Immediately defensive, she retorted hotly, 'Of course I know.'

But then Emma bit her lip. But did she? she asked herself. Did she really know how her future husband earned his living?

'Oh, a bit of this and a bit of that, you know,' Leonard had said airily when she had asked him what his business was and why he went to Lincoln so often.

'What? Do you mean a sort of dealer? Someone who buys and sells?'

Leonard laughed and tweaked her nose playfully. 'What a clever girl you are, Emma. That's it exactly. I'm a dealer.' And he had laughed again.

'What in?' she had persisted.

'Ooh, now let's think.' His blue-grey eyes were sparkling with mischief. 'All sorts of things. Anything from a spade to a diamond. Would you like to be dripping in diamonds, Emma darling? Maybe one day I'll make my fortune and dress you in diamonds.'

Then Emma had joined in his teasing. 'Hardly suitable for working in the mill or the bakehouse.'

Then Leonard had lifted her hand to his lips and kissed each finger, like a gentleman courting a fine lady. 'But it's hearts I'm dealing in at this moment. Your heart. Have I beaten all the other bidders to win your heart, Emma Forrest?'

'There are no other bidders, Leonard,' she had told him truthfully. And silently added to herself, not any more.

'And you don't – mind?' William was saying now. 'You don't mind what he does?'

She shrugged her shoulders. 'You can't blame a man for the way he earns his living, as long as it's honest.'

William looked doubtful as he muttered, 'Exactly. Is it, though?'

She knew that William must be referring to the sort of dealer who dealt on the fringes of the law, his way of trading not strictly honest, the kind who would pass off a fake antique as the genuine article or maybe ask far too high a price for something, taking advantage of folk's ignorance or simplicity. She hoped her future husband was not one of those.

'Ya pays ya money and ya teks ya chance,' she said mockingly, deliberately lapsing into broad dialect.

William's frown deepened so that for a moment he looked uncannily like his older brother. The fleeting similarity hardened Emma's resolve.

'What would you have me do, eh? Wait around 'til I'm an old maid for your brother to come to his senses? You know what the village folk say about me, don't you, William? That I'll only find a husband 'cos he wants to get his hands on my father's mill. And it's not only the gossips. It's what my father thinks – or rather used to think – too.' She saw William's face grow paler until his eyes were big and dark against his white skin, but he made no answer and ruthlessly, she went on. 'But Leonard's not after the mill. He doesn't know the first thing about milling. Shouldn't think he's even interested in it. So I know that's not the reason he's marrying me. And I don't exactly see a queue forming behind him, do you?'

William seemed about to speak, even opened his mouth to form the words but then he clamped his jaw shut as if deliberately cutting off whatever he had been about to say. There was a silence and he seemed to be struggling with himself. At last he said, 'But do you love him, Emma? And does he love you?'

She stared at him. Such a personal question, even from

William, startled her. 'We'll do very nicely together, thank you,' she said tightly. 'And my father is delighted by the match.'

'He would be, wouldn't he?'

'What do you mean by that?'

'Well, he's bedding the mother, ain't he?'

Emma gasped. 'Don't be so – so crude!'

The young man's white face was suddenly diffused with colour and he muttered, 'I'm sorry.'

'I think you'd better go, if you've said all you came to say. And that's been a mite too much.'

'Em, I'm sorry, really I am. It's only that . . .' His gaze searched her face as he moved towards her, his hand reaching out tentatively. With a shock she saw that his fingers were trembling. 'Please, Em, I – I only want you to be happy.'

Her expression softened and briefly she clasped his hand and squeezed it. 'Oh, William—'

'Emma, Emma? Where are you, girl?'

'Oh, that's me dad. I must go.' She began to pull away but found herself held fast now in his grip.

'Emma, just remember. If you ever need any help if things don't work out. Remember, I'm your – your friend always.'

'Oh, William—' she began again, but her father's voice came again, loud and impatient, 'Where's me breakfast, girl? Have I to wait all day? I've work to do even if you ain't.'

Emma pulled herself free from William's grasp and hurried from the bakehouse and into the kitchen.

Fourteen

William was not the only person to disapprove of her forthcoming marriage to Leonard. To Emma's dismay, Luke Robson was strangely tight-lipped and Sarah, who had been a second mother to her, seemed perplexed and troubled.

Trying to make light of it, Emma had asked her, 'What do the bees think, Sarah? Have you asked them?'

For once, Sarah, who usually took such teasing good naturedly, frowned and snapped, 'Dun't you mock, Miss Emma. I know I've got me funny ways, I'll be the first to admit it, but dun't you mock me.'

Immediately contrite, Emma put her arms about the woman's ample waist. 'Oh, Sarah, don't even think such a thing. I was only teasing.'

The fat arms came around her hugging her tightly. 'Oh, I'm sorry, lass. I should know you would never be unkind. I don't know what I'm thinking about, but Luke's got me so wound up and worried, I hardly know what I'm sayin'.'

'Luke? Why, what's the matter? He's not ill, is he?'

'No, no, it's not that.' The arms about her loosened and Sarah pulled away, her eyes avoiding meeting Emma's.

But the girl persisted. 'What then?'

'He – he's not happy about you marrying that young feller.'

'Why?'

Sarah's words came in a rush. 'Oh, Emma, dun't take it

wrong. You know he cares for you. You know how we both think of you as if you were our own.' The plump cheeks glowed red with embarrassment and she plucked at the corner of her white apron with pudgy, nervous fingers.

'I know you do,' Emma said gently, 'and I'm sorry he feels that way. I thought he'd be glad for me.'

They were silent a moment, standing in the yard near the back door in the early autumn sunshine, glancing across to where Luke lugged heavy sacks of grain down the steps of the granary.

'I didn't ought to be taking time off for a wedding just now,' Emma murmured. 'Not when we're so busy. I ought to go and help Luke. I ought to try to talk to him.'

'Leave 'im be, at least today. Mebbe he'll come around given time.'

'But why is he so against Leonard?'

'You hardly know the young feller. None of us do. "Marry in haste, repent at leisure," that's what Luke keeps saying, lass,' Sarah said worriedly, shaking her head. She glanced at Emma, a defensive note in her tone as she added, 'And since you ask, the bees aren't happy about it either, so there.'

With that parting shot, Sarah's bustling little body flounced back into the bakehouse and Emma could hear her banging the bread tins as she set them out for the following morning's batch of dough. She sighed and, despite Sarah's warning, was about to cross the yard towards Luke when a wagon, driven by her father, drew into the yard and pulled up near the granary steps. Flinging the reins over the neck of the horse, who stood docilely, Harry Forrest climbed down stiffly. Resting his hand on the rail at the side of the steps, he looked up as Luke, heavy-footed under the weight of a bulging sack of grain, clomped down the wooden stair.

'Ain't you finished yet? Farmer Popple wants his flour to tek to Lincoln this Wednesday.'

Luke, twisting his neck awkwardly under the heavy load glowered at his employer. 'We'd get on a dang sight quicker if you didn't keep doing ya disappearing act and kept the mill running when the wind's right, 'stead of going a'courting.' Luke sniffed and muttered. 'Man of your age and all. Must be in ya second childhood, I reckon.'

'And who asked you for your opinion?' Harry Forrest raged.

Emma, quickening her pace towards them, intervened, 'It's all right, Father. I'll give Luke a hand. Sarah's holding the fort in the bakehouse.' Without waiting for his approval or otherwise, she placed her foot on the bottom step, grasped the handrail and ran lightly up the steps. But as she reached the top her father's harsh voice reached her, 'You get back down here, girl, and see to your own business. Ya should be getting ready for ya wedding. There's enough for you to do in yon house to welcome ya new husband. This is men's work, so leave us to do it.'

Open-mouthed she stared down at him, whilst Luke dropped the sack he was carrying and gaped at Harry, who muttered morosely. 'Well, what's the matter with the pair of you, standing gawping like idiots?'

It was Luke who actually voiced what was in Emma's mind too. 'By heck, ya've changed ya tune, ain't ye? She's been good enough to hump these great sacks about for years, almost afore she were big enough to lift 'em, and with no thought from you for the fact that she's a girl. But now, all of a sudden, because you can suddenly see the chance of getting yarsen a grandson – another Charlie Forrest – ' sarcasm laced the old man's words now, 'now she's to be treated proper, like the woman she's been for years. Well, Harry Forrest, let me tell you summat. I've never held with how you've treated your lass in the past. She's pure gold, that girl.' His gnarled hand gestured upwards to Emma, still standing at the top of the steps, her hand grasping the rough-hewn wood of the rail so tightly that the splinters dug into her palm. She held her breath, stunned by the words spewing from Luke's angry mouth. 'You don't deserve to have her as your daughter,' he ranted. 'Ya never did. But how you can stand there and be encouraging her to marry the likes of Leonard Smith, well, it beats me.'

The two men stood glaring at each other like a couple of fighting cocks, whilst Emma stood, silent and still at the top of the steps, waiting. Her heart was thumping, but her father made no effort to deny Luke's accusation. So, she said to herself, that was the reason behind her father's sudden thoughtfulness for her. Harry Forrest wanted a grandson. He wanted another Charlie Forrest to inherit his mill and suddenly, with the arrival of Leonard Smith, he had at last seen a way to get what he most wanted and at the same time to defy the Metcalfe family once and for all. She didn't know whether to laugh or cry. The hurt went deep but she refused to let anyone, least of all her father, see it. Her chin came higher. Well, she thought, whatever Harry Forrest's motives were in encouraging her to marry Leonard, she had no doubt that the young man's reasons could not be questioned.

No young man, certainly not one as good-looking and smartly dressed as Leonard Smith, married a girl for any other reason than that he wanted to do so. Why, he could surely have the pick of all the girls he met in the city, if he'd a mind. But he'd asked her, Emma Forrest, to marry him. He'd taken her out, brought her flowers and chocolates and charmed her. She enjoyed his company and, under his flattery, she felt like a real woman. Leonard really wanted to marry her, she knew he did. So she lifted her chin and, as she spoke, the two men below her looked up in surprise, almost as if they had both forgotten she was standing there, listening to every word.

'You can stop your arguing because I shall be marrying Leonard a week come Saturday whether you,' she glanced at her father, 'like it,' her gaze swivelled to Luke, 'or not.'

And with that parting shot she turned, stepped into the granary and with a strength that had a lot to do with the angry humiliation burning inside her, heaved a sack of grain onto her broad shoulders. When she appeared in the doorway once more it was to see Harry Forrest marching towards the house and Luke struggling to pick up his sack again and stagger towards the mill.

The day of her wedding dawned bright and clear with that special sharp tang of autumn.

'You will come to the church, won't you?' she asked Sarah. 'I – I know you don't approve but I couldn't bear it if you stayed away.'

'Of course we'll be there, lass. Mebbe we're wrong. I hope to goodness we are. All we want is for you to be happy. Now, shall I help you get ready?'

'Oh – er . . .' Emma felt her cheeks glow hot.

Sarah pursed her lips. 'Oh, I see. *She's* coming, is she?'

'I'm sorry,' Emma said. 'It's been so difficult, what with Father . . .'

Sarah smiled, but Emma could see it was somewhat forced. 'It's all right. Don't worry about it.' She turned away. 'I've plenty to do, anyway.'

Now Sarah was hurt. Emma sighed. This wedding seemed to belong to everyone else but her, she thought.

*

Bridget arrived midmorning in a flurry of excitement. 'Where are you, my dear girl? Are you dressed and—?' She stopped in amazement as Emma came into the kitchen from the bakehouse, her face red from the heat of the fire, her hands covered with flour. Bridget gasped. 'Emma, my dear, what are you *thinking* of? The ceremony is in an hour and a half and you haven't even *begun* to dress. Now, come along, my dear, do.'

Emma allowed herself to be led from the kitchen towards the stairs, but as she did so, she glanced back towards the door into the bakehouse to see Sarah shaking her head and casting her eyes to the ceiling.

'Fancy your father expecting you to work on your wedding day. Really! I shall have something to say to him.'

An hour later, Emma scarcely recognized the face that stared back at her from the mirror. Bridget had brushed Emma's freshly washed hair until it gleamed. Then, with her nimble fingers, she had twisted, rolled and patted it, piling it high on the top of Emma's head in the most elegant style the girl had ever seen.

'Oh, Bridget?' she breathed, 'how clever you are.'

The woman beamed and laughed girlishly. 'I'm enjoying every minute of it, my dear. Now, let me show you how to put a little colour into your cheeks, though you scarcely need any. You really have perfect skin, Emma. Positively *glowing* with health.'

A few minutes before they had to leave for the church, Bridget said, 'Now for the final touch. Look, I've made you a little coronet of yellow roses to hold your veil in place and Leonard has sent you a bouquet to match. It's waiting downstairs for you. There . . .' She fastened the coronet on the top of Emma's hair and attached the trailing veil to it. 'Now, let me look at you. Stand up.'

Carefully, hardly daring to breathe, Emma rose from the

dressing stool and moved to the only space available in the cluttered bedroom.

'Turn round,' Bridget instructed and then she clasped her hands together. 'My dear, you look magnificent. Regal. Yes, that's the word, *regal*. Leonard really is a lucky boy and your father will be so proud of you. Now, I really must go and take my place in the church.'

She came forward and planted a delicate kiss on Emma's cheek, so brief it was like the touch of a butterfly's wings.

As she went down the stairs, Bridget's voice floated back to her. 'You should leave in about ten minutes, my dear.'

Left alone in her room, Emma stared again at her reflection in the mirror. With her hair piled on top of her head, she looked even taller, but the beautiful dress accentuated her generous bosom and slender waist and the delicate blush on her cheeks refined her face. Her violet eyes, the dark lashes long and curling, stared back at her. A tremor ran through her. For a moment the whole day was unreal. The person staring back at her was not Emma Forrest, but someone else. This elegant creature could not possibly be Harry Forrest's carthorse of a daughter.

And then the thought that she had managed to hold at bay pushed its way into her mind and threatened to be her undoing. She thought about Jamie Metcalfe. It should have been Jamie for whom she was making herself beautiful. It should be Jamie waiting at the church for her. But Jamie did not love her enough . . . Resolutely, Emma lifted her chin and moved towards the head of the stairs and descended, one step at a time, towards her father who waited in the yard to give her away in marriage.

Leonard had hired an open carriage to drive Emma and her father to the church and as she climbed into it outside the front of the house, she could see that all along the curve of the street ahead, the villagers stood waiting to see her in her wedding finery. She smiled and waved for there was not one face amongst them that she didn't know, that she hadn't known since her childhood. They were her friends, each and every one, and they had come out to wish her well.

As the carriage passed the open space of the market place on the right-hand side, her gaze went at once to the brick archway between the smithy and the wheelwright's yard. Framed in the archway, stood the tall, burly figure of Jamie, his shirt sleeves rolled up above his elbows, his waistcoat unbuttoned, as if he had just stepped out from the forge to see what was causing all the commotion. He was too far away for her to see his face but then, closer, standing half-hidden behind the corner of a wall as if he didn't want to be seen and yet could not help being there, she saw William. As she met the haunted look in his eyes, eyes that were huge in his white, pinched face, Emma's lips parted in a gasp.

She didn't think that if she lived to be a hundred she would ever, for the rest of her life, forget the look on William Metcalfe's face as she passed by him on the way to her wedding.

Fifteen

Married life was not quite what Emma had imagined it would be. She had known, of course, what to expect on her wedding night; Sarah had seen to that.

The older woman, blushing and stammering, had tried to explain. 'Don't ever refuse him, Emma. It's a wife's duty and if – well – if he's a kindly feller, then – then – it's not all that bad. In fact . . .' the blush had deepened, 'it can be very nice.'

But if Emma had fondly imagined caring for her husband, cooking, washing and cleaning their own little house and being a willing, even joyful, wife in their bed at night, then she was to be disappointed. The truth of her life as a new bride was very little different from what it had been before her marriage. Leonard, far from suggesting that they set up home together or even that she should move into the cottage he shared with his mother, just moved into the millhouse to share the double bed in the room which Emma had occupied for as long as she could remember. She still rose every morning just as early as she had always done to begin work in the bakehouse and, without it even being discussed, she continued to work in the mill. Indeed, the only difference was that there was now another man in the house to pander to and, although he shared her bed, even that side of married life was vaguely disappointing to her.

There was no one to ask, not even Sarah, as to whether what occurred between them in the privacy of their bed was normal or not. The act was very quickly over and performed in complete darkness. There were no words of love between them, no tender caresses before the thrusting and writhing of buttocks above her and his final grunt of either satisfaction or accomplishment. In her naivety, Emma could not know which, nor could she explain the feeling of unfulfillment as she lay sleepless and staring wide-eyed into the darkness whilst Leonard lay on his back beside her, snoring loudly, with his mouth wide open. And why, she wondered did he only make love to her when he returned home late at night from the city, when his eyes were bright with the success of a day's dealings and with the smell of liquor on his breath?

Strangely enough, in the days following her marriage, it was not Sarah who became Emma's confidante, but her new mother-in-law, Bridget. Although Sarah was as loving and devoted to her as ever, somehow, where her new husband was concerned, Emma felt a constraint between them. She knew that neither Luke nor Sarah approved of the match and the knowledge made it difficult for Emma to talk to either of them about Leonard. But with Bridget, there was, of course, no such restraint. So when, on the rare occasions she found herself with an hour or so to spare, Emma walked the mile to the other side of the village to the low, whitewashed cottage where her mother-in-law lived, Bridget's welcome was always ecstatic. On opening the door, she would fling her arms wide and enfold Emma in a hug. 'How *lovely*.'

Sitting in her pretty sitting room, Emma said. 'Leonard's so secretive. I wish he'd talk to me more about what he does.'

'Oh, men!' Bridget flapped her delicate hands and her laughter tinkled when Emma tried, tactfully, to ask what it was exactly that Leonard did and where he went, sometimes staying away overnight. 'They're a law unto themselves, my dear, and Leonard's worse than most. But a woman's duty is to look after her man, in *every* way.' And her merry laughter sounded again and her eyes twinkled coquettishly. Emma found herself smiling too. It was so easy to like Bridget and she couldn't quite understand why some of the villagers gossiped about her so scathingly. Now she was patting Emma's hand and saying, 'Don't ask him too many questions, Emma dear. He doesn't like it.'

A small frown creased Emma's forehead. 'But I don't understand what it is he does, exactly. I mean, some days he comes home in such a good mood, bringing expensive presents from town. At other times, he's in a black mood and borrowing a few shillings from me for the fare back to Lincoln. Is it because sometimes he pulls off a good deal and then another time, it doesn't work or – or something?' She was floundering, trying to ask the right questions and yet completely mystified.

Bridget blinked at her. 'Deals?'

'Yes, he's a dealer, isn't he? That's what he told me. I presumed he buys and sells things? Is that right?'

'Well, er . . .' Bridget hesitated and her glance shied away from Emma's direct gaze. 'Sort of, I suppose. I think he does a bit of all sorts, you know.'

Emma was shaking her head. 'No, that's just it, I *don't* know.'

She had never thought of herself as stupid nor even particularly naive and innocent, but suddenly Emma felt very ignorant of the ways of the world beyond the confines of Marsh Thorpe. She knew nothing, she realized, of town or city life, nothing about the world of men other than the lives of the few men she knew; her father, of course, and the local farmers and the craftsmen and shopkeepers in the village community.

Bridget shrugged her shoulders, 'Well, you know how men are. They don't think we can understand the world of – er – business. If you take my advice, dear, just don't ask questions.'

'I'm leaving this morning. I've matters to attend to in Lincoln.'

'Of course,' Emma smiled. 'I'll have your supper ready for when you get back, Leonard.'

'Eh?' He stared at her for a moment and then laughed. 'Oh, I shan't be back tonight, Emma.'

'Oh, I see. When will you be back then? Tomorrow?'

'Can't say. Depends.'

'On what?'

An irritated frown creased his forehead. 'Stop questioning me, woman. It depends how long it takes me. How long I choose to stay.'

She was silent and watchful as she waited for an explanation, but when none was forthcoming, she asked quietly, 'What exactly is it you do, Leonard?'

He turned away and said casually over his shoulder, 'I've told you. This and that. I have to be ready to travel, you know. To go where the best – er – deals are.'

'I see,' she murmured, her gaze upon him but he kept his face turned away from her, busying himself over the packing of his suitcase, each item folded and neatly laid in precise order in its depths. 'Would you like me to help you pack?' she offered.

'No!' His answer was like a pistol shot. 'Don't you ever touch any of my things, not my possessions nor my clothes, except those I give you to wash for me.'

Emma gasped and stared at him, and immediately he crossed the space between them and put his hands on her shoulders. He was smiling again, charming once more. 'My dear, what am I thinking of? Please forgive me. I'm not yet used to having a wife to look after me. I suppose it began in the army. You know, caring for one's own kit and that. Perhaps it's best if you allow me to continue as I always have. I'm so used to all the packing and unpacking and I know just how I like things done.'

She returned his look steadily. 'That's all right, Leonard. I was only trying to help.'

'I know,' he kissed her forehead and turned back to the suitcase, his sharpness of a moment ago gone as quickly as it had come. He was laughing now. 'Even Mother knew not to touch my things. Just one of my little foibles. You'll soon get used to me, Emma. Me and my funny little ways.'

'As you wish, Leonard,' Emma said evenly and turned to leave the bedroom.

So, Bridget's advice had been right. It was better that she did not question her husband and his comings and goings unless she wanted a full-scale confrontation. Emma sighed and went downstairs. It was time she lit the fires in the bakehouse anyway, she reminded herself.

'Where's he off to then?' Luke asked at her shoulder as she stood leaning over the yard gate a little later in the morning, watching the carrier's cart taking Leonard up the street, round the sharp corner and out of sight.

'Lincoln. On business.'

Luke sniffed. 'Oh aye?' His tone was disbelieving and though Emma twisted her head sharply to look at him, the older man had turned away and was hobbling towards the mill.

'Luke?' She hurried after him. 'What's that supposed to mean?'

'Nothing, lass, nothing,' he muttered and refused to stop or even to look at her. 'I've work to do. Ya'd better let me get on wi' it, else ya dad'll be after me.'

She laughed then, a clear sound in the early morning air. 'Since when did you ever take any notice of him?'

Luke shot her a swift smile, but a wary look came into his eyes. 'Aye mebbe you've a point there, lass. I'd better be watching mesen from now on, I reckon.'

'Whatever do you mean?' But he was gone, walking away from her and calling back over his shoulder. 'You go and help Sarah in the bakery. It's high time you stopped lifting these heavy sacks, now you're a married woman.'

She watched as he climbed the granary steps stiffly, hauling himself up as if every step pained him. She was about to turn and go into the baker's shop, but then she called out to him. 'You send them up on the hoist, Luke. I'll go up top. I've time to unload them into the bins. It'll save you a lot of clambering up and down.'

The old man continued his weary climb and she could not be sure whether he had heard her or not. She shrugged and went towards the mill to mount the ladders to the bin floor. He would soon realize she was up there, she thought, when he sent the sacks up on the hoist.

Emma was panting slightly as she arrived on the floor where a permanent dust haze seemed to hang. In a few moments the air would be thick with it as she tipped the grain into the bins. As she waited, she leant against the whitewashed wall and looked out of the tiny window overlooking the yard below. The day was still with hardly a breath of wind. If this weather kept up, Emma thought, they would be forced to start the engine to work the mill. Although the motor was kept oiled and greased and ready for use, her father always put off starting it. He hated the monstrosity, as he called it, and usually it was Luke who had the job of unwinding the thick belt and starting the engine, whilst Harry Forrest grumbled and groused and glowered at the sky as if personally willing the wind to come again. It was one of the few things Emma and her father actually agreed about; they both preferred to see the sails spinning to work the mill.

She saw Luke staggering out of the granary and down the steps, a bulging sack of grain on his back, and cross the yard towards the mill. As she turned away, she saw her father come out of the back door of the house and walk towards the mill too. From far below Emma heard the gentle chink of metal as Luke fastened the sack onto the hoist chain and began to operate it. A few seconds later the sack crashed through the trap doors and she caught hold of it. Just as she was about to shout down to Luke that she was up there and had the sack, their raised voices floated up clearly through the hollow silence of the idle mill.

'Well, if that's how you feel, Harry Forrest, I ain't working for you a minute longer. Given my life to you and Forrest's Mill, I have, and that's the thanks I get. You tek ya fancy son-in-law into the mill instead and see 'ow far that gets ye. What d'ya think he knows about milling, any road?'

'He's not coming into the mill. At least, not now, though it'll be his one day when I'm gone.'

Even from here, Emma could hear the shock in Luke's voice. 'His? His?' He almost spat out the word. 'You'd leave ya dad's mill to that – that – ' It seemed as if words failed him to find an appropriate adjective for his opinion of Leonard Smith, for he broke off and then said, 'What's it going to be then? Smith's Mill, is it? Cut out ya own flesh and blood, would ye?'

'No, that weren't the deal.'

There was silence for a moment and above them in the

dust of the bin floor, Emma held her breath and bent lower towards the hole in the floor so that she might hear better.

Luke's voice was lower now, but there was a menacing note in his tone. 'Deal? What deal?'

'The deal I had to make,' came her father's voice raised in anger, 'to get my daughter a husband.'

Far above him, Emma put one hand over her mouth to stifle a gasp and groped with trembling fingers to find the edge of a nearby bin to steady herself.

The tirade continued. 'How else would she have got one, eh? Answer me that!'

'Easily,' came Luke's sharp retort. 'She's a fine lass and young Metcalfe—'

'Oh, him!' Harry Forrest spat out. 'Over my dead body.'

'That'd've been better than the one you've wangled for her. He's a fortune hunter, if ever I saw one. Ya've taunted the poor lass for years that no one'd marry her except to get ya blasted mill. And then damn me if ya don't go and fall for that very thing yasen. He's a trickster. Can't you see it? Or are you blind 'cos you're getting ya way with the mother, eh?'

'Watch ya tongue, Luke Robson, else ya'll find yasen out of a job.'

'Suits me. I'm damned if I want to work with a man who sells his own daughter.'

Emma made an involuntary movement, opened her mouth to shout down and then clamped it shut again. She could not move, could not make a sound without revealing that she had overheard every word of their quarrel; a quarrel that had left her feeling more hurt and humiliated than she had ever felt in her life.

Luke didn't mean it, not about leaving his work, she was sure he didn't. In the heat of the moment they were both saying things that later they would bitterly regret. But it seemed that Luke did mean everything he said, for his final words were, 'Do ya own milling from now on, Harry Forrest.'

'If you walk out of here, Luke Robson, ya won't walk back.'

'Suits me,' Luke said again.

'And you'll be out of ya house an' all.'

There was a moment's pause, then a low growl from Luke that Emma could scarcely hear. 'By heck, Harry, after all these years.'

The hoist chain shivered and clinked and Emma drew back from the hole. For a moment she thought Luke had given in, but then she heard his boots on the stone floor and peeked out of the window to see him hobbling away across the yard towards the orchard and his cottage. Her father appeared in the yard just below her and stood watching Luke Robson as if seeing him off his premises, before he too marched across the yard and back into the house.

Wearily she leaned against the wall and then slid down to sit on a pile of sacks as her legs gave way beneath her. She felt sick and, closing her eyes, Emma dropped her head forward into her hands. The words she had overheard hammered round her brain. Her marriage was nothing but a bargain stuck between two men. And what exactly, Emma wanted to know, had that bargain been?

A few moments later she heard shouting below in the yard and pulled herself up to look out of the window again. Hurrying across the yard towards the gap in the hedge leading to her own cottage, her face flushed with anger and outrage in every bustling step of her round little body, was Sarah.

'No. Oh no,' Emma groaned aloud and sank back onto the sacks.

The mill was silent, the only sound the gentle clink of the hoist chain as it quivered. Outside the breeze stayed defiantly calm and the sails stood idle. With Luke storming off in a temper, her father's stubbornness, and Leonard half way to Lincoln, there was no one who could start the engine.

Farmer Popple would not get his grain ground this day.

She stayed in the mill for a long time, stunned by what she had overheard, what the few moments of anger between her father and Luke had wrought, though she had no doubt that once they all calmed down, Luke would return to his work and Sarah would go back into the shop.

At last she heard the back door of the house open once more and saw her father leaving the yard, crashing the gate shut behind him and setting off up the village street. Cold anger spread through her and hardened her resolve. She was glad now that she had not revealed herself and let them know she had overheard every word. Calculatingly, she decided, quite rationally and coldly, that she would keep her counsel. She would act as if she had heard nothing and she would express surprise to find Luke and Sarah missing. She would demand to be told what had happened. And then she would see what explanation her father gave.

Stiffly, her legs trembling with emotion even though her resolve was now quite firm, Emma climbed down the ladders and came out of the mill into the yard. As she reached the door into the house, she hesitated. There was no one about, no one in the yard and, thinking quickly, she realized that if she were to make her ignorance of the quarrel plausible, she would have to have a believable story. It would be easier to keep to if it was also the truth. If she could say that she had not even been there, that she had been to the market place, to the butcher's maybe . . . Come to think of it, she tried to gather her scattered thoughts, I do need to order a joint for the weekend.

She turned, left the yard and went out of the gate and up the road to the market place. It was market day and she would soon lose herself amongst the throng, would perhaps even talk to a few folk she knew, so that on her return she could chatter brightly about village news rather than what she had really overheard. A small, wry smile quirked her mouth. I'm becoming as devious as my father and Leonard, she thought, and unbidden, the saying, 'if you can't beat 'em, join 'em' slipped into her mind.

She wandered amongst the stalls until she found herself near the archway leading to the smithy. Even from here, with the bustling chatter of the market behind her, she could hear the heavy clang, clang of Jamie's hammer.

Oh, Jamie, Jamie, her heart yearned, if only . . .

'Em?'

She heard her name spoken and turned to find herself looking straight into William's concerned gaze. He was standing a few feet away from her at the entrance into the yard of his wheelwright's workshop on the other side of the archway. Her smile was swift and genuine and she saw immediately the worry in his eyes lighten as he smiled in return.

'It's good to see you,' he said. 'How are you?'

'Fine. Fine.'

Was her tone a little too bright, perhaps a little too brittle, to be convincing, for there was a sudden fleeting shadow in William's eyes again.

'Really?' he persisted. 'Are you really – happy?'

She put her hand on his arm. She could hear the concern for her in his voice, knew in that moment that in all of this, here was one person who was genuinely concerned for *her*.

She was on the point of telling him about the conversation between her father and Luke but suddenly pride stilled her tongue. Had she not been humiliated long enough knowing that all the village men laughed about her; how they had mocked Jamie Metcalfe in his tentative courtship. 'She'll mek a fine wife for a Metcalfe,' she knew they had said. 'Young Emma Forrest – and her mill! It's what old Josiah always wanted.' The village gossip had added fuel to his father's final letter and made the proud Jamie Metcalfe turn his back on her and any chance of happiness they might have had, even though she was convinced he still loved her if only he would let himself.

She wanted no one to know that those taunts had come true. Although it was not Jamie who had married her, her father had still struck some kind of bargain with her prospective husband, even though she did not know at this moment what exactly that bargain had been.

So, she smiled brightly, concealing the hurt and, neatly avoiding a direct answer to his question, for even now Emma found she could not lie, said, 'I'm fine. And you? Are you well? And Jamie? How – ' her voice faltered ever so slightly, 'is Jamie?'

William's eyes darkened. 'Well enough,' he said brusquely in tones that were quite unlike his usual self.

She stared at him. 'William? What is it? Is something wrong? Is – is he ill? Tell me.'

William shook his head. 'No, oh no,' he said harshly, his expression grim. 'He's not ill, unless he's sick in his head.'

Emma gasped. 'Whatever do you mean?'

He sighed and the anger seemed to drain from him leaving only a great sadness. 'We do nothing but quarrel. All the time. I'm not sure just how much more I can take. If it doesn't stop soon, I – I think I shall leave.'

'Leave? Oh no, William. You can't leave. I – I . . .'

As she hesitated, she saw a spark in William's eyes and his hand suddenly covered hers that still lay on his arm. 'What, Em?' he prompted ever so softly.

She swallowed and said, 'What about Jamie? You can't leave him to cope alone. Not after he's been through so much in the war. You know how hard it was for you. Things will get better. You'll see. He'll come around.'

The light died in the young man's eyes. 'Will he, Emma?' His voice was heavy with sadness and a kind of defeat. 'He didn't for you, did he?' For a long moment, amidst the bustle and jostling of the crowded market place, they stood and stared at each other. 'I wonder,' he said slowly, 'if my brother will ever realize what an utter fool he's been.'

Then, pulling away from her he turned suddenly, and was gone and, though she stood and watched him, he did not look back.

Sixteen

'Where's my tea? Where've you been gallivanting off to now, girl?'

'I've been to the butcher's, that's all,' Emma said, outwardly calm though her heart was pounding with anger she knew she must hold in check. She wanted to shout and scream and demand to be told what deal had been struck between Harry Forrest and Leonard, a deal in which she was the pawn.

'Well, I've work to do and I need me tea 'afore I start. The wind's getting up now. I'll be working all night.'

She turned away and busied herself at the kitchen range. Trying to keep her voice level, she remarked with apparent innocence, 'Luke will have started Ben Popple's grain.'

She bit her lip and held her breath. Had she given herself away already, revealing that she knew it was Farmer Popple's grain that was waiting to be ground? Emma chided herself. She really was no good at trying to be devious and was too honest for her own good sometimes. But her father, caught up in his own thoughts, did not appear to notice. His reply was a grunt and a doubtful, 'Mebbe so.'

He ate the meal she placed before him, rose from the table and, without a word of thanks, moved to the door. His hand on the latch, he glanced back at her. 'When will that husband of yours be home? I might need his help tonight.'

She shrugged. 'He went to Lincoln this morning but couldn't tell me how long he would be away. He took a suitcase with him, so I suppose he'll stay overnight at least.'

Harry Forrest frowned, grunted with irritation and left the kitchen.

Emma completed her household chores and turned down the lamp. She hesitated, pondering whether she should go across the yard to the mill to help her father, knowing that he was completely alone there. But for once, she remained coldly resolute and readied herself for bed, only to lie awake far into the night, listening to the rhythmic sound of the mills sails, turning, turning in the darkness.

What time she fell asleep she did not know, but she awoke with a start in the half light of early morning. Emma swung her legs out of bed and stood up to be overcome at once by a feeling of dizziness and nausea. It must be reaction from a restless night and yesterday's upset. She had scarcely reached the washstand before beginning to retch, leaning over the bowl until she felt pale and exhausted. She wanted to do nothing more than to creep back into bed until someone brought her a cup of tea.

But there was little chance of that. This morning there was not only no Leonard – as usual – she thought bitterly, but it was more than likely that there would be no Sarah or Luke either. She dressed hurriedly. Shivering and still feeling queasy, she went downstairs to a cold kitchen and a silent and deserted bakehouse.

Opening the back door she could see the sails still turning against the pale light of dawn. Her father had worked all night. She knew he must be exhausted, and felt a moment's guilt. But it was only for a moment when she remembered again the quarrel which had caused all this. Sighing, she bent to pick up the bellows to blow the embers in the range into life and set the kettle on the hob. At least she would make them both a cup of tea before she tackled the work in the bakehouse. Freshly baked bread would most definitely be late this morning and she well knew the grumbling that would cause amongst their customers.

As she carried a mug of tea across the yard, her mouth was pursed with disapproval at yesterday's quarrel, never mind the inner anguish it was causing her.

'Oh, you've decided to stir yourself, have you?' was the only greeting her father gave her. In silence she handed him the mug and turned to leave.

'I could use some help here. I've been up all night.'

'Have you really?' she said carefully. 'Well, Luke should be here any moment and then you can come across for your breakfast. He's late though. He hasn't even lit the fires in the bakehouse. Perhaps I ought to go and see if anything's wrong.'

'You'll do no such thing,' her father barked. 'Leave 'im be. We had words yesterday and I 'spect he's doing it to pay me back.'

'Oh well, it's not the first time,' Emma said airily, though she lowered her gaze lest he should notice the glint in her eyes. 'And with you two, I don't expect it'll be the last.'

His only reply was a grunt.

'I'd better go and get things started, but I shall be behind all day if I've everything to do.'

He blinked and stared at her. 'Eh?'

'Sarah's not come into work either. We're on our own. Father.'

'It was 'im I sacked, not her.'

Emma forced surprise on to her face as she said, 'Sacked him? You *sacked* Luke?'

'He were getting far too uppity. He had no right to say what he did.'

Keeping her voice level, Emma asked, 'And what was that, Father?'

'Never you mind, girl,' he growled. 'Ya'd best get into yon bakehouse if we're to have any bread to sell today. Go and fetch Sarah.'

'I doubt she'll come. If that's what's happened, she's going to take his side, isn't she?'

'Huh, so that's how it is, is it? And after all I've done for him over the years. I've a good mind to turn 'em out of the cottage an' all. But I tell you one thing, girl, I'll not tek him back, not now, not if he were to beg me on bended knees, I won't. And I'll mek sure he'll have to go cap in hand if he wants to work anywhere in this village again.'

'It'll likely you'll be the one going cap in hand, Father,' she flung back over her shoulder as she left the mill and went back towards the house.

'Never!' Harry Forrest roared into the sharp morning air. 'Never in a million years.'

'We don't need that nosey old beggar any longer,' Harry Forrest decided the following morning when once more neither Luke nor Sarah appeared. 'Just 'cos we grew up together he reckons he can let his mouth say what it likes and get away with it. Well, he's gone too far this time.'

'We can't manage to run things without Luke and Sarah, Father, and you know it.' Emma faced up to him. 'I can't possibly manage the bakehouse and the bakery on my own, nor can you manage that mill single-handed.'

'Bridget will help you in the bakery,' Harry Forrest decided. 'And I'll get a lad from the village to help me in the mill.'

146

'Why don't you ask Leonard—'

Almost before the words had left her mouth, her father snapped a reply. 'Yon lad's got his own affairs to attend to. He dun't want nowt to do wi' the mill. He told me that 'afore you was wed.'

'Did he indeed?' Emma said quietly and her eyes narrowed as she regarded her father thoughtfully. 'Why was that then?'

'Eh?' he grunted. 'Why? Obvious, ain't it? He dun't know owt about milling. You know he dun't.'

'But a young man like him can always learn, if he'd a mind.'

'Well, he hasn't,' Harry said shortly.

'But you were ready to ask him to help the other night,' she put in slyly. 'When you had to work all night on your own.'

'That was different. That was an emergency. If the lad 'ad been here, I'm sure he'd have given me a hand. Just the once.'

'Perhaps Leonard wouldn't mind helping you now and then. I'll ask him, if you like.'

'I've told you "no" and you'll do as I say.' He turned away. 'I ain't time to be standing here arguing with you, girl.'

Emma stood a moment longer watching him cross the yard, her troubled eyes watching him thoughtfully. Why, she wondered, was her father so adamant that Leonard was not to be involved in the mill now, even though in the quarrel with Luke he had said that the mill would be Leonard's one day? She had imagined that the deal must have been that if he agreed to marry her, Leonard would inherit the mill when her father died. She frowned. But that was what her father had always scathingly predicted would be the demand of any young man who could be persuaded

147

to marry her. Why, then, had he agreed to that very thing? Was it just because Leonard was Bridget's son and Harry Forrest, being besotted by the mother, was prepared to promise the son anything, even his family's mill? And why then, did Leonard want nothing to do with the mill? If he had no interest in the mill, what then had been in the 'deal' for him?

Emma gave a slight shake of her head, more confused than ever, sighed and went into the bakehouse to light the ovens.

'Luke won't let me come back to work,' Sarah stood awkwardly outside the back door three days after the quarrel had occurred, as if she dare not even cross the threshold. She shifted her weight uneasily from one foot to the other, her normally smiling face sober and her eyes troubled. 'I've tried reasoning with him – pleading. I even turned on the water taps, but he won't budge.' The woman bit her lip. 'How are you going to manage, Emma lass?'

Emma was surprised. Usually Sarah could win Luke round about most things in the end. This time, it seemed, was different.

'Goodness knows . . .' she began.

From the bakery at the front, came the sound of tinkling laughter and, hearing it, Sarah's eyes widened.

Emma nodded towards the shop. 'Bridget – Mrs Smith. Father has asked her to come and help out in the mornings.'

Sarah's mouth formed a rounded, silent 'oh' and she shrugged her plump shoulders. 'Oh, well then,' she said aloud, 'if you've got some help, then it's not so bad.' But there was a hurt deep in her eyes and her round face sagged into lines of sadness.

Emma gave a snort of wry amusement. 'She didn't get

here until ten o'clock. Day's half gone then – at least a baker's day.'

At that Sarah pulled a face in an expression of sympathy and said again, 'Oh.' And added, 'Like that, is it?'

'Yes. It is "like that".'

'Emma dear,' came Bridget's high-pitched voice. 'How much are these little bread bun things?'

Emma sighed. 'I'll have to go, Sarah, but I'll come over this evening to see you both.'

'I won't go back. He can throw us out on the street, if he likes. I don't care. I'm in the right – and he knows it.'

'What started it all anyway?' she asked, still pretending that she knew nothing.

Luke's frown deepened. 'Never you mind.'

Emma could not remember ever having seen Luke so incensed. The quarrel between her father and his lifelong friend and employee went deep, much deeper, Emma felt, than she or Sarah could understand.

She sighed. 'He'll not throw you out. He'd not do that.'

Luke grunted. 'Mebbe not. But I'm not sure I want to live in a place belonging to Harry Forrest any longer.'

'Oh, Luke, no!' Sarah's eyes were wide with fear. 'We can't uproot. This is our home. What about me bees?' Then as a fresh thought came to her, Sarah turned her worried eyes on Emma. 'Oh, Emma – I can still look after the bees, can't I? I – I mean by rights, they're yours, but . . .'

For the first time since the dreadful quarrel that was causing all this disruption in their lives, Emma smiled and gave Sarah a swift hug, 'Of *course* you can still look after the bees. We certainly don't want them deserting us just now.'

'Oh, thank you. I couldn't bear it, especially as they're a

bit unsettled now—' Sarah broke off and looked towards Luke who gave a slight shake of his head.

Emma glanced from one to the other and then back again. 'Unsettled? The bees? How do you mean?'

Sarah fingered the edge of her apron, running it between her fingers. 'Oh, it's nothing. Nothing really.'

'No, it isn't "nothing" to you, Sarah. Is it because of this quarrel? Please tell me.'

The two women looked towards Luke, but he was silent, refusing to look at either of them. He sat in his chair at the side of the range and packed his clay pipe with tobacco, his mouth a tight, unyielding line.

Suddenly he said, 'Mebbe, mebbe not.' Slowly he turned his head to look at Emma. 'The bees have deserted one of the hives. The one she put a piece of your wedding cake in.'

Emma stared at him, mystified. This was one custom she had not heard of before. 'Cake?' she asked. 'My wedding cake? Why?' She turned to Sarah. 'Why, Sarah?'

'We allus put a piece of funeral cake and a drop of wine in the hives when someone in the family dies. We did it when ya grandpa was killed and when ya mam died. It's a custom.'

Emma nodded. That much she did know. 'But I've never heard about doing it with wedding cake.'

'No more had I,' Luke stabbed the air with his pipe. 'That's 'er own daft idea and look where it's got her. All worried and upset now 'cos she thinks the bees don't approve of your marriage.' He sniffed. 'Mind you, mebbe them bees have got more sense than I've given 'em credit for, 'cos I don't approve of it either. But,' he added swiftly, 'if you're happy, Emma lass, then I'll say no more about it, 'cos you're the only person I'm bothered about now.'

'Oh, Luke,' Emma said sadly. 'Don't say that. Not after all the years you and my father have been friends.'

150

But the old man sat in his chair gazing into the fire, his teeth clamped stubbornly on his pipe, refusing to say any more.

Emma sighed and glanced at Sarah, who shrugged helplessly. Wearily, knowing there was nothing else she could do, Emma got to her feet. Suddenly, such a wave of nausea and dizziness swept over her, that she sat down again, holding her head in her hands.

'What is it, Emma? What's the matter?' Sarah was instantly at her side.

'I don't know. I just felt so dizzy. All the upset, I suppose. And I haven't eaten since dinner time.' She made as if to rise again but Sarah pressed her back into the chair.

'Sit there, love, and I'll get you a bite to eat.'

Emma did as she was told. A cold sweat broke out on her forehead and the room seemed to swim. She bent forward, her head was resting on her knees until the dizziness subsided. When she raised her head again carefully and opened her eyes, it was to see Luke watching her with troubled, guilty eyes.

Seventeen

'So, old Luke's not working for you any more then?'

Emma, bending over one of the market stalls to examine the fruit, felt the breath leave her body. Slowly she straightened up and turned to face the man standing behind her.

Outwardly calm, she said, 'Good morning, Jamie. How are you?' How she managed to keep her voice steady, she could not imagine, when her heart was fluttering inside her chest and her knees were trembling just at the sight of him.

Before her stood the scowling, bitter man that Jamie Metcalfe had become, and yet at the mere sound of his voice, Emma could not forget the laughing young fellow he had once been. Still, deep in her heart, she held the memory of the Jamie she had loved. Even she dare not question what her feelings for him were now. Without being able to prevent it, bright colour suffused her pale face. She tried to smile, and, deliberately avoiding his question, said, 'You look much better than when you first came home. More – more like your old self,' she could not help adding, though the catch in her voice threatened to give her away.

But Jamie was not about to allow her to avoid his probing. 'Your fancy new husband taken over then, has he, and pushed poor old Luke on to the scrap heap?'

'No,' she retorted hotly. 'Leonard is not involved with the mill at all.'

At this, Jamie's dark eyebrows lifted. 'Really?' he said and there was no hiding the surprise, nor the disbelief, in

152

his voice. 'Can't give up the bright lights of the city so easily, eh, to bury himself in the country?'

'Oh, *you*,' she began. 'Whatever he did, it wouldn't suit you, would it?'

With one stride he came close to her, his dark eyes looking down into her upturned face. Irrationally, she was reminded once again that he had always been, and still was, the only man she knew who was physically taller than she was; the only man whose very presence made her feel small and feminine. His frame had filled out again and the pallor of the trenches, though perhaps not the memory, was gone. His shoulders were broad and muscular, his waist slim and his legs long and straight and sturdy.

'I hate the very sight of him,' Jamie said through clenched teeth.

'Why?' Emma gasped. 'What harm has he ever done to you?'

His face was even closer to her, so close she could feel his breath warm on her cheek. 'He married my girl.'

Her eyes widened. 'But – but you . . .'

'Em – Emma!' She heard her name called and Jamie give a sigh of annoyance before he stepped back from her, but he made no attempt to move right away as his brother joined them.

William was smiling. 'Em, how lovely to see you. How are you?'

Fighting to gain her composure, Emma stammered, 'I'm fine – fine. How – how are you?'

Now it was William who leant towards her, his concerned glance raking her face.

'You don't *look* fine. You look very tired.'

'She's overworked,' Jamie put in before she could answer William. 'Her *husband* does little or nothing around the place and Luke's no longer working at the mill.'

'Luke? Why, what's the matter. Is he ill?'

Emma shook her head. 'No. He and my father quarrelled. They'll make it up eventually, but you know how stubborn they can be.' She glanced at Jamie, thinking fleetingly that it was not just her father and Luke Robson who could be stupidly bullheaded.

'And in the meantime,' William took the words from her mouth. 'You're trying to cope with all the work.'

She nodded.

'Right. I'll be over in the morning to give you a hand in the bakehouse.'

'Oh no, you won't,' his older brother thundered. 'You've enough work of your own. You let the business go to wrack and ruin once, I'll not see it happen again.'

Calmly, William said, 'I can spare an hour or two first thing in the morning.'

'No, you can't. Mester Leighton wants his wagon back by tomorrow afternoon.'

'Well, I'm not seeing Emma killing herself for want of a helping hand.'

She put out her hand and touched William's arm. 'It's all right. I don't want to be the cause of trouble between the two of you, please.'

William turned to her, his eyes on a level with her brilliant violet gaze. 'You won't,' he said softly. 'And I'll be over in the morning.'

Jamie turned on his heel and marched away towards the brick archway leading to the smithy, fury in every stride.

It was the first time, Emma thought as she walked home, that she could remember William standing up to his elder brother.

*

When Leonard returned home from his three-day trip to the city, he came loaded with presents. Tobacco for his father-in-law, a silk blouse and a soft, midnight blue velvet skirt for Emma. 'And chocolates too,' he teased, his eyes bright with good humour. 'But don't eat them all at once and get fat, will you, darling.' His hands reached out and his fingers spanned her waist. 'Hey, what's this?' he joked. 'I think you are putting on a little around here.'

'Well, it's surprising if I am,' Emma replied shortly. 'With all the trouble. I'm too tired to eat properly and I feel sick all the time.'

'Trouble, what trouble?'

She told him briefly what had occurred during his absence. 'Can you help us out a little, Leonard? Your mother's been – ' she swallowed on the slight untruth, 'a wonderful help.' At least, Emma thought to herself, Bridget had done her willing best. 'But Father really can't manage the mill on his own.'

A frown swept away Leonard's good mood. 'Work in the mill? Me? You've got to be joking, Emma.' He spread out his hands in front of her. Large, well-shaped hands though they were, she could see at once they had never done a day's manual work in their lives. The palms were smooth and white, the nails perfectly shaped, looking almost as if they had been professionally manicured.

Emma sighed and touched the soft velvet of the skirt he had brought her. 'Thank you for the presents, Leonard. They are lovely, but goodness knows when I'll get the chance to wear them now.'

'You can wear them next Friday. I'm taking you and Mother into Lincoln for the day. You two can go shopping and then we can all meet for lunch at . . .'

Emma shook her head. 'Oh, Leonard, it's kind of you,

but I can't. I can't leave here. There's no one to mind the shop now, let alone—'

His generous, expansive mood was gone in an instant. 'Oh, very well, then. Have it your own way. But I shall take my mother. You're not going to turn her into a drudge too.' He turned and strode towards the back door, flung it open, sending it crashing back and then marched across the yard towards the gate.

Emma bit her lip. He was running back to his mother, to be cosseted and pampered and spoilt like the small boy that he still was, she thought resentfully.

She took a deep breath. 'Well,' she said aloud to the empty kitchen. 'Looks like there's no help coming from that direction, m'girl, or from Bridget today.' With a sigh, she turned and went through to the shop, leaving her fancy new clothes lying in their boxes on the kitchen table.

The days passed and Emma still felt sick all the time, especially when she first rose in the half-light of the early hours to drag herself downstairs into the bakehouse. It persisted every morning, until white-faced, she went to see Sarah.

'Can't you persuade Luke to let you come back at least?' she said without preamble as she allowed herself to be ushered into the kitchen of the small cottage and pressed into a chair at the table. 'Bridget's a willing soul, but she's no idea. She spends most of the time chatting and laughing with the customers, and although William's been a brick coming to help first thing in the morning, it just isn't the same.'

'And what's ya dad had to say about *that*?'

'A Metcalfe coming to the mill, you mean?'

Sarah nodded.

Emma pulled a wry face. 'He hasn't *said* anything, but if looks could kill.'

The older woman shook her head. 'Aye, I know. But sit down a minute, lass. You look done in. Eh, I feel so guilty, but my Luke's adamant. We're not to set foot inside the mill or the bakehouse – either of us – till ya dad apologizes.'

'Then we'll all be waiting a long time.' She gave a groan and dropped her head on to her arms as they lay folded on the table. 'Oh Sarah,' she mumbled. 'If only I didn't feel so sick all the time.'

'Eh? What's that you say?' Sarah was patting her arm. 'Look at me, Emma.'

Slowly Emma raised her white face and looked up into the older woman's face. She knew there were dark smudges of weariness beneath her eyes and her skin, normally glowing with health and vitality, had given way to a white, unhealthy pallor. She felt so bone-weary she could cry and indeed, under Sarah's kindly scrutiny, tears sprang to Emma's eyes. To her surprise, however, Sarah was smiling.

'You're expecting, Emma lass. That's what's the matter with you.'

Emma's eyes were large and brilliant against the paleness of her skin. Stupidly she stuttered, 'You mean – a baby?'

Sarah nodded. 'Yes, lass. A baby. You're going to have a baby. Why, it's not so surprising, is it?'

'Well, no, I suppose not. But . . .' She stopped and was silent whilst she took in all that this meant.

A child. She was going to have a child. And that child could be a boy. A grandson for Harry Forrest.

Suddenly, without needing to be told, she knew what the deal – or at least part of it – had been between her father and Leonard Smith. 'Marry my daughter and give me a grandson.' But what had Leonard got out of the deal in return, she wondered, apart from the promise of the mill? A mill he did not seem to have any interest in at all. So, Emma pondered, there must have been something else. She could not begin to guess what that had been, but obviously it had appealed to Leonard, it had been sufficient to bribe the young man to marry her and produce a grandson for Harry; a future heir for the mill who would have Forrest blood in his veins. Unbidden, the thought thrust its way into her mind; that at the same time, her father's plan had prevented the mill from ever passing into the hands of the Metcalfe family. In one 'deal' Harry Forrest had brought about the two things he wanted most. But what, Emma still wondered, had he promised Leonard Smith in return? What was Leonard getting out of it now?

'Aren't you pleased, lass? You seem very quiet.' Sarah's question interrupted her thoughts.

Emma forced a smile on to her lips. 'Yes, yes, of course I am. I was just thinking, that's all.'

'Now don't you go thinking about what happened to ya mam,' Sarah patted her hand, misinterpreting Emma's preoccupied thoughts completely. 'You're built differently to ya mam. Childbearing hips you've got, me lass, an' no mistake. Ya mam was thin and delicate, not really made for it at all. No, you'll be fine. And besides – ' Sarah's grin broadened, 'I'll be there when ya time comes, don't you worry.'

'Really?' Emma looked up at her. 'Will you come?'

'Couldn't keep me away. Ne'er mind these stupid men and their quarrels.' She thought a moment and then said, ''Sides, this puts a different light on all that anyway. We can't let you go on trying to cope with all that work yasen. You leave it with me, Emma.' Again she patted Emma's arm. 'I'll speak to Luke.'

Emma hid her smile. Despite the fact that Sarah always led everyone to believe she obeyed and deferred to her husband in all things, the truth was that in reality she twisted the older man around her little finger. It had been a surprise to Emma that Sarah had not persuaded Luke to return to work before now.

'Oh, Sarah,' Emma said thankfully. 'What would I do without you?'

Sarah smiled and moved towards the back door and reached down her coat. 'I won't be a minute. There's just something I have to do.' Before Emma could speak again, Sarah had lifted the latch on the back door and hurried out. Through the window, Emma saw her scurrying towards the orchard.

Tears of laughter ran down Emma's face. 'Oh, Sarah, Sarah,' she murmured.

Even before her own husband or her father knew of Emma's forthcoming 'happy event', the bees would be informed.

Eighteen

Her husband was the first person to hear the news from Emma. He smiled, put his arms about her shoulders and kissed her forehead. 'Why, you clever girl. Your father will be delighted.'

She watched him carefully. 'What about you, Leonard? Are you pleased?'

'Of course I am.' Deliberately, it seemed to her, he puffed out his chest. 'Any man likes to sire a child, especially if it's a boy.' Then he threw back his head and laughed. 'Though I'm not so sure my mother will like being a *grandmother*.'

Emma felt her mouth twitching at the thought of the glamorous, flirtatious Bridget Smith becoming a grandmother. She was hardly everyone's picture of a typical grandmother.

'But she'll spoil it rotten,' he was saying. 'Mind you, I expect she'd like a girl to dress up in pretty clothes, but your father . . .'

He left the words unspoken, but Emma murmured, 'Yes, my father . . .'

They both knew full well what Harry Forrest would want the child to be.

'A son! A grandson!'

Emma watched her father's face. The deep, perpetual frown on his forehead lightened and his mouth stretched

160

into a wide, genuine grin. 'My dear girl . . .' He held out his arms and came towards her, enveloping her awkwardly in his embrace.

She could not remember when she had last seen her father quite so happy. Even his satisfaction at her marriage did not come close to his delight now. Emma stood rigidly, so unused to such a display of affection from him, that she did not know how to respond.

'I'm glad you're pleased,' she said faintly.

'Pleased? I'll say I'm pleased. At last, an heir for Forrest's Mill.'

'Father, I'm only two or three months gone. And it – it may not be a boy.'

'Of course it'll be a boy.' He rubbed his hands together, refusing to be thwarted in his hopes, not this time. 'At last,' he said again, more to himself than to his daughter. 'Old Charlie's dreams will come true. I shan't have failed him after all.'

Oh, Father, Emma moaned silently. Don't get your hopes up so much. It could all end in bitter disappointment. But she kept these thoughts to herself, not wanting to spoil the moment either for her father or for herself. It was something she wanted to savour.

'Have you told Leonard yet?'

'Yes, yes, I told him just before he went away.' She paused, remembering how it had been Harry Forrest's anticipated delight that had been Leonard's first thought, rather than his own pleasure at becoming a father.

She looked up quickly. 'Father, do *you* know just what his business is?'

Harry Forrest avoided her questioning gaze. 'Oh – er – I dunno. A bit o' this and a bit o' that. Ya know.'

'No,' Emma said quietly. 'That's exactly it. I don't know.'

'Women shouldn't trouble their pretty heads about such things.' He waved his hand dismissively in the air. 'You've got enough to do, lass, and now you'll soon have a babby.' He beamed again. 'You leave Leonard to his own affairs. He's a good husband, ain't he?'

Slowly, she said, 'Well, yes, I suppose so . . .'

'There you are, then. You be a good wife – and mother.' Now there was a note of pride in his voice. 'That's all I – we – ask of you.'

She looked at him sharply, but her father had turned away saying over his shoulder, 'You'll have to stop doing so much of the heavy work now, Emma.'

She opened her mouth to retort 'And how do you expect me to do that when you've sacked Luke?' but instead, she said with deliberate casualness, 'Why don't you ask Leonard to help out in the mill?'

Her father swung round, the frown back on his face. 'Now you leave things be, Emma. You hear me? You're still my daughter and this is still my house. You'll do as I say. Leonard's all right. He wants no part in the running of the mill. I've told you that 'afore. Don't keep going on about it, girl. It was all agreed 'afore you was wed—' Harry stopped abruptly, as if his sharpness had almost led him to let slip more than he intended.

'Was it indeed?' Emma's eyes narrowed. 'And what exactly was agreed?'

He stabbed his forefinger towards her. 'It's nowt to do with you. It's between him and me. I've told you, you attend to your womanly duties. The home and your child. I want a grandson, Emma, and you'd better not do anything to cheat me of one.' He turned and left the house, banging the door behind him.

There! It was said. His joy was not really for her. All he

wanted, all he had ever wanted, was a boy-child to fulfil old Charlie's dreams.

'Luke, won't you come back to work? Please? We really can't manage without you or Sarah. You know full well we can't.'

They were standing in the middle of the yard, all five of them: Emma, her father and Leonard, Luke and Sarah. There had been a moment's awkwardness as, in an uncomfortable coincidence, they had all come into the yard at the same moment. It was early one Monday morning. Leonard was about to leave for Lincoln and Emma was walking with him to the gate. Harry, too, had paused to bid his son-in-law goodbye before he crossed the yard to begin work in the mill. At that moment, Luke and Sarah appeared from the orchard and began to cross the yard towards the gate before they realized the presence of the other three. Seizing the moment, Emma had greeted them as they made to pass by without a word.

Luke stopped and Sarah, her arm through his, was obliged to do so too. The older man's glance flickered towards Harry Forrest. Slowly Luke answered her, but in a tone that made it obvious to them all that he was in no way apologizing. 'I will come back, aye, but only because of you, Emma.' Luke shook his fist towards Harry and Leonard. 'This poor lass'll pull 'er guts out for the pair of you selfish beggars. Aye, an' you'd both let 'er and all.' His eyes turned towards Leonard. 'I've no time for you, lad, as ya probably know 'cos I reckon there's more gone on between you and this new father-in-law of yours than any of us knows about.'

Emma saw the look that passed between her father and

her husband and she wondered afresh. Luke's sharp eyes had not missed the exchange either for as his tirade continued, he said, 'Ya might well look at each other. Time you acted as a husband and stayed home of a night wi'out gallivanting off to the bright lights of the city. And as for you – ' he prodded his forefinger towards Harry Forrest, 'you've never acted as a proper father to 'er, forever moping that you wanted a son.'

Harry's scowl deepened. 'And you have, I suppose?'

'I care for Emma as if she were me own. Both me an' my Sarah do. So, mek no mistake, Harry Forrest, it's for ya girl's sake I'm coming back to me work and for no other reason. You hear me?'

'And who ses I'll have you back, eh?'

Before either of them could speak again, Emma said firmly. 'I do.'

Harry raised his hand and pointed at her. 'Now you listen here, m'girl . . .' he began and then, as he met her steady, unflinching gaze, he faltered. His hand fell away and his glance dropped lower, towards the slight roundness of her belly. With a grunt, he turned on his heel and walked towards the granary to start heaving sacks about in a temper.

Luke grinned wryly and set off towards the mill, leaving Leonard standing in the middle of the yard dressed in his smart suit, a red flower in his buttonhole and his hair, parted in the centre, slicked down.

'Silly old duffer,' he muttered, then he turned, grinned broadly at Emma, pecked her on the cheek, set his Homburg at a jaunty angle on his head and said, 'Well, I'd better be off then. See you sometime, darlin'. Take good care of yourself – and our son.'

Emma watched as he walked towards the yard gate, a swagger in every step. He gave her a cheerful wave and set off up the road towards the market place, carrying the small suitcase that meant his absence was going to be at least one night and, she was learning, probably even longer. She sighed. Obviously, Leonard had no intention of changing his ways. Luke's words had certainly fallen on deaf ears as far as her husband was concerned but at least Luke, and Sarah too, were back.

She held out her arms and, with tears in her eyes, said, 'Oh, Sarah, Sarah, thank goodness!'

The weeks and months passed and they all settled back into the routine, though because of Emma's condition, there were changes for her. She was no longer allowed to do any heavy lifting and Sarah made sure she rested every afternoon. 'If you still insist on getting up so early, Emma, to start in the bakehouse, you must have a rest later in the day. Think of the bairn, lass, even if not yourself.'

Emma sighed. 'You're right, I know. I do seem to get dreadfully tired now.' And with every passing week, as she grew larger, she found her work more exhausting.

'Get a bit of fresh air, lass,' Sarah persuaded her. 'Go for a walk up to the market place. You're looking so pale. The heat in this bakery's too much for you.'

It was late September, just over a year now since they had been married and the last few days had been surprisingly hot and sultry. 'Do you know, I think I will,' Emma said and straightened up, pressing her hand into her aching back. She had only a week or so to go before her time and she was so big now that she could scarcely bend forward to knead the dough.

The previous evening there had been a thunderstorm that had cleared the air and today, though it was still warm, there was a hint of a breeze that was cooling and refreshing as she walked up the gentle rise of the street and turned into the market place.

'Em.' She heard her name being called and knew, even before she turned and saw him standing there, who it would be. Only one person ever called her 'Em'.

He was standing beneath the archway between the two workshops, but to her surprise he was not dressed in his working clothes on this weekday morning, but in his Sunday best.

'Hello, William. You're all dressed up. Are you off to town?' As she waddled towards him, she saw him glance down at the bulge she carried in front of her and then his embarrassed gaze flickered away.

He seemed ill at ease and, when he did not answer at once, she prompted. 'What is it? Is something wrong?'

Now he looked at her fully, returning her gaze steadily, but in his eyes was an expression of deep sorrow. Her heart missed a beat. She caught her breath as she asked unsteadily, 'Is it – Jamie?'

His mouth twisted wryly. 'No,' he said harshly and then added, 'well, yes, in a way I suppose it is. I . . .' He hesitated, glanced away awkwardly and then met her gaze again.

'William, what *is* it?'

'I was coming to see you this very morning.' His glance dropped away again and his head drooped. 'I'm – leaving.'

'Leaving?' she gasped, her mouth falling open in shock. 'Whatever do you mean?'

'I've got a job away from here.'

Her violet eyes were wide, staring at him. 'Oh no, William, you can't go away. What shall I . . .?' she began. His head jerked up and there was a flash of hope in his eyes. But already the next words were out of her mouth

166

before she could stop them. 'What about Jamie? You're really going to leave him?'

'I am,' he said, adding, with a hardness so unlike the gentle William, 'We'll see how he likes being left alone to run two businesses. Let's see if the marvellous Jamie Metcalfe can manage single-handed.'

'Oh, William,' she said gently, saddened by the bitterness she heard in her friend's voice. There was silence between them, then she asked, 'Where are you going?'

'I'm going to work for the millwrights in Bilsford. John Pickering. His son's about my age. I reckon I can make a go of it.'

Impulsively she reached out and touched his arm. 'Of course you will. But I – I'll miss you dreadfully.'

Now his intense gaze was upon her. 'Will you?' He took her hand in his and gently kissed the roughened fingers. 'I'll miss you, Em, more than you'll ever know.'

'Let me have your address and maybe after the baby's born I can get over to see you. Bilsford's not that far away.' But even as she spoke, she knew it would not be possible. With all the work there was to do and with the added responsibility of a child, there would be little time for Emma to go 'gallivanting'.

William knew it too but he smiled and said dutifully, 'That would be nice.' He nodded towards her bulging stomach. 'I hope all goes well with—'

Emma laughed. 'I can't wait for the day now. It feels heavier than a sack of wheat,' she pulled a face, 'but I can't put *this* down for a rest!'

He smiled, but the laughter did not reach his eyes. 'Take care of yourself, Em,' he said in a hoarse whisper. 'You know where I am if – if ever you need me.'

She nodded as the lump in her throat robbed her

suddenly of her voice. She watched in silence as he turned and walked away from her up the village street, around the corner and out of her sight.

Bilsford might only be ten miles away from Marsh Thorpe, but at that moment, as she watched her childhood friend walk away from her, to Emma it felt like a million miles.

Nineteen

'Oh, Sarah! It hurts!' She clung to the bed post, her knuckles white, sweat beading her forehead.

'Of course it does, lass,' said Sarah in a matter-of-fact manner.

Emma opened her mouth, then bit back the remark just in time. She had been about to say 'And how would you know?' But it would have been a cruel remark to the childless Sarah, and not quite true anyway. Sarah might not have suffered the pain of childbirth herself, but she had helped many a baby into the world and had seen the mothers suffer each in their individual way.

''Sides,' the older woman continued, knowing nothing of Emma's moment of inner conflict. 'Soon as you hold your babby in your arms, the pain goes,' she paused a moment and then added wistfully, 'so they say.'

Emma was even more grateful that she had managed to bite back the words from escaping her rash tongue.

'Have you sent for the doctor?'

'Aye, ya dad's seen to that.' Sarah smiled. 'Pacing up and down the bakehouse, he is. Left Luke to cope alone across at the mill. Anyone'd think he was the father.' She paused and wagged her finger in the air at no one in particular. 'Aye, an' that's another thing. The father *ought* to be here, and ain't!'

As the pains subsided, Emma allowed herself a wry smile. It was ironic. All her life, she had suffered her

169

father's taunts for daring to be a girl. She had never felt herself loved, nor even wanted, by him. Yet now, it was him pacing the floor beneath, he who waited to see if at last she could give him what he most wanted.

And her husband? Well, to be fair, Leonard hadn't known the child would come a week earlier than anticipated. He'd promised to be back by the weekend and then to stay at home until the child was born.

'I'm going up, Harry. Emma could do with another woman with her. One who's had a child.'

As she heard Bridget's high-pitched voice on the stairs, Emma cast a glance at Sarah's face. She must have heard the thoughtless remark, but the kindly Sarah's face remained placid. The bedroom door was flung wide and Bridget made her entrance just as another contraction gripped Emma, who screwed up her face in agony. With her long black hair flowing freely to her waist, her hands gripping the bedpost, her white nightdress stained with sweat and the groaning that escaped her dry lips, she must have presented the spectacle of a mad woman.

Bridget let out a small, ladylike scream and clapped her mauve gloved hand to her mouth. 'Oh, my dear, shouldn't you be on the bed – or – or something?' she finished weakly.

The pain receded and Emma gave a short laugh of amusement. She could imagine that Bridget had mounted the stairs with the thought of sitting at her bedside, soothing her brow, holding her hand. Perhaps Sarah was right. Perhaps you did forget the whole undignified business once it was all over. Certainly, the elegant, fussily-dressed Bridget standing wide-eyed in the doorway didn't look at that moment as if she had ever given birth in her life.

'Oh!' Emma's eyes widened. 'Sarah, what's happening? I'm all wet.'

Sarah beamed. 'Good girl. That's ya waters broken. Right, on to the bed with ya.'

Heaving and grunting and with Sarah's help, Emma got herself on to the high bed.

'Right, let's have a look at ya. Bend ya knees – legs apart . . .'

She flung back Emma's nightdress and bent over her.

'I think . . .' Emma heard Bridget say weakly, 'I'll just go back downstairs.'

As the bedroom door closed, Sarah muttered, 'Good riddance. We dun't want her flappin' about when there's work to be done.'

Emma lay back, propped up against the pillows, and closed her eyes. Aye, there was work to be done all right. It seemed as if the whole of her life she'd heard the words, 'There's work to be done'.

'Come on, lass. One more push and you'll do it.'

She was exhausted, drowning in her own sweat. Her whole body was shaking with the effort and pain engulfed her now without respite. It felt as if she'd been pushing and panting for hours. Emma summoned every ounce of energy left in her body and gave one great, last push.

'Aaaah . . .'

'There! That's it! Here it comes.' Sarah's jubilant voice penetrated the mists of pain. 'It's a boy. By, an' he's a big lad, an' all. Oh, Emma, lass, it *is* a boy.'

Emma lay completely spent of all energy, all emotion. She closed her eyes and allowed Sarah to bustle about and do whatever was necessary. She lay perfectly still, holding her breath and listening for the sound of her baby's first cry, but there was silence in the room.

The bedroom door opened and Emma heard her father's voice. 'What is it? Is it a boy? Is it all right?'

Then came Sarah's worried tone. 'Yes! Yes, it's a boy. But, oh Mester, he's not breathing!'

'What? 'Ere. Give him here to me.'

'But . . .'

'Don't argue, woman.'

Weakly, Emma raised her head from the pillow and watched as her father took the slippery, unwashed infant into his hands. Then she saw him tip the baby upside down, holding the child by its heels. 'Now, come on,' Harry said. 'This is ya Grandpa.' He raised his hand and dealt the still and silent infant a sharp smack on its tiny buttocks.

'Oh, Mester . . .' Sarah began, but whatever she had been going to say was drowned by the wonderful, beautiful, miraculous sound of a disgruntled wail.

Emma let out her breath in a sigh of relief and then smiled weakly. Even her newborn child already knew who it had to obey.

By the time the doctor arrived, Emma was washed and dressed in clean linen with her baby in the cradle at the side of her bed. She was very sleepy.

'You've done very well, Emma. You have a fine, healthy son and, for a first, you've given birth relatively quickly and easily.'

Emma managed a weak smile. It hadn't felt quick or easy, but now it was over, just as Sarah had promised, the memory of the pain was, even now, receding. Against some of the horror stories she had heard whispered amongst the village women, she had undoubtedly been fortunate.

'And of course,' the doctor was saying, 'it will be even easier next time.'

At that moment there came a knock at the bedroom door and as the doctor made his farewells, Leonard stepped into the room. He came at once to the head of the bed, bent and kissed Emma's forehead and laid a huge bunch of flowers by her side. 'My dear, I'm so sorry I wasn't here. You've taken us all by surprise, I really had meant to be here . . .'

She reached up her hand and he grasped it. 'I know, Leonard. It's all right, really it is. You couldn't help it. He came early.' She twisted her head and glanced towards the cradle. 'Say "hello" to your son, Leonard.'

He turned and bent over the cradle and, smiling, touched the baby's little cheek with his forefinger. 'He's a bit red. Is he all right?'

'He's only just been in the world about two hours and it was hard work,' Emma reassured him. 'He'll be all right.'

'Was it very bad? For you, I mean.'

Touched by his concern, Emma said, 'No. Not too bad, but I'm very tired.'

'Of course you are.' He straightened up and came back to the bedside. He patted her hand and was about to turn to leave, when she caught hold of his hand again. 'What do you want to call him? Leonard? After you?'

Her husband stared down at her for a moment before he said, with surprise in his tone, 'Oh no, Emma. There's only one name we can call him. Hasn't your father told you? It's all been agreed. His name is *Charles Forrest Smith*.'

173

Twenty

'Where's she taking him?' Harry Forrest appeared in the doorway of the mill and pointed towards Sarah carrying the baby in her arms. The child was scarcely visible, buried deep in a woollen shawl which Sarah had knitted. 'Where you takin' my grandson, Sarah Robson?'

But Sarah hurried on towards the orchard and Harry started across the yard after her.

'It's all right, Father,' Emma called, stepping out into the slanting sunshine of the warm autumn day, still bright enough for the mill to cast a deep shadow across the yard, the whirling sails making moving patterns on the ground. 'She's only showing him to the bees.'

'The bees?' Harry was scandalized. 'Has the woman no sense? If that little mite gets stung . . .'

Luke, coming up behind them, said, 'Now Harry, you know Sarah wouldn't harm a hair of the bairn's head. Besides, the bees won't sting a Forrest.'

'Well, I dunno about that,' the worried grandfather sniffed. 'I know that's what *she* thinks, but I don't like to risk it. Not with my grandson.'

The three of them moved towards the edge of the yard to watch through the wide gap in the hedge as Sarah moved beneath the trees, her head bent low towards the child in her arms as if she were talking to him.

'Tell me, Harry,' Luke said softly. 'Have you ever, in the

174

whole of your life, been stung by the bees in yon orchard? By *Forrest* bees?'

'Lot of old wives' tales,' Harry muttered, avoiding giving a direct answer. 'If owt happens to my little lad . . .' He moved forward, away from Emma and Luke, to hover protectively at the edge of the trees.

Emma watched her father, a pensive smile on her lips. Already, she felt as if possession of her baby had been taken over by him. She sighed inwardly, yet with the birth of her child had come a new understanding.

'Do you know, Luke,' she said softly, 'I hardly know my father these days.'

She heard Luke's low chuckle. 'He's a changed man and no mistake. Mind you, he's more like I remember him from the old days. He were a bright spark as a young feller, full of devilment and fight. Aye, in them days there weren't many young fellers hereabouts who liked to be on the wrong end of Harry Forrest's fists. But the last few years, he's been a bad-tempered beggar and no mistake. But now you're seeing him for the man he used to be. The man he might always have been if – if . . .'

Gently, Emma finished the sentence for him. 'If he'd had a son of his own, you mean?'

'Aw lass, you know I wouldn't . . .'

She put her hand on his arm. 'I know you wouldn't say anything to hurt me, Luke. Besides, to be honest, it doesn't hurt so much now. Not now we've got young Charles. I'm just so thankful, so very thankful, my baby was a boy.'

Luke laughed out loud. 'And so say all of us. I daresunt think what life would have been like if it had been a girl.'

Emma joined in his laughter and saw her father glance back towards them, a questioning look on his face. But his inquisitiveness was only fleeting, for almost at once his attention went back to the bundle in Sarah's arms.

'He's besotted with the little chap, ain't he?'

Emma nodded. 'Yes, that's a very good word for it, Luke. Besotted.' She giggled. 'I think even "the Merry Widow" has to take second place in his affections now.'

At the baby's christening, Harry insisted on carrying the child himself even though Emma argued, 'It should be the godmother who carries him, or even one of the godfathers, not you, Father.' But her protestations fell on deaf ears. Even the choice of godparents had almost precipitated a quarrel, not between husband and wife, but between Emma and her father.

'It's bad enough you wanting Luke and Sarah Robson, but to want William Metcalfe as the second godfather, now that I can't abide. What does your husband say to it?'

'Leonard doesn't mind,' Emma said evenly. In fact, Leonard couldn't have cared less. She did not add that, because her husband was not much of a chapelgoer, he viewed the whole proceeding as a waste of time.

'What does my son need godparents for when he's got me for his father?' Leonard had said. 'I'll teach him all he needs to know.' His sudden wide grin seemed to say, and a good bit more besides, but Emma was beyond arguing; there had been enough with her father.

William, however, was godfather by proxy. To Emma's intense disappointment, he had written to say he could not come for the ceremony, though he sent a silver christening mug that must have cost far more than the young man could afford on an apprentice millwright's wage. Emma set it in the glazed corner cupboard in the best parlour and during the following weeks, her eyes often strayed towards it when she thought of her friend and how much she missed him. As for Jamie Metcalfe, she saw little of him now, for her days were filled with caring for her child and, as her strength and vigour returned, with her work in the bakehouse and bakery.

They settled into a routine, Harry and Luke working the mill, Sarah and Emma in the bakehouse and shop, and between them they all cared for the child. Only Leonard, who spent long stretches away from home on business in the city, had little time for his son. 'I can't abide babies, Emma. He'll be more interesting to me when he's grown a bit.'

But as the child grew and became a sturdy, solemn-faced little boy, Leonard still seemed to have no time to spend with his son. 'When he's older . . .' was all Leonard would say. So it was his Grandpa Harry who took Charles for walks, who held out his arms when the boy took his first, faltering steps. It was Harry who bought him his first toy engine and taught him to ride their docile pony. It was his grandfather who took the boy's hand and led him to school on his first day there.

And it was Harry who took Charles Forrest Smith all over the mill, telling him day after day, 'One day, lad, all this will be yours.'

Twenty-One

'The miserable, conniving, cheating old beggar!'

'Leonard! Not in front of the boy and at a time like this,' Emma stormed. 'Have you no respect for my father when we've only just buried him?'

The five-year-old Charles, dressed in sombre clothes as befitting the day, watched the quarrel between his parents raging above his head. His eyes followed their movements that were quick and full of anger and he cringed under the raised voices.

'Respect? Respect, you say? For that old—'

'Leonard,' Emma said again warningly and cast a meaningful glance towards their son.

The child was perhaps the one person in the room, Emma thought, who would genuinely miss Harry Forrest. From the moment of his birth, Harry had idolized his grandson. The boy was the culmination of all the old man's dreams, the answer to a prayer, after the long years of waiting for the birth of a male heir for old Charlie Forrest's mill; a boy who must, and did, bear the name of the founder of the mill.

'Everything – every bloody thing – ' Leonard spat, 'in trust for *him*.' As Leonard thrust an accusing finger towards the boy, Emma saw her son wince and blink and knew that although he did not fully understand the furious words flying above his head, Charles knew instinctively that in some way he was the centre of his father's wrath.

Emma saw that the child's hands were trembling. He was a gentle little boy, quiet and reserved. His large, dark eyes were soulful and his face, even though he played outside for much of the time, was always pale. He was rarely in trouble. Indeed, he seemed to have little daring, no spark of devilment and perhaps this, Emma thought, was what made Leonard so irritable with his son. Overshadowed by his flamboyant father, in his presence Charles seemed to fade into the background, perhaps, Emma thought shrewdly, deliberately. The five-year-old had yet to learn how to deal with the man whose fleeting visits home were sometimes a whirlwind of fun and laughter with lavish gifts and outings to the fair or the beach, while at other times, Leonard ignored the boy or shouted at him for some insignificant misdemeanour that sent Charles, whimpering, to hide his face against Emma's skirts

'He's a mother's boy,' Leonard had said scathingly more than once. 'I can see I'll have to take him in hand.'

At this moment, seeing him standing there so wide-eyed and solemn, Emma felt compassion for her son. He had still not recovered from the awful shock of seeing his grandfather fall down one of the ladders in the mill. Emma could still hear the child's terrified screams, 'Mammy, Mammy, Grandpa's hurt!' If anyone knew how such a trauma left scars on a child down the years, then Emma did. She had witnessed her own grandfather, Charlie, falling to his death from the sails of the mill and to this day, there was something she could still not remember about it; something that her mind had shut out. Sometimes in the early morning hours she would awake from a nightmare, sweating and trembling, on the brink of remembering and yet still the memory eluded her. She had been twelve at that time and had known what death meant, but young Charles did not seem to understand and was still asking, 'Where is Grandpa?'

Now, standing in the room listening to the heated words between his parents, his young, confused mind, would be wondering what he had done wrong to make his father so angry. Had he done something bad in the church, he would be thinking, or when they were lowering that long box into the ground? He couldn't remember saying or doing anything that could have been wrong. He had stood quietly by his mother's side, holding her hand, not saying anything in his piping little voice, just silently watching the other people, all of them dressed in black from head to foot. And his mother had been very proud of him; she had told him so as they walked back to the mill. When all the visitors had come back to the house to eat sandwiches and cake he had sat quietly in the corner by old Luke's side and the only thing Emma had heard him say in all that time had been a whispered 'Where's Grandpa?'

Luke had looked at him with watery eyes and said, 'He's gone, lad.'

'Gone where, Mester Robson?'

'On – on a long journey.'

'When will he come back?'

The white head had shaken, 'He won't be coming back, Charles.'

The child's lips had quivered then. 'Not ever?' Luke had not spoken then, but had only shaken his head again.

All the other mourners had gone; Luke and Sarah back to their cottage and the strange man in the long black coat, who had sat at the table and read from a piece of paper, had climbed into his noisy motor car and chugged his way out of the yard. Now only his mother and father and the boy were left in the best parlour above the shop. Emma saw Charles bite his lip, his eyes blinking rapidly as if he were trying to hold back threatening tears. She saw his glance take in the sheaf of papers lying on the table. That was what was to blame for the quarrel between his parents. Emma could read the thought on his face.

As the lawyer had been reading, they had all witnessed, the child too, the change that had come across Leonard's face. His lips had tightened, his eyes had become a steely, cold grey. His face had been pink at first, then red, and finally, his skin had turned a blotchy, furious purple. But it wasn't until everyone had gone – even Bridget, dabbing at her eyes with a lacy, perfumed handkerchief – that Leonard's anger had exploded.

As he continued to pace the floor, shaking his fist in the air and ranting, Emma was aware that the boy had crept from the room. She heard him tiptoe down the stairs and the click of the latch on the back door as he reached up to let himself out into the yard.

'Your father's cheated me, that's what,' Leonard was saying. He prodded his finger towards his wife. 'And he's cheated you too, if you only realize it. To pass over his own daughter in favour of a *child*. I ask you? Had he lost his mind, d'ya reckon? Do you think we've grounds to contest the will?'

'Hardly,' Emma said drily, watching him. 'It was drawn up and witnessed five years ago, the day after Charles's birth.' She paused and regarded her husband steadily, her head on one side. 'What exactly is it that has upset you? We still have a home and the mill for our lifetime. It was too much to hope that my father would ever leave the mill to me. After all,' there was a wry twist to her lips and she gave a small sigh, 'I'm only a woman.' Then she shook her head, mystified by her husband's reaction, and added, 'You must have guessed he would leave it to Charles. It was what he always wanted. A male heir for the mill.'

181

'That wasn't what he promised me when I married you,' Leonard muttered, still pacing, so incensed that he forgot to guard his tongue.

In the five years since the birth of her child, Emma had given little thought – and then only fleetingly – to the overheard conversation about the 'deal' regarding her marriage. Her life had been filled with the work of the mill and the bakery, the birth and care of her son, until that awful day – was it really only five days ago – that her son's screams had rent the peace of a lazy summer afternoon. Luke had come hobbling across the yard.

'Emma, come quick! Ya dad . . .'

She had run across the yard and into the mill, pausing in the doorway as she saw immediately her father lying at the bottom of the ladder, his neck at an awkward, unnatural angle.

'He fell,' Luke wheezed behind her. 'I were on the bin floor. I heard him slip, cry out once and then the bumping and thumping. Oh, lass, I couldn't do anything.'

'No, Luke, I know . . .' she said, putting her hand out to him. 'But please, can you fetch the doctor?' Even as she said it, she knew it was pointless. And all the time, little Charles was screaming.

Now, facing her angry husband she remembered the quarrel she had overheard in the mill between her father and Luke years before, she said quietly, 'And what did my father promise you, Leonard? What was the "deal" if you married me?'

Leonard glared at her and then, as if unable to contain his rage any longer, he spat out the words, 'A hundred pounds a year and, when he died, the whole lot, the *whole* lot, would come to me for my lifetime as long as I – we – produced an heir. A *male* heir. The only thing *I* had to do was, in my turn, leave it all to the boy.'

182

Emma gasped. Despite the years of humiliation under her father's taunts, she had not thought that even he would stoop so low, would be so vitriolic in his resentment against her for being a girl. Her legs felt weak and she reached out for the corner of the table and sat down on the nearest chair. Her gaze was fixed, mesmerized, on her husband; the man who had been *bought* for her. 'I don't believe it,' she whispered. 'How could he? And how – how could *you*?' Anger spurted again, giving her strength.

Leonard stopped his restless pacing and turned to face her. 'How could I what?'

'Be – be *bought*. He bought you, didn't he? For a hundred pounds a year and the promise of an inheritance. It was all just another *deal* to you, wasn't it?'

'It wasn't like that, Emma. Not like you're making it sound.' He spread his hands. 'Haven't you ever heard of a dowry? Well, it was like that. I needed a home. I could hardly live with my mother forever, now could I? Her with all her fancy men—'

'Oh aye. And one of 'em was my father, wasn't he?'

Leonard shot her a look. But for all the gossip that surrounded Bridget, Emma could not find it in her to dislike the charming, frivolous woman who had shown her nothing but kindness, even if in a rather offhand way. It was the same kind of attitude which Leonard displayed towards her when he came home from his trips to the city which, over the years, had become longer and longer, and his visits home so infrequent and fleeting that she wondered if little Charles really knew who this dashing, well-dressed man was.

Quietly, she asked. 'Did you ever love me, Leonard?'

'Of course I did – do,' he corrected himself impatiently. 'Don't get all sentimental. It's not like you. It's one of the things I liked about you. You're not a simpering, silly female. You're tough and determined and – and dependable.'

'And,' she murmured flatly, 'I had a mill.'

'Oh, well, if you're going to fling that at me . . .'

'I'm not Leonard. I don't blame you as much as I blame my father.'

'Oh, very generous of you,' he said sarcastically. Then he sighed and added, 'But you're right, the old beggar's done it across both of us.'

Anger in every movement, he snatched up the copy of the will which the solicitor had left lying on the table. His mouth tight, his eyes glittering with resentment, Leonard scanned the pages, his fingers turning the sheets over one after the other. As Emma watched, she saw a sudden stillness come over him, saw him pause longer on one particular page as if reading and re-reading one section. Before her eyes, Leonard's manner changed. With deliberate casualness he tossed the will on to the table and said, 'Well, there it is then. Let's not quarrel any more, my dear.' He came towards her and put his hands on her shoulders. 'We'll make the best of a bad job, eh? You run the mill until Charles is old enough to take over and I'll continue with my – er – business interests.'

She stared at him, confused by his sudden change of attitude.

He kissed her forehead, turned and left the room. She heard him go into the bedroom, undoubtedly, she thought, to pack his suitcase once more.

Slowly Emma reached across the table and picked up the sheaf of papers. Her eyes scanned the stilted legal jargon, trying to make sense of it all. Then the words leapt off the page at her.

And I appoint my daughter, Emma Smith, to be Executrix of this my Will and Trustee for my estate until my grandson, Charles Forrest Smith, shall attain the age of one and twenty, with full Powers of Attorney . . .

She wasn't quite sure what the legal wording meant, but she had a shrewd idea. Until her son reached twenty-one, she, Emma, had full power over all the estate, including the handling of the money. With the will still in her hands she moved slowly towards the window overlooking the yard. Below, she saw her five-year-old son standing rigidly still, his gaze fixed upon the mill, its sails still and silent today. Faintly, through the open window and coming from the direction of the mill, she heard a low, continuous buzzing. A black cloud seemed to be clinging to the side of the mill about half way up; a heaving, moving, humming black cloud. Fascinated, the boy and his mother watched as the bees from the orchard swarmed on the side of the mill.

'The death of a Forrest,' Emma murmured.

Twenty-Two

'Leonard, I really need your help.'

Above the morning paper Leonard raised his eyebrows. Already he was dressed for the city in his smart check suit, a white shirt and a dark blue tie. As always, when there were any available, there was a fresh flower in his button-hole. In contrast, Emma felt weary and dishevelled. As usual she had been up since the early hours that morning and now, at seven thirty, it was the first time she had stopped to grab a slice of toast and a mouthful of tea and to call Charles for school.

'My help?' her husband asked. 'Whatever do you need my help for? Besides,' he added, his eyes going back to the Sales and Wanted column in the newspaper, 'I must be on my way.' He crumpled the paper and said, 'And that reminds me, it's high time I invested in a car. The times I travel on Tom Robinson's bus, I must have nearly bought the darn thing by now.'

'Never mind that just now, Leonard. Will you listen? I need your help with the mill.'

'The mill? Now look here, you know I don't—'

'Listen!' she snapped, worry shortening her patience. 'It's the machinery. It needs keeping in good order.'

'What about Luke? I thought he saw to all that.'

Emma bit her lip. 'Luke isn't well. He's getting dizzy spells. He's not worked for a couple of weeks.'

'Hasn't he? Can't say I'd noticed.' Emma glared at him

and bit back the sharp retort that sprang to her lips as Leonard added, disinterestedly, 'What's the matter with him?'

'After Father died, he seemed – well – he seemed to give up somehow. I don't think he'll ever be well enough to work again, not even if he improves a bit. Me and the lad from the village have been managing the mill between use but we're not getting through the work. Sarah's kept the bakehouse going, but we'll be losing business soon, if . . .'

'Get someone else, then.'

'But why can't you . . .?' she began, but her words were cut short by Leonard holding out his hand towards her, palm outwards, as if fending her off.

'You know I don't want to have anything to do with the mill. I know nothing about it, so it would be pointless me even trying.'

'You like the money it earns well enough, though, don't you?' she retorted.

'Well, if you're going to start that again, I'm going. I'll be back on Saturday.'

'Saturday?' Her eyes widened. 'But – but you usually come home midweek.'

'I've business in Sheffield on Wednesday and Thursday, so I shan't be home until the weekend.'

Emma's eyes narrowed and before she had stopped to think, the thought that had troubled her for several months now, formed itself into words and came out of her mouth. 'Leonard, have you got someone else? Another woman in Lincoln?'

'Eh?' He spun round and she had to admit that the surprise on his face was genuine. He stared at her for a moment and then let out a huge guffaw of laughter and came back towards her, his arms outstretched, to take her by the shoulders and give her a gentle shake. 'Heavens, no! I've got enough to handle with the one I've got.'

His eyes were dancing, his mouth smiling as he turned on the familiar charm. In spite of herself, Emma found herself smiling in return.

'Well,' she said. 'You can hardly blame me for wondering. You spend so much time away from home and—'

'My dear, I have my business to keep going. And I'm sorry I'm not more use to you here, but, well,' he shrugged his shoulders, 'my time's better spent doing the job I know how to do. Now you must see that, don't you?'

'I suppose so,' Emma murmured. Even after having been married to him for almost seven years, she still did not know precisely how her husband made his money. All she knew was that it was some kind of dealing. She supposed that meant buying and selling, for he always seemed to be scouring the newspapers. He was still the same; flush with money one week, penniless the next and borrowing from her. Although he always promised to pay her back the next time he pulled off a deal, he never did repay her and in the end she ceased to expect it. After all, they were husband and wife and all that was hers was, by law, his too. As, more than once, Leonard had reminded her. But whenever she tried to probe too deeply into his affairs, her husband became angry and eventually, Emma had given up trying. Whatever it was that he did to earn a so-called 'living', Emma decided at last, then let him get on with it. Shrewdly, however, she did not so readily hand over money every time he demanded it.

'I can let you have a little next week,' she would answer, becoming as evasive as Leonard himself, 'when Farmer Popple pays me.'

Then Leonard would frown and glare at her, but she

would stand firm and he would turn away muttering darkly about what might happen to people who did not pay their debts on time, though whether he was referring to Farmer Popple or to himself being in debt to someone, Emma could never quite be sure.

But now, Leonard was all smiles. 'Actually,' he was saying airily, 'I'm going over to Sheffield to look at a second-hand car. A mate of mine knows a bloke in the business.'

'Leonard, we really can't afford . . .'

'I'm not asking you for money, Emma. I had a bit of good luck last week so I thought I'd get one while the going's good.'

'I see,' she said flatly. No intention of paying back all the money he's had from me, she thought.

'Oh, come on, Em, cheer up. If I get this motor car, I'll take you out for a drive next Sunday – you and the boy. If the weather's nice, we'll take a picnic and go up the coast. How about that, eh?'

Suddenly, he looked so boyish, so anxious to please, that she hadn't the heart to spoil his fun. She forced herself to laugh, tapped his nose playfully with her forefinger and said gaily, 'You'd better.'

'That's the ticket.' He leant forward and kissed her forehead briefly. 'And don't worry, I'll try to find someone in Lincoln who knows about mills.'

'Oh, it's all right, don't bother. I've just remembered someone locally who might be able to help.'

His wide smile showed gratitude at being relieved of the responsibility, and he left the house with a jaunty step and his Homburg set at a rakish angle.

Now why on earth had she never thought of it before she asked herself? It had been Leonard's unusual shortening of her name to 'Em' that had reminded her. Only one person ever called her that; William. And now he worked for a millwright in Bilsford.

She only had to ask, she knew, and William would come.

When she had delivered her son to the village school only a few yards up the road from the mill, Emma crossed the road and went into the market place, striding purposefully across the square towards the smithy.

During the past seven years, she had, of course, seen Jamie about the village, at chapel, in the market, even in her bakery. She had spoken to him, enquired after his health and William's, but this was the first time since her marriage that she had visited him at the smithy, the first time she had deliberately sought him out. As she drew near, she could hear the roar of the furnace, could smell the tang of singeing hoof that always seemed to linger about the place, even when there were no horses there being shod. Then she heard the rhythmic clang, clang, clang of his hammer as he shaped a piece of metal on his anvil. From a safe distance she stood and watched him.

He must have caught sight of her out of the corner of his eye, for she saw him stiffen and then slowly straighten up to face her. For a fleeting moment, his feelings were naked in his eyes; brown eyes that were dark with longing. But then the mask of indifference clouded his face and the perpetual frown deepened. Against her own will, her heart quickened its beat.

'And what do you want?' he said gruffly and flung the piece of metal into a corner, its clanging sound echoing around the yard.

'Good morning, Jamie,' she said with emphatic politeness.

He grunted and then grudgingly replied, 'Good morning.'

'Do you know the name of the people William works for in Bilsford? He did tell me once, but I've forgotten it.'

Jamie wrinkled his brow, 'Er, something beginning with P – er – Pickering. Yes, that's it, Pickering.'

Feeling she owed him some kind of explanation, she added, 'I thought maybe he'd take a look at the mill for me. The machinery, y'know. Luke's not up to it any more.'

'Aye, I'd heard he was ill.'

There was silence and though Emma waited, gave him every possible chance, there was no offer of help from Jamie.

Sighing softly to herself, she turned away. 'Thank you,' she said. 'I'll write to him.'

'You do that,' the man said harshly. 'But he'll not come.'

She half-turned back towards him. 'Eh? Why not? Why won't he come?'

Jamie sniffed. 'He ain't been back here more than twice since he went six years ago. Too taken up wi' his new employers and his new job to think about his family; the *only* member of his family left now,' he added bitterly. He glanced at her and said, 'He lives with them, y'know.'

Emma frowned. 'So? Why is that so very dreadful?'

Jamie prodded the air with his finger. 'He should never have gone in the first place. His duty's here with me, in the family business our grandfather and his brother started. He'd no right to leave me here to cope alone.'

Softly Emma said, 'Maybe now you realize just how he had to struggle after your parents died and you were away in the war. And he was only a boy then, not even a man.'

'That's different,' he argued. 'I had me duty to me country to do. 'Sides, when I left, me mam and dad were well and strong. How was I to know what would happen?'

He fell silent, but the accusation against his younger brother still hung in the air between them.

'Maybe, Jamie,' Emma said gently, and there was an infinite sadness in her tone, 'if the same man who went away to the war had come back to us – the very same man – then perhaps a lot of things might have been different.'

The tears sprang to her eyes and lest he should see them, she turned away and hurried across the market square without looking back to see if he stood watching her.

She received a reply to her letter to William by return of post.

Of course I'll come over and oil and grease all the workings for you, Em. Do you want the stones dressing too? I'm a dab hand at that now. I could have come before if you'd said. I'll be there on Saturday afternoon. I was sorry to hear about your father and now you say poor old Luke's failing. Well, they always were very close despite the fact that they've had their ups and downs over the years. They grew up together, didn't they, let alone worked together? Maybe your father's death affected Luke more than he lets on . . .

She let the letter fall from her hands on to the table. She knew William was right. He understood the relationship between the two men as well as she did. A small smile curved her generous mouth as she thought about her childhood friend. Kind, considerate, so gentle, and always, she thought, ruefully comparing him to her volatile husband, the same. William had never been in one mood one moment, another the next. Dependable, reliable – dull, some might have said, but Emma at this moment felt the loss of his nearness keenly. But tomorrow, he would be here. How good it would be to see him again.

She made her way across the yard and through the orchard. It was a bright, breezy morning, white cumulus clouds scudded across a pearl grey sky. To the west, the sky was darker, threatening rain. She paused a moment as she passed by the hives and stood listening and watching. There were three rounded straw skeps on wooden stands. For years now, she had been trying to persuade Sarah to let her buy the more modern square, wooden hives, but Sarah was adamant.

'What was good enough for your grandpa Charlie, is good enough for me.'

'But they're so out of date now and so cumbersome. It's a wonder you don't get dreadfully stung every time you remove the combs. Now, these new ones . . .' Emma would begin, but Sarah would hold up her hands in horror and refuse to listen.

'What if the bees didn't like some newfangled thing? *Then* they'd sting me. Or worse still, they might leave us. Then what?'

Emma always covered her amusement. 'They're not newfangled, Sarah. Wooden hives have been on the go for – oh, years now. You can lift out each—'

'I don't want to listen and I certainly don't want any, so there.'

And there the argument always ended with Sarah having her own way as usual.

The bees seemed very active this morning, Emma thought, flying in and out with a sense of urgency as if there was not a moment to lose. Perhaps they were getting ready for winter. Smiling to herself, she continued towards the cottage where Sarah and Luke lived.

As soon as Sarah opened the door, Emma said, 'Whatever's wrong?'

Sarah looked away as if avoiding Emma's direct gaze. 'Oh, it's nothing, nothing. You'd only laugh.'

'Me? Now Sarah dear, have I ever laughed at you?'

'Well,' she said, 'no, not exactly, but I know what folks think of me and my silly superstitions.'

Emma put her arm around her friend's shoulders. 'Come on,' she said gently. 'What is it? Tell me.'

'The bees. It's the bees. They're very restless. It's as if something's going to happen. There's going to be trouble.'

'I did notice as I came by just now that they seem very busy,' Emma said and added quietly, 'and no, I'm not laughing.'

The two women exchanged a look then Emma felt the shoulders beneath her arm lift in a little shrug of resignation. 'Well, there's nowt we can do about it. We'll just have to wait and see. Come on through,' she said, trying to change the subject, 'and see Luke. He's feeling a little stronger today, even talking about coming back to work. He's that worried about you trying to manage everything on your own.'

Emma laughed. 'I'll talk to him. I've something to tell him, anyway.'

Moments later when Emma had given the old man her news, Luke leant back in his chair and let out a huge sigh of relief. 'I can't tell you how that's taken a weight off me mind. I've been whittling that much about that blessed mill 'cos the workings need checking,' he gave a wry laugh, 'ya'd think it were mine.'

Emma sat on a low stool and rested her elbows on her

knees, cupping her chin in her hands. She regarded him with her bright eyes. 'Well, Luke, to my way of thinking it very nearly is. You've given your whole life to it,' she said gently, 'to the mill and to the Forrest family.'

Tears welled in the old eyes and he reached out with calloused fingers that were crooked now with rheumatism. 'Eh, lass,' he said hoarsely, touched by her compliments. 'I'm just sorry that ya man dun't tek more interest and be a help to ya. If only them Metcalfes hadn't been so bloody stupid, ya'd be married into that family by now and well taken care of.'

Emma had rarely, if ever, heard Luke use bad language and coming from his lips it sounded more comical than blasphemous, yet she hid her smile. She tried to reassure him. 'Well, there's one Metcalfe who's not so bloody stupid,' she teased him. 'It's William who's coming on Saturday to look at the machinery for me.' She saw the old man glance towards his wife, saw the look that passed between them.

At once old Luke seemed to relax even more and settle back in his chair. 'Is it, be-gum? Well, then, that'll be all right. Them bees must have got it wrong, Sarah, me old dear, 'cos if it's William coming back, then everything'll be all right.'

Twenty-Three

By nightfall the wind had risen to gale force. It rattled the granary door on its loose catch, flinging it open, the wood splintering as it crashed back against the wall.

'I'll have to go and tie that door, Charles,' Emma said to her son, who was sitting huddled by the fire, his eyes huge and fearful.

'Don't go out in it, Mamma,' his child's voice pleaded. 'Stay here, where it's safe. You might get blown away.'

'Don't be silly, darling.' She fought to keep the vexation from her voice. She knew he was only six, yet even she was sometimes irritated by the boy's lack of spirit. Charles was always so solemn, his dark eyes huge in his pale face. And he didn't seem to laugh and play like other children. He was never naughty, never in childish pranks or scrapes and whilst she loved him with motherly protectiveness, at times, Emma wished there was some way in which she could instil some of her own mettle into her son. He was nothing, she thought, like his namesake, old Grandpa Charlie, if the tales that had been told down the years about him were to be believed.

Perhaps she had allowed the boy to be too much in the company of old men. First, her father and lately, with Luke. Perhaps it was her fault. She was so busy, so wrapped up in trying to keep the mill going that she had little time for her son. She would try to make more time for him, she promised herself, see that he had some playmates of his own age.

Contrite now for her sharpness, Emma hugged him swiftly to her and ruffled his hair. 'You stand and watch me from the back door, then I'll be safe, won't I? You must be the man of the house when your father is away.'

Picking up a length of line from under the sink, she opened the door. The wind blew into the house with a ferocity that made even Emma gasp in surprise. She stepped out into the yard, bending her head against the gale. She turned and saw Charles, his white fingers gripping the door frame as if to stop himself being blown away.

Sudden fear for his safety now – he was, after all, such a little chap – made her say, 'Now don't move from there. Promise me?'

His eyes were large ovals in his white face and his lips were pressed together as if to stop them trembling, but he nodded.

Clutching her coat around her, she staggered across the yard and, reaching the steps to the granary, grasped the rail and hauled herself up. Above her, the mill creaked and groaned. At the top of the steps she caught hold of the door and slammed it, leaning against it whilst she struggled with icy fingers to tie the piece of line around the catch to secure the door shut. As she turned away, the wind buffeted her and she grasped the rail to stop herself being blown down the steps. She looked up at the mill, a black shape against the stormy sky. The sails, silhouetted against the deepening dusk, shuddered as the gale blustered from first one direction and then another and the fantail struggled to turn the huge mechanism into the wind. But which way, which way now? She could almost feel the panic rising in her as she watched the neglected machinery fighting to do its job. Transfixed, she stared at the huge sails above her as a dreadful split-second premonition gripped her. In that moment, she knew exactly what was going to happen yet she was helpless to prevent the catastrophe.

The main sails were tail-winded and a great gust of wind with the force of a tornado got behind the huge sails and pushed them forward. Emma watched in horror as, in slow motion, the gigantic structure – sails, fantail and the onion-shaped cap – toppled into the yard, the wood of the sails smashing and splintering into matchwood, the canvas shades tearing into shreds. The noise seemed to go on forever. Shards of wood flew in all directions and Emma cringed against the granary door. Dropping to her haunches, she covered her face and head with her arms. She felt a piece of flying timber hit her forearm, then rattle down the steps, bouncing on every tread.

At last there was silence, an unearthly silence, with only the wind still howling triumphantly. Slowly Emma raised her face and saw the shape of the mill, a black, capless cone, stark against the sky.

'Oh, Grandpa. Grandpa Charlie,' she murmured. 'No! Oh no!'

And then, above the wind, she heard the wailing of her terrified child.

Struggling to her feet, she tried to call out to him. 'I'm all right, darling. Stay there. Charles, stay there.'

But she heard him clambering over the pile of wood that filled the yard. 'Mam, Mammy – where are you?'

'Stay there, Charles. I'm fine – I'm coming . . .' But the wind whipped the words from her mouth and tossed them away.

She tried to go down the steps but a huge spar of wood blocked her way. Then there were other sounds borne on the wind; Sarah, from the direction of the orchard, and even Luke, had struggled out into the night. From the gate into the road, there came the voices of other neighbours, who, hearing the horrific noise, had rushed out to see what had happened.

There was no way down the steps for Emma. The broken wood lay in a tangled heap of wreckage, blocking her way down the steps and across the yard.

'Mammy, Mammy,' came Charles's piping voice. 'I'm coming.' The voice was no longer panic-stricken, instead there was a note of reassurance.

Emma strained her eyes through the dusk and saw the small boy climbing over the wood, picking his way carefully, testing each foot and handhold until it felt safe.

'Go back, Charles,' she cried again, but above the howling wind he could not hear her.

She saw him totter once, as the wind buffeted him, but he held his arms out wide, instinctively balancing himself on top of the pile of wood.

Through the gloom she saw his mouth moving, but whatever he was saying was lost in the roar of the gale. She watched in awe, in admiration, until he reached the place beneath the steps and peered up at her.

'Mam – are you hurt?' he shouted. Closer now, she could hear what he said.

'No, darling, I'm fine.' She looked down at her son. 'Are you all right?'

'Oh, yes,' he almost dismissed her enquiry and glanced about him. 'But how are you going to get down?'

'I don't know, I—'

'Wait there, Mammy, I'll fetch a ladder.'

Emma listened in amazement to the confidence in the six-year-old's voice. How could she ever have thought him weak and timorous? He was turning away again, beginning to feel his way carefully over the wreckage. 'Stay there, Mammy. Don't move.'

Emma felt the tears, wet against her cheeks, and fought

the hysteria welling up inside her. He was using the very same words she had said to him only a few moments ago. But it was she, and not her son, who was trapped amidst the destruction; she, who might, had she been in the yard and not at the top of the steps, have been crushed to death.

'Em, Emma!' Above the wind, another voice came faintly from the direction of the yard gate; a voice she knew, a voice she was so thankful to hear.

'William, oh William,' she breathed but it was Charles, who, hearing the man's voice, shouted back, his high-pitched child's voice carrying above the storm. 'Here! We're over here, Mester!'

The boy stayed perfectly still and waited for William to clamber towards them both. Reaching Charles first, Emma saw William bend towards the little boy, obviously asking, 'Are you all right? Where's ya mam? Where is she?' for then she saw Charles point to where she was standing, marooned amidst the rubble.

William clambered closer. 'Oh, thank God, I thought . . . Are you hurt?'

'No, no, but I can't get down the steps. Part of a sail has lodged itself at the bottom and it's too heavy to move.'

'Can you climb over the rail?' William held up his arms. 'I'll catch you.'

Emma didn't hesitate. She pulled up her skirts and hitched herself up to sit on the top rail. She threw first one leg and then the other over until she was sitting on the rail above William's outstretched arms, clinging on lest the wind should blow her off.

'Right, now turn and let yourself hang down from the top rail and then just let yourself drop,' William instructed her.

Trusting him implicitly, Emma did as he suggested,

200

hanging by her hands momentarily until he said, 'Right, I'm just below you. Just let go, Em. I'll catch you.'

Emma released her grip and felt herself falling. William staggered and tottered backwards momentarily under her weight but then her feet were on the ground and she was turning in his arms and wrapping her own around him. 'You're hardly built to catch a great lump like me . . .' she began, and then his arms around her tightened and swiftly his lips brushed her forehead.

'Oh, Em,' his voice was hoarse. 'I thought for one dreadful moment, when I saw little Charles clambering over the heap and calling your name, that you were under it all.'

'I'm fine,' she said gently and as she felt her son hugging her skirts, she put out her hand to his head and held him to her.

William released her, reluctantly it seemed, and his voice was gruff as he added, 'Thank God you're safe – both of you.'

'Yes, we are, but the mill . . .' she half-turned towards the looming denuded shape in the darkness, her vision blurred by the tears that welled in her eyes. 'Oh, just look at old Charlie's mill. What have I done? Oh, William, what have I done?'

'It's not your fault,' William tried to reassure her for the twentieth time.

They were sitting huddled against the warm range in the kitchen. She was unable to think of going to bed and William refused to leave her alone. He had come from Bilsford to stay the night with his brother. 'So that I could get an early start on the mill in the morning,' he explained.

Tragically, there was no need for William's expertise now. It would take a great deal more than a bit of oiling and greasing to repair the destruction of the storm.

The neighbours had gone back to their homes, even Sarah and Luke, whose way across the yard to the bakery was barred by the heap of shattered wood. 'We'll come back in the morning, Emma,' had been her neighbours' unanimous promise. 'And help you clear this lot.'

Charles, thankfully, was safely in bed, remarkably unscathed by the night's events, Emma thought in surprise. She had seen something in her son this night that she had not seen before; courage in a crisis. She would ponder this more, but for now the loss of her mill was uppermost in her mind.

'It *is* my fault,' she countered William's statement, ranting at herself. 'I should have had the machinery checked weeks ago. I knew Luke couldn't get up there anymore. Oh, the shame of it too. In milling circles, it's the worst thing, the most disgraceful thing that can happen to a miller, you know it is, to allow his mill to get tail-winded. It's neglect, sheer neglect. And I'm to blame.'

William leaned across and took her hands in his own. 'Emma, listen to me. Try as you might, you cannot carry the whole world on your shoulders, even though . . .' even amidst the tragedy of the night, a small smile flickered on his mouth, 'you have a damned good try most of the time.'

In the flickering firelight, her violet eyes looked into his. 'What do you mean?'

'You can't carry the responsibility, or the blame, for everything that happens. Being a girl, for a start, and your father's only child. And – and – there was a catch in his voice as he said, 'and Jamie. All that was his fault. He's the biggest fool out and one day, he'll realize it. I can't—' now he seemed to be struggling to find the words, 'I can't even blame you for marrying Leonard Smith,' his voice dropped to a hoarse whisper, 'though I wish you hadn't.'

Emma sighed. 'Oh, he's not so bad, really. He's good to the boy and he treats me well enough on the whole. It's just—' She stopped, feeling suddenly disloyal, even though William was her oldest and dearest friend, apart, perhaps, from Luke and Sarah.

'Well, you deserve better, Emma,' William muttered, so low that she scarcely caught the words.

Impulsively she leant forward and kissed his cheek. 'Oh, William, my biggest regret is that I haven't got you as my brother-in-law.'

As she drew back, Emma caught sight of the fleeting pain in William's eyes, but he dropped his head quickly, hiding from her gaze, and when he raised it again, he was smiling. His expression was gentle as he said, 'Well, I'm still your friend, Em. I'm always your friend.'

'Sell it. It's the only answer,' Leonard stood in the middle of the yard and waved his hand towards the mill in disgust. The wood of the sails, smashed beyond repair, had been stacked as neatly as possible to one side of the yard by Emma's willing helpers the morning after the disaster.

In the late afternoon, Leonard had returned home and now in the deepening dusk he stood surveying the ravages of the previous night.

'I can't sell it, Leonard. You know I can't. Under the terms of my father's will—'

'Oh aye, the famous will!' He turned on her, his face thunderous. 'It's hardly apt, now, is it? What is there left for the boy to inherit? Sell it I say, and raise what money you can.' He turned and his gaze ran over the house and the bakery. He nodded towards it. 'That, at least, ought to be worth something.' Then his calculating glance swept around and encompassed the orchard and, beyond it, the Robsons' tiny cottage. 'And you own that, don't you?'

Emma gasped. 'I couldn't sell that! It's their home!'

Leonard shrugged. 'They'd have to find somewhere else,' he said heartlessly.

Shocked Emma stared at him, but his callousness hardened her resolve. Thank God, she thought, for my father's foresight.

'Leonard,' she said slowly, 'I cannot sell what is Charles' inheritance. Nor,' she added deliberately, 'will I. It is Forrest's Mill and it will always be a Forrest's Mill.'

Leonard stared at her, his face twisted with anger. 'If you believe that, then you're a fool, Emma.' He jabbed his finger at her, only an inch from her face, but resolutely Emma stood her ground, refusing to be cowed by his rage. The memory of old Charlie was strong within her.

'Mine,' he spat the words in her face. 'It should all have been mine. Your father promised me when I married you and then, because he got a precious grandson, he cheated me. But one day, Emma, I'll have what's rightly mine. You see if I don't.'

Leonard turned on his heel and marched into the house, slamming the door behind him and leaving Emma standing forlornly amidst the wreckage of her family's inheritance.

Part Two

Twenty-Four

The room in the huge Victorian house on the steep slope of the hill leading up to the cathedral from the sprawling city below was huge, fusty and cold. It was where Leonard stayed when he was in Lincoln in one large, high-ceilinged room, sharing the use of the bathroom and kitchen with the other tenants in the house. Emma surveyed it in dismay.

'We can't bring a family here, Leonard.' She moved to look out of the long window down into the narrow backyard where washing, grey with smuts, hung limply on a drooping washing line slung between two posts. Down three flights of dismal stairs every time she wanted to go outside and down one flight even to visit the bathroom or kitchen. She turned to face her husband who was standing, frowning angrily, in the middle of the room.

'Well, I didn't want you to come here. Of course it's no place for children. You'd have been better staying in Marsh Thorpe.'

'Oh yes, that would suit you, wouldn't it? You have a wife and a family now and it's time you took some responsibility for us.'

The quarrel had wrangled on for weeks and had achieved nothing.

The mill was irreparable. No, that was not quite true, Emma acknowledged. The truth was that she had not the money to pay for such extensive repairs. William had been wonderful, she thought fondly. He had offered to speak to

207

the Pickerings, to see if they could offer a special rate if he worked for nothing in his spare time. But even the estimated cost of that had been prohibitive. At first she had thought she might have enough of the money left in the bank after her father's death to meet at least the major part of the cost and, although it would leave her with no ready cash, at least her livelihood would be restored. But a shock awaited Emma on her visit to the bank in Calceworth.

'My dear Mrs Smith,' the manager explained patiently, as one might to a child, 'there is less than fifty pounds in your father's account. We have, of course, been awaiting your instructions since his death. Did you not receive our letter?'

Emma had stared at him in amazement. 'No – no, I didn't.' She bit her lip. 'I thought my father's savings would be much more than that. He was always – well – frugal.'

The manager eyed her keenly. 'He was,' he remarked drily, 'until about seven years ago. Let me see . . ' He leant back in his swivel chair and steepled his fingers together, the roundness of his belly stretching the buttons on his waistcoat almost to bursting point. His eyes looked up at the ceiling as if something there was commanding his attention. 'It would be about the time of your marriage that it began.'

Emma leaned forward. 'What "began"?'

'The depletion of his savings.' The man brought his gaze down again to her face and he leant forward, almost accusingly, and rested his arms on the desk. 'At that time your father had over seven hundred pounds in his account. A considerable sum of money, I'm sure you will agree, dear lady.'

Emma swallowed. Indeed it was, and would, she felt sure, have been enough to repair the mill. Even before the words, edged with a sneer, had left the man's mouth,

Emma knew exactly what he was going to say. 'Over the last seven years, your father has withdrawn one hundred pounds a year. I regret, dear lady, that I am not at liberty to disclose—'

'There's no need,' Emma snapped and, in one swift movement, rose and moved towards the door. 'I know *exactly* where the money went. I bid you good day, sir.'

She returned home in a temper and went immediately to Leonard's desk and rifled through his papers to find a recent bank statement. Holding it in her hands, she sank down into a chair staring at the figures before her. Forty-nine pounds, two shillings and three pence was all the cash that remained in her father's account at the time of his death. Again she scrabbled amongst the papers in the drawer and found a letter from the bank addressed to her that she had never seen before. The letter, dated two weeks after her father's will had been proved, informed her of the amount in his current account and asked that she 'acquaint them with her instructions'. They were, the letter said, 'her obedient servants'.

The following day, Emma returned to the branch in Calceworth and withdrew the money and closed the account.

Ever since their marriage, Leonard had received one hundred pounds a year from Harry Forrest and yet he had still, on occasions, borrowed money from her. She was not only humiliated by the 'deal' that had been made between her father and her husband, but angry too. Money that might have repaired the mill had been frittered away by her spendthrift husband.

Facing him now across the dingy room in the city dwelling, her resentment welled again. 'If you hadn't spent all my father's money, we could have repaired the mill.'

'If you'd insured it properly,' he began, but Emma cut in

again. 'I thought all that sort of thing was in your hands.' Sarcasm laced her tone. 'After all, you're the man of the house. How can a woman attend to such matters?'

They were glaring at each other, Emma's dark eyes flashing, but Leonard was not to be outdone.

'The running of the mill was left in your hands, and insuring it was *your* responsibility. If you weren't being so stubborn, we could all live in clover. Sell the damn place, woman.'

Emma's chin went a little higher as she said again, 'Never.'

Angrily he thumped one fist into the palm of his other hand. 'If it wasn't all tied up so bloody tightly, I'd sell it myself. Him and his blasted trust for his precious grandson.'

Emma felt Charles shrink against her skirts.

'I've no doubt you would,' she said with icy calmness, safe in the knowledge that at least Leonard could never do that. At first she had been hurt that her father had passed her by in favour of his grandson, but now she was beginning to see the wisdom of his action. 'But as it is,' Emma went on, 'you'd better start being a real husband and father, instead of a visiting one. And you can begin by finding us a better place to live than this. I don't intend to have Charles live here for long or the baby to be born here.'

She saw Leonard's smirk as he glanced down at the swelling mound of her stomach and wondered, not for the first time, if he had impregnated her deliberately as a kind of punishment. She tried to dismiss the idea as preposterous, yet the uncomfortable thought refused to die completely.

Emma had been dismayed to find herself pregnant. The last thing she needed now was another child. On top of her distress about the mill, her sadness at having to watch her old friend Luke wither visibly as he saw his life's work end up in a heap of smashed timber, the discovery of her husband's deceit and her father's manipulation even from beyond the grave, the added burden of another child was too much.

Without the mill, the bakehouse and the bakery began to lose business and Sarah, with an ailing Luke to care for, could not work the hours Emma needed her. Then had come the final blow, and Jamie had been the one to tell her.

One market day a few weeks after the disastrous storm, he walked across the road from the cattle market and leant on the gate leading into the mill yard. Emma saw him from the kitchen window and, unable to stop herself, opened the back door and walked slowly towards him, drying her hands on a tea towel as she went.

She saw his gaze roaming over the brick structure of the mill and come slowly round to meet her eyes. 'William not got it rebuilt for you yet then?' The sarcasm in his tone was not lost on her.

Holding her temper in check, Emma said evenly, 'No, nor can he. I can't pay for the materials needed, let alone his labour.'

A smirk twisted Jamie's face. 'I'm sure William would work for nothing if you asked him nicely.'

Emma remained silent. That was just what his brother had offered, but she was not going to give Jamie the satisfaction of knowing it.

He nodded towards the bakehouse. 'That'll not be going long either, if what I've heard is true.'

Emma stared at him. 'What? What have you heard?'

He jerked his head vaguely in the direction of Morgan's Mill at the other end of the village, the mill that had always occupied the prime site in the locality even from the time when Charlie Forrest had built his mill on the piece of waste ground he'd bought for a song. It was owned and run by a man called Fothergill now.

'He's building on to his engine house. Word has it that it's a bakehouse.'

Morgan's Mill had never had a bakehouse or a bakery, but now, Emma guessed without Jamie having to say more, that the present owner, Sam Fothergill, would be taking advantage of her misfortune. She sighed heavily. 'Well, I can't say I blame him. He's a businessman, when all's done and said.'

'So,' Jamie said, 'all's fair in love, war *and* business, is it, Emma?'

Stung to retort, Emma lifted her head high. 'Oh no, Jamie Metcalfe. All was not fair in love and war for *me*, was it now?' She turned on her heel and marched back to the house slamming the door behind her without even staying to see what effect her words had on him.

The very next morning she awoke feeling sick and knew instinctively that she was pregnant. Four months later she climbed into Leonard's Ford van – the vehicle he had been to Sheffield to buy on the day her mill had been devastated – and sat stiffly beside him as he drove up the village street, round the left-hand corner, past the church, round the sweeping right-handed corner, past Morgan's Mill and out of the village westwards towards Lincoln and a new life.

As they passed the market square, Emma did not even glance to her right towards the brick archway with the name P HWFDOIH emblazoned there, though it took every ounce of her will-power not to do so.

Now, standing in this damp, draughty place with the winter approaching, she felt sick and bone weary. The emotional farewell to old Luke, who she feared she would not see again, and the feeling that she was deserting Sarah, left alone to care for the sick old man, had drained Emma

212

of her energy. And worst of all, she had turned her back on Grandpa Charlie's mill. Yet from somewhere she dredged up her last reserves of energy and squared her shoulders. Her violet eyes shone with the light of battle as she faced Leonard. The marked contrast between his appearance and her own was not lost on her either and only served to fuel her anger. He was smartly dressed in a check suit with a matching waistcoat, a gleaming white shirt and, as always, a flower in his buttonhole. His brown hair was expertly cut, parted in the centre and slicked back. His shoes were highly polished and whenever he left the house to go to the city, he wore a Homburg hat and carried a cane. In contrast, she felt like a tramp. Her workaday clothes were drab and well worn, her long plait was wound around her head, and she felt dishevelled and grubby and tired from the long journey. Beside her, his eyes wide with tiredness, Charles looked ready to fall asleep on his feet.

'Well,' Leonard said with sarcastic nonchalance, moving towards the door, 'you'll have to make the best of it for the moment. It's all we can afford.'

He left the room, and she heard his footsteps running lightly down the stairs. Emma sighed deeply and then becoming aware of the small, cold hand still clinging to hers, she gave Charles a tiny shake and said, with more determination than she felt inside, 'Come along, darling, let's get you ready for bed. You look tired out.'

There was an old-fashioned truckle bed tucked beneath the huge double bed that dominated the corner of the large room that would be living room cum bedroom. It was all there was for the boy to sleep on.

On the floor below, Emma stepped into the kitchen and, glancing round, her lips tightened in disgust. To her eyes, the place was filthy. A woman stood at the stove frying something in an open pan, the fat spitting in all directions.

Not for the first time, either, Emma thought, by the look of the back panel above the top of the stove. It was streaked with congealed fat and brown splashes.

The woman turned and looked the newcomers up and down. She sniffed and turned back to her cooking without a word.

'Good evening,' Emma said pointedly.

'Evenin',' the woman said without turning round, again sniffed loudly and wiped the back of her hand across her nose.

'May I warm some milk for my son?' Emma asked firmly.

''Elp yerself,' the woman said but made no effort to move aside at the stove to allow Emma space at one of the gas rings.

The door across the landing from the kitchen opened and a raucous male voice made Emma jump and Charles grasp her skirt again. 'Ain't my tea ready yet, woman?'

The woman at the stove took no notice, made no sign of even having heard. She merely removed the pan from the heat and tipped the whole greasy concoction on to a plate on the corner of the table. With a clatter she dropped the pan into the deep sink, already half-full of unwashed pots and pans, picked up the plate and moved towards the door. As she passed through it, she said, 'It's all yours.'

The woman had left the gas ring she had been using still burning so Emma tipped some milk into a small saucepan she had brought down and set it on the ring. Charles moved towards a chair at the table as if to sit down, but Emma said, 'We're not stopping down here, Charles. We'll take it back upstairs.'

Whilst they waited for the milk to heat, the boy stood uncertainly amid the squalor, his eyes large and round in his pale, tired face. What a place, Emma thought and her resentment flared against her husband for bringing his family here.

She noticed Charles looking about him, then he went to the doorway and looked out into the passage, first one way, then the other, turning back to look at his mother.

'What's the matter, love?' she asked, seeing an unspoken question in the boy's eyes.

'I just thought Grandpa might be here.'

Emma gasped. 'Grandpa? But . . .' she hesitated, then added gently, 'Grandpa died, Charles dear. You know he did.'

The child's lower lip trembled. 'But Luke said he'd gone on a long journey, Mammy. And we've just come on a long journey, haven't we? I thought we'd come to find Grandpa.'

'Oh, my darling.' Emma squatted down and held her arms wide to envelop her small, lost boy to her. 'It was Luke's way of trying to tell you kindly. I'm sorry if you didn't understand.'

The boy's voice was muffled against her bosom. 'I won't ever see Grandpa again, will I, Mammy?'

She said nothing, but hugged him tightly and he understood her answer.

Twenty-Five

The bedding on the truckle bed was lumpy and damp. 'You'll not sleep on that tonight, Charles. You can snuggle in beside me.' In her thoughts she added, 'and your father can sleep on that thing if he wants'. The double bed was little better though it did not feel damp. The sheets were grey and the mattress hard and indented by the shapes that had slept upon it.

The exhausted little boy was asleep in moments, but Emma lay awake far into the night, staring sleeplessly into the blackness and reliving all the events in her life that had brought her to this moment. Lying there in the grubby room in a strange house, listening to the night sounds of the city, she resolved with a determination that she had not really recognized within herself that never again would she allow herself to be manipulated by others, certainly never again by her husband. She had always been obedient to her father's wishes. 'Honour thy father' had been so strongly instilled into her that she had never thought to question it or dreamt of rebelling against him.

Her love for Jamie Metcalfe and his rejection of her for reasons she herself could not, even yet, come to terms with, had driven her, foolishly she saw now, into marriage with a man who was superficially good-tempered and generous. But she had married him, and her strong sense of duty, for better for worse, still ruled her thinking. She felt the small mound that was the new life forming within her and felt a moment's fleeting guilt that she could not anticipate the birth of her next child with the joy with which she had looked forward to Charles' birth.

Gently she stroked the hair of the sleeping child beside her and, in the darkness, a smile touched her lips. She loved him dearly and was filled with pride for the bravery he had shown on the night of the disaster. But it was a courage that had been short-lived and now he was once again the pale, timorous child whose nervousness seemed to irritate his father so. In the darkness, Emma sighed. She was expecting too much of the boy, she told herself sharply. Charles was only six years old. Yet into her mind, unbidden, came the stories of old Charlie as a youngster, of his daring escapades, of his cheeky, lovable grin that disarmed everyone. His strength of character had been evident even then.

'Oh, Grandpa, Grandpa,' she whispered into the lonely night, 'I'm so sorry. So very sorry.'

Only one thought burned in her mind and hardened her resolve; I'll never part with your mill, Grandpa Charlie. Never. No one will ever make me do that. One day the young child sleeping here beside me – the next Charles – will inherit your mill, just as you always wanted.

In the darkness she frowned. The fleeting pictures haunted her still; the elusive memory that was always just out of reach. She was in her grandfather's arms and he was pointing towards the mill and saying something. Then she was standing on the ground and watching him begin to climb. And, as always, there was the awful sight, so vividly imprinted in her mind, of Grandpa Charlie lying in the yard beneath the mill.

She turned her face into her pillow and moaned. 'Oh, Grandpa, what is it that I can't remember?'

She awoke with a start to feel her husband pulling back

the bedclothes and climbing in beside her, the smell of the drink on his breath adding to the sour odour of the room. Emma turned on her side, away from him, protecting her young son with the curve of her body and drifted back into an uneasy sleep to dream of a dark cloud of bees swarming on the side of Forrest's Mill.

The following morning, Emma attacked their living quarters with brooms and brushes, hot water and carbolic soap.

Today Leonard was in a good mood, kissing her forehead and promising that this accommodation was only temporary and that they would move as soon as he could find somewhere.

'Well, it won't be a moment too soon. In fact, you can take Charles into the town and start looking now.' She glanced at her husband. 'Where do you look for places to rent?'

He shrugged. 'I'll ask around. Come on, Charlie boy, get your coat on and I'll take you shopping.'

As she listened to them clattering down the stairs, hearing Charles's high-pitched voice demanding excitedly, 'Where are we going, Father?' Emma tugged at the huge sash window which gave way reluctantly under her strength. Morning air blew into the room, but it was not the fresh, country air with the hint of the sea in it she knew so well. This was city air, with street smells and fumes from a thousand chimneys. She leaned out and glanced from right to left, seeing the backs of the neighbouring houses, each with their own identical tiny square of a backyard. Some, it seemed, still had the privy at the end of the yard. They were fortunate, she supposed, that there was a bathroom of sorts within this house. Once, it must have belonged to quite a wealthy family before being let off in rooms. She withdrew her head and surveyed the room behind her, took a deep breath and picked up her broom.

By the time Leonard and Charles arrived back, the room was smelling strongly of carbolic and disinfectant, but it was clean. As he came in the room, Emma could see that Leonard was hiding something behind his back. With a dramatic flourish, he produced a bouquet of flowers, expensively wrapped and tied up with blue ribbon and, for a moment, Emma was reminded of the first time he had come to court her. Once again, he was smiling that same disarming, charming smile that had so flattered her. She swallowed her resentment and acknowledged his gesture of peacemaking. She took the flowers and smiled, 'Thank you, Leonard. They're beautiful.'

Leonard wrinkled his nose as he stepped into the room and laughed. 'At least they'll help to disguise the smell of carbolic.'

'Mammy, we saw all sorts of things. Swans on the river and the shops. Oh, Mammy, you should see all the toys. And look – look what Father bought for me.' He held up a wooden train, painted red with a blue funnel. The boy bent and put it on the floor. 'You can pull it along and it makes a noise.' He glanced up at her again. 'We walked right down the hill and through an arch and over a bridge and then, guess what, Mammy?'

Emma smiled down at the excited child. 'No, darling, I couldn't possibly guess. You tell me.'

'A train. We saw a real live train. It went across the street. The big gates shut and all the horses and carts—'

'Drays, boy. They're called drays.'

The boy glanced at his father briefly. 'Yes, Father,' but he was turning back to her, anxious to tell his mother all that he had seen. 'And the people walking too, they all had to stop to let the train go across the street. We were that close, Mammy, right near the gates – ' again he held his arms wide, '*that* close to the train. And then when it'd gone, the man came and opened the gates and everything could go on. He's in a sort of house at the side of the track, high up, it is, with all sorts of levers to operate the signals. And his house is called a – a signal box.' The boy beamed as he remembered without having to be reminded. 'Father told me. And then . . .' his grin was even wider.

Emma shook her head and laughed. She could not remember seeing her son so animated. 'Go on. What then?'

'We had a ride on a – a tram.' Once more Charles glanced at his father for approval. 'It runs on rails in the street and stops every so often to let people get on and off.'

Leonard was nodding his approval. 'Good lad,' he said and Emma caught his glance. 'He's quite a bright little chap, isn't he?'

Emma agreed and the thought entered her mind that perhaps, after all, their coming to the city would have its compensations. If, here, Leonard was not such an absent father, he might take more interest in his son.

The shared kitchen and bathroom were more difficult for Emma to bring up to her own standards of cleanliness. Much of the equipment belonged to the other residents and whilst Emma always washed and cleaned up after herself, others were not so meticulous. From the first, she carried all her own pots and pans back to her room, leaving nothing in the kitchen that could be used by anyone else. But the incessant trailing up and down the dismal flights of stairs, began to drain even Emma's strength, and as the weeks of her pregnancy passed and the sickness showed no signs of abating, not even after the first three months were over, she began to feel ill. At night she dreamt of the clouds scudding across a clear blue sky, of mill sails turning and of the sound of millstones at work.

And in her dreams she saw Luke and Sarah – and William; William who had said he was her friend for ever.

Twenty-Six

'I can't find the silver christening mug that William gave Charles. I've unpacked everything now and I can't find it anywhere. I know I brought it.'

'Really?' Leonard said absently and opened his newspaper, his eyes scanning the pages.

'Leonard, you don't think that awful woman from downstairs can get into this room while we're all out, do you?'

"Course not.'

'I've a good mind to ask her, the nosey old—'

Leonard sprang to his feet with such a sudden, violent movement that the chair he was sitting on fell backwards. He crumpled the newspaper in his hands and flung it away from him in an untidy heap on the floor. Then he leant menacingly towards Emma, 'Now you keep your mouth shut, woman. You hear? Don't you go upsetting her. Don't you dare say a word about the wretched thing, you hear me?'

Open-mouthed, Emma stared at him. She regarded him steadily, then put her head on one side. 'Oh, and why not?'

'Because her husband's put me in the way of a nice little – er – deal, that's why not. And he might be helpful again.'

There was silence as she stood watching him set the chair upright, pick up his paper, sit down and open it again, shaking it to straighten the pages.

Quietly, never taking her eyes from him, Emma said, 'So, do you have any idea where the mug might be?'

'If you must know,' he growled. 'I've pawned it.'

'Pawned it!'

'I'll get it back, I'll get it back,' he raised his voice irritably. 'Next week when I'm a bit more flush.'

There was a loud knocking on the door and Emma, dozing in a chair by the fire, roused herself stiffly. The room was shadowy as dusk had fallen outside the long window whilst she slept. She levered herself up from her seat, the nine-month bulge slowing her movements. The banging came again, more insistent. She was alone for Leonard had taken the boy to the market and had told her they would be late.

'There's some good bargains on a Saturday night. When the market traders start to pack up, rather than take stuff back home, 'specially perishables like vegetables and chickens, the stallholders sell them off dirt cheap.' Leonard had smiled and nodded and tapped the side of his nose with his finger in a gesture of having inside knowledge. He looked incongruous in his smart city suit standing there in the middle of the one cluttered room, which, no matter how hard she tried, she could not keep tidy.

Emma, more tired than she could ever remember being in her life, had nodded listlessly. She'd be glad when this bairn was born. The pregnancy was draining her energy far more than had her firstborn. And the child seemed anxious to be born for it kicked and stretched within her.

'Have you asked around about other rooms, Leonard? I don't want the baby born here with only that old beezum to help.' She pointed downwards with her forefinger, indicating the floor below their room where the slovenly Mrs Biggins lived. If she'd asked him once during the last few months, indeed ever since they had set foot in this place, she had asked him a dozen times. Sometimes he got

223

angry and told her to be thankful she had a roof over her head. 'There's folks out there,' he had flung his arm wide vaguely in the direction of the factories down hill, 'getting put out of work, who'd give their right arm to have a room like this.' And then the same old quarrel would erupt. 'If you'd sell your blasted mill . . .'

Stubbornly, Emma refused.

But today, with the promise of a pint at one of the pubs near the Cornhill where the market was, Leonard was in an expansive mood. He patted her shoulder and said, 'Don't worry. I've got the matter in hand. Now are you ready, boy?' Leonard ran his glance over his son and Emma watched as Charles's eyes widened fearfully under the scrutiny. She could almost feel the boy's tension as he waited for the inevitable criticism. Emma kept silent, for she knew he wanted to go with his father. Charles was fascinated by the city streets, the hustle and bustle and, because Emma would not let him go out on his own, his world was restricted to the confines of the school play-ground and the half mile walk home to their lodgings. The promise of an evening wandering amongst the market stalls was a treat not to be missed.

But Leonard was smiling. 'I'll see if I can pick up some clothing for the lad, Emma. This jacket's seen better days.' He pointed to the frayed cuffs and her neat darning around the patches on the elbows. 'Can't have a son of mine looking like a street urchin, can we, boy?'

'No, Father,' Charles said, smiling back a little uncertainly, but with a growing confidence. He pulled up his knee-length grey socks and rubbed the toe of each boot on the back of his legs, then smoothed back his hair in an effort to be like his well-dressed father.

Emma, watching them together, hid her smile. The old Leonard Smith charm was being turned on his son for once, she mused. During the past few months her husband had grown a small, neat moustache that made him look a little older, much more the part of a successful middle-class man-about-town, and even more dashing. And today he was wearing a new dark suit.

As she had listened to their footsteps going down the stairs, Emma sank into the chair by the fire, thankful to have a few moments respite.

She awoke with a start at the sound of knocking and now, as she struggled across the room to open the door, she felt a sudden stab of unease. It was almost dark; they were later than she had thought. Oh, surely nothing had happened . . .

A strange man stood on the landing, a notebook and pencil in his hand, a leather strap slung across his shoulder which supported a deep leather bag resting against his hip. He was a small weasel of a man, with thin, sharp features and a scraggy neck that stuck up out of a stiffly starched collar.

'Yes?' she said uncertainly.

'Rent, madam,' the man said through thin, almost nonexistent lips, without preamble or greeting.

'Rent?' she repeated, blinking stupidly.

'Yes, madam. You're already two months in arrears. There was no one at home the last twice I've called.' The words were said with a hint of disbelief that was not lost on Emma.

'Well, you're out of luck again I'm afraid,' she said tartly. 'My husband pays the rent and he's out.' She made to close the door, but found the man had put his foot against the door jamb to prevent her doing so. Surprised she gaped at the booted foot for a moment and then raised her gaze to look into the man's mean eyes.

'Think I ain't heard that one before?' His thin lips

stretched. 'I want three months' rent, Missis, and I ain't budgin' till I have the money.'

'Please yourself,' Emma said and turned away from the door back towards the fire, leaving the man standing there. Unhurried and unconcerned she settled herself back in her chair, her mouth twitching with amusement. She raised her voice. 'There's a draught. Either come in or go out, but shut the door.'

Hesitantly, he stepped into the room and closed the door. He stood beside it, shifting his weight uneasily from one foot to the other. Obviously, in his vast experience, he had not previously encountered this sort of treatment. 'Er, if you'd just give me the money, Missis, I'll be on me way. I've other calls to make . . .' His voice petered out.

'I can't give you what I haven't got. If you want your rent money tonight, then you'll have to wait until my husband comes home.'

'Oh aye,' the man said with dry sarcasm. 'When the pubs shut, I suppose?'

Emma opened her mouth to say he shouldn't be long, he has our six-year-old with him, but something about the man's belligerent manner made her remain silent. She leant back against the chair and gave an exaggerated sigh and pressed both her hands on to her bulging stomach. 'I hope he's not long myself. I've been getting these pains . . .' She closed her eyes and gave a low moan.

'Pains,' the man's voice was a high-pitched squeak. She heard the door open and him say, 'Well, I'd best be on me way. I'll call again. Yes, I'll call again. Tomorrow – or – or the next day. Good day, missis.'

As the door closed behind him, Emma opened her eyes and looked into the firelight. Quietly she began to chuckle, then as the merriment bubbled up inside her, she clapped her hand over her mouth. The rent man could still be outside, hovering on the landing. She didn't want him to hear her laughing. But the more she tried to stifle her giggles the more insistent her mirth became until she was lying back in the chair, tears of helpless laughter running down her cheeks.

It was the first time since leaving Marsh Thorpe that she had laughed like this and that was how her husband and son, coming back into the room in a flurry of excited chatter, found her. As she told them of her run-in with the rent man, Leonard sat down in the chair opposite and stared at her in amazement. 'Well, now Emma Smith, if that don't beat all. You, of all people, tricking that little ferret, Forbes. I never thought I'd see the day.' There was a note of admiration in his tone that made Emma look up sharply, her laughter silenced.

'What do you mean? Tricked him?'

Leonard's shoulders lifted in a shrug. 'Well, you know, give him the run-around.'

'I did no such thing,' Emma denied hotly. 'I couldn't give him what I haven't got, could I? I told him that. But if I'd had the rent money here, I would have given it to him.'

At once Leonard's expression turned into a sneer and he rose to his feet. 'Huh, I might have known it was too much to hope that you were learning a bit of sense.'

'Leonard, what do you mean? And why are we two months' rent in arrears? He said he hadn't been paid the last twice he's called.'

Her husband waved his hand at her dismissively. 'Forget it, Emma. I'll see to it. Now come and see what we've bought.'

There was a new jacket and short, boy's trousers for Charles and two shirts.

'Oh, Leonard, they're almost new.'

'There's a good stall there on the Saturday. Secondhand stuff mostly, but it's usually very good.'

There was a box of chocolates for her, wrapped with a blue ribbon. She reached out her hand to pick it up, torn between the pleasure his gifts gave and the nagging thought that they could not afford such luxuries.

'And I got you this,' he said, pulling something wrapped in a piece of cloth from his pocket and beaming at her. He unfolded the cloth and there in his hands lay Charles's silver christening mug.

'Thank you.' She took the mug from him, far more thankful to have it safely back in her hands than for any other present he could have bought her.

As she went to the shelf in the corner of the room and reached up to put it in pride of place, Emma felt the first stab of pain low in her groin.

'I won't have that old beezum near me,' Emma shouted, writhing on the bed, alternately sweating and shivering as the spasms of pain gripped with increasing frequency. 'Get a doctor – a midwife – anyone, but not *her*!'

'Oh, I see, not good enough for you, aren't I?' Mrs Biggins, standing at the end of the bed, her flabby arms folded beneath her bosom across which was stretched a dirty, grey-white blouse, gave a sniff and turned away.

'No.' Leonard's hand shot out and gripped the woman's arm. 'No, please stay. She's – she's delirious.' He gave an exaggerated, hearty laugh. 'She must think you're my mother. Yes, that's it. They never did get on. Can't stand the sight of each other, in fact,' he added, warming to his theme.

'That's not true,' Emma tried to whisper, but her words were lost in the groan that began low in her stomach and forced its way up and into her throat. It was, in fact, a lie. Emma wished with all her heart that it *was* Bridget standing at the end of the bed at this moment.

She gave another moan and the pain caused her to bring her knees up, to grip her hands beneath them and bend forward over her bulging stomach. Through the haze of her pain she saw Leonard staring down at her and heard the woman say, 'Good God, she's getting ready to push. Look lively, man. Get down to yon kitchen and get some water boiling. Get my old man to help ye. He knows what to do. I've 'ad five o' me own and he delivered two of 'em when we couldn't afford a midwife. Go *on*.'

Roughly, she pushed Leonard towards the door and then gripped the bedclothes and flung them off. 'Now then, let's be 'aving a look at yer.'

Not one of them – not Emma, lost in the depths of her pain, nor the bewildered man, nor the blowsy, unkempt woman – noticed the young boy, cowering, terrified in the corner of the hot, stuffy room.

Twenty-Seven

By the time Emma was well enough to write and tell her friend Sarah the good news, the child's name had become Billy.

Tell William when next you see him that I've named the baby after him. She smiled as she wrote, her pen hovering over the page as she almost added, and don't forget to tell the bees. But the words remained unwritten. Sarah needed no reminding. Emma's gaze went to the window and beyond as she thought about her home.

The bees in the orchard would be the first to know.

Sarah replied by return.

> *Oh, Emma, another Forrest bairn and wouldn't your old dad have been that proud to think it's another boy? William Forrest Smith. It's a grand name. By the way, the bees are still here in the orchard. I was so afraid they might leave us, you know, after what happened to the mill and then you going away. But they're still here and that means one day you'll come back to us . . .*

A week after the birth, a knock came on the door.

'Oh no,' Emma groaned, remembering it was the day the rent man was due again and Leonard was once more, conveniently for him, not at home. She sighed and called, 'Come in.'

She was still in the huge bed in the corner although she now got up each day for a few hours, against the advice of the 'midwife'. Mrs Biggins, though without improvement in her appearance and slovenly ways, had risen in Emma's estimation. Emma was always ready to give credit where it was due, and whilst she bemoaned the fact that it could not have been Sarah once more with her at her confinement, she had to admit that without the ministrations of her neighbour, she would have been in great difficulty. And even afterwards, she was thankful when the woman levered her huge, bloated frame up the flight of stairs each day to help. Leonard disappeared every morning as soon as he could and even young Charles displayed a sudden keenness for school.

The door opened and Emma gave a delighted squeal and flung her arms wide in welcome. 'William!'

Grinning, he approached the bed, bent down and submitted himself to a rapturous hug.

'Oh, how lovely to see you. Sit down,' she patted the covers beside her. 'Tell me all the news. How's everything at home? How's – ?' she hesitated a fraction and then finished, 'everyone?'

He sat beside her, his eyes intent upon her face. 'How are you?' he said soberly. 'You look pale, Em.'

She smiled. 'Well, it is only a week since Billy was born.' She saw his glance take in the squalid room and said a little too brightly to deceive William, 'We're hoping to move out of here soon. These rooms were what Leonard had when he was on his own. They're not suitable for a family. They were always only temporary . . .' Her voice faded away. She could see that William did not believe her.

Emma lay back against the pillows and found herself confiding in her childhood friend. She hadn't meant to, but in the overwhelming joy of seeing someone from home, and especially as that someone was William, for a moment she was vulnerable. 'I've had a difficult time with this one. The labour lasted twelve hours. It'll be different when I get my strength back.'

'Is there anything I can do to help?' William asked, a worried frown creasing his forehead, his voice deep with anxiety. Suddenly, he stood up and turned away from her. 'This is no place for a newborn baby or for you,' he burst out angrily.

She watched him, her violet eyes dark and troubled. Tears welled up and she brushed them aside impatiently, but he caught sight of them as he turned to look at her again. 'Oh Em, don't. I'm sorry.' He sat beside her again and caught hold of her hands.

'Leonard's trying to find somewhere better for us, really he is,' but even as she spoke the words, she could hear the doubt in her own voice.

'Yes, yes,' William said, a little too quickly and patted her hand, but she could see that he had to force a smile on to his lips. 'Now, I'd better have a look at my namesake.'

Emma watched as he bent over the rough cradle and saw his expression soften, a small smile curve his mouth. What a wonderful father he would make; the thought came unbidden into her mind. He put out his forefinger, roughened and calloused by hard work, and gently, so very gently, touched the child's cheek. The infant stirred and snuffled and William straightened up. 'I'd better not wake him,' he whispered.

Emma laughed. 'He'll be waking soon to be fed. He's a greedy little devil.' She pulled a wry face. Her breasts were heavy with milk, and tender, and every feed was an agony for her.

'I don't know why this time's so different to when Charles was born,' she murmured and a frown creased her forehead. 'And talking of Charles, he ignores the baby. He won't even look at him.'

'I expect he feels pushed out a bit,' William said gently. 'After all, he's had you to himself for six years.'

Emma lay back against the pillows, her long, black hair spread around her and smiled up at him. 'Of course you're right. I should have realized. I must try to make more fuss of Charles.' She smiled and then added, 'Enough about me and my problems. Tell me about home? You haven't said anything about the village. Have you seen Sarah and Luke? How is poor old Luke?'

'I – ' he hesitated and then the words came in a rush, 'I don't go to Marsh Thorpe very often. Sarah sent word to me by the carrier about the bairn and I came straight here to see you.' There was silence as he seemed to be struggling with the next words. 'Jamie – Jamie and me – we still don't get on, you know.'

Emma sighed. 'I do so wish it was different,' she said sadly and once more she felt William's gaze upon her. He opened his mouth to speak, but whatever he had been about to say remained unspoken, for at that moment they heard the sound of raised voices on the floor below, then of footsteps mounting the stairs and the raucous voice of Mrs Biggins. 'Leave the poor lass alone, can't you? 'Er only a week past her birthing. 'Er man's not at home, I tell you.'

But the footsteps continued relentlessly up the stairs towards Emma's door.

'It'll be Forbes, the rent man. Please, William, just ask him to come back later. Leonard should be home then.'

William opened the door and Emma heard the man's surprised. 'Oh, good afternoon, sir. Is Mrs Smith at home?'

William's tone was polite, but clipped. 'She is, but she is not well enough to see you.'

'You the doctor, sir?'

'No, I'm just visiting. She's asked me to tell you to come back later when her husband will be here.'

'Oh aye,' the voice was not so pleasant now. 'You in on it an' all, mate?'

'I beg your pardon?' William began and Emma felt a sweat of embarrassment break out all over her. She pushed back the covers and put her feet to the floor.

William, hearing her movement, leant backwards to look at her around the open door. 'Get back into bed, I'll deal with this.'

He stepped out on to the landing with the rent man and closed the door behind him. Suddenly weakness gripped her and she felt dizzy and sick. She lay back and closed her eyes. She could hear them talking outside her door but could no longer hear what was being said.

'William . . .' she called weakly, but the murmur of voices continued for a few moments before the door opened again and William stepped back into the room, closing the door behind him once more.

Emma opened her eyes. 'Is he coming back later?'

William did not come back to the bed where Emma lay, but bent over the cradle once more. 'Er, he says he'll leave it until next week and try to call when Leonard will be at home. I made him see you weren't up to being bothered at the moment.' He looked up at her. 'Has a doctor seen you, Em?'

She shook her head, touched by his concern, his kindliness making her feel unusually weepy. 'I'll be fine in a day or two. I just feel so dreadfully tired.'

They talked a little longer and then William said reluctantly. 'I'm sorry, I must go else I'll miss the bus back.'

He stood uncertainly in the centre of the cluttered room; the one room where Emma's family lived, ate and slept. He was fishing in his pocket and pulled out two pound notes. 'Here . . .'

'Oh no, William, please . . .' she began, but he cut short her protestations saying, 'It's for the child – for Billy. And give this five shillings to Charles. Mustn't leave him out, you know,' he added, grinning at her.

'But so much . . .' she began again.

'Please let me. After all, you've called the baby after me, haven't you?'

She nodded as the easy tears threatened again. 'Oh, William,' was all she could say.

He stood there looking at her for a long moment, before he turned and placed the money on the mantelpiece under a candlestick. 'There, and don't let Leonard—' he began and then stopped and altered whatever he had been going to say, 'I mean, it's for the boys.'

'Thank you,' she said quietly, but they both knew that once Leonard knew about the money, it would never find it's way into the baby's money box or even into young Charles's pocket.

'I must go,' he said again and stood at the side of the bed looking down at her for a long moment, then he bent, kissed her forehead swiftly and turned away. 'Take care of yourself, Em. And if you ever need me, you know where I am.'

Then he was gone, moving across the room, opening the door and going through it before she could speak again.

As she listened to the sound of his steps on the stairs becoming fainter and fainter, she whispered, 'Goodbye William.' Then she turned her face into her pillow and wept.

*

Three days later, when she felt a little stronger and got up from her bed and dressed for the first time, she found that the money had disappeared from beneath the candlestick. Slowly, knowing what she would see, she turned her head towards the shelf in the corner. The space where the silver christening mug should have been standing was empty.

Twenty-Eight

Each day Emma grew stronger and was able to do a little more housework, but by the time she had tucked Charles into bed at night, she was thankful to crawl into the big bed in the corner and snatch an hour or two's sleep before the baby awoke, crying to be fed. Each time it happened during the night, she would hear a scuffle from Charles as the child pulled the covers over his head, trying to block out the sound of the squalling infant.

It was after midnight and Emma had just fed the baby and lay down again, listening to the peace in the big room, the snuffling breathing of the baby and the gentle deep breathing of the older boy, when she heard the front door of the house bang and feet pounding up the three flights of stairs. The door was flung open, crashing back against the rickety wardrobe that stood behind it, waking both children at once and startling Emma so that her heart began to pound and sweat bathed her body.

'Come on, look lively. We're moving.'

'Leonard, for Heaven's sake! Do you have to wake the children? I've only just got the baby . . . Leonard, what on earth are you doing?'

He was turning up the oil lamp and moving about the room, picking up clothes and heaping them together on the table. 'I told you, we're moving. Now. Come on.'

'Now?' she repeated stupidly. 'In the middle of the night? Don't be ridiculous.'

He came and stood over the bed, bending down towards her, suddenly a huge, menacing figure.

'Do as I say, else I'll leave you to fend for yourself.'

She gasped and her violet eyes widened. 'What – what do you mean?'

He straightened. 'Ever heard of a moonlight flit, Emma? Well, this is it. We're getting out of here. Fast.'

She didn't know what he was talking about. She didn't know what a 'moonlight flit' was, but his sense of urgency communicated itself to her and she swung her feet out of the bed, her mouth set in a determined line. Ever since she had set foot in this awful room, these dreadful lodgings, she had wanted to leave. Well, whatever the reason, they were leaving and she wasn't going to stand here and argue the toss with Leonard, she told herself. Not even if it was the middle of the night.

'Where are we going?' was all she asked as she pulled on her clothes and began to bundle clothes and bedding into a heap.

'Other side of town,' he said shortly. 'I've a cart downstairs. It'll hold all our stuff and you and the bairn. The boy'll have to walk with me.'

Her busy hands were stilled for a moment as in the low light from the lamp she stared at him. 'Cart? Where's your van? Why can't we use that?'

'Because I had to sell it weeks ago,' Leonard snapped, pulling out a trunk from under the bed and flinging back the lid. He pulled open the doors of the wardrobe, clutched all the clothes hanging there between his arms, tore them from the hangers and threw them into the open trunk.

Charles was sitting up in his bed, his eyes wide and fearful. 'Mam . . .' he began, but his father caught hold of his shoulder roughly and dragged him from beneath the warm covers. 'Come on, boy, get dressed and help. You're big enough now.'

Emma saw her son tremble, but he hurried to obey his father.

Within an hour they were all dressed and in the dark street, loading their possessions on to the handcart. Emma climbed up on to the cart holding the baby who was howling now, his cries echoing through the silent street, bouncing back from the row of houses, the windows all in darkness.

'Shut that brat up, for God's sake, else you'll have everyone knowing what we're about,' Leonard snarled as he grasped the handles of the cart and began to push it along the street. Emma opened the front of her coat and dress and pushed the baby's head against her bosom and was rewarded by silence as the child found her nipple and began to suck greedily. The wheels rattled on the wet street, and Charles walked beside his father. After what seemed hours of discomfort for Emma and every bone in her body seemed bruised by the jolting of the handcart, they turned into a long narrow street of terraced houses stretching as far as she could see through the darkness.

'Now, let's see,' she heard Leonard mutter. 'Number twenty three, we want. Ah, here we are, twenty-one, so it must be the next one.'

Suddenly, his good humour seemed restored. 'It's a house, Emma. You'll like it here,' he said as he helped her down from the cart. Her legs were stiff and cold. 'And all to ourselves too,' he went on as he produced a key from his pocket and opened the door leading into the house directly from the street. 'No sharing with anyone else. How about that, then?'

Emma stepped into the front room with Charles clutching at her skirts. By the light of the street lamp outside,

Emma could dimly make out the empty room, with a door leading further into the house. As she moved forward, her foot kicked a bottle which rolled across the floorboards making a loud rattling noise in the darkness.

'There's a bit of litter about. Scruffy beggars who had it before,' Leonard told her. 'But we'll soon get it cleaned up.'

I like the 'we' Emma thought wryly, but she said nothing. She moved carefully across the room and through the door opposite and saw that stairs went up on her right-hand side and another door led into the kitchen at the back. The house was cold, but not, she felt, as damp as the lodgings they had just left so hurriedly.

'There's no furniture, Leonard,' she said as her husband carried in the oil lamp from the cart, lit it and set it on the mantelpiece above the cold fireplace in the back room.

He rubbed his hands together and said, 'Don't worry. I'll soon pick up some bits and pieces from the market. We'll have it spick and span in no time.'

Emma was not so sure, but she said nothing as she spread out their bedding on the floor of the kitchen and urged a weary Charles to lie down, fully clothed, promising him that in the morning things would be better, even though in her heart she doubted the truth of her own words. The baby, replete from nuzzling and guzzling for the whole of the journey to this place, lay asleep in the cradle.

When he had unloaded the cart, Leonard took off his jacket, shirt and trousers and lay down beside her in his underwear. 'We'll be all right here, Emma,' he said, putting his arms about her. 'I had to get you out of that place. It was no good there for you or the youngsters.'

Long after Leonard lay snoring beside her, Emma stared into the darkness. What Leonard said had been true, she acknowledged, but she also knew that it was not the whole truth. They had already been at the lodgings several months, so why the sudden urgency? Why had they stolen away in the night, so secretly, so quickly? Oh yes, she thought grimly, don't take me for a fool, Leonard Smith. There's more to all this than you're telling me.

By daylight the house was even worse than it had seemed in the darkness. The upstairs rooms were virtually uninhabitable; the floorboards were rotten and damp patches covered the walls and ceilings. Spiders' webs hung in festoons from the corners and even the staircase leading to the upstairs was dangerous. In the kitchen, the sink was stained brown, the stove had the door hanging drunkenly off its hinges and everywhere was thick with dusty grease. Emma opened the back door and stepped out into the narrow yard. The wash-house and the lavatory were worse than the house, if that were possible, and in the lane that ran between the backs of these houses and those of the next street, a communal tap was the only running water supply. Three bare-bottomed children, no older than Charles, played in the dirt.

Emma fumed and went swiftly back into the house.

'Well, it's hardly what I would call an improvement on the last place. But at least we're self-contained now and we've an extra room.' She nodded towards the front room. 'That'll do as the bedroom. In the meantime,' she looked meaningfully at her husband, 'you can keep looking for something better.'

'So that's all the thanks I get, is it?' His frown deepened and he growled, 'We could live in a palace if you weren't so stubborn. What's the good of hanging on—'

Emma held up her hand. 'Don't start all that again, Leonard. Just take Charles to school, will you?'

'I've people to see. I can't be playing nursemaid to him.'

Emma looked down at the quiet little boy who stood solemnly waiting to be told where he was to go that morning. Suddenly, she was filled with maternal love for him and swept him against her. 'Don't look like that, Charles. It's the same school you've been going to and we're even a little nearer to it. You'll still have all the same playmates. That's good, isn't it?'

'Can't we go back home?' he said, his mouth muffled against her bosom.

'Oh, darling, it'll be much better here once I get it all cleaned up. Besides, you didn't like it in that one stuffy room, did you?' she asked in surprise.

He pulled back his head and looked up into her face. 'I don't mean *there*. I mean home – back to the mill.'

Behind them Leonard swore and moved towards the back door and out into the back yard. They heard the gate flung open and feet marching down the passage between theirs and the neighbouring house.

Swiftly Emma smoothed the lock of hair from the boy's forehead and said quickly, 'We'll talk about it later. I'll try to explain it all to you. But now you must hurry after your dad for him to show you the way to school. I'll meet you this afternoon.'

She hustled him out of the front door and watched whilst he scampered down the street after the tall figure of his father striding angrily away. Satisfied that he had caught up with Leonard. Emma pushed the door shut and turned to survey the work that awaited her.

At that moment young Billy began to wail.

After she had fed and settled the baby, Emma felt exhausted again. She had thought she felt stronger, but now the sudden upheaval in the middle of the night, their arrival in a cold, empty house and the thought that all her possessions, such as they were, were just dumped amongst the debris in the front room, overwhelmed her. She sat down on the floor on the bedding where they had slept for what had been left of the night and dropped her head into her hands. She felt lost and so lonely. Here in a strange city, removed from all her friends, still weak from childbirth, and with a husband who at one moment seemed good tempered and generous, the next moody, irritable and short of cash.

She heard a scuffle in the far corner and raised her head. What she saw made her mouth drop open in horror. Snuffling amongst the rubbish littering the corner, was a huge rat and only a couple of feet away lay her infant son in his cradle. Emma was by no means afraid of the creature – wherever there was grain and animal feed there would always be rats and mice – but the sight of a mangy sewer rat inside her home angered her. She scrambled to her feet and the creature scampered across the floor, running round her in a wide arc, seeking a way out. Emma threw her broom at it, but missed and the animal scuttled out of the open door into the scullery. Following, Emma opened the back door into the yard and then banged the broom against the sink until the rat appeared and ran for the open door. She tried once more to hit it, to kill it, but again she missed and the rat escaped.

Breathing hard she went back into the living room and looked about her. The place was filthy, worse than the accommodation they had just left and that had been bad enough.

'We're not staying here, Billy Boy,' Emma said and picked him out of the cradle. At his sleep being disturbed, the child whimpered. 'And you needn't start making that noise. I'm not in the mood.'

She wrapped him warmly in a blanket and carrying him

in the crook of her arm, she stepped outside the front door and looked up and down the street. 'Come on,' she said firmly. 'You and me are going house-hunting.'

Her temper carried her for two miles, down first one street and back up another. Up and down until fatigue overcame her again and she leant against a wall feeling sick and faint. Then she was angry with herself for allowing her stubbornness to make her act so foolishly. Her fury with Leonard for bringing his young family to such a place had spurred her out to walk the streets in search of a To Let sign. So far she had seen two, but the houses looked no better than the one they had come to the previous night.

'You all right, dear?' said a friendly voice beside her and Emma opened her eyes to see a woman, laden with shopping bags, obviously making her way home from the city centre, standing in front of her.

Emma smiled weakly. 'I'll be fine, thank you.'

The woman nodded and made as if to move on, but Emma stopped her by asking, 'I don't suppose, by any chance, you know of any decent houses to let round here, do you?'

The woman looked her up and down, as if assessing her, and, presumably liking what she saw, said, 'Sorry, I don't, but you could try the shop on the corner of the next street,' she accompanied her words with a nod of her head indicating the direction. 'Folks often put adverts in his window. Y'know, things they want to sell and that, and things they want. They often have rooms, or houses, to let an' all. You could try there.'

Emma smiled. 'Thank you, I will. You've been very kind.'

'Don't mention it, dear.' She nodded again. 'Mister Keenes'll make you a cuppa. He does sometimes for his customers. He's got a little table and chairs in one corner.' She grinned. 'Go in and sit there and mebbe he'll ask you, seein' as you look a bit peaky. He's a nice feller.'

Right at this moment, a sit down and a cup of tea sounded like heaven to the weary Emma. 'Thank you,' she said again, earnestly. 'Thank you very much.'

The shop door bell clanged as she entered. Inside it was a typical general store, a real corner shop serving the cluster of streets nearby. The shelves lining the walls were filled to overflowing with all manner of groceries and provisions to the point where they bowed in the centre under the weight. On the floor stood sacks of potatoes and carrots. There were two women in the shop, one being served by the huge, rotund man behind the counter, a copious white apron stretched over his paunch, the strings tied twice around his middle. His bald pate shone in the morning sunlight that slanted through his shop window and he beamed at her, his jowls creasing in welcome. The other woman waited for her turn and Emma, seeing the table in the corner near the window, squeezed past her and sat down thankfully on one of the chairs. As the rocking movement of being carried stopped, the baby began to whimper and the two women turned to look at Emma and her child. The one still waiting for attention moved closer and bent to look inside the folds of the shawl.

'Ah, poor little mite. Not very old, is he?'

'Four weeks,' Emma said.

The woman scrutinized the shadows beneath Emma's eyes and, straightening up, said, 'Mister Keenes, could this lady have a cup of tea, d'you think? She looks fair done in.'

'Right away, Mrs Porter. Whatever you say.' Emma saw the big man touch his forehead, as if touching a nonexistent forelock. He winked good-naturedly at Emma and then disappeared through a curtain into the back of the shop. The bell clanged and the first customer, who had now been served, nodded goodbye and left.

Mrs Porter, still standing before Emma and obviously

not in any rush to be served said, 'Not from round here, are you? I haven't seen you before.'

Emma shook her head. 'I'm house-hunting. I seem to have walked miles this morning. And the only places I've seen are as bad as the one I'm trying to leave.'

Suddenly she found herself pouring out her story to this stranger. 'We were in one room in a big house, you see, and it really wasn't suitable with another child. My husband found this house and we moved last—' she paused and altered her wording slightly, 'yesterday. But it's awful, worse than the room we left, and that was bad enough. A woman I met in the street,' Emma nodded her head through the window, 'said people often put advertisements in this shop window, but I had a look as I came in. I couldn't see any.'

Emma could no longer keep the weariness from her voice, nor stop the tears of fatigue and disappointment from welling in her fine eyes. Mr Keenes appeared from behind the brown curtain bearing a mug of tea and a freshly baked buttered scone. Emma couldn't remember ever having seen a more welcome sight.

'How – how much?' she stammered, realizing she had very little money in her pocket.

'Have this on me, lass,' the big man boomed with hearty kindness. 'Likely you'll be a good customer, eh?'

Emma smiled her gratitude. 'I'd like to be, Mr Keenes. Really I would, and thank you. You don't know how welcome this is.' She sipped the tea and took a bite from the scone and the baby began to wriggle in her arms. She glanced down at him, knowing he would be getting hungry again soon.

Mrs Porter sat in a chair opposite and beamed. 'Well, m'duck, this must be your lucky day. The advert's not gone in the window yet, 'cos it only happened yesterday,' Emma stared at her, holding her breath as the woman finished triumphantly, 'the house next door to me is empty. The beggars did a moonlight last night.'

Emma said nothing. She knew, now, what a 'moonlight' was and the scathing way in which Mrs Porter was describing her neighbour's hurried departure, made Emma shudder inwardly.

'So Mr Rabinski will be looking for new tenants. He's a good landlord. I can vouch for that 'cos he's ours an' all. I don't know how they'll have left the place though 'cos they were mucky beggars. I didn't have anything to do with 'em. Kids were rowdy and little devils, I wouldn't let our Joey play with 'em, even, and he's no angel.' She smiled fondly and Emma guessed she was referring to her own son. 'But he'll put it to rights for you, will Mr Rabinski. Lovely little man, he is. Poor soul. His wife died only a few months ago and he's no family. He owns three or four houses in our street and runs a bakery. Mr Keenes gets all his bread and cakes from Rabinski's, don't you, Mr Keenes?'

'That's right, Mrs Porter. He's a good man is old Rabinski. A real gentleman, always very correct and very polite. A bit formal, if you know what I mean, but a good man.'

'A bakery?' Emma murmured, feeling a sudden surge of hope. It seemed like a good omen. 'Do – do you think he would consider us, then?'

Mrs Porter's beam widened. ''Course he will, if I tell him I've found him someone.'

Suddenly, tears of thankfulness spilled over and ran down Emma's cheeks.

'There, there, m'duck. Don't take on so. You come along with me and we'll go and see him right now.'

'Thank you, oh, thank you,' was all Emma could say.

Twenty-Nine

Mr Rabinski was as nice as Mrs Porter had assured her he would be. A small, sad looking man whose age was difficult to guess for the wiry, grey beard that covered half his face. He was dressed in a long black frock coat and wore small, round, wire-framed spectacles half way down his nose, over which he peered at his customers, his head bent forward, his eyes slanting upwards. His English was excellent except for a slight accent that was the only reminder of whatever had once been his native country.

'You take the keys,' he offered at once. 'If Mrs Porter likes you, that is good enough for me.'

'Thank you, you're very kind,' Emma smiled as he waved her away.

'You move in wheneffer you want. Let me know if there is anything you need, uh?'

'Thank you,' Emma said again.

'I'll help you clean it, m'duck, if it's bad,' Mrs Porter offered, trotting along beside Emma. 'They were only in there three or four weeks.' She sniffed. 'Mind you, that's long enough for some folks to make it into a pigsty.'

The kindly woman had insisted on taking Emma to Mr Rabinski's bakery in the next street and now they were on their way to the house two streets away. In her arms, Billy whimpered and then his cries became more insistent.

'Hungry, ain't he?' Mrs Porter nodded. 'That's a hungry cry, that is.'

Sighing, Emma shifted the baby's weight in her arms. 'I'm afraid you're right.'

'Well, not far now, m'duck, and you can come into our place and feed him first and then we'll go and inspect next door.'

Once more Emma thanked her and glanced at the little figure walking beside her. Mrs Porter was thin but every movement was energetic. She was dressed in a black skirt and hip length coat. She wore black stockings and shoes, lace-ups with a small, cubed heel. From under her grey hat, pulled down low over her forehead, her sharp eyes missed nothing. She was carrying heavy shopping bags, but these seemed to be no trouble to her for she chattered nonstop, hardly seeming to pause to take in a breath.

Emma hid a smile; Mrs Porter was not quite what she would have imagined a guardian angel should look like but without a doubt, Emma thought, that was exactly what she was.

When Billy had been fed and Emma had rested, Mrs Porter, obviously enjoying her importance, ushered her next door.

The terraced house, separated from Mrs Porter's by a shared passage running between the two, was of much the same design as the one they had arrived at the previous night but the difference was noticeable the moment they stepped over the threshold from the street and straight into the front room.

'Rent'll be ten and six a week,' Mrs Porter said, 'and he comes on a Saturday afternoon every four weeks.' She laughed and nodded knowingly, ''Spect he reckons that's when he might catch most of the fellers at home.'

Not much chance in our house, Emma thought. Most Saturdays, Leonard disappeared after dinner and didn't appear again until the early hours of Sunday morning, flushed and walking very unsteadily. But she said nothing and listened as Mrs Porter extolled the virtues of the little house.

'This 'ere's the front room. We don't use ours much, 'cept at Christmas and if we have folks in, like. But there's a nice fire grate and it's furnished nicely, ain't it?' She looked at Emma for reassurance that her own standards were shared by her prospective new neighbour.

With genuine enthusiasm, Emma said, 'Indeed it is,' and she ran her hand along the back of the sofa, feeling the roughness of the brown moquette beneath her fingertips. The walls were papered with a darkish blue paper heavily patterned with a Jacobean design of flowers and leaves. A square of carpet covered the centre of the floor and around the edges, the floorboards were painted black.

Directly opposite the front door through which they had entered, Mrs Porter was opening a door leading further into the house. 'Come on, let's have a look at the rest of it'

They passed through a tiny hallway, with the stairs leading up on the left-hand side and into the living room.

'Oh yes,' Mrs Porter said with an air of definite satisfaction. 'Now that *is* a nice grate and . . .' she bent and opened a black iron door to one side of the fire basket, 'yes, the oven's in good order too. And that,' the woman pointed to the opposite side of the grate, 'that there is a boiler. You have to fill it and empty it by hand 'cos there's no tap, but it heats the water lovely, it does. Oh, Mr Rabinski is a good landlord,' she said again, straightening up and glancing round the room with a shrewd glance that missed nothing. Emma, too, looked about her. The room was square with the fireplace on the wall adjoining the next house. Another door led into what was more than likely the kitchen and in the far corner a long sash window looked out over the backyard towards the wash-house and lavatory at the far end. She was pleased to see that there was no lane running between this row of houses and the backs of the houses in the next street. Their yard was completely closed off and private.

Mrs Porter was pointing to the linoleum on the floor and pursing her lips. 'Y'know, I'm sure there was a strip of carpet down here and a peg rug. Them beggars must 'ave taken it.'

'Doesn't matter,' Emma said, 'I've a few bits and pieces of me own.'

Mrs Porter sniffed. 'Still, they 'ad no right to nick Mr Rabinski's stuff, now did they? Anyway, let's have a look how they've left the kitchen.' She opened the door and led the way again. 'Stove wants a good clean, just look at the grease on it. And the sink's bunged up, by the look of it.' She sniffed disapprovingly, then she smiled. 'Mr Rabinski's just bought me a brand new stove. Mebbe he'll do the same for you, once you've been here a bit.'

'It'll be fine once I've cleaned it up,' Emma assured her. 'Really, everything's wonderful. I can hardly believe my luck after what we've been living in. I really don't know how to thank you, Mrs Porter.'

The woman flapped her hand, embarrassed by Emma's gratitude. 'Don't mention it. I'm that glad to think we shall have some nice neighbours 'stead of that rowdy lot.' She laughed. 'I'm doin' myself a favour an' all. And call me Mary, 'cos I reckon we're going to be good friends.'

'It's nice of you to say so,' Emma murmured, a smile curving her mouth. She was ecstatic. In comparison to the other house, this was a palace. The place was even furnished, sparsely admittedly, she thought, but there was enough for her family to manage with for the immediate future.

Upstairs, there were iron bedsteads but no mattresses or bedding.

'The beggars have nicked them an' all,' Mrs Porter ranted. "Cos Mr Rabinski provides everything. You could move into one of his houses with nothing to your name and be all right. Oh, he'll be upset about that, I can tell you.'

'We have some bedding with us,' Emma said, 'and a feather bed. That'll do us.'

'But only temporary,' Mrs Porter insisted. 'Mr Rabinski'll see you right, don't you worry. Now,' she went on briskly, her movements quick and energetic. 'We'll go back to my place and you can leave the bairn with me, as long as you'll be back for his next feed.' She smiled. "Cos I ain't had baby things around my house since young Joey was born and he's nearly eight.'

Back in her spotless, though cluttered living room, Mary Porter opened the bottom drawer of a dresser, scooped out the conglomeration of years on to the floor and then pulled the drawer out completely. Taking two cushions from the old sofa and patting them down in to the depths of the drawer, she held out her arms for young Billy. 'There now, that'll make him a nice cradle till you get back. Off you go and fetch your things. Your little man'll be fine with me.'

As Emma walked back through the streets, she could hardly believe the turn in their fortunes that the last five hours had taken.

Leonard was marching up and down the cold, rubbish-strewn room in a raging temper. 'I thought you'd have got this place cleaned up a bit by now. Where the devil have you been, woman?'

'Doing what you should have done, Leonard. Finding a *decent* place for this family to live.'

'What do you mean? This place is good enough once we get it cleaned up—'

'I'm not staying here a moment longer. There was a rat running freely around this room this morning. With one leap it could have been in the baby's cradle. This place is worse than that awful room we've just left, to say nothing of having to fetch every drop of water from a tap in the lane out there—'

'We can't go back to those rooms, if that's what you're thinking.'

'I've no intention of going back,' she told him shortly. 'I've found us somewhere else, so you can get the handcart loaded up again and—'

'Oh yes? And where is this wonderful place you've found for us? Have you stopped to think if we can afford fancy rent?'

'Ten and six a week, and worth every penny,' she snapped.

'Well, if you think I'm paying that, you've another think coming. This one is only seven and six.'

'You stay here if you want to, Leonard. Me and the boys are going.'

She faced him squarely. Leonard was arguing with her over three shillings and she remembered how often he came home, his breath smelling of drink, with the telltale rolling gait that meant he'd drunk freely, Emma's mouth tightened. She thought of the times when he came home loaded with presents, flowers for her, toys for Charles. He was generous with his money when he was flush, she had to admit, and he was a great deal easier to live with when he was in that expansive mood. She didn't want to be too hard on him. She didn't want to spoil the good times they did have. And yet . . .

Quietly, she said, 'If you were a little more careful with your money when you have plenty, then—'

His fist was bunched only inches from her face. 'Don't

you dare to tell me how to spend my money, woman. I earn it, I'll spend it.'

Emma blinked, but stood her ground not flinching under his threat. 'The children and I are moving to this house I've found,' she said slowly and deliberately. 'It's up to you whether you come as well.'

For a long moment they stood glaring at each other, until shamefacedly, Leonard dropped his gaze. 'Where is it, then, this palace?' She saw that his anger had died as swiftly as it had come and she was determined not to let him spoil the moment.

'On a side road leading off one of the main roads, just opposite a park. And there's such a nice woman lives next door.' She moved towards him and put her hand on his arm, eager to dispel their quarrel, and launched into the story of her morning's efforts. She was still talking whilst they loaded their bedding back on to the handcart which still stood outside the front door.

'It was such good luck meeting Mary Porter in the corner shop and her saying her neighbours had done a moonlight.' She giggled and added, 'I didn't let on that we'd done much the same.'

Leonard glanced at her in surprise but said nothing, busying himself tying the load safely on to the cart. He picked up the handles. 'Ready then?'

Emma smiled brightly. 'Aye, I'm ready. We'll be all right there, Leonard. I know we will. Come on.' And with a newfound strength she marched ahead of him down the street leading the way to their new home.

Whether it was the relief at having found a decent place to live at last, or meeting the friendly Mary Porter, that had given Emma such a lift in her spirits, she didn't know.

Whatever it was, she felt her old strength flowing back into her and she set to work on their new home with renewed vigour. Keep busy, she told herself sternly, it will stop you feeling so homesick and wondering all the time what is happening back home in Marsh Thorpe. The next morning, in one corner of the wash-house across the backyard, she found a small heap of coal left by the previous tenant. She cleaned the range grate in the living room and lit the fire. Then she cleaned the gas stove in the scullery and set the kettle on the ring. The gas made a gentle popping sound and made the place more homely, she thought. Having placed the cradle out in the back yard in the morning sunshine, she cleaned her kitchen, scrubbing the shelves above the sink that would house her pans and the space beneath where she would keep the enamel washing-up bowl, scrubbing brushes and dusters.

In the living room she wiped the wooden table with its bulbous legs and the four chairs that fitted underneath it. She put down her own peg rug on the hearth in front of the range and swept the ceiling and the walls with a long-handled brush. She took down the thick brown curtains hanging either side of the window and out in the back yard she shook them vigorously till the dust rose in clouds and she glanced in alarm towards the cradle where the baby lay sleeping peacefully. Even little Billy seemed to have found a new contentment. As for Charles, he was already firm friends with Joey Porter.

When she had gone the previous afternoon to meet her son from school, Charles had walked beside her, dragging his feet as if reluctant to go home.

She took his hand and said, 'It's all right, Charles, I've found us a better house than the one we went to last night.'

As soon as they arrived at their new home, the boy rushed from room to room. 'Mam, it's great. Can that little bedroom at the front looking out on to the street be mine? Oh, please say"yes"?'

Emma smiled. 'Of course.'

'Great!' He dashed outside to inspect the backyard and its potential for ball games. After a few moments she heard his high-pitched voice and then another boy's and looking out of the window she saw Charles had hauled himself up to peer over the fence into the Porters' backyard next door. Only minutes later he was asking, 'Can I go out an' play, Mam? Joey's going to take me to play down the street with the other boys.'

Emma hesitated only a moment. She could not keep her young son close to her for ever. He was growing and needed to be with children of his own age. She sighed, wishing that it did not have to be a street playground instead of green meadows and sandy beaches, but she smiled at him and said, 'Of course. Off you go.'

With a whoop of delight he was out of the door and pounding down the passage out into the street. Emma opened the front door and stood watching as he trotted down the sloping street beside the older, taller Joey Porter. Mary's boy was seven years old, dressed in short trousers with braces over his shirt, knee-length socks that were permanently wrinkled and black boots with scuffed toe-caps. He was thin and wiry like his mother, but he walked with a swagger and whistled piercingly, the sound echoing down the street.

It seemed, she thought perceptively as she watched from a distance, that Joey Porter was the leader of the gang of boys, who were kicking a football about at the end of the street. The game was suspended for a moment, the boys clustering around the new arrival.

'This is Charles Smith. He's come to live next door to me,' she heard Joey introduce him. 'He can play with us.'

The next minute the ball was back in motion and, Emma noticed, the boys were aiming it towards Charles, immediately involving him in their game. There was no fuss amongst children, she mused, smiling to herself. They'd accepted Charles as Joey's new friend without question.

The following morning Charles had been up earlier than usual, eager to go to school. 'I'm walking with Joey,' Charles had informed her importantly. 'I don't need you or Dad to take me now.'

When Leonard too had left the house and she had settled the baby, Emma washed all her own pots and pans and arranged them on the newly scrubbed open shelves above the now spotlessly white sink. She had just started to sweep the red tiles of the kitchen floor when she heard the latch on the back gate and a moment later a cheerful voice shouted. 'Hello, anybody in?'

'Yes. Just a minute.' Emma stopped her sweeping, removed the scarf from around her mouth and went to the door. She knew she must look a sight with dust streaking her face and her long black hair plaited and wound around her head with a headscarf covering it.

Mary Porter stood there holding a tray with two mugs of steaming tea. 'I thought you might like a cuppa.' Her smile widened and she nodded towards the interior of Emma's home. 'I reckoned you'd have a bit of clearing up to do.'

'That is kind of you,' Emma said. 'Come in, Mary.'

Mary set the tray down on the table, still damp from Emma's scrubbing. 'By heck, m'duck, you've made a difference to this place already.' The woman looked at Emma with kindly concern. 'But don't you go mad, now. You look a bit tired. Overdo it an' you'll drive your milk away.' She nodded towards Emma's ripe and overflowing breasts. 'It's still not that long since you had the bairn, now is it?'

Emma smiled and sank thankfully into one of the chairs at the table. Mary pushed a mug of tea towards her and sat opposite.

'No, you're right,' Emma said. 'I've got the worst done now, with the kitchen and this room. The rest can wait its turn. Actually, the other rooms aren't so bad.'

'That's the way, m'duck. No good doing yourself in over the job.'

There was silence in the kitchen whilst the two women slipped their tea companionably. Mary Porter was a few years older than her, Emma guessed, and in some ways she reminded Emma of her friend, Sarah. Mary had the same blunt kindliness, but whereas Sarah had a round, comforting little body, Mary Porter was thin and energetic. For a moment, thinking of Sarah and reminded sharply of Marsh Thorpe, Emma felt suddenly homesick. But as she listened to her new friend launch into a ceaseless chatter about all her new neighbours in the street, Emma realized that at least she was feeling the happiest she had been since coming to the city.

Thirty

Emma and her family settled into city life remarkably well, more because of Emma's strength of will that determined her to make the best of her lot than that she actually took to the city. In moments of quiet, in that time of half-waking, half-sleeping, she would again imagine she was lying in her own bed at home, listening to the gentle rattle of the mill sails whirling outside her window, the smell of freshly-baked bread permeating the house. Then she would wake feeling vaguely disappointed and for a moment, lost.

Her new friend helped to dispel what might have been – indeed what had been during those early months in the dismal lodging house – a lonely and strange existence for a country-bred girl suddenly plunged into the city streets. Mary Porter took Emma to the market and taught her how to haggle with the stallholders. Then, together, they wandered through the grand stores in the High Street, marvelling at the clothes and jewellery.

'Too expensive for the likes of us,' Mary said without a trace of bitterness, 'but it's nice to *look*, ain't it?'

There had been one incident which had threatened to destroy Emma's hard won contentment which happened only a few weeks after they had moved into their new home. It was on the first day the rent for their new home fell due that she found out the truth about the man she had married.

Emma had been expecting Mr Rabinski himself to collect his rents, so when the Saturday came and she opened the door to find herself face to face with the same rent man, Forbes, who had called upon them in their previous rooms, she gave a gasp of surprise.

The thin man sneered. 'Oh, so this is where you've fetched up, eh?'

'But I thought—' Emma began and then stopped.

'And what did yet think, Mrs Smith?' The sneer was still there.

'Nothing,' Emma said shortly and clamped her mouth shut, thankful that she knew what the rent was and that she had it safely tucked away beneath her apron, had carried around with her for the last three days so that it should not disappear into Leonard's pocket and subsequently across the bar at the pub.

With a flourish she produced the money whilst the little man licked the end of his pencil and filled out a fresh page in his book for the new tenants at number fourteen. His beady little eyes kept flashing sly looks at her.

'S'pect you didn't think you'd see me again. Mind you, I couldn't understand why you did a moonlight,' he said, with calculated casualness and waited a moment. When Emma said nothing, he went on, 'After all, it's usually when folks owe that much rent they can't pay and they reckon I'm about to fetch the bailiffs in.' Emma could not prevent a gasp from escaping her dry lips and she knew she must have turned a little pale for the man said hurriedly, 'Don't worry, Missis. You didn't owe much at all – well, only the one week – not after that young feller visiting you paid me up to date and a couple of weeks in advance too.'

Emma's thoughts were in turmoil. So, that was what all

the whispering on the landing had been about. William had paid Forbes all the money owing, but because he had said nothing to her and Leonard had not known about it either, her husband had dragged them out in the middle of the night still thinking they owed over three months' rent.

And, she thought angrily, now she knew too just what 'doing a moonlight flit' really meant. How naive and stupid she had been. She had merely thought that it meant you left a place without giving the proper term of notice because you'd found something better. It had never entered her innocent and trusting head, she chastised herself, that it meant leaving suddenly and under the cover of darkness because you owed rent you could not pay. So, the previous occupiers of her present home, the Tomkinsons, had gone off without paying Mr Rabinski what they owed him. And no wonder Leonard had given her some funny looks. He couldn't understand why she had gone along with it so readily when normally she made such a fuss about being honest. What a fool she had been! She had imagined that her husband had been so eager to get them out of that dreadful place and into a house that he could not wait for morning, when all the time he had been rushing to escape the bailiff's men. She should have guessed, she castigated herself roundly, when the new house turned out to be worse than the rooms.

Grimly, she said, 'I knew nothing about owing a week's rent, Mister, but I'll have it for you next time you call.' She wasn't quite sure just how she was going to manage it, but she was determined that she would.

'Well, now,' the man said, leaning nonchalantly against the door jamb and leering at her so that Emma took a step back. 'Maybe we could come to some little arrangement about that. You and I. Maybe it's time we got a little more friendly like. My name's Forbes, but you can call me Peter.'

Emma felt the colour creep up her neck. 'Well! If you think—'

'No, no, not that,' he said hurriedly, putting up his hand out towards her as if to fend off the very idea. 'My wife'd kill me.' He smirked again, looking up and down Emma's handsome, womanly figure, her magnificent bosom and the trim waist that had returned surprisingly quickly after the birth of her second child. 'Although,' the little weasel of a man was saying reflectively, 'it might be worth it.'

Emma felt the palm of her hand itch and she had already begun to raise her arm, when he said laughingly, 'All right, Missis, all right. What I meant was, can your husband get me in on a game?'

Mystified, Emma repeated stupidly, 'A game? What sort of a game?'

'Aw, come on,' the man sneered. 'Don't play the innocent wi' me.' Then he bent closer, his beady eyes boring into hers. There was genuine surprise in his tone as he said, 'By heck, you don't know, do you?'

When Emma shook her head, he went on with ruthless bluntness, 'A card game. Your husband's a gambler. It's how he makes his living.'

And now Emma's mouth did drop wide open.

By the time Leonard weaved his way unsteadily into the house in the early hours of the following morning, Emma's anger was at boiling point. She had waited up all night, determined to learn the truth and with every hour that passed had grown more angry. Though whether it was all directed at her husband or at herself for her blind naivety, even she could not have said. Emma was being hard on herself, for what could she have known about the world that Leonard Smith inhabited? Born and bred in the small community of Marsh Thorpe, sheltered by the narrowness of her everyday life, what could she possibly have known beyond the confines of her father's domination?

'A gambler. You're a gambler! A card sharp.'

Leonard stood in the middle of the room, swaying slightly and staring at her with a vacant, half smile on his face. When he did not answer, she nodded slowly. 'So. It is true then.' It explained everything now, everything that had happened. 'My God, Leonard,' she burst out with uncharacteristic blasphemy. 'What more am I going to learn about you?' There was silence before she asked, more quietly now, for the anger had suddenly drained out of her. 'Tell me one thing. Just one thing. Did my father know what you did before we got married?'

Leonard ran his hand through his dark hair and with the other hand sought the support of the back of a chair. Then he lunged towards it and fell into it. He leant his head back and sighed deeply. 'Of course he did,' he said flatly. 'Harry Forrest was no fool.'

'The bitterness in his voice was not lost on Emma and she knew he was referring, yet again, to the terms of her father's will. Emma pressed her lips together tightly, refusing to let the tears fall, but inside, she was being torn apart. There was not one small shred of pride to be salvaged. Her father had knowingly and willingly married her to a gambler and, for that, she would never forgive him. Her humiliation was complete. In his bitterness against her for being a girl and not the son he wanted so passionately, her father had cared nothing for her. The only time that she had ever pleased him, she thought, was when she had given him a grandson.

She sat at the kitchen table, her rage against Leonard

dying to be replaced by a dull ache of sadness. But there was something else too; curiosity, and with her usual determination, she clung to it.

She mashed a pot of tea and poured out two cupfuls, hot and strong and sweet. Pushing one across the table towards her husband, she said quietly, 'Tell me about it. About what you *really* do. I'm intrigued.'

He sat up and reached for the cup, taking satisfying gulps, like a man thirsting.

'It's all I know, Emma. It's all I can do,' he said flatly, yet Emma thought she detected a hint of wistfulness. 'I never knew my father.' A wry smile twisted his lips. 'I sometimes wonder if my mother even knew who he was. My childhood was punctuated by a series of "uncles". Some stayed a few months, some only weeks. The one that stayed the longest – nearly four years actually – ' there was almost a note of surprise in his voice, 'when I was about ten was called Mick. I liked him – *really* liked him. He was the closest I ever had to a dad. And,' he spread his hands in explanation, 'he was a gambler. It's as simple as that. He taught me a lot and I was a quick learner. He got me into games dead easy 'cos fellers thought that anyone could beat a twelve-year-old. But when we got playing,' the smile broadened mischievously, 'they soon found out different. Oh, we 'ad some nasty moments, but I soon learnt to use my fists. He taught me how to take care of myself, did Mick.' Leonard leant back in the chair and closed his eyes. 'Oh, I liked Mick. I liked him a lot.'

'What happened to him?' she probed, beginning to feel more sorry for this man now than angry with him.

He sighed heavily. 'Same as all the rest, I expect. They died, or went back to their wives, or Mother got tired of them when she found a better fish. One day Mick just went out, and never came back.'

Emma stared at him incredulously. 'Just like that?'

'Yes,' he said and even now, after all this time, she could still hear the hurt of a bewildered young boy in Leonard's voice. 'Just like that.'

She stood up and went to stand on the peg rug in front of the fire. The red glow illuminated her face, casting shadows and shining on her skin, silhouetting her round, inviting figure in its soft light.

'Leonard,' she said softly. 'There's only one thing I want to know. Is what you do against the law?'

He sat up and leant forward, leaning his elbows on his knees, clasping his hands in front of him and staring straight into the burning coals. 'Yes – and no.'

She knelt in front of him on the rug and stared into his face. Slowly he raised his eyes and looked into hers. Suddenly sober, he said quietly, 'All I can tell you is that the card games are set up and all those who take part do so of their own free will. I don't cheat, either.' He grinned lopsidedly. 'I don't need to, I'm too good. The only time there might be a bit of a problem is if someone gets carried away and loses more than he can afford. But . . .' he spread his hands, 'it's their own fault if they do.'

'And is that all you do, Leonard? Just – play cards?'

'No,' he seemed to be picking his words carefully now. 'I do a bit of trading in other ways, buying and selling. Y'know.'

'No, Leonard, that's just it. I don't know.' When he said no more and seemed to be avoiding her eyes, she gasped and said, 'Oh, Leonard, no! You don't mean stolen goods?'

'Don't ask me that, Emma. It's best that you don't know. Really it is. What you don't know, can't hurt you.'

Can't it? she thought, but for once Emma remained silent.

At least I know the truth now, she said to herself and

sighed, but the knowledge didn't bring her any comfort nor make her future any more secure. Indeed, as the weeks and months passed, every knock on her door made her jump, made her peek out of the window before opening up to strangers. Any moment, she expected that the figure standing there would be dressed in a dark uniform. It made her realize just how precarious their living was and explained how Leonard had pockets bulging with winnings one day and was hiding from the rent man the next.

'Tek in a bit o' washing,' Mary suggested helpfully. In a moment of desperation when they already owed two weeks' rent and Mr Forbes was due to call again the following day for another four, Emma had confided in her friend though without telling her the details of why their existence was so precarious. 'There's plenty of posh houses uphill put their washing out to the likes of us living downhill. You might even pick up a bit of cleaning work now and then. I don't mind 'aving the little one now and again for you, if you like.'

A look of doubt crossed Emma's face. 'It's very kind of you, Mary. But Billy's a right little tyke. D'you really know what you're offering?'

Mary chuckled. 'I've had three lads of me own, m'duck, and our Joey's the youngest and the best of the lot. The older two were little beggars, I don't mind telling you.'

Emma had not met Mary's two older sons for they were grown up and had left home and were working in a factory in Sheffield.

'Well, if you're sure,' Emma said, her mind working quickly. If she could just earn enough each week to cover the rent, at least that would keep a roof over their heads.

''Course I am.'

Charles was still a quiet, rather shy boy, but he seemed happy enough trotting after the older Joey Porter with the devotion of a puppy. But over Billy, Emma shook her head. 'He was trouble with a capital T from the moment he was born. Before an' all, if you count the uncomfortable nine months and all that kicking.'

And as soon as the young Billy Smith started walking, Emma no longer knew where he was from one minute to the next. He was a street child from the time he could toddle, the ring leader amongst his peers, frightened of nothing and no one, a daredevil egged on by others to greater and greater deeds of daring.

'He'll come to a bad end, will that lad,' Mary Porter would shake her head. 'Mind you, he's got some spirit, I'll grant you.'

Emma would sigh and view both her sons with bewilderment, wondering just how they came to have the characters they did. Billy was his father's son with the same cherubic charm, the same temper and the same deviousness. As he grew, the boy would come home with the pockets of his short trousers jingling with the ha'pennies he'd won at marbles or conkers or some other game depending on the time of year.

'That's my boy,' Leonard would laugh proudly, ruffling the child's dark hair and Billy would look up at his father with a cheeky grin and in his eyes was a knowledge far beyond his years. Emma would turn away and catch sight of Charles melting into the shadows, no match for his charismatic brother. Surprisingly, though, the two boys were remarkably fond of each other, despite the difference in their ages and the complete antithesis of their characters. The amusing thing was that, of the two, it was Billy who was the natural leader, and, from the time Billy could walk, it was Charles who followed in his younger brother's wake.

Thirty-One

Once Emma had taken over the responsibility of finding the rent each week, she felt a little more secure, though Leonard's temperamental moods grew worse, rather than better. When he had money, he spent freely, buying presents for her and the two boys. At such times he came home decidedly less than sober most nights. When money was tight, his temper was short. If the boys annoyed him, he would raise his hand and take a swipe at them, uncaring on what part of their anatomy the blow landed. When his rages filled the small terraced house, Charles would creep next door to find refuge with the happy-go-lucky Porter family, but young Billy, even when quite small, would stand his ground, taking the blows and outstaring his father.

'Why do you do it, love?' Emma would ask with exasperation. 'Why don't you just keep out of his way, like Charles?'

'I aren't a coward,' Billy began and winced as his mother dabbed iodine on to the cut on his lip inflicted by Leonard.

Emma thought back briefly to the night of the storm that had wrecked the mill and said quietly, 'Neither is Charles, if push comes to shove. But he doesn't ask for trouble like you, young Billy. He tries to avoid it if he can. He's got a bit of common sense.'

He grinned up at her cheekily, his wounds forgotten. 'He's all right, our Charlie. 'Sides,' the seven-year-old swaggered, 'he's got me to look after him, ain't he?'

The irony of the fact that Charles, at nearly fourteen, needed a seven-year-old to 'look after him' was not lost on her. Emma sighed and turned away without answering. Oh yes, she thought grimly, and he's got you to lead him astray too.

Only Billy ever called his brother 'Charlie', for, to Emma's mind, there was only one Charlie – Grandpa Charlie Forrest – and her reserved elder son bore no resemblance at all to the ebullient man she remembered. If anything, she thought, Billy was closer to the daredevil her grandfather had reputedly been in his youth. Her younger son certainly had daring and charisma, yet there any similarity ended, for Billy had also inherited the darker, more devious, side of his own father's nature. There was a cunning about the young boy that was disconcerting, and to his mother, worrying, for she had not been able to prevent Leonard from teaching his son the tricks of his trade and the boy was fast becoming more streetwise than Emma liked.

'Oh, Grandpa Charlie,' she would murmur in quiet, reflective moments, 'why couldn't one of them have been more like you?'

Bridget had visited them now and again through the years, arriving unannounced in a flurry of excitement and laughter, leaving a waft of her flowery perfume wherever she went. She idolized Billy and whilst she was kind enough to bring presents for both boys, it never entered her pretty head that her obvious affection for the younger boy might hurt the older one. It was to Charles' credit that he never showed any jealousy at all towards Billy.

'Oh, Billy's just like his father,' Bridget would trill. 'Such a handsome, merry little chap.'

'And is Leonard like *his* father, Bridget?' Emma dared to ask once, holding her breath.

'Leonard's father?' Bridget's tone was mystified, almost as if she had forgotten the existence of such a man.

'Mm,' Emma said. 'Was he a dashing, man about town when you married him?'

'Me? Married?' The woman went into fits of laughter, until Emma, despite herself, was smiling too. Bridget wiped the tears from her eyes. 'Oh, my darling Emma. I've never been married, but don't you dare tell a soul, mind.' She patted the neat blonde sausage curls. 'Keep 'em guessing, that's what I always say. Keep 'em champing at the bit.' Her eyes twinkled with merriment. 'You'd have done better not to have married our Leonard. Once they've got a ring on your finger – and through your nose – ' she snorted with laughter at her own joke, 'they take you for granted. Expect you to wash and cook and clean for them.' Again she preened and glanced towards the mirror over the fireplace. 'That's not for me, Emma dear. Never was and never will be.'

'But,' Emma said hesitantly, 'what about Leonard's father?'

The woman's eyes widened. 'Leonard's *father*? Huh! I wouldn't have married him if he'd been the last man on earth! Never knew where you had him or *if* you had him at all. A real "Jack the Lad". I suppose that's where Leonard gets his bad habits from.'

Valiantly, Emma tried to hide her smile, but failed and Bridget wagged her finger playfully at her. 'Now then. I know what you're thinking. "Pot calling kettle black".' The smile spread across her painted mouth. 'Oh well, you're right, I suppose. I have been a bit of a bad girl in my time.' She sighed wistfully. 'But I'd do it all again. Every minute of it. I don't regret a moment of my life.' She paused, pondering for a moment and then added slowly, 'There was a time when I thought I did. When I found I was pregnant with Leonard. That was a mistake, I can tell you.'

Emma was speechless, unable to comprehend any woman not wanting to have children and at Bridget's next words, she could not stop the gasp of surprise escaping her lips.

'I thought about giving him away. You know, putting him up for adoption. But, well, when it came to the point, I couldn't do it.' She giggled as if surprised at herself. 'I must have more maternal instincts in me than I thought. Of course, he's been a pain at times. Some of my gentlemen friends haven't been too keen to have a kid tagging along.' Her grin widened and she winked broadly. 'But I soon changed their minds for them.'

Emma sniffed wryly. 'Well, he's a pain now, your Leonard.'

'Oh, don't be too hard on him. He's not a bad lad. He just likes a good time and you are a bit of a sobersides, now aren't you? Always worrying about money and paying the rent. No man wants to come home to a nagging wife, Emma.'

'Am I his wife?' She hadn't intended to ask the question but the words were out before she realized she had spoken them aloud.

Bridget's eyes widened. 'Of course you are. You can't think that big, fancy wedding could have been fixed?'

Emma pulled a face. 'I have wondered.'

Bridget laughed. 'Oh no, I'll say that for Harry Forrest, he had Leonard weighed up and tied up good and proper.'

'Yes,' Emma said grimly, and thought to herself, if only I had realized it at the time.

'Now,' Bridget was saying, dragging Emma's thoughts

back to the present. 'Where's Billy? I've a present for him.' As a hasty afterthought, she added, 'And for Charles as well, of course.'

As if on cue, they heard Billy's whistling and his boots thudding down the passageway between the two houses. The yard gate crashed back on its hinges and the boy came into the house.

'Hello, how's me favourite gran then?'

He stood before Bridget, bent forward and planted a sticky kiss on her cheek.

'You young scallywag,' Bridget laughed. 'I'm your *only* gran.'

Billy's cheeky grin widened. 'Where's me present then?'

'Billy . . .' Emma began, but Bridget only laughed and began hunting in the depths of her bag. 'But you've got to pay me for this, young Billy.'

'Pay you? Not likely!'

'Wait a bit and I'll tell you why. Ah, here we are.' Bridget pulled out two small thin parcels about four inches long.

'What is it?' the boy asked in spite of himself.

'Open it and see.'

Billy put his head on one side, a wary look on his face, meeting her teasing eyes squarely. 'Not if I've got to pay for it.'

Bridget laughed. 'Go on, open it first anyway.'

The boy unwrapped the present and in his palm lay a pearl handled penknife. 'It's great, but why have I got to pay for it?'

'If anyone gives you a knife, you're supposed to pay for it else it'll "cut" your friendship.'

Emma stifled her mirth. She had never thought of Leonard's mother as being superstitious. Sarah Robson, yes, but never Bridget. She watched, amused, as Billy's mouth curved in a sneer, but he was fishing in his pocket and pulled out a coin. 'Well, that's all I've got.'

Over his shoulder, Emma saw the coin – or rather what had once been a coin of the realm – lying on the flat of his palm.

Bridget smiled. 'Well, that'll do.'

'Wait a minute, young man,' Emma began, 'what is it?' She reached out and picked up the piece of metal that still had the imprint of the monarch's head on it, but it had been flattened and battered into twice it's normal size. 'What have you been up to now, Billy?'

She caught hold of the lobe of his ear and nipped it, holding it firmly between her thumb and forefinger until he squirmed. 'Ouch. It's only a ha'penny, Mam.'

She looked at it again. Yes, it was a halfpenny, or rather, it had been, but now it was the size of a penny. 'What have you done to it?' she asked suspiciously.

'We all do it,' he began, as if that made it acceptable. 'The older lads told us what to do. Jocy told us,' he added slyly, perhaps thinking that would make it all right. 'We buy some chewing gum with half our Sat'day penny, chew it until all the taste's gone and then we – we—'

He wriggled again, but Emma's grip was firm. 'Go on,' she said grimly.

'We stick it on the railway line. Y'know, where the track goes across the road in the High Street? Joey ses they used to do it on the tram lines but since the trams stopped running, we have to use the railway track. The train runs over it and it ends up like that.'

'And?' Emma persisted. 'Then what do you do with it?' The finger and thumb pressed a little harder.

'We – we go and put it in the slot machines on the station and get chocolate and stuff.'

Emma opened her mouth to upbraid her son, but before

she could say a word, Bridget was clapping her hands and laughing. 'Oh, how clever of you, Billy. You *are* like your father. That's *just* the sort of thing Leonard used to do.'

Thwarted in her outrage, Emma thought to herself, 'And he's still doing it.' Automatically, her glance went to the cupboard in the corner.

The christening mug was missing yet again.

Thirty-Two

Twelve years had passed since she had come to live in the city and in all that time she had not been back to Marsh Thorpe once. So when a letter arrived from Sarah telling her of Luke's death, Emma sat in her kitchen, the letter lying open on the table, and was overcome by guilt. 'I should have gone back more. I should have gone to see them,' she murmured aloud.

They had corresponded, she and Sarah, regularly, but Sarah had never come to the city and Emma, immersed in the hardship of her everyday life and burying the memories of her girlhood, had allowed the months and years to slip by. Perhaps, she thought, in a moment of honesty with herself, I've deliberately avoided going back. Marsh Thorpe held so many memories, happy and sad, that perhaps her innermost self had shied away from returning to open old wounds.

However, she knew exactly what had been happening in the village during all the years she had been gone, for Sarah's letters, an untidy, childish scrawl, were nevertheless newsy and a joy to read. Holding the pages of her ramblings was like talking to Sarah face to face and Emma had always eagerly awaited their arrival.

We've a new vicar come to the parish and he's
not married and you'd be surprised how many

young unmarried girls have suddenly found going to church of a Sunday a good idea . . .

Jamie Metcalfe's never wed, you know, Emma. Keeps himself to himself. If it wasn't for folk doing business with him, why, I don't reckon he'd set eyes on a body from one weekend to the next. William comes over now and again from Bilsford and always calls to see us. Oh, but he's a lovely man, Emma, and no mistake. Mind you, he was always a nice lad. Can't understand why some nice girl hasn't snapped him up years ago. Now I can understand Jamie not getting wed. Who'd put up with that mardy creature? But William, now he's a different kettle of fish . . .

By the way, I heard tell that Bridget got left a little cottage when that feller she went to live with passed away.

Luke's rheumatics are playing him up and his breathing is getting worse. Some days he don't even get out of bed. Since the mill went, he don't seem to have the heart somehow . . .

And now poor old Luke was gone.

The gossip about her mother-in-law was not news to Emma. She was very fond of her mother-in-law for Bridget made no secret of her way of life and was in no way ashamed of it.

'I've been fond of all my gentleman friends, Emma,' she would say, smoothing the silk of her skirt. 'Never mind what anyone says about me. And I've given them affection and pleasure,' she gave an arch look at the younger woman, 'in their final years, and if,' she waved her slim, well-manicured hand in the air, 'they want to show their appreciation by leaving me a little something, then I'm certainly not going to complain, now am I?' The latest 'little something' had been a small, thatched cottage in Thirsby, the next village to Marsh Thorpe. 'Of course, I may sell it and move back to the city,' she said dreamily, examining her long pointed fingernails with seeming intensity. 'But I'm in no hurry. There's this retired Colonel who's just moved into the village.' She looked up at Emma coyly out of the corners of her eyes. 'A widower, you know.'

Emma laughed aloud. 'Oh, Bridget, you're priceless.'

Bridget only shrugged her shoulders and laughed girlishly, adding, as always, 'Now where are my darling boys? Where's my little Billy?'

But this morning's letter from Sarah, Emma had not wanted to receive.

'Poor Luke,' she murmured. 'And poor Sarah. I ought to go to her. I ought—' With a swift movement she got up from the wooden chair and went to the mantelpiece and lifted down the pint pot where she kept a little housekeeping money. As she might have expected, it was empty. That meant Leonard was short this week, for he never touched her jar when he had money enough of his own to flash around.

So all she had was the rent money which she hid every week away from Leonard. Though she knew he had tried desperately on occasions to find it, pulling drawers open and scattering the contents, flinging furniture about in his frustration, she had always managed to keep it hidden from him. She would watch him with a thudding heart, determined to keep outwardly calm while all the time feeling the money tucked safely in the elastic of her knickers.

Her glance went to the cupboard in the corner where the christening mug stood. It was still there. So, things were not that tight at the moment. She bit her lip, debating whether to follow her husband's example and pop the mug to raise the fare to Marsh Thorpe so that she could go to Luke's funeral.

'No,' she said aloud to the empty kitchen. 'I'll not be dragged into his ways.' Her mouth tightened. Just for once, the rent man would have to wait. She was going to Marsh Thorpe to attend old Luke's funeral and Mr Forbes would have to whistle for a week. She quelled the shudder that ran through her, smothering the thought that it would be dangerous to get into that man's clutches too often.

'Oh, Emma, Emma lass. I'm that glad to see you. Thank you for coming. Let me look at you.'

Emma returned the swift hug and then allowed herself to be scrutinized by the puffy eyes that spoke of Sarah's recent loss. 'Luke would love to have seen ya again before . . .'

'Oh, Sarah. I'm so sorry I haven't been back. I should have—'

'No, no, lass,' the older woman was shaking her head. 'I didn't mean it like that. We knew you couldn't get away, what with ya family an' all. 'Sides, we realized it must be difficult for you to come back here . . .' Her voice trailed away and she glanced swiftly at the looming shape of the mill behind them.

Emma found she was holding her breath as her eyes went beyond the plump little figure of Sarah and she allowed herself to look at Forrest's Mill for the first time in twelve long years. It was still there, standing tall, a black shape against the morning light from the east, remarkably unscathed by the years that had passed.

'William came and – what did he call it? – capped it, I think he said, to stop the weather getting in and rotting all the floorboards.'

Emma glanced at her old friend in surprise. 'William?'

Sarah nodded and looked at her keenly. 'Oh yes.' Now it was her turn to show surprise. 'Didn't you know? I thought you must have asked him to do it.'

When Emma said nothing but merely shook her head, Sarah's puzzlement deepened. 'Oh that's odd, then, 'cos he comes every month to see to it. He goes all over the mill and does any repairs. To be honest, at first Luke and me thought you must have sold it to him, but we asked him one day – he always comes in for a cuppa, y'know – but he said no, he was only keeping an eye on it for you, to keep the machinery right, an' that. And the house, Emma, it's all just as you left it. I go in every week and keep it nice. It's all ready if you should ever want to come back.'

Emma hardly heard Sarah's prattle. She was standing perfectly still, just staring at the mill, her mind hammering out his name. William, oh, William.

Then something in Sarah's tone caught her attention again. There was a catch in the woman's throat as she said, 'But – but there's just one thing I'll have to tell you now. It's something mebbe I should have told you in a letter, but I could never bring myself to write the words. I kept hoping, you see . . .' Her voice dwindled. Even now she was putting off the moment of the actual telling of something unpleasant.

'What is it, Sarah?' Emma said gently, putting her arm around the older woman's shoulders.

The words came out in a rush then. 'It's the bees. They've gone. The hives, they're all empty.'

'Oh,' Emma said flatly. 'I see.'

Sarah was shaking her head sadly. 'I was so afraid they *would* go, y'know. But for the first few years after you'd gone, they did stay. And I was that pleased because I thought it meant that you would be coming back.' Her face slackened into lines of defeat. 'And I've tried everything I can think of, baiting the hives, all that. But they've never come back.'

There was nothing Emma could think of to say.

As she left the pew at the end of the funeral service to follow Luke's coffin out into the churchyard, with Sarah clinging to her arm and snuffling into her handkerchief, Emma searched for sight of William. It seemed as if all the village was there, packed into the church standing on the rise towering over the houses clustering round it. There were a lot of faces she recognized, older, certainly, but then no doubt hers was too. There were some strangers amongst the congregation; people she presumed had come to the village in the past twelve years and who had come to know – and to like – old Luke. Then she saw Jamie, standing rigidly tall, his gaze fixed upon the altar as the family mourners processed slowly down the aisle. But there was no sign of William Metcalfe and the fact surprised and disappointed Emma in one swift stab.

They buried Luke in one corner of the churchyard in a plot beneath a yew tree and, as Emma lifted her gaze from the deep hole with the mound of earth to one side, she saw the mill and knew that Luke would have been happy with the place Sarah had chosen for him. He would lay within sight of the mill where he had lived and worked all his life. No man could have loved that mill more, she thought, if he had owned it.

Only a handful of mourners came back to Sarah's cottage after the interment. Jamie was the last to leave and Emma walked with him out of the cottage, through the orchard and into the mill yard. They were ill at ease with each other. Neither seemed to know what to say nor even how to open up a conversation.

'How are —?' 'Do you see —?'

They both began to speak at once and then stopped, looked at each other, smiled awkwardly and then Emma said, 'You first.'

Jamie twisted his cap through his fingers. 'I was only going to ask how you are? You *look* fine.'

She glanced up to see those dark brown eyes upon her, but in their depths his expression was difficult to read. She smiled brightly, perhaps a little too brightly, and said, 'I'm fine. I've got used to life in the city. I never thought I would but, well, on the whole it's not so bad. I have a lovely neighbour, Mary Porter.' She laughed. 'She's very like Sarah in some ways.' Emma was prattling, she knew she was, to cover up her embarrassment. She was talking about anything and everything save the one thing she knew Jamie was really wanting to ask.

But he was not one to be put off. 'Are you – happy – Emma?'

She looked at him then, turning to face him, her brilliant eyes holding his, not allowing him to look away. Quietly, she said, 'As happy as I'm ever likely to be, Jamie.'

They stood in the middle of the yard just looking at each other until Jamie let out a sigh that came from the very depths of his soul.

'Oh, Emma, Emma,' was all he said.

Thirty-Three

'What on earth?' Emma began in surprise as she watched Leonard struggling through the back door with a huge wireless set in his arms.

He set it on the kitchen table and turned to face her, his eyes shining with excitement. He was breathing rapidly but not only from carrying the heavy piece of equipment from the handcart down the passage and into the house. There was excitement in his voice and his eyes sparkled as he said, 'Haven't you heard? The Prime Minister is to speak at a quarter past eleven this morning. This is it, Emma. It's going to be war again.' To her amazement, Leonard actually rubbed his hands together.

'And you mean – ' she spluttered angrily, pointing at the brown box with knobs and dials on the front sitting innocently on the table, 'you mean, you've actually gone and bought a wireless – just to hear the Prime Minister tell us what we already know? Have you taken leave of your senses, Leonard Smith?'

Leonard grinned cheekily at her. 'I haven't bought it exactly.'

She held up her hands. 'I don't want to hear. I don't want to know.'

But Leonard was too exhilarated today for her reproaches to upset him. Ignoring Emma's furious face, he began to play about with wires and cables, muttering to himself. 'Now let's see, where does this go?'

There was a knock at the back door and through the window overlooking their back yard, Emma saw the Porter family en masse, Mary, Alf and Joey, now a tall, broad-shouldered young man, standing there and peering in through the window. Tight-lipped Emma beckoned. 'Come in. Come in all of you. Why don't we fetch the whole street in to listen? Make it really worth your while,' she finished, glaring at Leonard.

The Porter family trooped into the kitchen and stood around watching Leonard fix up the wireless. Emma folded her arms under her bosom and tapped her foot angrily on the floor.

'Picked it up on the market, Alf,' Leonard said, ignoring his wife. 'It'll be useful to know what's going on.'

The big man nodded and said, as briefly as always, 'On at quarter past eleven, ain't he?'

'That's right. Now, let's see . . .' Leonard bent towards the wireless and twiddled the knobs. Strange noises interspersed with crackling came from the brown fabric of the speaker as he tried to tune into an interference-free wavelength.

There was the thumping of feet on the stairs and Billy charged into the room, followed by Charles. 'Aw, Dad, you've got a wireless!'

'Be quiet, then. Let's listen.'

'It's just gone eleven. He'll be on in a few minutes.'

As they all waited in the room, standing awkwardly, Emma noticed Charles move to stand beside Joey. A young man now, tall and thin, Charles was still quiet and rather reserved, his eyes large in a pale face. He had done so well at school that he had stayed on to take his Higher School Certificate examination and was now waiting to see if he had a place at a university, whereas Joey Porter had left school and was working in a local factory.

'He's a man now,' Leonard had stormed. 'He should be out earning a living, not still a lad in short trousers at school.'

'He's not in short trousers,' Emma had retorted. 'He's a chance to go to a university, a chance to better himself.'

'Better himself. Huh!' Leonard had sneered. 'He'd do better to get a trade.' There had been a pause, then he had added slyly. 'What about the milling trade, Emma? After all, he's destined to become a miller, isn't he?'

Emma had glared at him, her lips tight, but she had made no reply.

Now as they waited in the kitchen for the momentous words to issue from the wireless, Emma was filled with dread. What did the future hold for her quiet, studious son? What, indeed, did the future hold for any of them?

'Well, that's it then,' Leonard said, glancing round everyone in the room as the voice died away. He switched off the wireless and turned to look at Alf Porter. 'You joining up again, Alf?'

'Eh?' Mary Porter's voice came, high-pitched with fear, her eyes wide as she stared at her husband. 'You won't have to go, Alf, will you? You're too old, aren't you?'

Alf shrugged his huge shoulders. 'Dunno.'

Mary looked around at the others standing in the room, her eyes wild. 'He's too old and the boys are too young. No, no, they won't have to go . . .' There was silence. No one spoke as she added, her voice a terrified squeak. 'Will they?'

'Well, I wish I was old enough to go,' Billy said. 'You'll be going, Dad, won't you? You could be an officer if you went back in the army, couldn't you?'

Emma watched her husband's face, saw the calculating look on his features, the excitement in his eyes. Casually he rested his arm about his younger son's shoulders. 'Maybe so, son, maybe so.'

'Cor, Dad. I wish I could join up,' Billy said again, his worshipping gaze on his father. 'I wish I was as old as our Charles. He can go, can't he?'

Before she could stop herself, Emma gasped and looked towards her elder son. She hadn't realized, hadn't thought, that Charles at eighteen, might really have to go to war.

Standing behind them at the back of the room, the colour seemed to drain from Charles' face. He was silent as Billy said again, 'I wish *I* was Charles.'

Joey Porter, burly like his father, put his arm about his friend's shoulder. Quietly he said, 'If we have to go, Charlie, we'll stick together, eh?'

Charles said nothing but only nodded.

'They won't have to go, will they?'

If she'd said it once in the three weeks since the announcement that Britain was at war with Germany, Mary Porter had uttered the same words a hundred times, Emma thought. Biting back her rising irritation, she said, 'To be honest, Mary, I think that eventually, yes, they will be called up. At least Joey and Charles. We'd best get used to the idea.'

'But they won't send them to fight, will they? I mean they're so young.'

Emma, standing at the white sink in her scullery, her arms deep in soap suds, leant on her hands, the warm water lapping around her elbows. She was remembering the last time when she had been what? Only fifteen. The picture was in her mind of Jamie Metcalfe, her sweetheart, marching off proudly to war; the war they had all said was to 'end all wars' and yet here they were again with another generation of young men having to do it all over again. Fleetingly, she wondered if Jamie would volunteer for this one, but then her mind was dragged back to the present and to the agitated little woman beside her. Poor Mary, Emma thought with sudden compassion. Her family were her whole life as indeed were Emma's to her. If anything were to happen to any of them . . .

Emma dried her hands and arms and said firmly, 'Come on, Mary, let's have a cup of tea.'

They were sitting at the table, talking softly and drinking tea, when they heard footsteps in the passageway. They fell silent, staring at each other and listening for which back gate should open. It was the latch on Emma's that was lifted and heavy boots came into her yard and to the door. Mary rose as the knock sounded. 'I'd best go, m'duck. You've got a visitor. I'll see you later.'

As Mary Porter, her eyes wide with fear, went out, the policeman stepped into Emma's kitchen.

'Mrs Smith?' the officer asked, removing his helmet. His huge bulk seemed to fill the room.

Emma swallowed. Billy, she thought, it's Billy got himself into trouble. Well, she'd been expecting it.

She sighed as she said, 'Yes, that's right.'

'Is your husband at home, Mrs Smith?'

'No, he's gone down to the market.'

'Really?' The tone of the constable's voice as he said the one word made Emma stare at him. She watched as his glance went around the room and came to a stop on the wireless set now sitting on a low shelf in the corner. 'Can you tell me how your husband – er – came by that there wireless?'

Emma gave up a silent prayer of thankfulness that she was able to say truthfully. 'No, I have no idea.'

Emma felt his glance upon her appraisingly but she returned his look unflinchingly.

'Hmm,' was all he said and, replacing his helmet, added, 'Well, I'll be calling back to see your husband later, Missis. I'll bid you good-day – for the moment.'

For some reason, Emma felt that there was a veiled threat in the last three words, but she managed to remain outwardly calm as the officer left the house. She stood motionless in the middle of the kitchen, her heart pounding as she listened to his heavy tread going slowly up the passage again.

As dusk fell, Emma pulled on her hat and coat and walked to the bottom of the street to stand on the corner where the long road from town ran at right angles to their own. Standing outside the off-licence, she waited, stamping her feet in the cold.

'What you doing here, Mam?' She heard Billy's voice out of the darkness and when she beckoned him he detached himself from the other lads, shouting a cheery, 'See ya,' to his mates.

Emma gripped his shoulder and without preamble demanded, 'Where's your dad?'

'In a card game in the back room at one of the pubs near the market.'

'Fetch him.'

'Aw, Mam, he'll kill me if I interrupt his game.'

'Tell him it's me sent you and tell him it's urgent. I've never yet fetched him out of a game before – and he knows it.' She nodded grimly. 'He'll know it's urgent.'

The boy seemed to consider for a moment, then he shrugged his thin shoulders and said, 'All right, then. What's it all about anyway?'

'Best you don't know, young Billy. Just fetch him here.'

He turned to go and then glanced back as she made no move to go home. 'You staying here then?' he asked incredulously.

'Yes. Just you get off and look sharp about it.'

'Right,' Billy said and began to run, his socks wrinkling around his ankles as his boots pounded along the pavement. In the deepening gloom she heard the echo long after he had disappeared from her sight.

It was almost an hour later and she was stamping her icy feet and rubbing her deadened fingers before she heard two pairs of footsteps approaching along the street towards her.

'About time,' she muttered crossly.

'What on earth's the matter, woman, that I have to be dragged away from a game? And I was winning too.' His voice reached her out of the darkness before he did.

'You'll not be winning, m'lad, if you come home tonight. But why I'm bothering to save your thieving hide, I'll never know.'

He was close to her now, his eyes on a level, boring into hers. 'What the hell are you on about?'

'I had a visitor today. A bobby.'

She heard him pull in a sharp breath. 'Oh aye,' he said carefully.

'Asking,' Emma said with slow deliberation, 'about your wireless.'

'Aaah.' She heard him exhale, long and slow, and then he said again, 'Well now, that puts a different light on it.'

She felt him grasp her arm and give it a quick squeeze. 'You're a good 'un, Emma. Thanks.' He paused and then he put his face close to hers. 'Though, I have to admit I'm a bit surprised.' She heard his low chuckle as he added, 'I'd have thought you'd have let me swing and stood back laughing.'

288

In a low voice she said, 'No, Leonard. I may not approve of what you do and we have our ups and downs, I know, but you're still my husband and – and the father of my children.'

'Dad?' Billy's voice came out of the darkness and both Emma and Leonard jumped.

They had forgotten he was there, no doubt listening to every word. 'Dad, shall I get shut of it for you? I've got a mate who . . .'

'No,' Leonard's voice was like a pistol-shot, then more quietly and reaching out his hand to touch his son's shoulder. 'No, lad, you keep out of it.' He turned back to Emma. 'Look, Emma. I'll have to disappear for a while. They'll not do anything to you or the boys, though they'll maybe come and take the wireless.'

'That'll not bother me,' Emma said tartly.

'Right then. Pack me a few clothes and my razor and Billy can bring the case to the station.'

'But where—' she began, but his only answer was to squeeze her arm again and to say quietly in her ear. 'It's best you don't know. But I'll be back.'

She felt his lips seek hers, felt his warm mouth on hers and his wiry moustache gently scratching her cheek. And then he was gone, striding away in the darkness.

'Come on, Billy. Let's get home and pack a case for him before that bobby comes back.'

Several weeks passed and no word came from Leonard. The police visited again and took the wireless set away, just as Leonard had known they would, but after that, though they questioned her as to his whereabouts they seemed to believe that she did not know where her husband was and left the family in peace.

'Let that be a lesson to you, young Billy,' Emma said, and though the boy was subdued for a while, she doubted if the salutary lesson would obliterate the years of teaching him to live on the fringes of the law that he had received from his father. For months, even years after, Emma's nights were broken by nightmares and even in her waking hours she came to dread the sound of heavy footsteps in the passageway and every unexpected knock that came upon her door.

Thirty-Four

'Mam, I've – I've got my call-up papers.'

Charles was standing on the peg rug in front of the fire in the living room, the official document in his hands. Emma had just dressed and come downstairs to start the day. As she opened the door into the kitchen, she knew something was different this morning for normally Charles had left for work by the time she came downstairs.

She stared at him, her violet eyes suddenly wide. 'Called up? But – but you can't be. You're going to university in October. You got a place. You'll have to tell them—'

Charles had left school and had taken temporary work for a year until he could take up the place he had been offered at a university.

'Mam, listen.' He came and put his arms about her, holding her close with the gentle tenderness that had always been his nature. Quietly, he said. 'The truth is – I volunteered. Joey and me, we went together to the recruiting office.'

She pulled back a little, just enough so that she could look at him. Her searching gaze scanned his face and, for a moment, she was seeing not the young man standing there, pale but with a newfound determination, but the little boy clambering over the smashed timbers of the mill, his anxiety for her driving away all fear. Her gentle, reserved, studious Charles was far more courageous than a dozen loud-mouthed braggarts, she thought.

She nodded and a deep sigh escaped her lips. 'You're a brave lad, Charles Forrest Smith.'

He tried to smile but, standing so close, she could see it trembling on his mouth. 'Am I? I don't *feel* very brave.'

'It's like the night the mill blew down. You were dreadfully afraid then and yct when you thought I was hurt, you forgot your own fear and came climbing across all the wreckage to reach me.'

He looked into her eyes and frowned slightly. 'Did I? I don't remember.'

'Don't you?' She was surprised. Because every moment of that dreadful night was etched so sharply on her own memory, she had expected it to be so for everyone else, even for Charles, especially for Charles. But then, she reminded herself, he had been only a little boy, although a very heroic little boy. She had no doubt that her eldest son would act with that same courage in battle. Her only fear was that his very bravery might lead him into even more danger.

Emma shuddered inwardly, but on her face her smile of encouragement was serene and confident. 'I was proud of you that night, Charles, and I'm proud of you now.'

She voiced nothing of her innermost fears, the terror shared by thousands of mothers. At this moment, her son needed her to be brave for him.

She made a pot of tea and they sat at the table and talked until Billy clattered his way down the stairs to disturb their last few precious moments together.

When he heard the news, Billy slapped his brother's back, his eyes gleaming. 'Cor, our Charlie. You lucky sod!'

'Billy!' Emma began, although her reprimand was half-hearted. At this moment her mind was filled with her eldest son.

'Emma. Emma! Where are you?'

'I'm here, Mary, upstairs. Wait a bit. I'll come down.'

But already Mary was half way up the stairs to meet her. 'It's our Joey. He's volunteered. Him and your Charles. Did you know?'

'Oh, Mary,' she came down and put her arms about her friend, and together they went down again and into the kitchen.

'*Did* you know, Emma?'

Emma shook her head. 'Not until early this morning. Charles got his papers.'

Mary's lip trembled and easy tears filled her eyes. 'Joey too.'

'Well, you know what they said. They wanted to stick together. Maybe they'll be able to after all.'

'Do you think so?' Mary said, clinging to any vestige of hope. Her hair, liberally flecked with grey, was flying, wild and uncombed, around her face. 'Oh, do you really think so?'

Emma patted her hand. 'Let's hope so.'

But in the event, Charles and Joey were not able to stay together. Joey Porter was drafted into the Navy and Charles into the RAF. The news brought fresh anguish to Mary. 'The Navy. Oh, I don't want him in the Navy, but he seems set on the idea.'

Listening, Billy's eyes were bright. 'How old d'you have to be to join the Navy, Mam?'

'What?' Emma glanced at him absently, her mind still on what Mary was saying. 'What did you say?'

Billy repeated his question and added, 'That's where I'm off then. The sea. That'd be great!' He went towards the back door and was through it and gone before the word, 'Billy!' had escaped Emma's lips.

The two women listened as they heard the two back gates, first one and then the other, crash open and shut.

'He'll have gone to find our Joey,' Mary said flatly and her eyes filled with tears. 'He has to go on Sunday. It's – it's not long, is it?'

'No,' Emma said quietly. 'No, it isn't. That's when Charles goes too.'

'You don't get much a week with rations for only two, do yer?' Mary commented mournfully, holding open the two ration books for herself and Alf with the tiny squares with different letters and numbers on each page.

'No,' Emma sighed.

'I don't suppose,' Mary said slowly, her head on one side, 'your Billy knows how to get hold of a bit extra, does he?'

Emma snorted. 'I don't doubt he would know, Mary, but I've no intention of asking him. He runs enough risks without me encouraging him and I'd be glad if you'd say nothing to him about it, either.'

''Course I won't,' the woman bristled a little and then realizing it was she who had been in the wrong even to suggest it, said swiftly, 'I'm sorry, Emma. I wasn't thinking. It's just that I get so fed up having to queue even for things that *aren't* on ration. D'you know, I waited nearly an hour at the greengrocers yesterday and when I gets me turn, all the decent stuff had been picked over?'

'Don't you go to Mr Keenes?'

'The corner shop where we first met, you mean? Oh aye,

I go, but his stuff's gone before ten every morning. Mind you,' she laughed, 'there's one person we can rely on to put a bit under the counter for us . . .'

They chorused his name together. 'Mr Rabinski!'

Mary was sighing again. 'It almost makes me wish I lived in the country. I don't expect they feel the rationing there quite so bad as us.'

'We-ell,' Emma said slowly. 'We could go, you know. It'd be safer.'

'Oh no, Emma,' Mary Porter was suddenly adamant. 'I was only joking. Alf'd never agree to go and I couldn't think of leaving Alf.'

Emma was silent. She had never told Mary much about her life before coming to the city and so her friend was quite ignorant of the fact that, if she wanted, Emma had a home in the country still waiting for her.

But the more she thought about it, the better the idea seemed to be. She and Billy would go back to Marsh Thorpe. She didn't like the thought of leaving Mary, but she would offer for her and Alf to go too and, if they refused, well then, it was hardly her fault, she argued with herself.

Emma began to make plans, began to feel excited at the thought of going home. She would be back at the mill. She would be with Sarah. Maybe she could even open up the shop again. A recent letter from Sarah had prompted this idea.

> . . . *I've had to let the orchard be dug up, Emma, I hope you don't mind. The trees are still there, of course, but the whole village has got caught up in digging every bit of grassland to grow potatoes and other vegetables. William came with a machine to dig it the first time for me and now I can manage.*

*He helped me work out a plan so that in my own bit
of garden, and now with the orchard too, I'll be able
to grow vegetables nearly all the year round. It
seemed such a shame not to let the orchard be used,
specially as the bees are no longer there.*

Emma could sense Sarah's sadness at the loss of her
beloved bees, yet now she seemed to have found a new
outlet for her energies in the garden. And if I was there to
help her, Emma mused . . .

'I aren't going.'

'Oh yes you are.'

'I aren't going to live in the country. I don't care about
the bombs. I'm staying here. Besides, none of me mates are
going. We're getting kids from Leeds and Coventry come
here,' Billy argued fiercely. 'So you're not packing me off
anywhere.'

He was right, of course, about children being evacuated
to Lincoln, rather than from it. She'd seen the lines of
youngsters arriving at the station, clutching their small
suitcases and bags, each with the box containing a gas
mask around their shoulders and a label around their necks.
They'd had one boy from Leeds billeted with them soon
after the war had begun, and Emma had been glad of the
extra ten shillings and sixpence a week, but by June 1940
several children had returned home again and their evacuee
had been among that number.

'Oh yes, you are going,' Emma argued. 'We're both
going back home to Marsh Thorpe.'

But the boy was gone, his boots pounding down the
passageway, the back gate still shuddering on its hinges. He
did not return home until the following day.

Billy was adamant and each time Emma packed their suitcases, tied his gas mask around his shoulders and marched him to the railway station, at the last moment, he gave her the slip and darted off through the city's back streets until the train was long departed and it was safe to return home. Once she even got him aboard the train, but he got off at the next station and hitched a lift on an army lorry back to Lincoln and she had to alight at the next station and wait two hours for a train to take her back to Lincoln. That escapade had earned him a sharp clip around the ear, but Billy only grinned.

'Oh, I give up,' she said at last in exasperation. 'But you can help me put this wretched Morrison shelter up in the front room then and you're to promise me faithfully, Billy, that every time there's an air-raid you'll take cover. And if you're out, you're to go to a public shelter.'

''Course I will, Mam.' The cheeky grin and the charm of his willingness to agree now that he had got his own way, were pure Leonard.

Emma wrote to Sarah.

> I've tried everything, but I can't get him to come and, of course, I can't possibly come without him. He just won't leave the city. He's a real streetwise kid and no mistake. I never thought I'd say it, not about one of my own, but I can't control him. All he can think about now is going to sea. Joey Porter, Mary's son, came home on leave last week and when Billy saw him in his uniform, well, that was it. I've heard about nothing else since . . .

Emma's pen paused over the page and she lifted her head to look out of the window into the backyard and, beyond to the backs and roofs of the terraced houses in the next street. There were no flowers, no trees, not even many birds save the occasional pigeon that landed on her wash-house roof. Suddenly she had an overwhelming longing for flat fields of waving corn as far as the eye could see and whirling mill sails against white scudding clouds in a clear blue sky.

Emma awoke in the night with a start and sat up suddenly, her heart pounding. The bedroom was lit by the soft light from the street lamp outside. Throwing back the covers, she swung her legs out of bed, her feet touching the icy linoleum. Opening the bedroom door, she again heard the noise that had woken her; a bump downstairs, this time swiftly followed by a muttered oath.

'Billy? Billy, is that you?'

But from beyond his bedroom door she heard her son's gentle snoring. Then who, Emma thought wildly, was creeping about downstairs in the dead of night? She swallowed her fear and was about to start down the stairs, one hand gripping the rail, the other splayed against the wall to give her support. The door at the bottom of the stairs leading into the kitchen opened and a figure began to mount the stairs.

A scream escaped her lips before she could stop it and the figure stopped.

'Don't come any further,' she began. 'I—'

'Emma, Emma, it's me. Don't wake the whole street, for Heaven's sake.'

'Leonard!'

As he reached her, she flung her arms about him, almost knocking him back down the stairs.

'Hey, steady on, old girl! I didn't expect a welcome like this.' With surprising ease, for Emma was no lightweight, he picked her up and carried her into the bedroom, kicking the door closed behind him.

It was not until the following morning when she awoke and saw his discarded clothes strewn across the chair in the bedroom, where he had flung them in his haste the previous night, that Emma realized her husband was in uniform.

Beside her, Leonard stretched and grinned.

'You've joined up,' she said, rather unnecessarily.

'Yup. I reckoned it was the best idea. I've joined my old army regiment and guess what?' His grin widened. 'They've given me the rank of major.'

Emma smiled, then the smile became a chuckle until she was lying back against the pillows, tears of laughter rolling down her face. 'Oh, Leonard, if that don't beat all. And I thought the British Army knew what it was doing.'

He was laughing with her, then he said, 'Best years of my life, they were, in the last lot.'

'I don't doubt it,' Emma snorted wryly, wiping her eyes. 'There's plenty of card-playing goes on, I don't doubt.'

Leonard threw back his head and guffawed. 'By God! You're not the little innocent I thought you were, are you?'

'Not after living with you for over twenty years, I'm not,' she retaliated, and then as he leant over her and began to unfasten the buttons on her nightdress, she chuckled and added, 'But just mind how you go, Leonard Smith, 'cos I'm not quite sure just who's going to be in the biggest danger from you. The enemy – or our own side!'

Leonard laughed again and pulled her to him.

Alf Porter found that his job came under the category of a reserved occupation. He would not have to go into the armed forces because the factory where he worked now made war machinery and his job was every bit as important as the soldiers who manned them at the Front.

'Well, you've still got your Billy and I've got my Alf,' Mary said, trying to be brave, but Emma could see the ill-concealed terror in the other woman's eyes for her youngest son; a terror that would never go away for as long as the nightmare lasted.

Aloud, Emma said, 'Well, yes, but if our Billy had his way, he'd be off too. Did you hear about him trying to join the Merchant Navy? Told 'em he was seventeen.'

'He didn't! The young tyke! He's not fourteen yet, is he?'

'Not quite.' Emma shook her head in despair of her younger son. 'I don't know what'll happen to him, I'm sure.'

Mary said nothing. Over the years, her response about young Billy's madcap ways had always been, 'He'll come to a bad end, that one,' but now the words, so often said in fun, seemed all too terribly real.

'What about your older boys?' Emma asked. Although they had never met she knew a lot about them for Mary never tired of talking about her family.

'One's in a reserved occupation like his dad, but our Tommy might well have to go. He might go in the army like your Leonard.' Emma felt her friend's glance and now there was laughter in Mary's voice as she added pointedly. 'Maybe he could be a major too.'

Emma stared at her as realization began to filter through. 'Oh – I get it. You mean, Leonard's having me on?'

Now Mary spluttered with laughter. 'My Alf ses that if Leonard Smith's a major, then our Joey'll be a ruddy admiral.'

They wiped tears of merriment from their eyes as Emma

said, 'Oh, it's good to have something to laugh about for once, Mary, even if it is Leonard up to his tricks.'

'Well, m'duck, we might be doing him an injustice, y'know. He was in the last lot when all's done and said.' She lifted her shoulders in a gesture of doubt. 'Maybe they have given him a rank of some sort. But a Major? I ask you!'

They laughed again and then Mary nodded knowingly, 'Still, you'll see what you get when they start sending you part of his army pay.'

Emma's eyes widened. 'Oh, do I get his pay? He won't like that.'

'I'm not really sure how it works exactly, but you'll get some sort of marriage allowance. I think he has to agree to send you part of his pay.'

Emma sat down on a kitchen chair and held her side, now aching with laughter. 'Oh, that's priceless.' She shook her head. 'To think that the army is actually going to get money out of Leonard Smith – for me!'

'It might not be much, Emma, so don't get too hopeful.'

Emma shook her head. 'Oh, I wouldn't, Mary, believe me, I wouldn't.' She paused, then added, 'Tell you what, though, we ought to do some kind of war work. You and me. It'll take our minds off things.'

'Do you think so?' Mary sounded doubtful.

The previous day Emma had seen a poster showing a woman with her arms spread out wide, and behind her the buildings of a factory with tall, smoking chimneys. Emerging from the factory and flying into the sky above her was a long line of aircraft. The caption read, 'Women of Britain – Come into the Factories'.

Telling Mary about it now, she added, 'You have to go to the employment exchange for details. Shall we go?'

'Might as well,' Mary said dully. 'I'm not sitting about me house waiting for bad news, and that's a fact.'

'That's the spirit,' Emma said. 'We'll go tomorrow.' She giggled. 'We'll "join up" an' all, Mary.'

They found work in a factory making diesel engines that were shipped all over the world to provide power in all sorts of military establishments. The two friends felt they were doing something useful and despite the hardships of rationing, the blackout and the constant nagging fear of bad news, there were compensations.

'They're a good bunch, aren't they?' Mary often said, and Emma was relieved to see that some of the anxiety left her friend's face when they were working alongside their cheerful, if rather raucous, workmates. They all joined in singing along in loud tuneless voices to the music programmes blaring out over a tannoy system from the wireless. Everyone was dressed alike in overalls and trousers, their hair tied up in scarves.

'Can't have that lovely hair of yours getting caught in a machine, Mrs Smith,' the foreman told her. 'Mind you keep it well tied up.'

Emma smiled but said nothing. Her lovely hair, as he called it, was not the shining colour of jet it had once been. With all the worry, she was sure she could see a new white hair appearing every day amongst the black.

'It seems an awful thing to say, Emma, seeing as what's brought it about,' Mary said as the women workers flooded out into the streets at the end of a shift, laughing and calling to each other, 'but I really enjoy working here. They're such a friendly lot.'

'We're all in the same boat, Mary. We've all got husbands, sons or even fathers out there.' As she saw the worry crease back into Mary's face, Emma could have bitten off her thoughtless tongue. 'Well, you know what I mean. We all try to jolly each other along.'

'Have you had any news from Charles, Emma?'

Emma shook her head. 'No, you know I'd tell you if I had.'

Mary's shoulders sagged. 'I know, I'm sorry. But it seems such an age between each letter. What about Leonard? Does he write?'

Emma glanced at her friend and shook her head. Good friends though they were, even Mary Porter did not know the whole truth about Emma's marriage. But her friend was not about to let the matter drop. 'What?' she asked, scandalized. 'Not at all? Not since he went? It's all of three months.'

Emma shrugged her shoulders and forced a laugh. 'Oh, you know Leonard. He's no letter writer. He'll turn up on leave without warning, just like a bad penny. You'll see.'

But as the weeks turned into months and the months into a whole year of war, apart from the regular arrival of a portion of his army pay, there was no word from Leonard Smith himself.

Thirty-Five

Emma wrote frequently to Sarah, thirsting for news of home.

> *Have many of the young men gone from the village? Oh, Sarah, isn't it awful? Doesn't it make you think of last time?*

She paused, remembering how she had watched with such pride, with such stupid, blind pride, as her young sweetheart marched off to the war. 'I'll wait for you, Jamie,', she had whispered to herself. 'I'll wait for you forever.'

Emma sighed and tried to banish her melancholy thoughts of a past that was long gone, but the memories evoked made the pen move once more across the page.

> *Has Jamie Metcalfe volunteered again? And have you seen William recently?*

Sarah's reply was reassuring on one point.

> *Jamie says he had enough in the last lot. Can't say I blame him, can you?*

No, Emma thought as she read the letter, no I certainly don't blame him.

*As for William, no one round here has heard
a word of him recently and the last time I saw
him was when he came to dig up the orchard for
me. He hasn't been since – not even to see to the
mill . . .*

'Oh no,' Emma groaned aloud, praying that her child-hood friend had not been foolish enough to volunteer just because he had been too young for the last lot and had felt a failure. 'Oh, William, *no!*'

There were of course lighter moments amidst all the worry and the bad news that crackled out of the Porters' wireless set, legitimately purchased with Alf Porter's hard earned cash. Emma could not bear to have one of her own, even if she could have scraped the money together to rent or buy one, though when she heard the music and the laughter issuing from the Porters' front room and heard Mary singing along to Vera Lynn and Gracie Fields, she was sorely tempted.

'I'll get you one, Mam,' Billy offered and earned himself a light cuff on the side of the head.

'You'll do no such thing, Billy Smith.' Her eyes narrowed as she added, deviously, 'The Navy won't take anyone who's been in trouble with the law, y'know.'

Emma wasn't sure whether what she was saying was strictly true, especially in wartime, but she was relying on the fact that Billy would not know either. The young eyes regarded her calculatingly. She could see he was assessing whether she was being truthful or just saying it to make him mend his ways.

Emma got up. 'That reminds me. I'm off next door to listen to the news.'

305

At news bulletin time, half the street seemed to find their way to the Porters' back door with one excuse or another.

'Come in, come in,' Mary would smile. 'Reckon I ought to start charging.' But of course she never did because her neighbours did not abuse her hospitality. If she gave them cups of tea, she would find little packages of tea and precious sugar put on her kitchen table from time to time in return.

No, it wasn't all bad. Amidst the tears and the ever-present worry about their menfolk in the services, there was laughter and some of the most unexpected people turned up in a uniform. On the day Mr Forbes came to collect the rent dressed in his Air Raid Warden's outfit, Emma clapped her hand to her mouth and spluttered with laughter. 'My, my Mr Forbes, you do look smart.'

The weasel-like eyes glittered. 'You laughing at me, Mrs Smith?'

'Oh, Mr Forbes.' Emma said. 'As if I would.'

The man sniffed and glared at her, then, boldly, he stepped across the threshold. 'I reckon I'd better just come inside and check your blackout.'

'What on earth?' Emma began, but before she realized what was happening, Mr Forbes had grabbed her by the arms and was attempting to hustle her from the back kitchen into the living room.

'I know you're on your own, 'cos I've just seen that lad of yours off up the street. Up to no good, as usual, I'll be bound. And I heard about that husband of yours joining up to get himself out of a charge for receiving.'

'Mr Forbes . . .' she began, struggling to free herself.

'And I could tell the police a thing or two about that lad of yours. Following in his father's footsteps, he is. But then,' his smile became sycophantic, 'how can a poor woman on her own be expected to cope with a lad like

him? Now, if you were to be nice to me, Mrs Smith –
Emma—'

'How dare you?' Emma's brilliant eyes flashed. 'Get out
of my house this minute.'

But his grip only tightened on her arms. 'By, but you're
a fine woman. First time I clapped eyes on you, I thought
to myself. There's a fine woman.' His bony fingers were
digging into her arms, and he stretched his thin neck
towards her, planting his wet mouth against hers.

'Ugh!' She gave a cry of disgust and repulsion and,
gathering all her strength, heaved him away from her. He
tottered backwards and fell against the table. Pulling himself up, she saw his eyes bright with lust in the glow from
the fire.

'I like a woman of spirit.' His gaze was roaming greedily
over her body. 'I've always admired you, Emma. And I've
been good to you, you know I have. Why, I could have
reported you a dozen times for being late with your rent.
But I never did, did I?'

Emma faced him squarely, not realizing that her magnificent bosom, heaving now as she breathed hard, and her
flashing violet eyes, only served to inflame the man's desire
even further. The smirk twisted his mouth and he took a
step closer again. 'And there was that little matter of the
unpaid week from your previous place, now wasn't there?'

'That's nearly fourteen years ago!'

'Maybe so. But I've got a long memory, see.' He paused
and then, his voice low with menace, he said, 'And now, of
course, there's young Billy.'

'You leave my son out of this.'

'Well, now,' he said, with the smoothness of a snake,
'I'd like to, of course, but – well – I hear such tales on my
rounds. You know how people talk, don't you, Emma?'

She felt the colour drain from her face as the man went on

relentlessly. 'Quite the little entrepreneur, isn't he? Well known already for his black-market dealings. Oh aye, if you want anything, ask young Billy Smith. He'll get it. Mind you,' his tone was oily, 'best not to ask *how* he'll get it. A real chip off the old block. Carryin' on where his old man left off.' In the firelight the man's face took on a frightening, vindictive expression. His bony fingers dug into the warm flesh of her arms once more. 'So, you see, my lovely Emma, you ought to be a little nicer to me, else I could make it very nasty for you – and your boy.'

He was leaning towards her, his bad breath wafting into her face. Anger gave her strength; a strength she had not known still remained with her since her days as a young girl heaving heavy sacks of grain. She pressed her hands against his chest and pushed, and at the same time brought her knee up catching him in a very tender part of his anatomy. He gave a howl of pain and rage and fell back against her sideboard knocking over a vase which crashed to the floor.

'You bitch,' he snarled. 'I'll get you for this.' Clutching his groin with one hand, he shook his other fist in her face and lurched out of the house.

Emma slammed the door behind him and leant against it, breathing hard. Tomorrow she would go to see Mr Rabinski and tell her side of the story before Forbes could turn her amiable landlord against her.

Slowly, Emma opened the back gate leading into the Porters' yard and walked round to their back door. The piece of paper she was holding fluttered in the breeze that whistled down the passage, under the gate and into the back yards.

The burly figure of Alf opened the door. He was holding a towel and mopping his face, grey stubble covering his jaw. He was wearing only a vest and trousers, the braces hanging down in a loop on either side.

'What's up, Missis?' A man of few, brusque words, there was, nevertheless, immediate concern in his gruff voice. He held the door open and she stepped inside and into their kitchen before she said, 'Alf, where's Mary?'

'Next door. Old Mrs Beale. Fell and broke her leg. Mary's just gone—' The big man stopped as he searched Emma's face. 'I'll get her.'

He went into the backyard and Emma heard him shouting over the fence. 'Mary? You there, Mary? Can yer come?'

A few moments later he came back inside. 'She's coming . . .' and almost before the words were out of his mouth they heard her light footsteps trotting down the passageway.

Then she was there, in the kitchen, her eyes wide with fear. 'Oh, Emma, what is it? What's happened?' Her glance went to the piece of paper Emma was holding and Mary's hand fluttered to her mouth. 'Oh no!' she breathed.

Emma nodded and swallowed, but her voice was surprisingly steady as she said, 'It's a telegram from the War Office. It's Leonard. They – they say he's missing, presumed killed.'

'Oh no!' Mary's eyes filled with tears. 'Sit down, m'duck, and I'll – I'll—' But for once even Mary could not think what she could do to help her friend. Not this time.

Emma stood there, unable to move, fighting a tumult of emotions. She was trying to feel some grief and feeling guilty because she could not. Then a fresh wave of guilt washed over her, for at this moment all she could think was, 'Thank God it's not my son. Thank the Good Lord it's not Charles.'

'He'll be all right,' Billy said, refusing to believe that anything could happen to the father he idolized. 'He'll be tucked up in some hole in the ground somewhere, playing cards and keeping his head well down. Don't you believe it, Mam. He's not dead. I know he isn't.'

'I hope you're right, Billy,' Emma said flatly. She didn't wish Leonard any harm, truly she didn't, but now more than ever before, she dreaded the arrival of any official letter or telegram.

For next time, it might be Charles.

Thirty-Six

The air raids were getting worse and every time the mournful wail rose over the city heralding the hum of enemy aircraft, Emma felt her heart leap in fear. More often than not, Billy was out in the streets somewhere, for now, at fifteen, the boy was scarcely ever at home and goodness only knew what he got up to. Since Mr Forbes' threats, she feared the dreaded knock of officialdom at the door even more.

'Alf's on duty,' Mary Porter said as she crawled into Emma's Morrison shelter, 'so I thought I'd keep you company. Is yer blackout all right, Emma? Then I can light this little lamp. D'yer know, I reckon it's what I hate the most, ferreting about in the pitch black.'

Mary struck a match and lit the child's tiny night-light that Emma kept in the shelter. Then she put out the torch she carried, to save the battery. 'I've brought sandwiches and some tea in a flask,' Mary said and then laughed. 'If you can call it tea. It's only coloured water. Eh, this rationing's the very devil, ain't it? An hour and a half I queued yesterday for a bit of brawn and when I gets to the head of the queue, it'd all but gone. Just a few bits of gristle was all I got.'

They sat in the dancing shadows cast by the lamp, listening to the thud, thud of bombs falling, talking about anything and everything to try to keep their mind off the air raid. Emma told her friend of her encounter with Mr Forbes.

'He's a slimy toad that one,' Mary sympathized. 'I wish he weren't the warden for this district. Did you go and see old man Rabinski then?'

'Yes, he was fine about it and told me not to worry.' In the darkness, Emma smiled thinking of the contrast between the two men. Mr Rabinski, her landlord, was a gentleman.

'You haf no need to concern yourself, my dear Mrs Smith. He is not a man I like myself.' He had spread his hands and shrugged his shoulders. 'But he is a good rent collector.' Then he had chuckled. 'You see, that way, I can remain friends with all my tenants.'

Emma had laughed with him. Old Mr Rabinski was indeed a gentleman, but he was also a shrewd businessman and Emma could not help but admire him for it.

'So have you seen Forbes since?' Mary was asking.

'Yes, but he didn't try anything this last time he came for the rent, although he was making pointed remarks about me being on me own. I suppose word's reached him about Leonard being posted missing.'

'If it happens again, you shout for my Alf. He's twice the size of Forbes. He'll see him off.'

They heard the whine and then the crash of a bomb. The windows of Emma's house rattled and the ground shuddered beneath them.

'That was a bit close,' Mary muttered.

'Billy's out,' Emma said, her voice tight with anxiety. 'I haven't seen him since this morning.'

'He'll be all right,' Mary reassured her. 'He's streetwise. Did you know he's setting up card games, just like his dad used to?'

'Oh no!' Emma groaned. 'He'll be getting himself into bother. You've always said he'd come to a bad end.'

Mary's laugh came out of the darkness. 'Well, maybe I was wrong, 'cos he seems to have the luck of the devil. They reckon at the first hint of any trouble, young Billy just melts into the shadows and disappears. He's a crafty little tyke, all right.'

'Mm.' Her friend's remark about Billy did not offend Emma. It was the bald truth.

'Is he still on about going to sea?' Mary asked.

'On about it? Huh! He talks of nothing else. Ever since your Joey came home in his uniform.'

Emma heard Mary's sigh. 'Oh, but he does look handsome, my lad, doesn't he?' There was a note of wistful pride in her tone but, barely audible, she added, 'God bless and keep him.'

In her own thoughts, Emma echoed the prayer of a million mothers.

The two women huddled in the indoor shelter for over two hours listening to the thud of bombs dropping. Emma found she was holding her breath, counting the seconds and trying to gauge if the bombs were coming nearer. But the next sounded further away and the next a little fainter still.

'They're going.'

'Thank God,' Mary muttered thankfully. 'I hope Alf's all right. He'll be having a busy night. He's on fire watch duty and with this lot . . .'

'I wonder where Billy is?' Emma murmured. 'I'll skin the little devil alive when he gets back.'

Billy did not appear until late the following day to be greeted by a smart smack on the side of his head by his overwrought mother.

'Where on earth have you been? I've been worried sick.'

Billy rubbed his ear and glared balefully at her. 'You shouldn't hit me on the head. You might do me an injury.'

'I'll do you an injury, m'lad, before you're much older. Where were you? Up to no good, as usual?'

A sly look came across his features and Emma's sharp eyes noticed his right hand go furtively into his pocket.

'What have you got there? Come on, empty your pockets.'

The look became stubborn. 'Mek me, then.'

For the second time in a few days Emma called upon reserves of strength, taking her adversary completely by surprise. Her son found the scruff of his neck grasped by her strong hand and his left arm pinioned behind him in a vicelike grip.

'Ow, Mam, ya hurting.'

'I'll hurt you, ya little bugger,' Emma said, her intense fear and anger making her use language she normally disapproved of, especially from a woman's mouth.

Whether it was the tone of voice, the swearing, or the fact that he could scarcely move in her grip, Billy emptied his pockets at once. On to the kitchen table came an odd assortment of items; the penknife Bridget had given him, a small screwdriver, a piece of Plasticine and then Emma's eyes widened. Lying amidst the normal collection one might expect to find in a boy's pocket, lay a gold watch.

Emma groaned. 'Oh no. Oh, Billy, where did you get that? Have you stolen it?'

Squirming beneath her grasp, he said, 'No, 'course I ain't. I found it.'

'Where?' she snapped.

'In a bombed-out house.'

She gasped. 'Looting? You've been looting poor beggars that have lost their homes? You little runt!' she spat, her rage and fear spilling over at the thought that Billy was no better than a common thief. 'You're taking it back.'

'How can I? There's no house left. They're all dead, they must be.'

'That's not the point. It's stealing.'

'Don't talk daft, Mam. Everybody does it.'

She thrust her face close to his. 'No, they don't. We don't. Not this family, Billy Smith.'

'If me dad were here—'

'Oh aye. Ya dad! Bit too much like him, you are. Well, he isn't here, so you've got me to contend with, m'lad. And I say you take it straight back and if you can't find the rightful owners, then you're taking it to the police station.'

Billy looked frightened. 'I aren't going in there. You can forget it.' He tried to wriggle free but Emma still held him firm.

'Oh no, I shan't forget—' she began but at that moment the back door burst open and a dishevelled Mary Porter burst in.

'Have you heard – ' she began and then stopped as she saw Billy. 'Oh, he's all right then. You've 'ad your poor mam going out of her mind, ya little devil . . .' she began, but then smiled and ruffled his hair, pleased to see him safe. She looked at Emma, seeming not to notice anything amiss between mother and son, as the news she brought obliterated anything else. 'Have you heard?' she repeated. 'Old man Rabinski's bakery's been burnt down and the rooms above where he lives.'

Emma's mouth dropped open. 'What do you mean? Bombed?'

Mary shook her head and her mouth tightened. 'No, all his windows were smashed and then someone threw petrol in. It's 'cos he's foreign.'

315

'But who'd do such a thing?' Emma was shocked and angry. 'Everyone round here likes the old man.'

'They don't reckon it's anyone local. They reckon it's a gang of fanatics from away.'

Emma felt Billy stiffen under her grasp and slowly she turned to look at him. The boy was hanging his head and shuffling his feet. Suddenly, she knew exactly where Billy had found the watch.

Thirty-Seven

'Aw Mam, leggo. You're hurtin' me ear.'

As soon as Mary had gone, Emma rounded on her son. 'Not likely, m'lad. You're taking that watch back and I'm going to see you do it.'

'But he's probably dead. Old man Rabinski wouldn't have minded me 'aving his watch if he's dead.'

She bent close to him. 'I want to know exactly what you had to do with all this, Billy. Were you with the gang that burnt his place down?'

'No, no, Mam, I swear I didn't do owt. I wouldn't do that. Honest.'

'Then what did you do? How did you find that watch? Come on, I want the truth.'

'I was coming home and I saw all the flames and went to look what was happening. I thought it had been bombed but someone said it had been set on fire deliberately.' The boy shrugged. ''Spect they thought if they did it in an air raid, everyone would think it had been a bomb, but no bombs fell round here last night—'

'Oh, very unlucky then, weren't they?' Emma said sarcastically and added grimly, 'Go on.'

'I stood and watched till they'd put the fires out and then the firemen got called away to another fire and when everyone had gone, I – I went into the house.'

'Oh, Billy, it could have collapsed on you.'

317

'I found this tin box and inside were some papers and this watch.'

'Where's the box now?'

The boy was reluctant to give away his secret hiding place, but even the bold, brash Billy Smith was no match for his mother in this mood. 'In – in our wash-house.'

'Right.' Still holding him, Emma marched him out through the back door across the backyard and into the wash-house. 'Right, let's be seeing this hiding place of yours. What else have you got there, eh?'

'Nothing,' he said morosely.

'Huh, got rid of it all, I s'pose?' When the boy did not answer Emma sighed, deeply saddened.

Billy reached up into the space between the brick wall and the tiles of the roof and pulled down a small tin cash box.

'That it?' she demanded and when he nodded, she said, 'Right. We're taking this back to Mr Rabinski right now.'

'But he's dead. I heard the firemen say so.'

'Did they find him?'

Billy shuffled uneasily 'Well, no, but I heard them say nobody could have still been alive in that lot.'

'Well, we'll go and see. Right now.'

A determined Emma marched her wayward son through the streets, keeping a firm grip on his shoulder. When they arrived at the end of the street where Mr Rabinski's bakery had stood, Emma stopped and gaped in horror, feeling an indignant anger flooding through her. This stupid, stupid war, she railed inwardly. Wasn't it bad enough that the enemy destroyed lives and homes without gangs of vigilantes taking the law into their own hands? How could anyone have done such a thing to a nice, harmless old man like Mr Rabinski? She shuddered. And if he had perished in the fire, what would become of her now at the mercy of

Mr Forbes? She pushed the selfish thought away and urged Billy towards the blackened shell, the smell of smoke still hanging like a pall.

An elderly man in a long black coat stood in the middle of the road staring at the destruction, his shoulders hunched with misery, his hands holding his hat in front of him as if paying his respects at a funeral. A playful breeze lifted the wisps of his grey hair but the man, unaware, stood quite still.

'That's him!' Emma cried. 'That's Mr Rabinski! He's alive!' She hurried forward, hustling Billy along with her, ignoring his protests. A few feet from the bent old man she stopped and said gently, 'Mr Rabinski.' The old man did not move until she came nearer and touched his arm. 'Oh, Mr Rabinski, I'm so sorry.'

As he turned to look at her, she could see tears streaming down his wrinkled cheeks. 'Ah, Mrs Smith. How could they? I haf never harmed anyvon. Who could do such a thing? I thought the people round here, they like me . . .' In his distress, his normally perfectly spoken English was thick with the foreign accent.

She took hold of his arm. 'They do. They do, Mr Rabinski. It wasn't locals.'

He shook his head gazing sadly at his former home. 'My life's work. My business, all gone.'

'But you've other property, Mr Rabinski,' she urged. 'You can open up another bakery.'

Again he shook his head and said flatly. 'No, no, I'm too old and too tired to start again.'

'Have you somewhere to go, because if not, you can come home with me?' Ignoring Billy's gasp of protest, she hurried on. 'There's a spare room – now that Charles is away in the forces.'

The old man's wrinkled hand covered hers where it lay

on his arm. 'You are so kind, Mrs Smith, but I have a house to go to. Some tenants in the next street, they haf just moved out.' He nodded. 'I have a house to go to.' With a dignified movement he put on his hat but his eyes still brimmed with tears and Emma knew that although the old man might still have a roof over his head, his home had gone.

She turned and pulled Billy forward and, sparing him nothing in the telling of it, said, 'I never thought I'd have to say this of a son of mine, Mr Rabinski, and although he swears blind he didn't have anything to do with setting fire to your place—'

The old man was not listening for he had seen the tin box in Billy's hands. 'My box, oh, you haf my box. Oh, my boy, thank you, *thank* you.' He reached out with trembling fingers to take it from a very surprised Billy.

The boy cast a sly glance at his mother and grinned at the old man. 'I came past, Mister, when they were putting the fire out and then the firemen got called away. Well, I thought, there'll be looters along any minute, so I thought to mesen I'd see what I could rescue for you.'

Emma took in a swift breath. The lying little toad, she thought, but she kept silent.

'Most of ya stuff's burnt, Mister. But I found this and thought you might like to have it.'

The old man was opening the box with an awed kind of reverence. 'My papers and my vatch. Oh, I am so happy not to haf lost my vatch.' He reached out and startled Billy by patting his cheek. 'You are goot boy. You are goot family. I'll not forget this.' He turned away and clutching the box to his chest moved slowly up the street. 'I'll not forget this.'

When he was out of earshot, Emma rounded on her son, 'You lying little toe-rag,' she hissed and raised her hand to

320

clout him, but this time Billy was too quick and he scampered up the road.

Emma lifted her skirt and chased after him, shaking her fist, the pins working loose from her hair until her long plait unwound itself from round her head and unfurled down her back. The boy darted away and disappeared round a corner, his mocking laughter floating back to her. 'I'm a hero, Mam. Our Charlie's not the only hero now.'

Billy was still not home by the time darkness fell, and Emma alternated between being outraged and worried sick.

'Oh, Mary, what am I to do with him?'

'He's missing a father's hand,' she said and then bit her lip, but the words had come out before she had thought to prevent them. 'Lots of the kids are with the menfolk away.'

Emma snorted derisively. 'Well, in Billy's case that's hardly true. I blame Leonard for leading Billy into bad ways in the first place.'

'But Leonard's never done – well – y'know.' The woman wriggled her thin shoulders in embarrassment.

'Thieving, you mean?' Emma said bluntly. 'No, not as such. But I reckon he's sailed pretty near the wind at times. All that business about the wireless. It was stolen property all right, even if Leonard didn't do the stealing himself. He's taught our Billy all about cards and betting and dealing and of course now, with the black market and that, the lad's in his element. I shudder to think what he does get up to.' She sighed and shook her head sadly. 'I don't mind telling you, Mary, though there's not many I'd admit it to, I dread hearing a knock on the door and opening it to find a policeman there.'

'I think we all dread opening the door to bad news of any sort at the moment,' Mary said quietly.

Emma was silent a moment and then said slowly. 'Aye, you're right. Perhaps I ought to be thankful if that's the only bad news I do get.'

'Aye, but you've had your share of that an' all, if the War Office is to be believed. I don't suppose there's been any more news? About Leonard. I mean?'

'Only another letter confirming the first one. They found his dog tags but they – they couldn't identify his body.' Her voice faded to a whisper. 'It was unrecognizable.'

Mary patted Emma's arm and sighed heavily. 'Well, at least they've found his tags. Surely that's enough, ain't it?'

Emma shook her head. 'I don't know. I really don't know.'

'Well, I bet before this lot's all over there'll be many a wife who never will know if she's a widow or not. Not for certain.' Mary gave a low moan and shuddered. 'Oh, Emma, isn't it all dreadful?'

The two women sat together, each thinking of their two sons in constant danger.

'At least your Charles and my Joey are all right,' Mary said, 'because as me old mam used to say, "No news is good news."'

Emma smiled at the daft, though strangely comforting, remark, and gripped her friend's hand swiftly. 'Oh, Mary, what would I do without you?'

Thirty-Eight

There was a whine, a whoosh and a loud bang and the ground shuddered beneath the foundations of the houses. Emma clutched the kitchen table and held her breath, automatically looking to the ceiling as if she would be able to see the next bomb. Then she heard the whine, louder this time and coming closer . . . closer . . . She gave a small scream and, with no time even to get through to the front room and the Morrison shelter, dived under the sturdy kitchen table.

The whole world seemed to erupt, noise blasted her ears and she heard the crumbling of masonry and the splintering of wood and brick. She heard a high-pitched scream and realized it had come from her own mouth. She was choking with dust as the house caved in upon her. The noise seemed to go on for ever and then suddenly there was silence with only the occasional shifting and settling of rubble. The hum of aircraft seemed to be receding and, mockingly, the all-clear sounded.

'Fat lot of good that'll do now,' Emma muttered crossly for there had been no warning sounded. The air raid had been swift and unexpected and devastating. In the pitch black Emma put out her hands to find herself feeling the sharp edges of smashed bricks and mortar. She coughed and covered her mouth with her apron. Dust was every-where, stinging her eyes, clogging her nose and throat and she could see nothing. And what unnerved her the most

323

was the deathly silence. She might have been alone in all the world.

She tried to quell the fear that she was buried beneath a huge mound of rubble and that she would suffocate. With trembling fingers she felt all around her in the blackness, but everywhere her hands touched sharp stone or splintered wood. Then, on one side of the table, she found a small space. Emma reached out and felt the wood of a beam that had fallen against the table and held up some of the brickwork. Feeling her way carefully she crawled forwards, pushing rubble out of the way as she went. Every few moments, she stopped to listen, but there were no sounds, no shouting voices, no pounding feet coming to her rescue. Nothing. The world was black and silent.

In the darkness, coughing the choking dust from her throat, Emma gave a little sob. Her hands and knees were cut already and she could feel the stickiness of blood in the palm of her hand. With every movement, sharp edges bit into her flesh. She felt something on the floor lying flat and smooth. Running her fingers along it she felt a door knob and knew that the kitchen door had been blown from its hinges. Clambering over it, she felt for the frame and cautiously hauled herself upwards, surprised to find that she could now stand upright. Arms outstretched, and with tentative fingers feeling the way all around her, she inched forward step by step, until she felt a cool draught of air from the back door. Her foot caught against something and she almost plunged forward into blackness but steadied herself and picking her foot up higher this time, she took another step.

This is what it must be like to be blind, she thought, and for a moment understood completely the sufferings of those bereft of sight.

Then she was out of the house and into the night air,

but even in the yard, the ground was littered with debris and the way was just as precarious. Glass crunched beneath her feet and a jagged piece cut through her shoe and stabbed her foot.

'Mary! Mary!' she tried to call, but her voice was a hoarse, quavering sound that even she would not have recognized as her own. She found the gate to her backyard, miraculously still intact and even fastened. She clicked up the catch, her sight now becoming accustomed to the dusk, so that now she could discern vague shadows. Pushing at the gate leading into Mary's backyard, she found the wooden door would only open a few inches before it hit something solid. 'Mary! Mary! Are you all right? I can't get in. Mary . . .'

Emma stood and listened for a moment. Not a sound came out of the grey shadows. The silence now, after all the noise, was uncanny and unnerving.

'Mary!'

Behind her in the passageway between the two houses, there was a noise, the sound of rubble moving as someone climbed over it.

'Mary?'

'Wait there,' a man's voice said.

Emma drew a swift breath. The shadowy figure came closer, until she felt him reach for her, his fingers clasping her arms, pulling her closer. She began to struggle, thinking that it was Forbes on duty as air raid warden in this district. Emma struggled to free one arm and, blindly, she lashed out, her hand striking against the side of his face.

'Em – it's me.'

Emma gasped. There was only one man who called her 'Em' and as she recognized the voice, that dear, beloved voice from her childhood, she flung herself against him. His arms were tightly about her. He was holding her close and his lips were kissing her face, her cheek, her forehead and then searching for her mouth. She was clinging to him, weeping and laughing and crying his name over and over.

'William! William! oh, William . . .'

'The Lord giveth and the Lord taketh away.' The words ran through her mind like a never-ending prayer as Emma stood in the street the following morning and watched the men carrying Mary Porter's lifeless body from the mound of rubble that had once been the Porters' home. William, his strong arm supporting her, stood quietly beside Emma, who gripped his hand in her own, oblivious to the curious stares of her neighbours, not caring who saw.

The night had taken her dear friend Mary from her, but, like a miracle, it had brought William to her when she needed him most.

They had pushed open the back gate into Mary's yard and had seen that the Porters' house had been demolished. Emma began to scrabble at the pile of bricks, crying, 'Mary, Mary . . .' the tears streaming down her face until she felt William's strong hands on her shoulders lifting her up and away. For a brief moment she struggled against him, but then gave way and buried her face against him.

She heard the deep rumble of his voice in his chest as he said, 'Em, if she was in there, there's no way she can still be alive.'

'But she might be under the table or—'

The Porters had no shelter, they shared Emma's, but the air raid had come with such unannounced ferocity that there had been no time for Mary to run next door. Even Emma had not been able to go the short distance from her own kitchen to the shelter in her front room. What chance, then, had Mary had?

'There's nothing we can do till we get more help,' William had assured her. 'If we go plunging about and disturb more rubble, we could do worse damage than has already been done.'

She knew the sense of his statement but it was hard to turn away. It was hard to wait when her friend might be lying dreadfully injured beneath the debris and no one was trying to reach her. 'Ought we to find the wardens? What about Alf – her husband? Oh, we ought to find Alf.'

'Where is he?' William asked.

'He'll be on fire watch duty.'

Through the deepening darkness she heard William's sigh. 'Then there's no knowing where he'll be.' William was silent a moment before he said, 'Em – the raid was a bad one coming so unexpectedly. The rescue teams will be fully stretched.'

'But we must do something.'

'Come on, then,' he said, finding her hand. 'Let's go out into the street. See if we can find anyone.'

Clinging to William, she climbed over the debris blocking the passageway. In the street, neighbours were gathering.

'Someone's gone to find Alf Porter,' someone said.

'There's nothing we can do. Thank God there's no fire.'

'You come to my place, Mrs Smith,' a voice came out of the darkness

'No, no, thanks. It's very kind of you, but I must stay here in case Billy comes home.'

'All right, love. But if you want owt, just knock on our door.'

One or two men started to move some of the wreckage, but as they did so part of a wall still standing crumbled.

'Look out! It's coming down!' the shout went up and the men scuttled back out of the way.

'We'll have to wait for daylight.'

The decision was taken and although it was the sensible one, no one there liked it. Worriedly, Emma allowed William to lead her back into what was left of her house. There was nothing more anyone could do until the light of morning.

'Where is young Billy?' he asked.

'I – I don't know. He's been gone three days now. I can't control him, William.'

William's only answer was an understanding squeeze on her arm.

They spent the night back in Emma's house beneath the kitchen table, a refuge, a haven that became, in those few short hours, a heaven. The night was a tumult of emotion, her love for William spilling over and engulfing them both.

'I can't believe you're here.'

'No miracle, Em.' His deep chuckle came out of the darkness. 'I have been here before – several times.'

'Oh, and I missed seeing you. Was I out? At work?'

She felt a small movement as he shifted uneasily. 'No.' In his voice there was a strange shyness. 'No, I never came to the house. I just stood in the street and – and—'

'Oh. Oh, William,' she breathed and laid her head against his chest, a tremor running through her as his arms came about her and his mouth brushed her forehead. She lifted her face to his and amidst the carnage and the destruction, they were lost in their own blissful world, shutting out for a few moments her desperate grief for Mary, and anxiety for Billy.

'I've always loved you, Emma. You must know that.'

'No,' she murmured. 'No, I didn't. I never even thought about it.' The realization surprised her.

328

He gave a wry laugh. 'No. You wouldn't. You could think of no one but Jamie.' There was silence between them, before he murmured sadly, 'Jamie, always Jamie.'

She snuggled her head against him. 'But why did you never say anything? Why didn't you tell me?'

'Now, how could I?' he said reasonably.

She thought back over the years, remembering her life back at Marsh Thorpe when she had been so obsessed with Jamie Metcalfe that she had been blind to the love William had carried for her even then. This man she lay with now was twice the man his brother had ever been, yet she had been so blind. And even when she had realized there was to be no future for her with Jamie, even then, she had turned to a stranger, wooed by Leonard's charm and carried along on the tide of her father's approval, for the first time in her life, basking in his approbation. And look where that had led her.

'Oh, William,' she breathed again, her voice full of sadness and regret.

Hearing it, he held her closer. She felt his arms tighten around her as if, amidst all the devastation and the sadness the morning might bring, having found her again, he would never, ever let her go.

Now in the cruel light of day, as they stood in silence, watching Mary Porter carried from the wreckage, Emma realized how close she too had come to death. She clung to William's arm, her dark eyes wide with fear, scanning the devastated street. Half the houses on her side of the street had been damaged, three beyond any repair. They would need complete rebuilding. Six others were so badly damaged that for the moment they were uninhabitable until some repairs could be carried out.

They heard the pounding of hobnailed boots on the pavement and turned to see Billy flying down the slope of the street, his jacket open, his eyes wild, his mouth gaping. 'Me mam! Oh, me mam! Where's me mam?'

She made an involuntary movement towards her son, but felt William hold her back and heard his whispered, 'Wait, Em. Watch.'

Billy had not seen them standing quietly on the other side of the street. Now he was thrusting aside the restraining arms of the air raid warden, pushing his way through the little knot of men who were digging amongst the debris for survivors or bodies. Billy saw the door the two men were carrying as a makeshift stretcher, saw the covered form lying on it.

'No,' he yelled. 'No, oh no . . .'

He caught hold of the rough blanket covering the body and ripped it away, staring down wide-eyed and fearful at Mary's body. For a moment he was motionless as the realization that it was not his mother dawned, then he turned away scrambling over the rubble, clawing frantically at the bricks and stones with his bare hands.

Now Emma broke free from William's arms and stepped forward.

'Billy, Billy love. I'm here.' Slowly he straightened up and turned round to stare at her. She saw his white face, his dark eyes wide with terror. 'I'm all right, Billy,' she said gently.

He stumbled down the pile of bricks and began to run towards her, opening his arms wide as if to scoop her into them. 'Oh, Mam . . .' she heard the break in his voice and, as he reached her, she saw the tears brimming in his eyes. 'I thought you were dead.'

He flung himself against her, for a moment no longer the swaggering, rebellious youth despising any emotion as weakness. For those few anguish-filled moments he was her little boy again, her Billy.

'It's all right, love. It's all right.' She rocked him in her arms, holding him tightly against her. Above his head she met William's steady gaze. 'Everything's going to be all right. We're going home, Billy, we're going home.'

Thirty-Nine

'What are you going to do, Alf?'

With her own immediate future decided, Emma was concerned for the big man whose whole world had been devastated. They were walking out of the gates of the cemetery after Mary's funeral. On her other side, with his hand on her elbow, supporting her, loving her, walked William.

'Have you somewhere to go, because . . .?' Emma said gently.

'S'all right,' the big man said, a slight tremble in his deep voice. 'Me eldest lad says I'm to go to theirs.' He jerked his head over his shoulder towards the family mourners following them. 'For a while anyway. I can get a job there, an' all, he reckons.'

Emma nodded. She was relieved. Alf would be with his family. She hadn't wanted to leave without knowing that he had somewhere to go, somewhere to live, yet she was anxious to be gone. She couldn't wait to go home.

'Have you heard from Joey?'

The big man shook his head. 'No, but I've sent word.'

They walked in silence until, at the top of their street, they stopped and faced each other.

Alf seemed to be struggling to find the words. 'She liked you, Emma. My Mary thought a lot of you. I hope everything – ' he glanced briefly towards William, 'works out for you. Mary would have been pleased.'

Her voice husky with emotion, Emma said. 'Thank you, Alf.' For a moment, they clasped hands and then, with the awkwardness of knowing they were parting, probably never to meet again, they hugged each other. 'Goodbye, Alf. And thank you – for everything,' she whispered and then turned away, tears blurring her vision. She tucked her hand through William's arm and he led her down the street towards his truck, already loaded with all her possessions, standing outside the wreckage of the terraced houses.

'Billy,' she called, spotting him at the bottom of the street, kicking a ball against a wall. 'Come on, we're going.'

Billy's caring attitude had not lasted long. He had very soon reverted to form and now he picked up the ball and came slowly up the street towards them, reluctance in every step.

'Why do we have to leave? Old man Rabinski said you could have another house as soon as one comes vacant,' he grumbled as he climbed into the front of the truck to sit between them. With every mile that took him away from the city where he roamed the streets freely, his indignation grew. 'I don't want to live in a bloody village.'

Emma's, 'Watch your language, m'lad,' was accompanied by a sharp slap and it was all William could do to hide his laughter and keep the truck straight on the road.

'I'll run away again,' was all Billy muttered morosely and fell silent between them.

But Emma, sitting on the far side of him, had a contented, placid smile on her face. She was on her way home. The few belongings they had been able to salvage from the devastation of her home were packed in the back of William's vehicle and on her knee, wrapped in a soft cloth, she held the silver christening mug. There was only the tiniest dint in the rim, caused the night the house had been bombed, that would tell generations to come –

Charles' children and grandchildren – of its chequered history.

As the truck rattled and bumped over the miles, Emma felt excitement mounting within her. Rounding the final corner that took them down the gently sloping hill within sight of the mill, she found she was holding her breath.

Except for her brief return to Luke's funeral, just over fifteen years had passed since she had lived here, and yet when the black shape of the mill, still standing forlornly without its proud sails, came into view, it was as if all the intervening years fell away. She was back home, back where she truly belonged. Above Billy's head she felt William's glance upon her face as he turned the vehicle into the gate and came to a halt in the yard of Forrest's Mill.

She climbed down and stood in the middle of the yard staring up at the mill above her. Silently she said, 'Oh, Grandpa Charlie, I deserted you, but I'm back now and I'll never leave you again.'

Almost as if reading her thoughts, William came and stood beside her putting his arm about her waist. 'Welcome home, Emma Forrest.' His arm tightened. 'We'll rebuild it, Em, you and I.'

She looked at him, her eyes on a level with his. 'Do you mean it? Can we? Do you *really* think we can?'

Steadily he returned her gaze. With sober sincerity, he said, 'Emma, I'd do anything in this world for you. Anything.'

Hearing the love and devotion in his voice, the lump that rose in her throat robbed her of her voice, so, in answer, she laid her head against his shoulder.

A cry from the direction of the orchard made her lift her head again to see Sarah hurrying towards them as fast as her legs would carry her plump little body. 'Emma, my little Emma . . .' and in a moment Emma found herself clasped against her soft bosom.

She hugged Sarah in return. 'It's so good to see you and this – ' Emma turned to pull a reluctant Billy forward, 'is young Billy.'

As Sarah made to envelop the boy in her embrace, Billy stepped smartly backwards to avoid the fat arms. The woman laughed, understanding. 'Too old for cuddles, eh?'

Turning back to link her arm with Emma's, she said, 'Is this a flying visit or have you come to stay? I've a spare bed all made up and Billy can sleep on me couch.'

There was a moment's pause before Emma said carefully. 'I've come home, Sarah.' She glanced at William and then added, so that there should be no mistake in anyone's mind from the very start, '*We've* come home.'

The woman's eyes widened as she glanced from one to the other and then back again. 'Oh,' she said and then again, '*oh!*'

Suddenly the yard of Forrest's Mill was filled with the sound of laughter.

Of course, in the village, Emma's return was a nine-day wonder. The gossips were having a field day.

'Come back, she has, and William Metcalfe has moved into the mill an' all. Of course, he's rebuilding it for 'er, leastways that's what the story is, but there's more to it than that. There's got to be.'

'And 'er husband away at the war, an' all.'

'He's been killed though, ain't he?'

'Ah, but they never identified his body, did they? What if he turns up after the war, eh? What happens then? You tell me that?'

And when Emma's belly swelled with William's child,

the gossips nodded, satisfied that their predictions had been correct.

'Do you mind?' she had asked William.

'Do you?' he had countered and when she had shaken her head, he had kissed her and said, 'Well then,' and that had ended the matter.

As for Emma, anyone had only to look at her face to see the happiness shining from it. She was loved by a wonderful man, she still had the loyalty of the devoted Sarah and she was home; home at Grandpa Charlie's mill.

To Emma, the village had changed little in all the years she had been away, except that now, like everywhere else, the war was making its mark. All around the village, the kerbs were painted white so that they could be seen in the blackout. Nearly every backyard or garden had a trench shelter and now, where once pretty flowers had nodded their heads, every inch of ground grew vegetables. Even the grass verges had been ploughed up to grow potatoes. William was soon part of the Auxiliary Fire Service and Emma found herself pressed into joining the Women's Institute and helping out in the large room at the pub which had become the NAAFI canteen. In their own way, the villagers were welcoming Emma back amongst them.

'There's far worse things going on while this war's on,' Sarah nodded sagely, 'for any of 'em to be casting stones at you, lass. What with a lot of our menfolk away at the war and the village full of soldiers.' She straightened up and looked at Emma. 'Well, then?'

Emma returned her gaze, puzzled. 'Well – what?'

'When are we opening up the bakehouse again?'

'The bakehouse?' Emma said stupidly, mystified by Sarah's sudden change in their conversation. 'But – I mean – I thought Sam Fothergill opened up a bakery after we finished?'

'Oh aye, he did and he's still going strong. But there's enough business for two of you now.' Sarah leant towards her. 'There's all the soldiers billeted in the village, then there's the camps and the airfields close by, not to mention—'

'All right, all right, you've made your point. And I thought nothing much had changed in Marsh Thorpe,' she laughed.

Sarah snorted. 'Aw lass, you don't know the half of it. The place is awash with the military, and as for the whole area hereabouts, well, I don't reckon anything will ever be the same again. Why, Jamie Metcalfe's never been so busy in his life. Different work to the old days, mind you, but it's work for him, none the less.'

'Really?' Emma said and her eyes narrowed. Perhaps Jamie was now finding out just how hard it was to cope single-handedly.

They were quiet for a moment, each busy with their own thoughts. Then Emma said slowly, 'So, you think we ought to start up the bakery again do you?'

'Yes, I do,' was the prompt reply.

When she spoke to William about the idea, he was reluctant at first. 'I don't want you overdoing it, what with our baby coming. If Billy would help, then . . .'

'Billy?' She gave a wry laugh. 'Billy won't stay five minutes, William. I know that and I've got to face it.' She sighed. 'He'll go to sea, I know he will. Just as soon as he can lie his way in to one of the services.'

'So? What do you want to do then?'

'Well,' she said slowly, her mouth twitching. 'There's this little man I know in Lincoln and he might, he just very well might, be the answer to our prayers.'

*

They found Mr Rabinski living in two rooms in a house that had only been partially repaired since the bombing. The old man was pathetically glad to see Emma again.

'I haf nothing now,' he spread his hands. 'People haf been kind to me. Very kind, but it is not the same as when I had my little shop, you know. Oh, how I miss the smell of the bread and...' He waved his hands in the air and smiled a little sadly. 'We vill say no more about it. It is done and I am lucky I am alive and still haf my strength.'

Emma glanced at William then, who, unseen by the old man, nodded.

'Would you like to be a baker again?' Emma began.

The old man was shaking his head. 'Oh, but I am too tired to start all over and—'

'No, I don't mean here, Mr Rabinski, and I don't mean on your own either. But would you be prepared to leave the city?'

Mr Rabinski blinked at her in puzzlement. 'I don't understand...?'

Swiftly she explained and when she had finished, tears were coursing down the old man's cheeks. He clasped Emma's hand in both of his, raised it to his lips and kissed it again and again until Emma found herself glancing towards William in embarrassment.

'Oh, thank you, thank you. I vill come with you. I vill come with you this day, this minute...'

So Mr Rabinski had packed his belongings and had travelled to Marsh Thorpe sitting in the front of the truck between William and Emma.

'You should let me sit in the back, dear lady. It is not – er – goot for you.' His glance had shied away from her growing bulge, but Emma had only laughed and said, 'I wouldn't dream of letting you sit in the back. The wind would blow you away.'

The old man smiled. 'I vould hold my hat on very tight,' he said and, impishly, he pulled his broad-brimmed black hat low down over his forehead to demonstrate.

The three of them were still laughing when William drew into the yard of Forrest's Mill and Sarah came bustling towards them.

A week later, she said, 'Mr Rabinski can move in with me if you like, Emma. He'd be company for me. He's a nice old boy. I like him.'

'Ooh, Sarah,' Emma's eyes glinted teasingly. 'Now, now . . .'

The round face beamed and the cheeks grew pink. 'Aye well, let's give the gossips summat else to chatter about, shall we?'

As he had threatened, Billy ran away again and again. It had nothing to do with the arrival of Mr Rabinski, although when the boy had seen him climbing down from the cab of William's truck, his face had been a picture.

'Oh, my boy. It is Billy. See, Billy,' the old man opened his coat to display the watch chain looped across his waist-coat. 'I still haf my vatch.' The boy had given him a sickly smile and his glance had gone straight to his mother, a glance that said, 'Have you brought him here on purpose?'

'What's all that about?' William whispered to Emma, who, trying desperately to hide her mirth, said, 'I'll tell you later.'

The third time Billy ran away, he did not return. A brief letter in his untidy scrawl informed them that he was going to sea on a ship out of Grimsby.

Holding the scribbled note in her fingers Emma murmured, 'Just like Grandpa Charlie's brother . . .'

Three weeks later, Emma was standing looking out of the scullery window, watching William at work in the yard on the last sail of the mill. Soon, she thought, soon the sails will be turning once more on Forrest's Mill.

A black cloud, a moving, humming black cloud, came from the fields and drifted towards the mill, nestling against the black slope of the mill side.

Emma caught her breath, then opened the back door and began to walk across the yard, her hands protectively covering the swell of the child she carried.

'Keep back, love,' William called coming towards her. 'It's a swarm of bees.'

As he spoke, Sarah came bustling from the direction of the orchard.

Her face wreathed in smiles she said happily, 'They're back. Oh, Emma, the bees have come back now that there's a Forrest at the mill again. But of course, I knew they would. I've had a skep baited ever since you came home.'

Emma said nothing, her gaze fixed upon the heaving mass. She was very much afraid that for once in her life, Sarah Robson was wrong. Much as she respected the country woman's quaint beliefs and superstitions, and would never dream of ridiculing her, Emma was very much afraid that there were occasions when Sarah believed what she wanted to believe. And at this moment, Emma was remembering the last time she had seen a swarm of bees on the side of Forrest's Mill.

It had been on day her father had died.

Forty

'Those bees, they do not like me. I am stung *again*.'

In the bakehouse, Mr Rabinski held up his hand for Emma and Sarah to see the swelling on the back of his purple veined hand. Sarah bustled towards him. 'Oh dear, oh dear. Let me see. I can't understand it, really I can't.'

On the day the swarm had arrived, Sarah had busily arranged the old-fashioned straw skeps in the orchard, placing them lovingly between the trees and the hawthorn hedge. 'Now everything's all right,' she had said happily. But much to her disappointment the bees refused to take possession.

'I'll make you some modern ones,' William had offered. 'Those old things have seen better days. They're nearly falling apart.'

Two days later he had presented Sarah with three square shaped, wooden hives, fashioned with the help of instructions in a book on bee-keeping.

'They're very nice, William,' Sarah had said dutifully, and baited the brand new constructions, but the expression on her face exposed her doubts. But by nightfall, she came hurrying through the orchard to the millhouse to report that the bees had settled in one of the hives.

Her happiness was complete, at least, almost, for to her chagrin her beloved bees did not seem to welcome the newcomer in their midst – Mr Rabinski.

'I vill come the other vay to the bakehouse,' he said

firmly, 'I vill *not* come through the trees anymore. I vill go out the other side of your cottage, round by the road and come in by the big gate.'

'I'll speak to them. It'll be all right. I'll tell them you're part of the Forrest family now.'

'Uh?' The old man was puzzled.

'The bees,' Sarah explained patiently. 'They don't realize you belong to us now.'

Mr Rabinski, completely mystified, lifted his shoulders and rolled his eyes, and Emma turned away to hide her mirth.

A little later, she saw Sarah hurrying towards the orchard and, gripping William's arm, she said, 'Oh, the bees are in for it now.'

'What's she going to say? Shall we go and listen?' he grinned.

'Oho, not on your life. I wouldn't dare!' was Emma's reply.

Four days after the swarm had taken up residence in the new hives, a telegram arrived informing her that Charles Forrest Smith had been killed in action.

Much later Emma was to admit, to herself if to no one else, that if it had not been for the strength of William's love at the time of hearing of her son's death, she would have given up.

'Why? Just tell me why?' she railed tearfully. 'Why all the Forrest sons? It was all Grandpa Charlie ever wanted – a Forrest at Forrest's Mill. And what does he get?' she cried through her tears of anguish. 'A *granddaughter*. Then I thought at least I'd given him great-grandsons. I even put Forrest as their second name just to keep the name alive. Charles Forrest Smith, I called him, and not just because my father demanded it. It was what *I* wanted for my Grandpa Charlie. And now . . .' her shoulders sagged with defeat, 'it's all come to nothing.'

William put his strong, loving arms around her. 'My darling,' he said gently but there was a note of firmness in his tone, 'it's time you stopped carrying this ridiculous burden of guilt for having been born a girl.' There was sadness in his smile as he touched her face with gentle fingers, lifting her chin to make her look up into his face. 'Grieve for Charles as any mother does for her son, but don't – I beg you, my love – make it even more unbearable with such bitterness. Besides, you don't know what the future holds. None of us do. Young Billy might come back and run the mill.'

She sniffed and said sadly, 'No, Billy will never come back, not here, even if he survives the war.'

William said nothing. He could not argue, for he knew she was right. Billy was not a 'country boy' and never would be.

'Oh, William,' Emma laid her face against his shoulder and sobbed, her arms going about him, clinging to him. 'I'm so frightened. I'm losing everyone – everyone I loved. What if I lose you, what if . . .?'

He stroked her hair. 'Oh, you're not going to lose me, Emma Forrest.' He said her maiden name without thinking. To him she was always Forrest, never Smith. 'Not when I've waited all these years to have you for my own.'

She raised her head and looked into his eyes and saw the undying love there that was her salvation.

The two women stared at each other.

'Thank you for – your letter. Thank you for letting me know about Charlie.'

Bridget – and Billy – were the only ones who had ever called Charles, Charlie. Emma watched the older woman, standing in the middle of the yard, dressed as always in up to the minute fashion. However did she manage it in wartime? Emma wondered irrationally at such a moment. Then she saw Bridget's chin tremble suddenly. She moved swiftly across the space between them and put her strong arm around the woman's slim shoulders that looked suddenly too fragile to bear the burden of grief. Bridget sagged against her, resting her head against Emma's shoulder.

'Oh, Emma, first Leonard and now young Charlie. I've lost them both. My boys, I've lost my darling boys.'

'Come along in and I'll make you a cup of tea.'

In the warm kitchen, Emma pressed Bridget into a chair by the table and then busied herself making a pot of tea.

'I had a letter the other day,' she told Bridget, 'saying they're awarding Charles a medal for bravery.' She stumbled over the word, 'Posthumously.'

She glanced at Bridget and saw the surprise in her eyes before she smiled tremulously and murmured, 'It's a small compensation for the greatest sacrifice of all.'

'I suppose so,' Emma said quietly and sighed, 'But that's war, isn't it?' The medal for her quiet, studious son was no surprise to Emma but she could understand that others would not have recognized his underlying strengths. Oh, how she was going to miss her firstborn.

Bridget from her chair said, 'But we still have Billy. Where is he? Where's my Billy?'

Not looking directly at the older woman. Emma said, 'There's something else I have to tell you.'

Even in her sadness, a little smile touched Bridget's mouth. 'If it's about you and William, then I know,' she began, but Emma interrupted. 'No, no. There is that of course, but – no, it's about Billy.' She met Bridget's eyes. 'He's run away to sea.'

Even beneath the make-up, Emma could see that Bridget turned pale, the only colour in her cheeks being the carefully applied rouge. 'Oh no! Not him too.' She paused and then said, 'But he's not old enough, is he?'

Emma shrugged and sighed. 'You know Billy. He'd lie his way in.'

A small, fond smile trembled on Bridget's mouth. 'Oh, Emma,' was all she could say.

As Emma placed the tea before her and sat down herself on the opposite side of the table, Bridget took a deep breath, dabbed at her watery eyes with a delicate lace handkerchief and smiled with a determination that surprised Emma.

'Well, now. I see you're – er – in a delicate condition.'

Emma felt the colour suffuse her cheeks and she glanced down in embarrassment, but then she felt Bridget's slim fingers reach out and touch her hand.

'My dear,' the woman said softly, 'who am I to judge you, or anyone else for that matter?' and Emma looked up into the blue eyes to see not a trace of censure in them. 'I don't blame you, not for one minute. You have to take your happiness where you can find it in this life and especially in these dreadful times we're living in. I hope you'll be happy, you and William. Really I do. Leonard's been away, what is it now, three years?'

Emma nodded.

'And if the War Office is to be believed,' Bridget said softly, 'he's not coming back.' She paused and then, bravely putting her own sadness aside, added firmly, 'No, you carry on with your life and good luck to you I say.' She flapped her elegant hand. 'And never you mind all the gossips. You and William and your little one,' she nodded her head towards Emma's stomach, 'you just be happy together.'

'Oh, Bridget,' Emma found there were tears in her eyes. 'You really are a lovely person.'

As Bridget took her leave, the two women hugged each other.

'Be happy, Emma dear,' were Bridget's parting words. 'This sadness will ease, given time. Then, be happy, my dear girl.'

Emma gave birth to William's daughter on the very day that the last sail was hoisted into position on the mill and the following day as she lay in bed, watching out of her bedroom window, the sails began to turn again. Beside her in the cradle the baby lay sleeping, blissfully unaware of the tumult of emotions her mother was experiencing.

When William came to her in the late afternoon, smelling of sweat, his eyes shining with exultation, she put up her arms to him, 'Oh, William, thank you, thank you for everything.'

As they held each other, they both looked towards the cradle. 'I suppose,' William said softly, 'there's only one name we can call her really.'

Her eyes shining, Emma chuckled. 'I'm afraid so. You don't mind, do you?'

William's face, full of happiness, told her the answer, but he said gently, 'Of course not. Charlotte Forrest Metcalfe, it is.'

Emma leant her head against his shoulder. 'It's what I wanted. For – for Charles, as well as for the obvious reason.'

The question that had been worrying her had been answered without her even having to ask it aloud. Even though they were not legally married – how could they be until the law decreed that she was free to remarry – William wanted his daughter to bear his name.

A small smile played at the corner of her mouth but for once she did not share the reason for her amusement with William. She was imagining how his father would be dancing with glee to think that at last there was a Metcalfe at Forrest's Mill. And how angry her own father would be!

Forty-One

'You know, we ought to have a party now the war's over,' Emma threw her arms wide. 'For the whole village.'

'Eh?' Sarah gaped at her and then clicked her tongue against her teeth. 'Never do things by half, do you? And where might I ask are we to hold this big party?' She tossed her head towards the window. 'In the yard here?'

'No,' Emma grinned. 'In the market place. Where else?'

'And what if it rains? Everyone's best hat gets drenched and we end up eating soggy sandwiches.'

'Oh, don't be such a killjoy, Sarah. We ought to do something to welcome the boys back.' She paused as unwelcome memories of the last time invaded her happy plans. Resolutely she pushed them away and went on, 'Everyone's so happy that it's all over.'

'What about those who've lost their menfolk?' Sarah said quietly.

'There's a lot of us lost someone,' Emma said soberly. 'But it would be a tribute to those that have sacrificed so much as well as a thanksgiving for those who have come back, wouldn't it?'

The plump shoulders wriggled. 'I don't know. I'd see what William ses, if I was you.'

Sarah trusted William and his opinion on anything and everything implicitly. From the moment he had moved into the millhouse, Sarah had been his staunch supporter fending off all the village tittle-tattle with such vehemence that

348

very soon it had ceased. Emma knew she had Sarah to thank for the fact that the villagers now accepted them.

Emma stifled a laugh. 'Oh, I will, don't worry.'

But William was all in favour of the idea and once Sarah knew that, she soon became the instigator of the whole affair, adopting the idea as having been her own.

'I vill bake the biggest cake you haf ever seen.' Mr Rabinski, too, was soon caught up in the excitement. He could not do enough to thank, not only Emma and her family, but the whole village who had welcomed him into their midst without question.

'I had some bad moments, ven the var started, you know, dear lady.' Since the day they had brought him to Marsh Thorpe and he had realized what the situation was between Emma and William, Mr Rabinski had always called Emma 'dear lady', neatly avoiding ever calling her 'Mrs Smith' again. 'Someone started a rumour that I vas a spy. Me? A spy!' He lifted his shoulders and spread his hands. 'Ven I haf lived here for over twenty-fife years.'

'Well, nobody round here thinks you're a spy, Mr Rabinski. They'd better not,' Sarah bristled with indignation, 'else they'll have me to answer to.'

Mr Rabinski beamed.

On the morning of VE Day, Emma watched as William climbed on to the roof of the engine shed, where the sails missed the roof by only a foot or two as they turned. As a sail drew close William yelled down, 'Right, Em,' and she opened the shades so that they slowed.

'Do be careful, William,' she called up, craning her neck backwards to watch him as he leaned out to tie a union jack on the tip of the sail.

'Right,' he called down. 'Same again.'

They repeated the operation until a flag fluttered at the end of each of the five sails.

'Leave it running now,' William said as he climbed down the ladder and stood beside her in the yard. 'Now that's a fine sight for you, ain't it, Em?'

'Oh yes,' she said, linking her arm through his. 'We're lucky the wind's in the right direction so you could reach the sails from the roof.'

William grinned. 'I ordered it specially.'

Emma threw back her head and laughed. 'I don't doubt it, William Metcalfe. Come on, we'd best be getting to the market place, else we'll miss all the fun.'

At that moment the church bells began to ring and the party began.

In the market place long trestle tables had been carried into the square, covered with tablecloths and spread with all manner of food. Bunting was festooned between lampposts and flags fluttered from chimneys and roof tops. Near Metcalfe's brick archway, the band sat on stools and played all the songs that had blared from the wireless throughout the war, lifting spirits and giving hope. Children ran around, shouting and laughing, heady with a freedom that some of them, too young to remember pre-war days, had never known before.

'Oh, William, no more bombing, no more blackouts, no more rationing . . .'

'Well, I think we'll have that with us for a while yet,' he remarked. 'But I know what you mean, love.'

She gave a huge sigh, 'And Billy's safe too.'

A letter had come two days earlier telling them he was staying in the Merchant Navy, but promising them that he would be home to spend Christmas with them. 'Must meet this new little sister of mine. . . .'

'Oh look! Look at Lottie.' The fond parents laughed as their young daughter toddled towards them, holding a sticky jam bun in each hand. 'She's like a little doll, isn't she?' Emma said. 'She reminds me so much of my mother, sometimes. The way she smiles, the way her cheeks dimple.'

William chuckled as he bent to lift Lottie into his arms. 'Oh, she's going to be a heartbreaker one day, and no mistake. And just where, young lady, did you get *two* sticky buns from?'

'Mister Rab,' Lottie said and smiled, her blue eyes sparkling and her blonde curls dancing. Unable to get her child's tongue round his unusual name, Lottie always called him 'Mister Rab'.

'I thought as much and, talk of the devil,' William said, 'just look at this pair, Em. They look like a couple of cats that's been at the cream.'

Coming towards them, weaving their way through the happy throng and arm in arm, were Mr Rabinski and Sarah. They stopped in front of Emma and William, glancing and smiling at each other. Sarah's cheeks were pink as Mr Rabinski removed his hat and began, 'Mr William, dear lady, I have the honour to inform you that this wonderful lady at my side had consented to be my vife.'

Emma clapped her hands together and threw her arms about Sarah. 'Oh, how wonderful. That makes today absolutely perfect.'

When all the congratulations had been said, Sarah, glancing impishly at her husband-to-be said, 'There's only one thing, Ezra, you will just *have* to make friends with the bees.'

As Mr Rabinski threw his hands in the air in horror, Emma and William leant against each other, weak with laughter.

A man was standing before her. A tall man who stooped slightly now from his years spent over the anvil. His skin was leather brown and the once black hair was now speckled with grey.

'Hello, Jamie,' Emma said, surprised at how calm and level her voice was. 'How are you?'

They had not met – not face to face – for many years. Even since her return to Marsh Thorpe with William, Jamie had never once visited them at the mill. For all she knew, the brothers had never even spoken to each other for William had never mentioned Jamie's name. It was strange, she thought, that even in a small village community, people could live only a few yards from each other and yet never speak. She found the realization very sad. She had seen Jamie, of course, in the market place or in the chapel, but never had they exchanged more than a brief, awkward nod.

'Well enough,' he said, and then fell silent, his brown eyes were upon her face, holding her from turning away. He twisted his cap round and round in his hands with a strange nervousness. 'Emma,' he began, his words coming haltingly, 'I've wanted to say something to you for a long time, but I haven't known quite how.'

She waited, watching him, unable to help because she wasn't really sure what it was he was trying to say.

'I was a fool,' he blurted out and her eyes widened. 'A blind, stupid, damned proud fool. And I've spent a lifetime regretting it.'

'Oh, Jamie,' Emma said and there was a wealth of sadness in her tone. For the first time in years she looked at the man she had once loved so desperately with all the passion of her youth. Through the years, she had carried the heartache of his cruel rejection that had thrust her into a most unsuitable marriage. Because of him, she had thought herself unloved and unworthy of being loved. But now, for the first time, she realized that at last she could let him go, bury all the bitterness, the age-old longing. Jamie had been her first love and there would always be a special place in her heart for him, but William was her last love, her greatest love. It was William who had healed her wounded heart and given her back her own pride; William who staunched her grief over the death of her eldest son; William who had given her a new beginning with the birth of their daughter. And it had been William who had brought her home to Grandpa Charlie's mill and his love that had rebuilt it for her.

He was coming towards her now, weaving his way through the throng to reach her side, a worried frown on his face when he saw her talking to his brother. As he came and stood beside her, Jamie nodded a greeting. 'I wanted to tell you, tell you both, that I'm sorry. Sorry for how I behaved when I came home after the last lot.'

Emma felt William glance from one to the other, but she said nothing now. Later, she would tell him everything and she would tell him too that the ghost of her first love had finally been put to rest. But now she allowed Jamie to struggle with the words he had been withholding so long. 'I – I've realized now, through this war, what it must have been like for you, William, when Mother and Dad died, and you only a lad. I – I should have been more understanding.' Between his nervous fingers, the cap continued to twirl like mill sails.

Emma smiled and stepped forward to reach up to kiss his cheek. 'It's all water under the bridge now, Jamie. Let's start anew. Today's the day for new beginnings. The past is dead and – and buried.' She faltered a little over the words, for fleetingly, the vision of her son, Charles, came into her mind. Her dear boy was buried somewhere in France, and she knew not where; perhaps she would never know exactly where. But she smiled tremulously through unshed tears. Deep in many hearts today, there was an ache for loved ones who would never return, yet life had to go on and today the whole village was trying to put the bleak, dark days of war behind them and look to the future.

Emma's future clutched at skirts. She swept the child up into her arms. 'And this sticky little urchin, is Lottie. Say "hello" to your uncle Jamie, Lottie.'

The child, her face smeared with red jam, regarded Jamie solemnly, her clear blue eyes seeming to assess him. Then her mouth curved and two dimples appeared in the round cheeks. She reached out her chubby arms to be held and as Emma passed her into his arms, both she and William chuckled at the look of consternation that appeared on Jamie's face.

It had been a good day, a happy day. As they walked home in the dusk, Lottie walked between them, but her little feet dragged with tiredness.

'It's a lick and a promise for you tonight, little one,' Emma murmured, 'and into your bed.' But she paused in the yard and looked up at the mill, Lottie leaning against her knee. 'Oh, William, I don't know when I ever felt so happy. But I feel guilty at feeling it.'

'Why?'

'Well, Charles and – and Leonard too,' she said softly. 'I didn't wish him dead, you know.'

William's arm tightened about her. 'Of course you didn't. And stop feeling guilty. Charles wouldn't want you to grieve for ever. He'd want you to be happy. And Leonard too. For all his faults, I believe he cared for you in his own way.'

Emma smiled. 'Dear William. You're such a kind, understanding man. I'm so lucky, so very lucky.'

As she stood there in the yard, looking up at the mill

now restored by William's clever, loving hands to its former glory, Emma was filled with a tumult of emotions, of memories flitting through her mind. She remembered the night the mill sails had blown down, of little Charles's bravery. Further back, she remembered Luke and his constant concern for her, a girl, having to work as hard as she did. And she remembered her father, his bitterness at not having a son, and then his joy when she gave him a grandson. And now that grandson was gone too.

She felt her daughter pull at her skirt and she lifted the child into her arms and as she did so, it was like a locked door in her memory being released and suddenly opened. Clearly, almost as if he were standing beside her, she heard her grandpa Charlie's deep, gravelly voice.

'You're a miller's daughter, Emma Forrest, never forget that. There are no sons to carry on the name, but that's no matter. You carry Forrest blood in your veins, that's what counts, and one day, all this will be yours.'

At last, she had recalled the memory that had lain buried in her mind, blotted out by the dreadful event which had happened only moments after he had said those words to her. Now, she remembered it all so clearly, so vividly that the returning memory almost robbed her of her breath. Her grandfather had been holding her in his arms, had lifted her up and pointed to the mill and said the words; '*You are a miller's daughter, Emma Forrest.*' Then he had set her on the ground, walked towards the mill and begun to climb up and up and up . . . Moments later he was lying, smashed and bleeding on the ground beneath the mill's sails.

The child in her arms, wriggled and whimpered. 'Mum, you're squeezing Lottie.'

Emma felt the world reel and the feel of William's arm about her and his concerned voice saying, 'Are you all right, Em?' brought her crashing back to the present.

She passed the back of her hand across her forehead and smiled tremulously at him. 'Yes,' she said. 'I am now. Now – everything's all right.'

With, their arms about each other, they turned to go into the house; Emma felt as if a great burden had been lifted from her shoulders. Grandpa Charlie hadn't minded at all that she, Emma, had been a girl. And now, in her arms, she carried her only hope for the future, another *miller's daughter*.

From the shadows across the street, a man stood watching the tender scene; a man with bitterness in his heart.

'One day,' he vowed, 'I'll have what rightly belongs to me, Emma Forrest – Smith – Metcalfe – or whatever you call yourself now. If it takes a lifetime, I'll have what's mine. You see if I don't.'

Part Three

Forty-Two

'Mum, there's this new boy at school. He started a few months back when he came to live with his grandmother in Thirsby. He's dishy.'

Thirsby was a small hamlet about three miles from Marsh Thorpe but still within the catchment area for the Grammar School Lottie attended in Calceworth.

'Oh yes?' Emma said, absently, starting to add a column of figures for the third time.

Lottie bent and kissed the frown of concentration on her mother's forehead. 'Like me to do that for you, Mum? Maths never was your strong subject, was it?'

'Oh, please. I get a different answer every time.' Thankfully, Emma pushed the sheaf of papers towards her daughter and watched in admiration as the girl picked up the pen and ran her glance down the column adding up the figures in her head. 'Yes,' she murmured. 'He's dishy. I could really go for someone like him.'

Emma smiled fondly at the short, blonde curls bent over the figures. Small and slender with blue eyes and a clear, smooth porcelain skin, Lottie was like a precious china doll. And William, bless him, treated their daughter as if that was exactly what she was.

'However a great carthorse like me produced such a daughter, I'll never know,' Emma would laugh. Now, with the passage of time and secure in William's never-failing love, Emma could joke about herself.

'To me,' he would say, cupping her face in his hands and stroking the now short, pure white hair, 'you were beautiful and you always will be.' Then he would put his arm about her thickening waist and his gaze would go towards their daughter and Emma would see adoration in his face. It brought her joy every time she saw a father's love for his daughter.

'She's like my mother,' she would say softly. 'Sarah always says so. I can't remember her very clearly, but I have fleeting memories of a sweet face and a sunny nature.'

She heard William's deep chuckle. 'Well, that's Lottie to a point, but the sun goes in and the storm clouds gather now and then when she can't get her own way.'

Emma laughed. 'She can be a stubborn little madam, when she wants to be.'

'Aye, and then we're all running for shelter. Still, even if I'd been given the choice, I wouldn't change a hair of her lovely head. Would you?'

'No,' Emma said slowly, biting her lip.

'Do I hear a "but" in there somewhere?' There was surprise in William's voice.

'It's just that I worry about her, now she's older. I mean, I know she's still at school but she almost seventeen. She's a young woman.'

'Well, all parents worry about their daughters. About their children whatever their sex, if it comes to that.'

'Mm.'

'It's more than just that with you, though, isn't it, Em? Come on, tell me, love.'

'Sarah's right. Lottie is like my mother. Very like her. And I worry that – that if she gets married and – and has children ... Well, you know what happened to my mother?'

'Oh, darling,' William's reassuring arms came around

her now. 'Things are very different nowadays for women in childbirth. For a start, they're not left at home with little or no proper medical attention.' He touched her cheek and said, teasingly, 'It's nearly sixty years ago, my old dear, since you were born and your poor mam was losing all her other babies. You've no need to fear for Lottie, not now, I'm sure.'

'I hope you're right,' Emma murmured. 'Oh, I do hope you're right.'

Now, deliberately casual, she asked Lottie, 'What's his name, this – er – dish?'

Charlotte laughed. 'Micky.'

'And what's he like?'

Lottie looked up and smiled, her delicate pink cheeks dimpling. 'Oh Mum, come on. I'm not getting the third degree, am I? You'll be asking next what his father does and are his intentions towards me "honourable"?'

Emma laughed. 'No, I didn't mean it like that. I just meant – well – is he good-looking?'

'Would I go for anything less?' Lottie countered saucily. 'Well, now, let me see. He's tall.' She giggled. 'I only come up to his shoulder. He's got sort of bluey-grey eyes and dark hair and, yes, he's vey good looking.' She sighed ecstatically. 'And he's a right charmer. All the girls are after him. I shouldn't think I'll even get a look-in.'

Thoughtfully, Emma watched the bowed head. *That* she did not believe, not for one minute.

'And you say he's come to live in Thirsby with his grandmother?'

'Thirty-six, forty, fifty-seven,' Lottie murmured, her pen still running up the columns. 'Yes.'

For some unaccountable reason, before she even voiced the question, Emma knew the answer, 'What – what's his surname?'

'Smith,' Lottie said absently, her concentration still on the figures.

A cold hand clutched at Emma's heart. 'Smith?' she squeaked. Oh, it couldn't be, could it? Smith was a common name and yet ... Emma swallowed painfully, remembering suddenly that Bridget Smith lived at Thirsby. And Lottie had said he had come to live with his grandmother. Emma stared at Lottie's bent head and her tone, when she spoke, was sharper than she intended. 'Well, you're too young to start thinking about boyfriends yet anyway. You've your O levels in two months' time. I don't want any silly nonsense over boys ruining your chances.'

She saw the pen stop, her daughter's head come up slowly, saw Lottie's blue eyes widen and her pretty mouth open in a gasp of surprise. 'Mum . . .?'

But Emma turned and hurried out of the kitchen and into the shop at the front of the house. Thankfully it was empty and she leant against the counter and closed her eyes. Suddenly Emma felt dizzy with fear. Oh no, she prayed fervently. Not that, please not that.

'It can't be anyone related to Leonard, can it?' she asked William, following him from the granary across the yard to the mill and back again, taking anxious little running steps at his side.

'I shouldn't think so, love,' William said, calm and matter-of-fact as ever. 'Did Leonard have any brothers or sisters?'

Emma stood, perplexed, fingering the hem of her apron. 'No, oh no. Bridget said – I mean – she told me once that she hadn't really wanted Leonard . . .' Her voice trailed away.

'So, you're saying Micky is Leonard's son, are you?'

'I – I don't know what I'm saying. I've just got this awful *feeling*.'

William picked up another sack and heaved it on to his shoulder. From his semi-stooping position, he grinned up at her. 'Why don't you go and ask the bees, love? They'll know for sure.'

'William! Don't you dare laugh at me.' To her chagrin, tears sprang into her eyes. Seeing them, William at once dropped the sack to the ground and reached out to her.

'I'm sorry. I didn't realize you were so serious. Whatever are you getting yourself so worked up about? Leonard was killed in the war.'

There was a silence between them, the only sound the rhythmic rattle of the rotating sails above them.

Emma met William's steady gaze. 'So we've been led to believe, but even though the court granted us that – that Presumption of Death Order so that we could marry, we can't ever be really sure, can we?'

William sighed. 'Does Lottie know anything?'

'She knows I was married to someone else and that he was killed in the war, because she knows Billy and she's heard about – about Charles.' Even now the loss of her firstborn still hurt Emma. Billy Smith had made a career in the Merchant Navy after the war, but some years ago now he had gone to live in Australia and had married out there. He wrote regularly and sent photographs of his wife and family, but Emma doubted she would ever see her younger son again.

'Does she know what your married name was?'

Emma wrinkled her forehead and sighed. 'I really don't know. Probably not. Billy's just – well – just "Billy" to her. What she certainly does not know,' Emma went on slowly, 'is that we were not married at the time she was born.'

'Well, I'm surprised that someone hasn't told her

already. You know what this place is like for gossip. It's a wonder if some kid hasn't teased her about it at school if nothing else.'

Emma shrugged. 'Oh, I don't know. Once they'd accepted it, I've always thought the villagers have been very loyal to us. Besides, we did all the right things and were married as soon as we—' Her eyes widened and her mouth rounded in an 'oh'.

William nodded grimly. 'Exactly. If Leonard is still alive, we may not be married at all.'

They stared at each other.

'Look,' William said reasonably, 'we might be worrying for nothing. We don't even know if this lad is anything to do with Bridget. The best thing we can do is to let things take their natural course. Make the boy welcome if she wants to bring him home. Just like you would any of her friends, just like you always have and,' he added pointedly, 'just like you would any *other* lad.'

'But what if . . .?'

'Wait and see, Emma,' William said firmly. 'Just wait and see.'

She knew he was right, but it didn't make it any easier, the 'waiting to see', as he put it. Worry kept her awake at night, staring into the darkness seeing all that they had built up in the past seventeen years crumbling before her eyes. They had worked hard, the two of them, with the ever faithful Sarah and Mr Rabinski – for some reason they could never come to call him Ezra – alongside them. The mill and the bakery had prospered in a modest way.

Now, Mr Rabinski was too old and frail to work the long hours in the bakehouse and Emma and William employed a young lad from the village to do most of the heavy work, though still under the direction of the old master baker. The shop itself had changed too. Although they still sold their own bread, it had become something of a general store now and for the past five years had also been the village post office. The work of the mill was changing. They ground a small quantity of wheat for their own bakehouse, but the bulk of their work now was producing animal feedstuffs. But at least they had enough work coming in to keep the sails turning.

Jamie's work too had diminished and changed over the years with little for the smithy and even less for the wheelwright side of the business. Now he fashioned fancy wrought iron gates and fences.

'What would our father have said?' Jamie would moan. 'All the old crafts are dying out, all the old ways.'

'Aye, well,' William would say, 'it's what they call progress.'

And Jamie would give a disgruntled, 'Huh. That's what you call it, is it? But you're all right, aren't you?' he'd say nodding towards the shop. 'Little gold mine you've got there with all the passing trade you're picking up.' And he would gesture towards the road where traffic now buzzed through the village on its way to the coast.

'You have to move with the times,' William would answer and then he would bite back the next few words that always sprang to his mind, 'and not stay buried in the past.'

Poor Jamie. They felt sorry for the embittered man, now in his mid-sixties, who had spent his life working so hard and yet seemed to have nothing to show for all his labour.

'He'd have been so different if he'd married you,' William would say softly, tracing his finger round the line of her face. 'But what would I have done then if I'd had to spend my life as your brother-in-law?'

A lot of things would have been different, Emma thought wryly, if I'd married Jamie Metcalfe. Though she no longer regretted the fact that she had not, she could not prevent the thought from slipping into her mind that if she had spent her life as Jamie's wife, she would not at this moment be worrying herself sick over a boy called Micky Smith.

Forty-Three

'Mum, you didn't really mean what you said, did you?'

Pretending ignorance, Emma said, 'What about, love?' But her heart was pounding inside her breast. She knew only too well what Lottie meant.

'About me and – boyfriends?' The girl gave a nervous laugh and touched her hair in an affected gesture that was totally unlike her. 'I mean, it's not that I want to get serious with anyone. But, well . . .' The words came out in a rush. 'All our class are going to a dance in the Castle Gardens in Calceworth. You know, that place on the seafront? And, well, this lad's asked me to go with him.'

Emma swallowed and tried to keep her voice steady, 'And which lad might that be?'

'Micky. Micky Smith.'

Emma let out the breath she had been holding, wishing vehemently that William was here with her. He would handle it so much better than she could. But William had taken Mr Rabinski to Lincoln on a business matter. The old man was too frail to go alone and William would have to spend the whole day with him. But Emma seemed to hear her husband's gentle voice inside her head, 'Let it take its course, Em.'

With a valiant effort, Emma plastered a smile on her face and turned to face her daughter. 'Of course you can go to the dance, love. But your dad will want to fetch you home?'

'Oh, there's a bus being organized to drop all of us off at our doors. Honestly, Mum, it's being done properly. And besides, Micky will see me home safely.'

That is exactly what I'm afraid of, Emma thought, but she managed to hold back the words and say instead, 'We'll see what your dad says.'

'Mum, this is Micky.'

Emma turned round slowly, knowing what she was going to see even before she found herself looking directly into a pair of blue-grey eyes that made time take a tilt.

He was tall for his age, taller than Leonard had been. Micky had the same eyes, the same dark hair and the same engaging smile. Completely unaware of the tumult of emotions the sight of him was causing her, the boy was holding out his hand towards her and saying politely, 'Good evening, Mrs Metcalfe. I hope we're not late. The dance went on a bit.'

'No, no, it's all right,' Emma heard herself saying mechanically and adding lamely, 'as long as we know where she is.'

She saw the two youngsters exchange a glance and could almost read their thoughts. Parents!

Oh, yes, m'lad, Emma was thinking. Parents, it is indeed, but not in the way you're thinking.

With relief she heard the back door open and William, returning from locking up outside for the night, came into the kitchen. His glance went immediately from his daughter to the boy and then his gaze swivelled to meet Emma's. 'Well, now,' he said, rubbing his hands together. 'Come along in and have a drink before you go, lad. Far, is it?'

'No, sir.' The boy was all courteousness. Too courteous,

Emma thought suspiciously. 'Only about three miles and it's a fine night.'

Lottie was smiling up at him, her blue eyes shining. 'I told him to stay on the bus, but he would insist on getting off and seeing me to the door.' Emma noticed that the girl's hand fluttered out and touched his, the lightest, feather touch. Micky turned swiftly and gave Lottie a broad wink.

'Oh!' Emma's hand flew to her mouth and the tiny cry escaped her lips before she could prevent it. A hot sweat spread through her and she closed her eyes. Forty years ago Leonard had stood in this very room and winked at her, a naive, inexperienced nineteen-year-old. And now, if what she believed was really true, Leonard's son was standing almost on the same spot and flirting with her daughter in the same way.

'Mum? What is it? Are you all right?' As if from a great distance she heard Lottie's voice. 'You've gone ever so white. Come on, sit down.'

Emma opened her eyes and took a deep breath. 'I'm fine, love. A bit tired, that's all.'

'I'd better go,' Micky began, but Emma waved his protestations aside. 'No, no, really. Go upstairs with Mr Metcalfe and we'll bring some coffee up.'

As William led the young man upstairs to the sitting room above the shop, Lottie whispered, 'Well? What do you think? He *is* a dish, isn't he?'

'Yes, oh yes, he's a dish all right,' Emma replied, finding it difficult to keep the resentment from her tone.

'What is it, Mum?' The girl's voice trembled. 'Don't you like him?'

There was a moment's pause and then Emma shook herself and forced a smile on to her mouth. She was being so unfair to Lottie, who was completely ignorant about who the boy might be. It wasn't the girl's fault, but Emma sighed inwardly, things would have to be stopped before they went too far.

'It's not that, darling. Don't worry. He seems a very nice boy.' Emma avoided meeting her daughter's shrewd gaze. 'Come on, butter some plum bread. Boys of his age are always hungry, I know.'

Sitting slightly apart from the other three, watching and listening to them talking, Emma could not help feeling how nice it was to have a young man in the house again. She had missed her boys more than she had realized, and she could almost imagine it was Charles or even young Billy sitting there laughing and teasing Lottie. But Charles was dead and Billy, settled in Australia, had not been home for years. Lottie really did not know her half-brother at all.

The cup trembled in her hand and rattled in the saucer as, with a sudden jolt, Emma realized that if the boy sitting with such ease in her front room was indeed Leonard's son, then, although he was no blood relative of Lottie's, he was her son Billy's half-brother, just as Lottie was Billy's half-sister.

'We've got to put a stop to it before she gets in too deep.'

William frowned worriedly. 'How can we do anything unless we tell her the truth? And that means telling her *everything*.'

Emma met his gaze and her chin rose a little higher in defiance. 'Then,' she said, keeping her voice steady, 'we'll have to tell her everything.' She leant closer. 'Don't you see, William, if this boy Micky really is his son, Leonard might still be alive?'

'That's exactly what I do mean. And maybe we're not legally married. That's part of what we've got to tell Lottie.'

370

Emma let out a long sigh. 'I know.' She put her hand on his arm and with great sadness said again, 'I know.'

Almost inaudibly, William murmured, 'And you know what that makes our daughter?'

Now rebellion sparkled in Emma's brilliant eyes. 'There's worse things in this world than being illegitimate. She has two parents who love her dearly and besides, it was hardly our fault, now was it? And another thing, maybe Leonard's married again.'

William gave a bark of wry laughter. 'Well, we can plead ignorance, but he can't, now can he? He would knowingly have been committing bigamy.' He was thoughtful for a moment and then said, 'But what grounds have we to stop Lottie and Micky being, well, whatever they want to be? I mean, they're not related, are they?'

'Not by blood, no. But you know what Leonard was. A gambler, a con-man living only just on the right side of the law.' Remembering her life in the city with him, the dread of hearing a knock on the door and then the final fiasco over the wireless set, Emma muttered, 'Scarcely that at times. That's not the sort of life you want for Lottie, is it?'

William spread his hands. 'But that doesn't mean to say this lad is the same. You can't condemn him—'

'If he is Leonard's son, then of course he'll be like him.'

'Charles was his son,' William reminded her gently. 'And a finer lad you could not have met.'

Emma smiled, remembering, then her smile faded. 'But young Billy was his double. Leonard *trained* him, William. He wanted his son to be like him. He was proud of it.' She wriggled uncomfortably as another memory thrust its way into her mind. 'And Bridget, she indulged Billy too. He – he was her favourite. "Like father, like son," she used to say.' Emma leant towards William and added, 'And that's exactly what she'll be saying with *this* son too.'

Helplessly, William shook his head. 'Darling, we're still not even sure Micky is Leonard's son.'

'There's something else I've remembered too. I once asked Leonard about his father, but he couldn't remember him. It seems Bridget never actually married at all. But he said there was one man who stayed with her longer than the rest when he was a boy. Leonard said that man was the closest he'd ever had to a father figure. And he was a gambler. "Taught me everything he knew." Leonard actually said those words. He was *proud* of it, William, as if he'd idolized the man. And I could tell from the way he spoke that he still, even after all that time, felt the hurt of that man leaving.'

William was frowning, obviously wondering what all this had to do with their present concern.

'That man's name,' Emma said slowly and deliberately, 'was Mick.'

'Oh,' William said. 'I see.' He was thoughtful for a moment and then said, 'But it still doesn't prove anything. Not really.'

Emma swallowed. She could hardly tell her husband just why she was so certain that Micky Smith was Leonard's son, but she knew he was. Oh yes, she knew as certainly as she knew the sun would rise over the sails of Forrest's Mill the following morning.

Quietly, she said, 'You know, I could settle this one way or the other.'

'How?'

'I could go to Thirsby to see this boy's grandmother.'

William stared and then nodded slowly. 'And if it is Bridget – then, then at least we'll know.'

Forty-Four

Emma sat behind the wheel of the truck and started the engine. William, his hands on the door where the window was wound down, said, 'Are you sure you don't want me to come with you?'

She shook her head and tried to smile but the nervousness in the pit of her stomach felt like fluttering butterflies. 'No, no, I'm better going on my own, though I'd love you to be with me. You know that.'

William smiled, touched her shoulder, saying, 'Well, good luck, then.' He stepped back and raised his hand in farewell as she let in the clutch and the vehicle moved slowly towards the gate into the road.

If it hadn't been for her errand, Emma would have enjoyed the short drive through the countryside between the two villages. The day was scorching, without a breath of wind, and in the lanes, bordered by high hedges, the heat shimmered above the surface of the road. In the fields, cows congregated under the trees seeking whatever shade they could find.

She had no idea where Micky's grandmother lived so, as she approached Thirsby, she slowed down looking for a post office or a village shop. She knew how often strangers called into her shop to asking for directions.

The bell clanged as she stepped inside the tiny shop. Like her own premises, it was part of a double-fronted house. The woman behind the counter beamed a welcome.

'I'm sorry to trouble you, but I'm looking for Micky Smith. I believe he lives with his grandmother. Do you know him?'

The woman laughed. 'Well, I should do. He's our Sunday paperboy. He's a nice lad,' she said. 'Yew Cottage. That's where he lives, as you say, with his gran.'

Emma held her breath. 'And her name is?'

'Mrs Smith, of course.' The woman stared a moment, then laughed. 'Oh, I see, it might not be the same name if it was his mother's mother. But, in this case, it is the same.'

Emma's heart sank.

'Yes,' the woman was saying. 'She's his dad's mother. Young Micky's been living with her, oh now, let's see? Since last September time. His dad visits from time to time, though.'

Emma felt a sweat that had nothing to do with the heat of the day break out all over her body. Her voice was a croak as she said. 'His – his father?' Then she clung to a vestige of new hope. Perhaps, after all, Micky wasn't Leonard's son, perhaps he was nothing to do with Leonard or Bridget or . . . But at the woman's next words her hopes sank even further.

'Oh yes, he comes two or three times a year to see his mother. Lovely lady she is, pretty as a picture even at her age. He's a nice bloke too, but,' she leaned over the counter as if imparting a confidence, 'a bit on the flash side for us village folk. But he's a real charmer.' She winked and nodded, 'Know what I mean?'

'Oh yes,' Emma murmured, 'I know what you mean,' and added bitterly in her own mind, only too well!

'Where do I find Yew Cottage?'

The woman pointed, 'Carry on up the street, take the first left and it's the last cottage on the left as you leave the village. You can't miss it 'cos it's got a huge yew tree in the front garden.'

Murmuring her thanks, Emma left the shop and followed the woman's directions. In a few moments she was drawing up outside the cottage. She pulled on to the grass verge and switched off the engine. She sat a minute summoning up the courage for what, she was more than ever sure now, she had to face.

It was a pretty little thatched cottage. The neatly-kept borders were edged with white alyssum and purple lobelia in alternating clumps, alongside bright yellow shrubs. But the garden was dominated, overpowered almost, by the huge yew tree which stood in the centre of the lawn, the ground beneath its thick branches so hidden from the light that the grass no longer grew there.

'Why, Emma, my dear. How lovely.' The woman's delight was genuine, Emma knew. She sighed. This was going to be even more difficult than she had imagined. Bridget was so disarmingly open, so transparently guileless. Surely she could not know about Micky's friendship with Lottie?

'Come in, come in.' The door was pulled open wider and Emma found herself stepping out of the bright sunlight and into the contrast of a shadowy, tiny hallway. Bridget led the way into a sunny sitting room and towards the French windows thrown open to the sun and leading out on to a paved area.

'I love to sit here in the summer, as long as I don't get too much sun,' Bridget patted her smooth cheek, her laughter tinkling and Emma, despite her errand, found herself smiling. It had always been difficult, impossible really, to resist this woman's charms. 'Sit down, sit down, let me make you a cup of tea. Oh, Emma, it is lovely to see you again.'

She reached out and clasped Emma's hands in her own slim fingers. Amazingly, she looked little changed, still slender in her floating chiffon dress and high heeled shoes.

'No, no, don't trouble, Bridget. Really. Please – ' the words came out stiffly, haltingly, 'please sit down. There's something I want to talk to you about.'

Bridget's mouth made a small, silent 'oh' but, obediently, she sat in the chair opposite and folded her hands neatly in her lap, looking like a naughty school girl about to be scolded.

Emma looked at her properly and saw that beneath the carefully applied make-up the wrinkles were there. The golden hair looked so perfect that Emma wondered if it was a wig. And Bridget's hands, still slim and elegant, had the tell-tale purple veins of age on the back. What age must she be now? Emma's mind clutched at another thought, any other thought, to put off the moment when she must face the reason that had brought her here. Bridget had to be eighty at least. If so, then the woman was incredible.

She was leaning forward saying gently, 'What is it, my dear? Not bad news?' Even her voice was not the quavery tone of an octogenarian. It was still light, almost girlish.

'Well . . .' Emma began and then hesitated. No, she told herself sharply, it was not bad news at least not the kind Bridget meant. 'Not really, I just want to talk to you, to ask you something. About Micky.'

The woman's eyes glowed with tenderness and she clasped her hands together. 'Oh, he's the joy of my old age, Emma. Such a dear, dear boy. And so clever too. He goes to the Grammar School in Calceworth, you know?'

'Yes,' Emma said slowly and added, with deliberate emphasis, 'and so does my daughter, Charlotte.'

'Does she? How nice . . .' Bridget began and then her eyes widened. 'Oh, you mean, they know each other?'

Her mouth tight, Emma nodded. 'They know each other very well. Too well.'

Bridget looked puzzled for a moment. 'But Micky's never mentioned anyone called—' Suddenly she clapped her hand over her mouth in the childish gesture Emma remembered so well. 'Of course – *Lottie*. She's your daughter?'

'Have you met her? Has he brought her home? Here?'

Bridget shook her head. 'No,' she said slowly and added, 'but he talks of no one else. You're right Emma. They are close. Very close.'

The two women stared at each other.

'I presume,' Emma said carefully and felt her heart thudding painfully, 'Micky is Leonard's son.'

Suddenly, Bridget looked a little old woman. She seemed to shrink before Emma's eyes. The joy seemed to go out of her face and she leant back wearily against the cushions.

'Yes,' she whispered. 'He's Leonard's boy.'

Emma rose slowly. 'Let me make you some tea, Bridget. I think we could both do with a cup now.'

The older woman nodded and Emma found her own way into the neat kitchen, finding all she needed readily to hand for an afternoon tray of tea things was already laid out in the kitchen. Minutes later, when she carried it back outside the French windows, she tried to say lightheartedly. 'I could almost imagine you were expecting me.'

Bridget, the colour back in her face, smiled though her voice was a little tremulous as she said, 'I always have a cup of tea and some cake waiting for Micky when he gets home from school. You know what boys are, always ravenous.'

She made no move to pour out the tea herself but sat back leaving it to Emma.

Handing her a cup, Emma said gently, 'Bridget, why did

377

you never come and tell me that Leonard was alive?' She was finding the realization that Bridget had known for years but had never told her, rather hurtful.

'Now, how could I, Emma dear? He was a deserter who could have been arrested. Besides, you were – are still, I hope – happy with William and your little girl.' The elegant shoulders lifted. 'Why stir up trouble?'

'But I would like to have known,' Emma murmured reproachfully. 'You could have trusted me, you know.'

The china blue eyes, still remarkably clear, were regarding Emma steadily. 'Leonard said you were always so honest. He wasn't sure how you would react.'

Emma gasped and felt the colour flood her face. She could well imagine that such a remark had been made with a sneer.

'That's not fair. How could he say that? I never let him down. Not even,' she added bitterly, remembering the wireless set again, 'when it was against my own instincts.'

Sipping the tea, Bridget said, 'Leonard's a rogue, Emma. I can't deny it any longer.'

Startled, Emma's cup rattled in the saucer and she gave a gasp of surprise. Even from the ingenuous Bridget she had not expected such honesty.

'Oh, I love him, I always have, I always will. He's my son. But I'm not as silly and feckless and blind to his faults as people believe.' Her steady gaze met Emma's. 'I know I've been painted a scarlet woman most of my life, Emma, but I've never deliberately hurt anyone. I had a lot of fun and I had a lot of love. But *I gave* a lot of love, yes, and fun, too.' Her mouth quirked. 'Even to your poor old dad, eh? And I never went with married men, whatever anyone says. I never took another woman's husband away from her. And there were times when I could have done.' Her eyes were dreamy looking back down the years. 'There was a Major once. He showered me with flowers and gifts, but I wouldn't have any of it. He had a wife and three children.' She shook her head, 'Oh no. Whatever else I may have done – may have been – ' she shot a mischievous, almost coquettish, glance at Emma, 'I never took another woman's man. Actually, that's how I came to Marsh Thorpe – to escape the Major.'

'So,' Emma said gently, trying to pull Bridget's reminiscing back to the present, 'Leonard did not die in the war?'

Bridget bit her lip and twisted her hands in her lap. 'No, no. But – oh, Emma, you won't give him away, will you, if I tell you? Promise?'

'Give him away? I don't understand.'

Bridget was silent a moment as if struggling with her conscience. 'He – he deserted. Goodness knows how he evaded capture by either the enemy or our side, but he did. So, legally he *is* dead.'

'Did he change his name?'

Bridget shrugged her shoulders. 'Didn't seem a lot of point really. Smith is a name other people use to *become* incognito.'

Emma could see the reasoning in that. 'Did he remarry?'

'Oh no. He lives with Helen, Micky's mother, but they never married. At least as far as I know.'

'So why is Micky living with you?'

Now there was puzzlement in the clear blue eyes. 'Leonard said he wanted him to come to live in the country. He told me the lad had asthma in the city. Leicester, they live now. But . . .' a small frown appeared on her forehead, 'I've never seen the slightest sign of Micky having asthma. He seems a particularly healthy lad to me.'

'Mm,' Emma said and there was a wealth of meaning in the sound.

'What? What are you thinking, Emma?'

'And Leonard comes here? To see you?'

'Well, yes, of course. Two or three times a year. Why?'

'Then he knows all about me. About me and William Metcalfe and that we have a daughter?'

'Well, yes. He's happy for you. Said he never meant you any harm.'

'Really?' The word was laced with sarcasm. 'Then why did he let me think he was dead?'

'He thought it best . . .' Bridget's voice trailed away. 'By the end of the war he'd got Helen. He met her in France. I think she sort of – hid him, you know. And they'd got Micky by then too.' She flapped her hand. 'But of course you must have realized that, because he's a similar age to Lottie. When I told him about you and William and your little girl, then he said things were best left the way they were for all concerned. Those were his very words, Emma.'

In fairness, Emma thought, it would have made things very awkward if her husband had returned from the dead – for all of them.

Emma sighed as she stood up. 'Well, perhaps for once I am misjudging Leonard. I thought he'd sent young Micky here for a reason.'

'What? What reason could there be?'

'I don't know.' She sniffed derisively. 'But I know Leonard of old and I'm going to stop Lottie seeing Micky.'

'Oh, Emma, Micky's going to be so upset. He really likes Lottie.'

As she walked back down the path towards the gate, she was acutely aware of Bridget watching her from the doorway, a troubled look on her sweet face.

'You're not to see Micky Smith anymore, Lottie.'

The girl's bright eyes were wide and her generous mouth

dropped open. 'Not – see – Micky? But – but why? He's nice. I thought you liked him. Dad did. You got on like a house on fire, didn't you?' Her frantic gaze was darting back and forth between her parents.

Emma bit her lip and avoided meeting her daughter's eyes. Resolutely she kept to her decision, but inside what she was doing was tearing her apart. 'No. You're too young to be having a boyfriend.' As the words left her mouth, the excuse sounded weak even to her own ears. She went on relentlessly, knowing she was only making matters worse, not better. 'You ought to be concentrating on your school work. If your O level results are good, you'll be staying on into the Sixth Form.'

'So will Micky. Just because I have a boyfriend doesn't mean I won't work hard. And I'll still help you in the shop on a Saturday.' The girl's face was growing pinker by the minute until her cheeks were fiery with anger. 'Why, Mum, just tell me why?'

When Emma made no answer, the girl turned resentful eyes upon her father. 'Dad? Do you know what this is all about?'

William ran his hand distractedly through his hair. Of course he knew. There were dark shadows under Emma's eyes for they had sat up talking half the night and even then sleep had been impossible. He didn't agree with the way Emma had decided to deal with the situation. He thought Lottie should be told the truth, the whole truth. There was nothing he could say, nothing he could do. Emma had been adamant.

When she received no answer from either of her parents, the girl whirled around and headed for the back door. 'Well, I won't stop seeing him, so there. And you can't make me. And if you do then – then I'll – I'll run away.'

The door slammed behind her and they heard her

running feet crossing the yard making for the gap in the hedge, through the orchard towards Sarah's cottage to lay her head against the older woman's plump shoulder and sob out her heart. Sarah would be on her side, Lottie would be thinking, Sarah would tell her why her mother was being so unreasonable.

But Sarah already knew what it was all about and Emma had sworn her to secrecy.

Forty-Five

'She's late home again. The school bus went through half an hour ago and she wasn't on it. Where is she?'

'I'll give you three guesses,' William said flatly.

Emma twisted her apron through her fingers. 'You don't agree with what I'm doing, do you?' she blurted out.

'You know I don't. You should have told her the truth from the start. This way, you're driving them together even faster. You know what youngsters are these days. The more you tell them *not* to do something, the more they want to do just that very thing.'

Emma passed the back of her hand wearily across her forehead. 'Oh, I suppose you're right.'

'I know it means telling her that we weren't married when she was born and that, maybe, we're not even now, but . . '

Emma sighed heavily. 'I really didn't want her to have to know.'

'She'll have to sooner or later,' he said reasonably. 'It's all part of growing up.' He put his arm about her shoulders. 'You can't keep them young and innocent. You can't protect them for ever. And I seem to remember you saying not so long ago that there were worse things than being illegitimate.'

Emma nodded. 'Yes, I did and I suppose you're right.' She laid her head against his shoulder. 'But I dread telling her.'

383

He gave her shoulders a little squeeze. 'We'll do it together. Tonight.'

But by nightfall, Lottie still had not returned home and Emma was almost frantic with worry. 'She must be with him. At his home – Bridget wouldn't see anything wrong in it.'

'Didn't you tell Bridget that you were going to stop them seeing each other?'

'Well, yes, but she's a very old lady now, William, and maybe—'

Emma made a sudden movement, snatched the keys to the truck from the hook on the back of the door, where they always hung.

'Where are you going?'

'Bridget's.'

'I'll come with you.'

'No, you stay here in case she comes home.' She pulled open the back door. 'I'll phone you from there. I don't think Bridget will be on the phone, but I remember seeing a phone box outside the little shop in the village.'

Most of the houses were in darkness as Emma drove into Thirsby but as she drew up outside Bridget's cottage she could see that a light still burned in the sitting room window. Emma walked up the paved path to the low front door and rapped on it with the brass door knocker. She didn't want to frighten the old lady at this time of night, but she had to find Lottie. She heard the rasp of a bolt being pulled back and as the door opened, Emma opened her mouth to say, 'Is she here? Have you seen Lottie?' But the words never came and she merely stared at the person standing there, her mouth gaping open. The blood pounded in her ears. Her legs trembled and threatened to give way beneath her.

'You!' She hardly recognized the strangulated croak as her own voice.

'Hello, Emma,' he said smoothly, almost as if he had been expecting her. 'How are you?'

'How . . .? How am I?' Her composure was returning a little, but with it came an almost uncontrollable anger. 'How dare you? How dare you stand there and ask me how I am?'

His hair was a little grey at the temples and the neat moustache was liberally peppered with white hairs. The handsome face had a few more lines than she remembered and there was a purple tinge to his nose, but it was still the same charming, smooth-talking Leonard; the man who was perhaps, she supposed with a sudden shudder, in the eyes of the law, still her husband.

'Do come in.' His grin broadened and his eyes glittered. It was a look she remembered well. Oh, how very well she remembered that expression. He was up to something, she knew. He *had* been expecting her.

In the sitting room, he said, 'Please sit down. Can I get you a drink?'

Emma ignored his offer and the question she had been going to ask Bridget burst from her lips. 'Where is she? Where's Lottie? And don't pretend you don't know anything about it.'

The smirk on his face sent a shiver down Emma's spine. 'I wouldn't pretend with you, my dear Emma.'

He sat down with a nonchalant air of satisfaction that Emma found more disturbing, more frightening, than she had ever felt of his anger, his swift changes of mood.

She sank down on to the sofa, her gaze fixed upon him.

'You do know where my daughter is, don't you, Leonard?' she asked quietly now.

'She's quite safe, Emma, my dear. I wouldn't harm her. In fact, I'd do everything in my power to keep her very safe. After all, she's part of my family.' Sarcasm lined his tone.

'What – what do you mean? She's no relation to you.'

'Oh no?' His lips stretched and his eyes narrowed. 'Perhaps not a blood relative, no, but very soon, she'll be my *daughter-in-law*.'

Emma felt the blood draining from her face and the room seemed to tilt. She put her hand to her head and lay back against the cushions. She felt Leonard pushing a glass into her hand.

'Here, have a sip of brandy. I never took you for the fainting type, Emma.' There was little real concern in his tone, but she took the brandy and sipped it. The sharp taste revived her and warmth crept back into her. She had never felt this way in the whole of her life and then she remembered that she had not eaten since lunch time and it was now almost midnight.

'Leonard, what do you mean? Where is Lottie? Please tell me.'

It went against the grain to have to beg anything of this man, but her maternal love for her daughter made her bury her pride.

'Micky and Lottie have gone away to be married.' His lip curled. 'And then one day, the mill will be Micky's. *My* son will own Forrest's Mill.'

Emma gasped. 'So that's what all this is about.'

'Yes, it is. I've waited a long time to get my revenge on your old man – and you for that matter. I came back here, you know, after the war.'

'Came back? When?'

'VE day, when the village was having one big party in the market place. I saw you with him, with Metcalfe, and I saw your little girl. I knew then I couldn't come back. It was too soon after the war to be safe. I wouldn't have put it past Metcalfe to turn me in.'

'Turn you in? Oh, you mean because you'd deserted?'

'Desertion in the field was a serious crime. There was this big push, you see. It was chaos, absolute hell. More than half my unit were killed. I was in a crater with only one other feller left alive and he was in a bad way. I'd had enough. So, I left my dog tags on a body that was so smashed up it was unrecognizable and I legged it out of there. I roamed around France for a while and then I met Helen. She was trying to run her small farm single-handedly. Her husband had been in the resistance and had been shot by the Germans. I worked on the farm and eventually – ' he grinned now, 'moved in with her. It was the perfect cover until the war was well and truly over.'

Emma was only half-listening but enough had penetrated her stupefied brain to ask, 'So why have you come back here now?'

His face was suddenly ugly. 'I want what is rightfully mine. I never could stand to be beaten, not at cards, nor in a deal, not at anything.' The sudden smile was vulpine. 'By the way, it was very good of your lover-boy to restore the mill for me. I must remember to thank him personally.'

Anger gave Emma back her strength. She leapt up, standing over him, shaking her fist in his face. 'You'll never get my mill, Leonard Smith. Over my dead body—'

'That's exactly how I will get it, or at least how Micky will. It's not that I want to live in it, or run it. I'm doing quite nicely in the Midlands. Oh no,' he stood up slowly and stood close to her, 'I just want to see justice done.'

'Justice?' Emma hissed. 'What about you? What about you, the deserter? There ought to be justice in that.'

His smile was confident. 'There was a case two years ago where a man was brought to trial for desertion in the war. They'd only just traced him. The case was dropped. Lack of evidence. And with a name like mine? Smith? Who could possibly prove anything?'

'I could. I've got the telegrams and the letters from the War Office.'

'And I'd tell them I came back after the war to find you had married another man while I was serving my country. You'd be had for bigamy.'

Suddenly, it was a war of nerves, a battle of wills.

'What about you? Haven't you married Helen?'

He laughed. 'Oh no. We're not married. And neither are you, Emma, my dear. At least – not to Metcalfe.'

She tried another tack. 'Lottie – and Micky – they can't get married. They're too young. They need parental permission.'

Leonard's smile was a sneer. 'Never heard of Gretna Green, Emma? They're on their way there right now. On a train bound for the Scottish border.'

'I'll go after them. I'll stop it . . .' Her voice rose and they heard a creak of floorboards from the room above them.

'That's Mother. Damn it, Emma, you've woken her.'

'I'll wake the whole bloody village, if I have to,' Emma screamed, deliberately now. 'You'll not get away with this, Leonard!'

They both heard the querulous voice from the top of the narrow stairs. 'Who's there? Leonard, are you there?'

He opened the door of the sitting room and called out to her. 'Go back to bed, Mother.' But Emma grabbed his arm, pulled him out of the way and pushed past him into the narrow hallway.

'Bridget.' She looked up the stairs to see the old woman standing there, her hair ruffled, her thin bare feet poking out from beneath her long cotton nightdress.

'Emma?' There was surprise in her tone. 'Is that you?' She started down the stairs. 'Whatever are you doing here?'

Behind Emma, Leonard said harshly. 'Mother, go back to bed. It has nothing to do with you.'

With asperity, Bridget said, 'Be quiet, Leonard. I'll not be ordered about in my own house,' and moments later she was downstairs demanding an explanation, quite unaware of the unusual appearance she was presenting to Emma. Without her make-up and the blonde hair that was, Emma realized now, a wig, the old woman actually did look the age she must be. Her own hair was thin and wispy white and her face was lined with tiny wrinkles. Without the frilly, high-necked blouses or dresses she always wore to hide it, Emma could see now that the skin around her neck sagged in folds. But her eyes were bright and knowingly sharp.

'Come along, Leonard. I'm waiting.'

Emma dragged her gaze away from Bridget back to Leonard and then back and forth between them. 'Do you mean you don't know what's going on, Bridget? Does she?' This to Leonard, then she turned back to Bridget, 'Do you know where Micky and Lottie are?'

'I know where Micky is. He's gone on one of these survival courses. He's camping somewhere in the Lake District.' Now Bridget stared at her son. 'Isn't he?'

'According to Leonard,' Emma said, 'Micky and Lottie are on their way to Gretna Green to be married.'

Bridget gasped, her wrinkled hand fluttering to her

throat. 'Don't be ridiculous. They can't. They're only children. Can't you stop them, Leonard?'

Emma bent over her and said slowly and deliberately, 'Apparently, it was all Leonard's idea – to get his hands on Forrest's Mill. *My* mill. But if he thinks that, he's got another think coming.' Now the initial shock of seeing her husband once more, of learning of his devious manipulation of her young and naive daughter, had worn off, Emma was once more in control of her emotions and her resolve. She faced Leonard. 'No one, *no one*, will ever take my grandfather's mill from me.'

Leonard smirked and said with a confidence that sent a fresh sliver of ice down her spine. 'Even you can't live forever, Emma – ' he paused and then added pointedly, '*Smith*.'

Emma drove through the darkness back to Marsh Thorpe. There had been nothing more she could do. Not even Bridget could move her son to put a stop to his plans.

Emma had spoken briefly to William from the call box outside the village shop, reassuring him that she had found out what had happened, that Lottie had come to no physical harm.

'But what is it? Where is she?' Even down the crackling telephone wire, she could hear the anguish in his voice.

'I can't explain now. I'm coming straight home.'

He was waiting for her in the yard, holding a storm lantern. Almost before she had pulled the vehicle to a halt, he was opening the driver's door. 'Are you all right? Where's Lottie? Isn't she with you?'

Stiffly, Emma climbed down. Tiredness washed over her in waves. She put her arms about William and leant her head against him. 'Oh, Em,' he said huskily. 'What is it? What's happened?'

She lifted her head and said wearily. 'Come inside and I'll tell you everything.'

When she had finished, William ran his hand distractedly through his hair. 'What ought we to do? Tell the police?'

Emma covered her face with her hands and groaned, 'I don't know. I just don't know what to do. Will the police help in a case like this? *Can* they?'

'I'm not sure. I would have thought so.' He came and put his arms around her. 'Look, let's not panic yet. She's obviously with Micky. He'll look after her.' He paused and then added, as if seeking reassurance himself. 'Won't he?'

'Oh yes, he'll look after her. That I do know. They want her alive and well and married to Micky,' she finished bitterly.

'You think young Micky's in on it all then?'

'He must be. Oh, I know he's not planned it. That's Leonard. But he must know what's going on. He must be party to it.'

'Mm.'

She looked at him. 'You're not sure, are you?'

He sighed heavily and shrugged his shoulders. 'I suppose you're right. It's just – well – a disappointment, that's all. I actually liked the lad.'

'Yes,' Emma murmured. 'I think that's the worst part. So did I. I daren't think what Lottie will do. She's crazy about him. It'll break her heart. But she's young. Maybe it's only infatuation. She'll get over it.'

William ran his finger gently down her face, tracing the line of her cheek. 'Will she?' he said huskily. 'Can you be sure of that? I never got over my youthful infatuation. She was – is – the love of my life.'

Emma closed her eyes but the tears still squeezed out and trickled down her cheeks. 'Oh William.'

They went to bed for a couple of hours but there was no sleep for either of them. They lay in each other's arms. There was no passion, merely a mutual comfort.

'I'd better go and tell Sarah,' Emma said heavily about eight o'clock. 'Lottie always nips across to see them before catching the bus to school. Sarah will be watching out for her. I can be back for nine to open the shop.'

Emma felt as if her feet were leaden as she walked across the yard and through the orchard. Then she stopped. Sarah was standing beneath the trees, a short distance from the wooden hives, watching the comings and goings of her beloved bees. 'You know,' she said without looking round, 'they seem very excited this morning. Now, I wonder what's going on?'

'Sarah,' Emma said gently and the older woman turned.

'Oh, it's you. Emma. I thought it was Lottie.' Concern flickered across the kindly face. 'She's all right, isn't she?'

Emma nodded. 'I've got something to tell you and there's no easy way to put it. Lottie has run away with Micky Smith to – to get married.'

Sarah stared at her for a moment then smiled and half-turned back towards the hives. 'You knew, didn't you?' Then, turning back to Emma, she said triumphantly, 'They knew even without me telling them.'

Emma sighed. Sometimes Sarah and her superstitions about her bees could become irritating, rather than a country woman's beliefs fondly viewed. Now was one of those times. Quelling the urge to speak sharply, Emma took a deep breath and explained what had happened the previous night. A worried frown deepened the lines in

Sarah's forehead. She glanced back over her shoulder once again and all she said was, 'Then why are they so pleased about it? That's what I can't understand. *They* seem to think it's all going to be all right.'

Emma said nothing, but thought, what wouldn't I give at this moment to be able to believe the bees too!

Forty-Six

The following two days were lived through, though afterwards Emma wondered how they had managed it without going out of their minds with worry.

'Can't we go after them, William?'

'We could. But where do we start looking?'

'Gretna Green.'

'What, camp outside the blacksmith's until they turn up? It could be days – weeks even.'

Emma blinked. 'Why?'

'Don't they have to live there for so long before they can get married?'

'I haven't the faintest idea,' Emma said bitterly then sighing deeply, she added, for the hundredth time, 'If only she'd ring.'

'She knows if she does we'll only try to stop her getting married and make her come home.'

'It shouldn't be allowed. It all sounds so romantic when you read about people eloping, but it's not so funny when it happens in your own family. Not when you know what's behind it.'

As they sat at the kitchen table late that night nibbling bread and cheese, with no real appetite, bone-weary but dreading having to go to bed to lie awake though the hours of darkness, William said again, 'We'll drive up there if you want to, Em. We might be lucky and find them and be able to talk to them.'

'I doubt Lottie would believe us, she'd think—' Emma began and then broke off, listening. 'Did you hear something outside?'

'No.'

'I thought I heard a noise in the yard.'

William got up from the table, his chair scraping on the tiled floor, to open the back door. In the light that flooded out into the night, Emma, rising from the table, saw the white, tired faces of the two young runaways.

She flew round the table and through the door. 'Oh, Lottie, we've been worried sick. How could you?' She stopped as she saw that her daughter's face was blotchy, her eyes swollen. It was obvious that she had been crying and the boy's face was pinched and white, his eyes large, his dark, curly hair ruffled. But, she noticed, he had his arm about Lottie's shoulders as if to protect her from the expected recriminations. Emma's hand fluttered to her bosom as beneath it her heart beat painfully. She felt William put his comforting hands on her shoulders. 'Steady,' he murmured in her ear. 'Let's give them both a chance to explain.'

Glancing from one to the other, Emma could plainly read the distress on both the young faces and her anger fell away. She swallowed and tried to smile, forcing brightness into her voice as she said, 'You young scallywags. Come on inside, sit down and I'll make us all some cocoa.'

'Mum . . .' Fresh tears were welling in Lottie's eyes as she allowed herself to be drawn into the warmth of the kitchen. Even in the summer night's air, Lottie was shivering uncontrollably. 'Mum, we – we need to talk to you.'

Emma busied herself at the stove, not wanting to hear what Lottie had to say, but behind her she heard William's calming voice. 'Sit down, sit down both of you.'

'Please, Dad, listen—'

William sighed. 'We know all about it, love. Your mam went to see Micky's father. It's you who doesn't know what's behind it all.'

Emma turned slowly to look at the boy's stricken face and knew in that instant that whatever Lottie did or didn't know, Micky Smith at least knew the truth.

'Yes, I do. But you don't know *our* side of it all,' Lottie cried, and Emma and William exchanged a glance.

The boy spoke for the first time. 'Please, Mr Metcalfe, will you listen to us. We – I – don't want to deceive you any longer.'

For a moment silence fell again, the only sounds in the kitchen being Emma rattling the mugs, the sizzling of the boiling milk and Lottie's sniffling.

At last, unable to put the moment off any longer, Emma sat at the table. 'Well,' she began bluntly, 'are you married?'

The two youngsters glanced at each other then Micky said quietly, 'No, we're not—'

Interrupting, Lottie burst out, 'But we will be – whatever you say – we will get married. You can't stop us.'

Emma felt the colour drain from her face. She opened her mouth to speak but before she could utter a word, the young man put his hand over Lottie's and said calmly, in a surprisingly mature way, 'Let me handle this, Lottie. Please.'

His gaze turned to face both Emma and William. 'We know what you'll say – ' a small smile quirked the corner of his mouth, 'that we're too young, and apart from that . . .' He stared straight into Emma's bright eyes. 'If, in the last two days, you've been speaking to my father then perhaps you know that there's a lot more to it than just the fact that *we* want to get married.'

'Oh yes. Your father left me in no doubt that it had all been his little plot to get his revenge on me and my father.

He means to have what he believes is his inheritance by whatever means it takes.' She paused and looked deeply into Micky's eyes, eyes that were like Leonard's and yet they lacked that cold, greedy glint. This young man returned her look unflinchingly. 'What hurts,' she said softly, 'is that you could have been part of his wicked scheme. That you could hurt Lottie so—'

'But that's just it, Mum, he hasn't, he didn't—'

Again, Emma saw Micky pat Lottie's hand as he said steadily. 'My father brought me over here to live with my grandmother nearly a year ago. At first, he told me it was because he was concerned about my grandmother living on her own as she's getting old.' The boy shrugged. 'I didn't mind. I've always loved my gran and I enjoy being with her. I wasn't all that happy at the school I was in and the Grammar School here offered better choices in the A levels I want to do.' He grinned swiftly, 'Providing I get what I need in the O levels, of course. Dad came over a couple of times a year and each time he came, he would ask me about school and any friends I had made. I thought, at first, he was concerned that I was happy here.'

'Bridget said you came because you had asthma badly in the city and that this air suited you better,' Emma cut in.

The boy sighed and said flatly, 'I've never had asthma in my life and, although she is getting on a bit, my grandmother scarcely needs looking after. I've never seen anyone of well over eighty so sprightly.'

'Are you telling us,' William asked quietly, 'that you didn't know what your father was planning?'

Micky sighed. 'Not then, no, I didn't. It was when I mentioned knowing Lottie that he started to get really interested. It's funny really, looking back,' Micky shook his head slowly. 'Of course I didn't think anything of it at the time, but he almost rubbed his hands.' Micky's expression was comical. '"You get yourself a nice girlfriend," he said. "Never mind all these flashy pieces, you stick to the nice, steady sort of girl. Never mind if they're not pretty, it's what they bring to a marriage that counts, boy."' Micky glanced apologetically at Lottie, who smiled.

Safe in the knowledge of her own prettiness, Lottie could brush aside the insult. But for Emma, sitting there listening to the words falling so innocently from the boy's lips, she felt again the humiliation of her own girlhood. Micky couldn't possibly know how his words could dredge up the cruel past, but she felt William reach out and take her hand into his. William knew. She gave his hand an answering squeeze.

"'This girl", Dad said, "this girl called Charlotte Metcalfe? She's sounds a nice girl. You stick with her. And if her parents run a mill and a shop too, well, you'd be well set up for life, boy."'

Emma's hold on William's hand tightened, but she said nothing. How many more times would poor Grandpa Charlie's mill become the centre of such bitterness and greed?

Micky leant towards them. 'You know, Mr Metcalfe, I must have been stupid, because I didn't realize until afterwards that I'd never told him that Lottie's parents owned this mill.'

There was silence in the kitchen for a moment, then William said flatly, 'But you still went along with what he wanted? You still became friends with Lottie?'

'Only because *I* wanted to. If I'd known – or even guessed – what he was really up to I'd have run as fast as I could in the opposite direction. Trouble is,' the boy bit his lip, 'I really do care for Lottie. But I suppose he's wrecked it for us now. There's no chance you'd ever agree—'

'No, don't say that,' Lottie butted in, unable to keep

silent any longer. She turned pleading eyes upon her parents. 'We do love each other, Mum – Dad. And you must believe Micky. He wasn't part of it.'

Emma and William exchanged a glance and when she gave a slight nod. William said, 'We do believe you, lad. But I'm still wondering if you know the whole story?'

'Last week Dad arrived at Gran's unexpectedly,' Micky went on. "'What's this about you and the Metcalfe girl?" Gran must have said something in a letter that we'd been going out together. I thought I was in for a right telling-off. Because of it being exam time, you know. But it was just the opposite. He asked me if we wanted to get married and when I said yes, when we were older, he said, "Why wait? Why don't you run away together? Girls like to be swept of their feet. I'll help you."'

Micky shook his head, surprised at himself. 'I must have been thick, I still didn't think there was anything, well, odd about it all. Not even when he said it again, "That mill will be hers one day."' The boy was obviously feeling awkward at the telling of this part of his story, but he took a deep breath and went on, 'I told him that wasn't the reason why I wanted to marry Lottie, but he only laughed and said, "But you have to think of these things and besides you'd be righting a wrong that was done to me years ago." When I asked him what he meant, he said that the mill was rightly his and therefore should always have been mine one day anyway.' The boy looked from one to the other of them. 'But I don't understand what he meant. Lottie says that the mill has always been in your family, Mrs Metcalfe. That your name was Forrest.'

Emma took a deep breath 'You don't know, then, that I was – still am, maybe – married to Leonard Smith, your father.'

Shock, incredulity, and finally disbelief flitted across the two young faces in front of her. 'Married to Micky's father?' Lottie squeaked. 'You don't mean – oh, you can't mean – that we're brother and sister?'

'No, no,' Emma put out her hand swiftly. 'William is your father and obviously Helen is Micky's mother. You're not related by blood at all, only connected by a peculiar set of circumstances.'

She told them everything, sparing neither herself, nor William, in the telling of it. She told them about her girlish love for Jamie Metcalfe, how she had married Leonard Smith and how she had found out afterwards the terms of the agreement between her father and her husband.

'When my father died, he left everything to his grandson, Charles Forrest Smith, cutting out Leonard completely. Charles was killed in the war and under the terms of the will, the mill reverted to me, not to Billy. Billy was not born, you see, until after my father had died. Leonard never forgave my father, or me, for what happened. And this,' she glanced at their shocked faces in front of her, 'is his revenge.'

Lottie's quick mind was working. 'You say we're not related, me and Micky, but how come . . .?' Her glance went from one to the other of her parents.

William sighed. It was his turn to do the explaining about what had happened in the war and at the end of it, he said, 'I really don't know how we stand legally. We'll have to consult a lawyer.'

'But – but that would let everyone know my dad is still alive,' Micky burst out. 'Could he still be arrested for desertion?'

Grimly, Emma said, 'Frankly, I don't know, but it wouldn't bother me if he was.'

When she saw the boy's anxious face, she shook her head sadly. 'Why couldn't he just let things be? Surely, his new life and the farm in France were enough?'

Quietly Micky said, 'He and my mother aren't married. I did know that. It came out at school when I was little. You know how cruel young kids are? My mother is English. She was married to a Frenchman who was killed working with the resistance. She continued to run his farm, but it was never legally hers. My dad was on the run from the army, met her and moved in with her. As soon as the war ended, her husband's family fought her for possession of the farm. She lost and that's when we came to England.'

'So,' William said, 'Leonard no doubt felt himself cheated for a second time.'

Micky looked uncomfortable. 'There's – there's something else. After we left the farm, the next day, it – burnt down. The farmhouse, the barns, everything.'

'You don't mean – ?' Emma breathed, 'Leonard?'

The boy was embarrassed. 'I don't know. My mother told me about it years later. Nothing was ever proved, but . . .' He left the words hanging in the silence.

It was Lottie who broke it eventually, saying, 'So you will let us get married?'

'Darling, you're both far too young.' Emma reached out to touch her daughter's hand, but the girl snatched it away. To see the sunny-natured, pretty Lottie with her face blotchy with weeping was like a knife piercing Emma's heart. She leaned forward. 'Lottie. Why all the rush? Are you – pregnant?'

The girl's eyes widened and a small gasp escaped her lips. 'No, I am *not.*' Her indignation was enough. They could see she was telling the truth. The two youngsters glanced at each other and then Micky said determinedly, although the slight tremor in his voice and the pallor of his face told his listeners of his nervousness. 'We mean to marry and – one day – we will.'

'At least I will be properly married,' Lottie said.

'Now, now, Lottie. That wasn't necessary, love.' William's deep, calm voice remonstrated gently.

Micky, his face colouring slightly, said, 'I really have come to care for Lottie and I do want to marry her, but for all the right reasons and not just because my dad had this hare-brained scheme of getting back what he thinks belongs to him. I just hope you're going to believe me.'

William and Emma glanced at each other. 'Well,' he said softly. 'What do you think, Em?'

Suddenly, the relief making her feel almost lightheaded, Emma's brilliant eyes sparkled with mischief as she said, 'Well, unless young Micky here is a very clever manipulator trying to pull some kind of double bluff, then, yes, I think I do believe him.'

Lottie gave a squeal of glee, sprang up and rushed around the table to fling her arms around her mother. 'Oh Mum, thank you, thank you.'

'Now wait a minute,' Emma began. 'I've said I believe him, but that doesn't mean I agree to you getting married now.'

'Oh no, we don't intend to – at least not yet,' Lottie said excitedly. 'Micky's decided to leave school and get a job. And me, well, there's a job going at the main post office in Calceworth. I'd have to go away for a few weeks' training, but then,' she beamed ecstatically, 'we'd both be working. And after about two years, perhaps then we could get married.'

'Well now, what sort of a job were you thinking of, young man?' William, happier than he had been feeling for two days, winked broadly at Emma.

'Anything. Maybe I could get an apprenticeship somewhere.'

William leant across the table. 'Ever thought of becoming a *miller*?'

When the mouths of the two young people sitting opposite them dropped open, William and Emma leant against each other and laughed.

'Are you serious?' Micky said. 'After all that's happened, do you really mean it?'

William nodded and Lottie hugged her mother again and then her father. Emma went on laughing until tears ran down her face.

'Whatever's got into you?' William said as her infectious laughter spread to them all and in turn they each began to giggle too, even though they were not really sure what they were supposed to be laughing at.

Emma wiped the tears away with the back of her hand. 'I've just thought of something else. I was just wondering just how old Sarah's going to explain all this – ' she spluttered so that her final words came out in a high-pitched squeak, 'to the *bees*.'

Forty-Seven

'So, they're getting married on Lottie's eighteenth birthday?' Sarah asked.

Almost two years had passed and during that time Lottie and Micky had remained devoted to each other. They had both achieved good results in their GCE O Levels and had shown Emma and William they possessed a growing maturity that demanded respect. And now they wanted to be married.

Emma linked her arm through Sarah's as they walked from the shop through the orchard towards Sarah's cottage. 'Yes. We can't find a good excuse to make them wait any longer.'

'Do you really want to? I know they're young, but if they're half as happy as you and William . . .'

The unspoken words hung in the air between them and Emma smiled, savouring yet again the memory of the day William had returned from the town after consulting a solicitor regarding the legality of their own marriage. 'I'll put it tactfully,' he had promised. 'I'll not give Leonard away.'

Emma had remained silent. She had no feelings for Leonard now, not after the latest devious stunt he had tried, but there were others involved about whom she did care, Lottie, Micky and even Bridget. No, she did not want to bring trouble on Leonard, yet she had needed to know about her own marriage. She couldn't bear it if . . .

But William had returned home beaming, spreading his arms wide as he crossed the yard towards her and folding her into his embrace, quite oblivious to anyone who might see them. 'It's all right. You're my wife, my own darling wife.'

She had clung to him and breathed a sigh of relief.

'That court order we got before getting married,' he explained, 'it's like a divorce so even if the first husband turns up again, we're still all right. Mind you, if we hadn't followed Mr Revill's advice at the time and done it properly, then we might have had problems.'

'But we did, we did. Oh, God bless dear Mr Revill.'

Now, as she held the door of the cottage open, Emma answered Sarah's question. 'No, we don't want to make them wait any longer. He is a good lad and we're both very fond of him. Now, are you sure you're all right?'

'Yes, yes, I'll be fine. I've lived on my own before you know.' Sarah patted Emma's hand. 'And now you've had the telephone put in for me, I've only to ring for you. Mind you, I will miss old Ezra. We've been happy together, you know, Emma.'

'I know. He was such a lovely gentleman.'

'He did so want to be at Lottie's wedding.' Sarah sighed. 'But it wasn't to be.'

'And he wanted to make her a cake.'

'Oh, he did, he did,' Sarah's eyes filled with tears.

They had buried Ezra Rabinski in the village churchyard three days earlier and since then Sarah had stayed with Emma and William at the millhouse, but tonight she was insisting on returning to her own cottage. She gave another heavy sigh. 'I know how you must be feeling though, Emma. They are still very young.'

Emma smiled reminding herself that at the very same age she had been waiting for her sweetheart to return from the war and imagining herself as a spring bride. The thought of the first war which had altered the whole course of her life, made her think of the second which had taken her son. 'My boys were younger than Lottie is now when they went to war,' she murmured.

'That's true. At least you're not going to lose Lottie. They're going to settle here, aren't they? I mean, they're not even leaving home to go miles and miles away, like your Billy. Where are they going to live?'

'With us to start with. There's plenty of room and Lottie's leaving her job in Calceworth and going to run our little post office.'

'Oh, now that is nice. And with Micky at the mill, you will all be together.'

'Ah, now that's a bit more difficult. He tries very hard, you know, but he's not really cut out to be a miller. William was trying to show him how to dress the stones and the tools slipped and the lad cut his hand quite badly.'

'Well, they're difficult to do, Emma.' Sarah remarked. 'My Luke used to curse every time he had to help ya dad dress the stones. Even he'd come home with cuts on his hands and you know how good he was.'

'Mm,' Emma agreed then began again, 'Are you sure . . .?' but Sarah reached up and cupped Emma's face in her plump hands.

'Yes, I'll be fine. Now off you go, back to William. You've got a wedding to plan.'

'Oh, Lottie, do stop getting in such a tizzy. You don't want to keep Micky standing at that church forever, do you?'

'Oh, Mum, what if he's not there? What if he doesn't turn up?'

'What!' Emma began and burst out laughing. 'Charlotte

Metcalfe. How can you possibly even *think* such a thing? The boy is besotted with you.'

Lottie was smiling again. 'I know, I know. But I'm just so terrified that something is going to go wrong.'

'My darling, you look a picture.'

And she did. Her blonde curls framed her sweet face, the blue eyes were sparkling with happiness and the long, lace wedding dress hugged her tiny waist and then flared out in a full skirt. Gently, so as not to disturb the finery, Emma bent forward and kissed her daughter. 'Now I must go, before I start to cry. Your dad's downstairs waiting for you and I must go with the bridesmaids. Come down in about five minutes.'

She hurried away, down the stairs, calling to William who was standing stiffly in the kitchen, unused to the pin-striped suit he was obliged to wear. 'She'll be down in a moment and the car will come back for you.' She paused a moment, fussed with his tie and then suddenly planted a kiss on her husband's cheek. She was anxious to be gone. She knew that when William saw his daughter in her wedding dress, even he would shed a tear.

Fancy me having such a beautiful daughter, she marvelled yet again. More than ever today, Lottie reminded Emma of her own pretty, feminine mother. As the car drew out of the gate and turned to go the few yards up the village street and round the corner to the church, any morbid thoughts were driven from Emma's mind by the nervous giggling of the two bridesmaids, school friends of Lottie's, who sat beside her.

In the front pew, Emma sat beside Jamie.

'You look grand, Emma,' he whispered to her and she turned to smile at him. Her figure was matronly now. But her pure white hair was neatly set beneath a frothy pink hat that matched her suit. She wore gloves to cover her work-roughened hands and, today, she felt almost elegant. She glanced nervously over her shoulder to where Bridget, slim in blue chiffon, sat. Emma let out a sigh of relief. 'Thank goodness,' she murmured.

'What?' Jamie wanted to know. 'Summat the matter?'

Emma's violet eyes, still their brilliant colour, sparkled at him. 'No, everything's wonderful. I was so afraid that Leonard might show up, but there's no sign of him. Thank goodness.'

The two brothers had buried their differences on VE day and over the years Jamie had become a frequent visitor to their home. He knew all about Micky and whose son he was. He seemed about to say something more, but there was a stir at the rear of the church, and the organist launched into the Bridal March. The congregation rose and Emma saw Micky stand and turn to greet his beautiful bride.

At her side, Emma heard Jamie say softly, 'Emma, oh Emma.' She glanced at him and saw the depth of longing in his eyes and knew that he realized just what he had thrown away all those years ago. She smiled at him, a warm smile of understanding, of forgiveness, and then turned to watch as William gave away his daughter in marriage.

'Oh, what a day. My feet!' Emma sank into a chair at the kitchen table.

'Well, the pub did us proud with the reception, didn't they?' William said.

'Where've they gone on honeymoon, then?' Sarah asked, easing her stout frame into another chair.

Emma chuckled. 'I wouldn't dare ask.'

William grinned. 'Well, they don't need to go to Gretna now,' and they all laughed.

They sat together chatting about the events of the day until the shadows lengthened in the yard and Sarah levered herself up again. 'Well, I'd best be on me way. Now where's that bit o' wedding cake. Ah, here it is in me bag.'

From her new patent handbag, Sarah pulled out a small square of cake wrapped in a paper napkin.

'You could have brought a bigger piece than that home, Sarah,' William said. 'There's plenty left.'

'Oh, 'tain't for me,' she began and then smiled coyly, 'it's . . .' But before she could finish, Emma and William joined in and the three of them chorused at once, 'it's for the bees.'

Forty-Eight

'A boy. Oh, William, it's a *boy*.'

Tears of joy were running down Emma's face as she turned towards her husband. She still held the telephone receiver clutched tightly in her hands. She was shouting into the mouthpiece again. 'And Lottie? She's all right? You're sure she's all right?'

Gently, William took it from her. 'Hello? Hello, Micky? That you?'

The young man's voice came excitedly down the phone, so loud that they could both hear him clearly as they bent their heads together close to the receiver. 'Yes. Isn't it wonderful? They're both fine. He's a grand little chap. Yelling loudly already. He's got lots of black hair that sticks up in spikes, just like a brush.'

'Give Lottie our love and tell her we'll be in tomorrow afternoon to see her.'

'Is Lottie all right?' Emma hissed. 'Ask him again.'

'She's fine,' Micky said. 'Honest. It was a long labour and she's tired, but really, she's fine. It's only fathers are allowed to visit at night, but I'll tell her you'll both be in tomorrow to see her and – our son.' He paused as if realization was only just beginning to dawn. 'I'm a father. I'm really a father. And almost a year to the day since our wedding. Isn't it absolutely wonderful?'

'And we,' William was smiling broadly as he replaced the receiver in its cradle, 'are grandparents. Can you believe

410

that, Emma Metcalfe? And you still looking scarcely old enough to be a mother.'

Emma, dabbing ineffectually at her tears, laughed and cried all at once. 'Oh, go on with you, you old softie. With all this white hair?' Then she shook her head wonderingly. 'No, no I can't take it in really. It's silly, isn't it? Babies are born every day, yet it still always seems like a miracle.' She was silent a moment, thinking back. 'I never thought when we had all that trouble with Leonard three years ago that things could turn out so well.'

'No, nor did I. But Micky's a good lad and he really does love Lottie.' William smiled. 'What really makes me laugh, though, is the thought that Leonard reckons he's got his own way at last, when all the time it's what we all want too.'

'Well, it's only right, I suppose, that they should have the mill one day, yet somehow I just can't bring myself to hand it over legally, not just yet. Perhaps I'm being unfair. Maybe I'm still letting Leonard cloud my better judgement. I mean, now they have a family, maybe we should start to take things a little easier ourselves and let them take over.'

'Hey, I'm not ready for the scrap heap yet and they're still only nineteen. Let's leave it another few years. See how things shape up, eh?'

'You're right, of course,' she said, kissing his leathery cheek. '*Grandad.*'

He caught her by the waist and swung her round. 'I'll give you Grandad!'

Emma giggled, broke free of his grasp and ran to the foot of the stairs. Then laughing, she scampered up them with the sprightly agility of a woman half her age and several pounds lighter. William pounded after her with the eagerness of a first-time lover.

*

They lay in each other's arms, his head resting against her plump breast listening to the beat of her heart. In the aftermath of joyful lovemaking, they were quiet together each thinking their own thoughts, even though no doubt those thoughts ran along similar lines.

'A son,' Emma murmured at last. 'I can hardly believe it. At last, a boy to carry on the mill.'

William stirred and shifted his weight. She heard him sigh. 'As long as there's something for him *to* carry on.'

Again there was silence between them for Emma knew full well that their milling business was in decline.

'Jamie was only saying yesterday he's no work at all on the wheelwright side, hasn't had for years, and very little on the smithing. It's mostly his fancy wrought iron work now. There's a few folk still bring their horses to be shod. He gets quite a bit from that riding stable that's opened up in Thirsby, but if it wasn't for them . . .' He left the words unspoken but Emma knew his meaning only too well. Her eyes strayed automatically to the bedroom window where she could still see the sails of the mill.

'Grandpa Charlie said there'd always be a Forrest at Forrest's Mill,' she murmured.

William covered her hands. 'Well, there will be, my dear. Sadly, the only thing in question now in this modern era is – how long will there be work for the mill to do?'

She sighed and then turning her eyes away from the window smiled and said, 'Let's not get morbid. Today, we have a grandson. And wouldn't Grandpa Charlie have been tickled pink?'

'Aye, and your dad.'

She gave him a playful push on the shoulder. 'And yours,' she reminded him, almost accusingly. 'He must be up there in Heaven rubbing his hands with glee.'

They laughed together and then Emma said pensively, 'I wonder what Lottie will call him.'

'Now then, Em, don't go getting your hopes up. He's *their* son, not ours.'

'I know,' Emma said wistfully, remembering her own boys, though she said nothing aloud for they were not William's sons. 'I know, but it would be nice.' She shook herself and threw back the covers. 'I don't know, William Metcalfe, lovemaking in the middle of the afternoon, whatever next?' She slid off the bed and glanced at him archly.

His deep chuckle rumbled and he said, 'Aye well, I'd best get back to me work and you,' he wagged his finger at Emma, 'had better go and tell Sarah the good news.'

Despite William's warning, the moment Emma held the child in her arms she knew in her heart that he was 'her boy' and when Lottie told her the names she and Micky had agreed on for their son, Emma's happiness was complete.

'Oh, thank you, Lottie, thank you,' Emma murmured, gently placing her lips against the black downy hair of the baby. She looked down at him and the child stared solemnly back at her with dark blue eyes. 'My own precious little Boydie,' she whispered.

But Lottie's sharp ears had heard her mother's endearment and laughed. 'I like that, Mum. His proper name's a bit of a mouthful for such a mite, isn't it? But Boydie?' She tried out the name again. 'Yes, yes, I like that.'

Even after his christening three months later he was always known as Boydie, and, as the small party returned from the christening service in the Chapel, Emma carried him across the yard and stood beneath the towering shape of the mill. 'Look, Boydie, look. See the mill? Your great-great-grandad built this mill with his own hands. And one day, it will be yours.'

Was it her fond fancy or did the baby's eyes focus on the sails, his hand wave in the air, his fingers outstretched towards it?

'Now, Mum, he's a bit young to be a miller yet.' She heard Lottie's voice behind her and Emma had the grace to laugh a little shamefacedly. 'I was just telling him . . . Ah well, time enough, but if you don't mind, I'll just pop into Sarah's with him. She's so disappointed she couldn't make the christening, but her legs are that bad today.'

'Ok, but mind him going past those bees. There are hoards of 'em buzzing about the orchard today. I reckon they must be on double time.'

As she walked towards the cottage, Emma held the child close to her, shielding him. She paused a moment and listened. The still summer air was filled with the sound of the bees, the buzzing came closer and three bees rose from a yellow flowered bush nearby and circled her head. In her arms the child gurgled and waved his chubby arms. One bee flew closer, diving towards the baby. Emma gave out a small gasp of surprise and fear and stepped back. But the bee merely circled the child's head and flew away.

'She's right,' Emma murmured, 'Your Mummy's right, Boydie, they are busy today.'

'Of course they are,' Sarah said a few moments later when Emma related the encounter in the orchard.

'I thought they were going to sting him.'

'Emma, oh Emma. What are you thinking of? Have you

414

learnt nothing in all these years? Our own bees sting a
Forrest? Tut-tut. Fancy you even thinking such a thing?'

Emma smiled tenderly, considering herself rebuked by
the elderly woman whose faith in the bees was eternal. She
was taking the child into her fat arms and bouncing him.
'Now my little fellow. You know better, don't you? The
bees will never sting you.' The wrinkled old face bent closer
and whispered to the child, who crowed with delight and
reached out with tiny fingers to clutch at the wisps of her
white hair.

Old Sarah was right; it seemed as if the boy had a charmed
life and from the moment he began to take notice, he was
besotted by the mill. Lying in the sunshine in his pram, his
legs kicking with growing strength he would watch the
mill's sails turning and, if anyone mistakenly placed his
pram so that he could not see the mill, his screams of
protest could be heard along the village street. His first
tottering steps were made in the yard, straight towards the
mill and his first word – after the obligatory 'Dada' – was
'mill' and later when he began to string words together,
'Boydie's mill'.

'What *would* old Charlie have said?' Emma would often
remark, watching the boy with doting, grandmotherly love.

'He's a chip off the old block and no mistake. He even
looks like him,' William would say with surprise in his
voice, 'if those old pictures of Grandpa Charlie are anything
to go by. You wouldn't think it's possible four generations
later, would you?'

'Anything's possible,' Emma would say.

'Now then, Em. I know you,' William would say
warningly, but his loving tone was filled with concern for

her; concern that she should not be hurt yet again. Life had dealt his Emma many blows, but this would surely be the cruellest yet. 'Don't go getting your hopes up about Boydie and the mill. By the time he's grown, Emma, there's going to be no milling business left.'

'I know, I know,' she would sigh. 'But I can dream, can't I?'

He knew she heard what he said, knew she knew it to be the truth with her rational mind. But in her heart? Now that was a different matter. There was nothing more William could do, but he could foresee more disappointment and heartbreak for his Emma.

Although the arrival of their child had been a joy and a living proof of their love, Lottie and Micky were so wrapped up in each other, so determined to succeed, that they happily handed Boydie over to Emma during the daytime. As soon as she could, Lottie resumed her duties running Marsh Thorpe's village post office which still formed part – the major part now – of Emma's shop. On leaving school, Micky had begun to work in the mill but a few months after their marriage, it had become obvious to all of them that there was not going to be enough of a living to support them all.

'The lad tried and tried hard,' William had told Emma. 'But he's not cut out for it. His heart's not in it. I don't think he really likes the hard physical work. He's always seemed to like doing the paperwork though.'

Emma had snorted contemptuously. 'Well, he's welcome to it. I can't abide all that side of business. It all seems such a waste of time when there's real work to be done.' She had sighed. 'What's he going to do then?'

'He's applied to work in a bank in Calceworth. I reckon that would suit him fine.'

It had and it did. Micky had got the job and had embarked upon a career to which he seemed well suited, being promoted during his first year so that he and Lottie were able to put a deposit on a small house a few doors up the street from Emma and William, even though Emma fought desperately with every excuse she could think of to keep them, and more importantly now, Boydie, under her roof.

They saw Bridget Smith almost every week for she was getting very frail now. But her laugh was still as merry and her smile as warm. Much to Emma's relief, they saw nothing of Leonard.

'Let him live in cloud cuckoo land,' Micky would grin, unrepentant. 'He wouldn't know the truth if he saw it staring him in the face.'

Emma stared at her son-in-law, marvelling at his perspicacity where his own father was concerned. Then his face would sober as he would say with quiet solemnity, 'Besides, there's not really much of a future in the mill. You know, you'll have to sell it eventually, Mother, don't you?'

Though it was never spoken of between them – it would have been a serious breach of the rules of banking if Micky had breathed a word outside the walls of the bank – he knew better than anyone just how severely depleted their savings now were.

'Over my dead body! Never, never. I'll never sell Forrest's Mill. It's to be Boydie's, you know that, young Micky.'

And Micky would put his arm about his mother-in-law's shoulders and say softly, 'I know, I know.'

What he did not say was that, in his view, she would be leaving the young boy a mountain of debts and a useless pile of bricks.

Forty-Nine

The growing Boydie had no idea of the gloomy predictions of his own father. From the time he could walk, he roamed the yard, the mill and the orchard with complete freedom.

'Oh, watch him, do watch him, William,' an anxious Emma would call from the bottom of the rough wooden ladder as she saw his chubby little legs climbing far above her, up and up and round and round. She would hear William's chuckle from the bin floor above and hear him say, 'You come to help, young'un?'

Then would come the child's piping voice asking questions, and William's deep rumble as he answered, patiently explaining what he was doing and just why he was doing it. A smile upon her mouth and shaking her head fondly, she would watch with fascinated wonderment as the boy stood on an upturned box, reaching out to gauge the flowing flour between his finger and thumb, a slight frown of concentration on his forehead. Then he would reach up and, on tiptoe, grasp the tentering gear lever with his other hand, easing it gently until he was happy with the fineness of the flow.

'He's a natural,' William never tired of telling her. 'He's got a born instinct for it.'

Emma's smile would broaden.

With the increase of traffic passing their gate, rushing towards the seaside, Emma's anxieties for Boydie grew, but the child made no attempt to go out of the gate. The world beyond the mill yard held no fascination for him.

She had not thought to ban him from the orchard, but the day she saw the seven-year-old trotting purposefully towards the hives beneath the trees, she gave a cry of alarm and began to run after him, her heart pounding, her once strong legs suddenly feeling old and feeble. 'Boydie, Boydie, no, don't go near the bees!'

The boy took no notice and Emma watched in horror as he lifted the lid of one of the hives.

'Hello, bees. Have you got any honey for me today?' Emma pressed her hand over her mouth to prevent herself from crying out again. A sudden noise might startle the bees and make them angry. They were swirling around the child's head now, buzzing, diving and then swooping away. Away? Emma's eyes widened in disbelief as she watched in fearful fascination.

A voice spoke behind her. 'They won't sting Boydie, Emma. You needn't fear. He comes nearly every day to look at *his* bees.' Leaning heavily on the two sticks she now used to get about, Sarah was standing a few feet away from her watching the boy. She shook her head gravely. 'It's as if old Charlie had been born again, Emma. But don't you tell our Minister I said so, else he'll think I'm forgetting me good Christian upbringing.'

'No,' Emma said softly, her gaze turning back to watch the child, still not quite able to believe what she was seeing. 'And I know what you mean. I've thought it often myself and the more he grows, the more I see it.'

Sarah chuckled. 'Mind you, your grandad was an old rogue.'

Emma laughed, 'Oh yes, but a *lovable* old rogue, Sarah.'

'Aye, that's true. That's true.'

Emma held her breath as she watched the boy gently let

the lid fall back into its place and come towards the two women. His dark blue eyes sparkled with mischief and when he smiled, two dimples appeared in his cheeks. His black hair, ruffled into curliness by the summer breeze, shone in the sunlight.

'They haven't got enough for us to take any today, Grannie.'

Emma stared in amazement. Already, the boy knew that only excess honey, not needed by the colony, could be removed from the hives.

The dimples on his rounded cheeks deepened. 'Hello, Grannie Sarah. How are you? Have you come to tell the bees some news today?' The question was said in all seriousness, without a hint of the derision with which some of the villagers viewed old Sarah's beliefs.

'You know, Boydie,' Sarah was saying, 'I'm finding it difficult to get out now, 'specially in the cold weather, so I was wondering if you could help me out by taking over the job of telling the bees anything they ought to know.'

The boy put his head on one side and regarded her thoughtfully. 'But how do I know what I ought to tell them?'

'Oh, you'll know,' Sarah said confidently. 'Anything important that happens in the family and even in the village.' She nodded and winked. 'They like a bit of gossip do Forrest's bees.'

'Have we always had bees, Grannie Sarah?'

'As long as I can remember and before that. Luke used to say that your great-great-grandad started with bees when he built the mill. Bread and honey, old Charlie used to say, the Forrests will never go hungry if they always have bread and honey.'

'And have there been bees here ever since?' The question was innocent enough, but it prompted a swift look of resentment to cross Sarah's face as she glanced at Emma. 'There was a time a while back now, when they – went away.'

'Why?' came the expected question. 'Why did the bees go?'

Emma saved Sarah the awkwardness of having to answer. 'Because for some years there were no Forrests here at the mill. It was my fault, Boydie. I went away, but when I came back,' the surprise was still in her voice for she had never ceased to wonder, 'the bees came back too.' Yet the memory caused her sadness too, for the bees' return had heralded the news of the death of a Forrest, her son, Charles.

But Boydie accepted this statement without further question, as if it was to be expected. 'That's all right then.'

In the early autumn of Boydie's eighth year, Lottie said, 'Mam, I've got some news for you.'

Emma looked at her daughter's pink cheeks and waited. 'We're going to have another baby.'

Emma flung her arms wide open. 'Oh, darling, how wonderful. I'd begun to think you weren't going to have any more children.'

'Well, we've been trying for a while but nothing seemed to happen. But I saw the doctor yesterday and he's confirmed it.'

'And everything's all right?'

'Oh yes, fine. He says I can continue to work in the post office until about a month before the birth.'

'Oh, well, I don't know about that.'

Lottie laughed and her eyes twinkled. 'Now then, don't start fussing. I've got enough coping with Micky.'

'I bet he's pleased, isn't he? Does he want another boy?'

Lottie shook her head and, completely unaware of the memories her words would evoke in Emma, said, 'Oh no. He's hoping for a daughter.'

A small smile curved Emma's mouth and she shook her head wonderingly. How times had changed!

'Lottie, you look very tired. You ought to go home and rest.'

'I feel so dreadfully sick all the time. I thought that was supposed to go after the first three months and yet here I am almost seven months gone and still getting it.' She shivered. 'And I seem to feel the cold so. And today,' she placed her hand beneath her rounded belly, 'I keep getting a niggling pain.'

'Oh, do go home and rest, love,' Emma persisted, worried by Lottie's pale face and dark rimmed eyes.

'I'll be all right.' She sat on the chair behind the post office counter and leant her head on her arms. Her voice muffled, she said, 'I can't leave the cashing up. You know what it's like on pension days.'

'Can't I help?' Emma asked, fingering the edge of her apron.

Weakly, Lottie laughed and sat up again. 'Oh, Mam, you and your adding up? No thanks. I'll manage,' and she flapped her hand at her mother, indicating that she should go away and leave her to her calculations.

Biting her lip, Emma left the shop and went through the kitchen and into the yard. 'William,' she shouted. 'Where are you?'

Shading her eyes against the bright sunlight, she saw him open one of the windows high up on the top floor of the mill.

'Here, Em. What's up?'

She walked across the yard, 'Can you come down and talk some sense into your daughter. She's . . .'

It was then that she heard Lottie's screams. Emma turned and ran. She found her lying on the floor of the shop, clutching her stomach and writhing.

'Mam, oh Mam! Something's awfully wrong! Oh, the pain, the pain.'

'Oh, my darling girl. Oh no!'

'What is it? What's happened?' Panting, William appeared in the doorway and Emma turned wide, terrified eyes towards him. 'Get an ambulance. Quick.'

He paused for the briefest of moments to stare down, with horrified eyes, at his lovely daughter, then he turned and disappeared.

'Lie still, darling, try to lie still. Oh no!' she breathed as she saw the blood beginning to seep through Lottie's clothing.

From the dark recesses of her memory came the awful picture of blood-soaked sheets and the cries of agony from her mother's room.

It was some time after midnight when Emma walked alone into the orchard. Beneath the trees, where the moonlight dappled the grass, she stood motionless watching the hives. She lifted her head once and looked towards the mill, half expecting to see a swarm already there.

But there was nothing and in the cold, black night, there was only silence.

Her voice low, she said aloud, 'How could you let it happen? To Lottie? To my darling girl. Why? Why? Oh, *why*?' She sank to her knees, the frosty grass crunching beneath her, oblivious to the cold soaking through her dress.

Half an hour later, it was where William found her, kneeling on the ground, just staring at the silent bee hives.

Holding his own grief in check, he said firmly, 'Come along, Em. Micky's come back from the hospital. He needs you. And so does Boydie.'

As if the weight of her misery hampered every movement, she lifted her head slowly and stared at him with unseeing eyes. 'Boydie?' She blinked and said again, 'Of course, Boydie. Does he know?'

William, his voice hoarse with the tears he was trying to hold in check, said, 'The little lad's still awake and asking questions. Micky's telling him now.'

'I must go to him.' William put his hand beneath her elbow and urged her to get up from the icy ground. Stiffly, she unbent her body and clinging to him, dragged herself to her feet. She stood a moment until the feeling returned to her legs and then she murmured, 'My poor little Boydie . . .'

Freeing herself from William's supporting arms, she set off towards the house, leaving him to follow.

Fifty

They buried Lottie in the churchyard on the hillside overlooking the mill near to where Harry Forrest and Luke lay,
and in sight of old Charlie Forrest's grave. At the funeral
Micky was inconsolable and it was Emma's hand that
Boydie clutched. He stood beside her, white and solemn-
faced. His dark blue glance went from the grave to his
weeping father and back again and his grip on Emma's
hand tightened.

It had all happened so very quickly that none of them
could believe that their beloved Lottie was really gone.

'She was, in the end, just like my mother,' Emma said to
Sarah sadly. 'I'd thought, when Boydie's birth went so well,
that she would be all right.'

'Aye, aye,' the old lady, shrunken in her own sadness for
the loss which touched them all, shook her head. 'You
never can tell.'

'By the time she got to hospital she'd already lost so
much blood that – that she went into shock and – and . . .'

Sarah patted her hand. 'I know, I know, Emma lass.'
Heavily, she added, 'Poor Micky, and Boydie.'

Emma sighed. 'It's William I feel so for. He's taken it
very badly.'

'She was his only child, don't forget. You've suffered the
loss of a child before, Emma, and, terrible though it is,
you've come through it once and you can again. But this is
the first time for William.'

'I know. But you don't ever get over it, you know. Not really. You just learn to live with it. I don't think I could have coped when Charles died if it hadn't been for William's love and support.'

'Well, this time you've got to help each other. And Micky, well, he's heartbroken now, but he's young.'

A cold hand touched Emma's heart. Yes, Micky was young. Young enough to love again. Young enough to find a new mother for Boydie.

'Why don't you both come back to us for a while, Micky? You'll have to get back to work and I can look after Boydie, so you don't have to worry about him.'

Micky looked suddenly very young and vulnerable. Robbed of his cheery smile and the light in his eyes, he seemed lost.

'I suppose so,' he said listlessly and just seemed to sink deeper into the armchair.

'That's settled then,' Emma said briskly, taking his disinterest for agreement. 'I'll meet Boydie from school this afternoon and take him home with me. All right?'

'Whatever you say.'

The boy walked slowly across the playground towards her, ignoring the other children, skipping and shouting all around him.

'Hello, Gran,' he said, slipping his hand into hers. 'Where's Dad?'

'At home, love. But you're both coming to stay with us for a while just till, well, till your dad feels a bit better.'

'At the mill? We're going to live at the mill – for ever?'

She looked down into the upturned face and, for the

first time since he had been told the news of his mother's death, there was a spark in Boydie's eyes. They stopped walking and, still hand in hand, turned to face each other.

'Is that what you would like, Boydie?'

'Yes, oh yes.'

She said no more, for she was very afraid that, in the long term, Micky would not agree.

The months that followed were difficult for them all. Micky turned to his work as his salvation and gradually, life began to return to something approaching normality.

'Mother, you've been wonderful,' he said at last, putting his arm about Emma's shoulders. 'But it's time Boydie and I made a home for ourselves. I – I still can't face returning to the house up the street. I don't really want to live there again.'

'You can stay here. You know you can . . .' she began, her hopes rising, but at his next words the fragile world she had clung to since Lottie's death began to crumble.

'I've been offered a Head Cashier's job in Lincoln. It's a wonderful promotion for someone of my age and I think it could be just what I'm looking for. Boydie and I can make a fresh start.'

Emma knew the colour drained from her face and she felt suddenly weak and sick and every minute of her seventy years. But she said nothing. She could not. Boydie might be the child of her heart, the boy who was, to her, her grandpa Charlie reborn, but he was not her son. There was nothing she could do to stop Micky taking him away.

With a hand that trembled, she reached out and clasped Micky's hand. 'Just promise me one thing, Micky?'

'Of course. What is it?' he said, infinitely tender, knowing how his decision must be hurting her.

'Don't ever let him go to live with your father, will you?'

Micky's smile was amused and yet sad at the same time. 'Oh no, Mother. That I can promise you.'

The boy faced his father, his face mutinous, his dark eyes resentful. 'I won't go. I'm staying here with my gran. I'm staying at the mill.'

Micky's eyes clouded. 'You're my son and you'll do as I say.'

At eight years old, there was nothing the boy could do, but the day his father forced him into the back seat of his car, slammed the door and got in behind the driver's seat, would live in Emma's memory for the rest of her life. Boydie's white face, streaked with tears, watched her from the rear window of the car, his little hand waved as the car drew out of the yard and turned into the road. She raised her hand and found her sight of his face was blurred by her own tears.

'I've let him down. I've failed him,' she wailed, turned and buried her face against William's shoulder. 'I should have fought Micky to let him stay here. How can he look after a little boy and do his job properly?'

'There's nothing we could do. He's Micky's son, and we've no say in the matter.'

'But I've lost all my children, one way or another,' she mourned. 'And now I've lost Boydie too.'

This time, even William could not comfort her. Emma was beginning to wonder just how cruel the world could be.

Fifty-One

In the three years that followed Boydie ran away from Lincoln a total of five times. On the first two occasions he was spotted by a friendly policeman in the city who thought that a boy of eight or nine should not be out alone. The third time, Boydie caught the bus to Calceworth but had money for only half the distance and Micky travelled to Horncastle to take him back home.

By the time he was eleven, Boydie planned his escape with meticulous care.

'Is he with you?' Micky's voice came distantly down the wire to Emma, but she could hear the anxiety in his voice.

'Oh no, not again, Micky,' she groaned and then said, 'no, he's not here.'

'He must have gone this morning. The school says he's not been there all day. I dropped him off at the gate on my way to the bank, but...' Micky sighed heavily. 'Oh, Mother, I've got to admit it. I can't control the lad. Even when he's not actually running away, he roams the streets, doesn't come home till all hours. He's only eleven for Heaven's sake, yet I can't do anything with him. I'm so afraid he'll be getting into trouble, real trouble.'

For Emma, it was like an echo from the past. Years ago she had said the same words about Billy, and yet she had always had such faith in Boydie. She could not believe that he would turn out like Billy, a runaway *and* a rogue. She sighed heavily. But, she reminded herself, Boydie did, of course, have Leonard Smith's blood in his veins too.

'What are we going to do, Micky?'

'I don't know. I'm at the end of my tether with him. If he comes home safe and sound, I'll try and have a talk with him at the weekend. We can't go on like this. We'll have to try and sort something out.'

Emma replaced the receiver slowly and turned to answer the question in William's anxious eyes. When she had finished telling him, William shook his head.

'Poor kid,' he murmured. 'I can't help but sympathize with him, y'know. Micky does his best, and I'm not criticizing him, but it's not the same as if . . .' He left the words hanging between them.

'No,' Emma said quietly. 'It's not the same as having a mother around, is it?'

Emma folded her arms under her bosom and moved to the kitchen window. Her glance roamed over the mill, the sails were idle today. There was not only no wind, there was also very little work.

'Do you think there'll be much of a milling business to leave the lad, when the time comes?' she asked suddenly. 'He loves this mill, you know. That's what all this running away from home is all about, isn't it?'

William came to stand beside her, his arm resting casually about her. He sighed heavily and, answering her first question, said, 'The way things are looking there won't be much of a business left, no, if I'm honest.'

Her glance followed the sweep of the sails, the stark black outline of the mill, the tiny white-painted windows.

'I don't suppose—' she began and then stopped, bending forward, squinting up at the mill. 'Why, the young scallywag!'

431

'What? What is it? What have you seen? I can't see anything.'

She was laughing with relief and pointing. 'Look, look at the window on the granary floor, the small one right at the top above the bin floor. The young monkey's hiding up there. He knows we rarely go up on to that floor.' She giggled mischievously. 'I reckon we ought to play the little rascal at his own game. We'll leave him up there for the night.'

'Are you sure you saw him?'

'Oh, I saw him right enough. He's there, all right.' She chuckled again. Now she knew the boy was safe, she was enjoying Boydie's escapade as much as he was. 'I'll ring Micky.'

Minutes later, when she had reassured the boy's father that he was hiding in the mill and told him of her plan, she came back to stand beside William.

'Maybe by the time he's spent a night up there in the cold and with mice and spiders for company, he won't be so keen to run away again.'

William said nothing but his glance out of the corner of his eye told her that he did not quite agree with her.

The following morning, from her kitchen window, Emma watched for Boydie to appear. He emerged from the white double doors and, to her surprise, sauntered jauntily across the yard whistling loudly.

'Well, I'll be . . .' she began and, behind her, William chuckled.

'You know, Em, I think even you've underestimated that lad this time.'

The back door opened. 'Morning, Gran.' The grin was stretched across his mouth and his eyes challenged her. A flop of curly, black hair fell untidily across his forehead and he flicked it back expertly. 'Any breakfast going?'

'Well,' she said and, 'well, I never.' And then she was laughing and scooping him against her in such a bear-hug that the young boy wriggled with embarrassment.

She stood him back at arms' length. 'Let's have a look at you. My, you've grown. Come on, sit down. It's all ready.'

The boy's eyes widened. 'You knew I was here?'

Now it was Emma's turn to tease him. 'Oh yes, I saw you up there last night.'

'Well, I'll be . . .' he began and then the three of them laughed together.

'So, what are we going to do with you, Boydie?'

They were gathered around the table in the sitting room on the following Sunday afternoon. Emma, William, Boydie and Micky, who had arrived on the Friday night to stay the weekend.

'We can't go on like this you know,' Micky continued.

There was no anger now, just a loving concern for his boy's welfare. As if he felt this, Boydie acted with a maturity far older than his eleven years.

'Dad, I hate the city. Why can't we move back here, to Marsh Thorpe?'

Micky sighed. 'My job's there and besides,' he shot an awkward glance towards Emma and took a deep breath, 'I hope this won't hurt you,' he began, 'but I've met someone who could become very important to me – to us. Her name's Angela.'

Emma reached across the table swiftly and took Micky's hand in hers. 'We're glad. We wouldn't expect you to spend the rest of your life alone.'

The relief was written on Micky's face. 'Thank you,' he said briefly, but then their attention came back to the boy.

Gently, Emma said, 'Don't you like Angela, Boydie? Is that the trouble?'

The boy shrugged. 'No. She's all right.' Then he grinned broadly. 'Well, better than all right, really. No, it's just that I want to live here, in Marsh Thorpe, near my mill.'

William and Micky said in unison. '*Your* mill?'

The boy looked from one to the other of them, his expression genuinely innocent. 'Well, isn't it? I mean, won't it be? One day? It's what Gran's always told me, so I want to come back here to the mill. And to you, Gran, of course,' he added, but it was obvious to them all that his grandparents were secondary in his boyish list of priorities.

It amused, rather that distressed Emma but, with a supreme effort, she managed to say, 'That rather depends on your father.'

And all eyes were turned on Micky.

He sighed and spread his hands, palms upwards. 'All right, you win. All of you,' but he was smiling as he said it. 'Boydie can come and live here.'

The words were scarcely out of his mouth before the boy gave a loud yelp of joy, jumped up from the table and was hurtling down the stairs and outside. Moving to the window, Emma watched him as he raced across the yard, not, as she had imagined, towards the mill but into the orchard. She could just see him as he darted amongst the trees and came to a halt in front of the hives.

She laughed and turning back, said, 'You'll never guess what. He's gone to tell the bees!'

Fifty-Two

At eleven, Boydie was tall for his age, but sturdy and strong too, so that he looked much older. Even more of the lovable rogue than Sarah had once predicted, he walked with an air of supreme self-confidence, yet without conceit. He was ever cheerful, a wide grin stretched across his face and his dark blue eyes dancing with merriment.

'He's going to be a real heartbreaker when he grows up,' Emma said, leaning her chin on her hands as she sat at the kitchen table watching him walk across the yard towards the mill, her fond gaze following him.

William gave a heavy sigh and sat down, pulling the mug of tea towards him. 'I'm not so sure he's isn't now. Did you see him leaning over the yard gate last night talking to two young girls? Giggling and laughing they were, the two young lasses. Flirting, I'd have called it. But at eleven years old! I don't know what the world's coming to, really I don't.' But he was laughing as he spoke.

Emma said nothing. She could well remember being eleven. Even then she would watch the road for a glimpse of Jamie.

Suddenly, her eyes widened. 'William, what's he doing?'

Boydie had stood for a moment watching the mill sails turning, then he had gone towards the engine shed and shinnied up a drain pipe. Now he was balancing himself on the end of the roof, standing in the guttering. He inched himself sideways towards where the sails swooped past the slope of the roof within a foot or so.

'The silly little . . .' William muttered, beginning to rise out of his chair, but before either of them could move to the door and out into the yard, they saw Boydie take a flying leap. He caught hold of the tip of the sail and was carried round in the wide circle.

'Oh – my – God!' Emma breathed and rushed to the door.

'Emma! Don't shout at him. Don't startle him,' William put a warning hand on her arm to stop her rushing headlong out and yelling up at the boy.

They stepped into the yard and stood watching as the sail swept him up, hanging by his arms, his legs dangling against the sky. Pictures from the past flashed before Emma's horror-stricken eyes. Pictures of her grandfather high on the side of the mill, turning to wave to her standing below in the yard, slipping, grasping desperately at thin air and then falling, falling on to the yard below.

'Grandpa Charlie,' she murmured. 'Oh no, not again.'

He was at the very top of the arc now, nimbly changing his grasp as the length of his lithe body stretched down the sail. So small, it seemed, and so high up. Then, as the sail came round again, Boydie shifted his grasp, glanced over his shoulder and, as the tip passed close to the roof, he leapt back on to the slates. He landed on all fours like a cat, slithering down until his feet lodged in the guttering. He turned an engaging, mischievous grin upon his grandparents, but for once Emma was not amused by his daring antics.

'Get down here, you little devil!' she shouted, shaking her fist at him. 'I'll skelp the livin' daylights out of you.'

He jumped from the edge of the roof landing lightly on his feet on the yard. 'Don't be cross, Gran. It was great.'

Her hand was raised above his head, ready to strike him, but when their gaze met and locked and he stood unflinchingly before her, her hand fell away without the blow being delivered. Instead she leant towards him and said, 'You trying to give me or your Grandad a heart attack? Don't you ever do that again, you hear me?'

The boy grinned roguishly. 'Well, maybe not for a week or two.' Then, as he saw her hands trembling, he said swiftly, 'All right, Gran. I promise. But,' his bright eyes so like her own, sparked mischief, 'it was fun.'

'Oh, you young scamp.' And suddenly she swept him into a tight embrace until the boy wriggled and said, 'Leave off, Gran. Someone might see.'

Later, she saw William with his hand on the child's shoulder talking earnestly to him. She was too far away to hear what they were saying or even to read the expressions on their faces, but from their stance, it was a serious conversation.

As she was laying the table for tea, Boydie came up behind her and put his arms about her waist, a waist that was no longer slim and shapely as it had once been. 'Gran, I'm so sorry. I didn't know about your Grandpa Charlie falling off the mill. I'd never have done it if I'd known it was going to frighten you so much.' She turned and hugged him to her, tears smarting the back of her throat so that she could not speak. 'Grandad's just told me about it. I won't do it again, I promise, but – ' he leant back a little away from her so that he could look at her and there was the cheeky grin on his face once more, 'but *my* mill would never hurt me.' And suddenly they were laughing together.

Over the next five years, there was less and less work for the mill.

'You're burying your head in the sand, Mother,' Micky would try to tell her when he visited every other weekend. 'And beside, Dad's getting too old to be climbing up and down those ladders. If you're not careful . . .'

Emma put her hands over her ears. 'I won't listen. I don't want to hear it. The mill is for Boydie.'

Micky leant closer. Gently he tried to explain. 'There's nothing to give Boydie now, Mother, just a heap of bricks and wood that won't ever earn him a living.'

'Micky, don't you dare speak of Forrest's Mill like that. Why, if my Grandpa Charlie could hear you . . .'

'Mother, dear, stop living in the past. Grandpa Charlie's been dead over sixty years. This is a new generation, a new age. Windmills are dead. The best thing you could do would be to sell the mill and the yard. Keep the house and the shop. There's enough coming in from the post office and the shop to give the two of you a living. But any profit you make now in the shop is being poured back into the mill. Mother, you've eaten into your savings just to live, haven't you, and now you've scarcely anything left?'

Emma glared at him. 'You've no business prying into our private affairs, just because you work in the same bank. I could have you dismissed for that.'

Micky sighed and shook his head. 'But you won't, will you?' he said wearily. 'Because you know it's only that I'm worried about what's happening. Worried for you. You know it's no more than the truth.'

'Micky Smith, I never thought I'd hear myself say it, but you're beginning to sound like your father. He always wanted me to sell the mill. But he was always just after one thing. The money!' She was silent a moment and then, belligerently, she said, 'Besides, who'd want to buy it? Who could make a better living out of it than we can? Answer me that?'

'Well . . .' he began slowly, aware that what he was about to say would cause a storm to break about his head, 'if you sold the mill, the yard and the orchard, there would be just under an acre of land and building land is fetching quite a good price at the moment.'

Deep in their conversation, neither of them heard the back door open.

'Building land?' Emma was frowning already, even though she still did not fully understand exactly what it was Micky was suggesting. 'How can anyone build anything in the yard, there wouldn't be room enough—' Her eyes widened in horror as realization slowly began to seep into her reluctant mind. 'You don't mean – pull down the mill?'

They heard a slight movement and looked round to see Boydie standing in the doorway, his face ghostly white, a stricken look in his eyes. Stiffly, he moved forward to stand facing them both across the kitchen table.

'Gran? What are you saying? What are you thinking of? Don't listen to him!' The boy's voice rose until he was shouting. He stabbed his forefinger towards her, punctuating every word. 'Don't – you – dare – even *think* – of pulling my mill down!'

Micky was on his feet. 'That's enough. How dare you speak to your grandmother like that?'

The young man, his blue eyes flashing fire, turned on his father. 'And how dare *you* interfere?'

'Boydie, it's not a viable proposition. There's no work—'

'Don't give me your "banking talk", Dad. I'm not interested in "viable propositions". That mill,' Boydie said slowly and deliberately, leaning towards his father and pointing out of the window as he spoke, 'has been in the Forrest family ever since her grandpa built it. And it's *staying* in the Forrest family.'

'Then what are you proposing to do with it?' Sarcasm lined Micky's tone. 'How are you going to keep it running with nothing to grind? Gran's money's – all her life savings – have all but gone. She's hanging on to a worthless heap of bricks and wood just so she can hand it on to you.' His tone softened and he shook his head sadly. 'Just think a minute, Boydie, please. Is that fair on your grandparents?'

For a moment, the boy looked unsure, glancing from his father to Emma and William.

'Boydie—' Emma began, rising from her chair, but he put out his hand towards her as if fending her off.

'I don't want to hear it, Gran,' he said bluntly, 'whatever it is, I don't want to hear it.'

He dragged open the back door, slammed it behind him and then they heard his feet pounding across the yard towards the mill.

'Oh dear, oh dear,' Emma said, her voice breaking as tears threatened to overwhelm her. 'Go after him, William. Tell him I—'

William's arms were about her. 'Leave him be, Em,' he said gently. 'Just wait.'

'But I can't let him think I mean to pull down the mill.'

There was silence in the kitchen as the two men looked at each other, whilst Emma's wild glance went from one to the other. 'Oh no, no, that's not what you think too, William?'

When he did not answer, she sank back into her chair. 'Forrest's Folly,' she murmured.

'Eh?' Micky said. 'What do you mean?'

She sighed heavily, thinking back down the years to the tales old Luke used to tell her. 'When Grandpa Charlie built the mill, the villagers called it "Forrest's Folly". Perhaps,' her voice quavered, 'it was.'

She was lost in her own thoughts remembering – no son

to carry on the Forrest name as Charlie had wanted, then the destruction of the sails through her neglect and the years of desertion. And now, when at last they had a male heir who loved and wanted the mill so desperately, now there was no work for it to do.

'Oh Grandpa Charlie,' she whispered inside her mind. 'What am I to do?'

Fifty-Three

Boydie stayed in the mill all day and only when Emma herself went across the yard and pleaded with him to come into the house, did he climb down the ladders. But he refused to speak to any of them and the following morning he stood in the yard dressed in his best suit and holding a small suitcase.

'I'm going back to Lincoln with Dad,' he said bluntly.

'Why? Oh, Boydie, don't go. Not like this. Please . . .'

For a moment, the angry, determined look in his brilliant eyes softened. Gently, he kissed her wrinkled cheek. 'Don't worry, Gran.' He patted her arm. 'Don't worry about anything.'

He eased his lanky frame into the front seat, slammed the door of the car and rested his arm on the frame of the open window.

'He'll be all right,' Micky said, kissing her goodbye. 'I'll talk to him when we get home. I'll explain it all to him. It's high time he understood.'

She shook her head, her eyes still on the figure sitting in the car, waiting for his father. 'I won't ever allow the mill to be pulled down whatever you say – not while there's breath in my body.'

'But it'll fall into ruin again,' Micky protested. 'It'll become a danger and an eyesore.'

'No, it won't. William will keep it in working order, even if there's no work for it to do.'

442

Micky sighed again and shook his head. It was like swimming against the tide. 'Mother, that's all part of what I'm trying to tell you. Dad can't go on much longer. It's too much for him.'

'Then Boydie can do it. If only he'd stay. He's old enough now. He'll be sixteen in a few weeks. He can leave school then.' She was frantic, clutching at straws. 'Why won't he talk to us and why's he suddenly decided to go back with you? What did you say to him last night, Micky?'

'Nothing. He won't talk to me either. But maybe he's seeing sense at last.'

'It's what you said about it being unfair to us,' she said suddenly. 'That's what's done it. Micky, you shouldn't have said that.' She tried to push past Micky to get to the car, to talk to Boydie. But Micky's arms held her fast.

'Mother. Leave it. You're both upset.'

'Micky's right, Em,' came William's gentle, but firm, voice behind her. 'Let them go.' She stood in the yard, for the second time watching her beloved Boydie leaving her. This time he did not look back out of the rear window, did not even raise his arm in farewell.

'Oh, William,' the tears were running down her cheeks. 'He's gone. This time he's really gone for good.'

'Now, now. Just wait and see.'

Emma was inconsolable. Even Sarah's blind faith in the bees was shaken.

'I can't believe it, Emma. That he's just gone off like that. Given in to his father so easily. What's he going to do in Lincoln? Stay on at school or leave and get a job?'

Defeated, Emma shrugged. 'I don't know. I can't believe it myself. That he just packed his bag and went off.'

The old head shook and Sarah's gaze went to the hives

in the orchard. 'I don't understand it. I don't understand it at all,' she murmured.

'You know, I never thought Boydie would run away,' Emma said, again and again, unable to think of anything else in the days that followed Boydie's going.

Despite their shared anxiety, William smiled. 'He hasn't. That lad wouldn't run away from anything. 'Specially not the mill.'

Emma blinked and stared at him. 'But he did before – from Lincoln.'

'He didn't run *away*, Em. He was running *to*. To the mill.'

'But this time he has,' she said.

'Wait and see,' was all William would say.

'We might as well pull it down as Micky wants,' she said bitterly. 'There's no future for the mill *without* Boydie, that's for sure.'

She stood in the yard looking up at the mill as, throughout her long life, she had done so often. The sails were idle, and so, if she were honest, was the mill itself. She put her hand on its side, feeling the black-tarred brickwork beneath her hand. But there was no pulse. Its heartbeat was silent. The heart had gone out of the mill just as her own heart was gone along with Boydie. If he was gone, then there was nothing left to go on fighting for any more. Nothing else mattered. She was old and tired and, now, she felt defeated. She had struggled for so long but now she felt that the battle was no longer worth the effort.

She went into the mill, breathing in the familiar dusty air. No bulging sacks of grain waited at the bottom of the chains to be hoisted to the bin floor. Emma climbed slowly up the wooden ladders towards the very top, pausing on

Fifty-Four

The rumours were flying around the village.

'Micky's fetched his lad back, then? So much for Emma's high hopes.'

'But there's no future in milling.'

'What's going to happen to the mill?'

'Pull it down, that'd be the best thing. Why, they'd mek a fortune selling it for building land.'

And then, like echoes from the past, 'Ya missed out there, Jamie, all them years ago, didn't ya?'

'I don't want a fortune,' Emma wept. 'I just want Boydie back.'

Late in the evening of the third day, she heard a knock at the back door and her heart leapt. When she flung it wide open, it was not Boydie who stood there but, to her surprise, Jamie Metcalfe.

'Come in,' she said flatly, turning away listlessly, hardly able to bear the disappointment when each time a knock came on the door and brief hope fluttered in her breast.

Still a tall and fine looking man despite the years, Jamie stood there awkwardly, twisting the cap he held in his hands. He stepped into the kitchen, his frame seeming to fill the room. 'He's not come back, then?'

Emma bit her lip and shook her head. 'No,' she whispered.

With his large, work-worn fingers, fingers that trembled ever so slightly, Jamie touched her white hair. His deep

447

voice was husky as he said, 'Poor Emma. You don't deserve all the sadness you've had in your life. And,' she heard him swallow painfully before he said very softly, 'I'm not proud of the unhappiness I caused you all those years ago. I was a fool, Emma. I've spent a lifetime regretting what my life – what our lives might have been together if I hadn't been so blindly stupid and proud.'

Impetuously, Emma took hold of his big hand between hers and briefly she held it to her cheek. 'Oh, Jamie, how much I loved you then. It's all such a long time ago now but at least now we're old . . .'

'You'll never be old to me, Emma. You'll always be the young girl I loved.'

'There, there,' she patted his hand and let it fall. 'Come on up,' she said and led the way upstairs into the living room, where William was sitting beside the fire. The newspaper he was pretending to read had slid down his knees, where it lay unread whilst he stared into the coals, his mind anywhere and everywhere but in this room.

'William . . .'

At the sound of her voice, he turned his head slowly and stared for a few moments at his brother. Then he struggled to his feet asking, 'Is summat wrong?'

'No, no,' Jamie said, hastily, putting his hand up, palm outwards, to reassure William. He sat in the chair on the opposite side of the fireplace. 'But I'm sorry to hear about Boydie leaving. I know how it must hurt both of you.'

William sank back into his chair. 'Aye well,' was all he said.

Emma watched them for a moment; the two men whom she had loved most of all in her life. Jamie, her first love, whom she had adored and worshipped with the passion of youth. And William, her last love, the man who had loved her and only her his whole life through. The generous, kindly man who had buried his own feelings for her, knowing she loved his brother. Who had waited through the years until he had found her again.

As she stood watching them talking softly, she realized that William had not found her by accident again during the war, he had never, ever, lost sight of her. He had known all the time what was happening to her and when the time was right to seek her out he had come, as he always did, when she needed him the most. In that moment, Emma found new strength. Though her heart was aching for Boydie, she still had William. Dear, faithful, loving William. As long as she had William, all was not lost.

'What about a nice cup of tea?' She smiled and, as William looked up at her, she saw some of the anxiety in his own eyes fade as he heard the renewed vigour in her voice.

Emma went back down to the kitchen where she filled the kettle under the tap and plugged it in, comforted by the murmur of their voices from the living room above. She was stretching up to reach down cups and saucers from the shelf in the cupboard when she heard it. The sound of whistling. She could hear whistling.

Boydie's whistling.

Before she could move towards it, the back door opened and he was standing there, the cheeky grin on his face, his black hair glistening from the light drizzle that had begun as darkness fell. He wiped his feet on the door mat and closed the door. 'Hello, Gran. Just in time for a cuppa, am I?'

She was still staring open-mouthed at him when William, followed by Jamie, came down the stairs and into the kitchen. William, too, just stood looking at the boy, but Jamie pushed past his brother and made for the door.

As he passed Boydie he put his hand briefly on the boy's

shoulder and said gruffly, 'Glad to see you, lad, but I'd best be off.'

As the door closed behind Jamie Metcalfe, Emma turned away quickly to hide the tears that suddenly sprang to her eyes. Brushing them away impatiently with the back of her hand, she reached down another cup and saucer and said, in a voice that was none too steady, 'My, you know how to time it, Boydie. Sit down.'

He did as she bade him, but she could sense an excitement about him. The boy could hardly sit still in his seat. 'Gran,' he began, as if he had some news that would keep no longer. 'Gran, I went back to Lincoln with Dad because I had an idea, but I couldn't tell you anything about it because – well – I didn't know enough.'

'Idea?' she said slowly, sitting at the table and pouring the tea. 'What sort of idea?'

William, too, sat down, pulling a cup towards him and scarcely noticing as the liquid slopped into the saucer. His gaze was fixed on Boydie.

'Do you remember me going on a bus trip with the school?'

She nodded. 'Yes, you went for the whole day.'

'We went to a museum in Yorkshire. I thought it would be awfully dull, but when we got there, it was great. It was a farm, but a *working* farm, so that the visitors could see what it was really like to have been farming at the beginning of this century.'

Emma found she was holding her breath. She was staring at him, but she could not speak.

'Well,' Boydie went on with an air of triumph. 'I've been in Lincoln seeing folks. I've been to the County Council offices, to a museum, and I've talked to all sorts of people. I've been asking their advice, and do you know what we're going to do with the mill?' Now, he was beaming happily.

'We're going to keep it, but we're going to turn it into a museum – a *working* museum, just like that farm. People will be able to come and see what it was like to be a miller in your Grandpa Charlie's day.' His excitement was rising with every word, shining out of his brilliantly blue eyes. 'And we'll open up the bakehouse again and bake bread and sell it. Maybe we could even open a tearoom with homemade jams and scones. Now, what do you think to that, eh?'

'You mean the Council want to buy it off us?'

'Well, they might, but we can do it ourselves.' For the first time a note of doubt crept into his voice. 'Can't we?'

Again, Emma glanced at William but his gaze was still fixed on the boy's animated, eager expression. 'Now, tell us again, Boydie, calmly . . .'

They talked far into the night but by the time Boydie yawned, stood up, and kissed his grandmother's forehead, it had all been decided.

As they listened to the sound of Boydie's feet going up the stairs to bed and heard his whistling, Emma and William looked at each other across the kitchen table.

'Do you know, Emma,' William said, with a slightly bemused expression on his face. 'If you were to tell me that your Grandpa Charlie had been reincarnated in Boydie, do you know, I think, at this very moment, I would believe you?'

'Oh, William!' Emma said, not knowing whether to laugh or cry as she held out her arms to him. 'Oh, *William*.'

Fifty-Five

William was sitting contentedly on the seat in the orchard, his eyes closed, his face lifted towards the sun.

'You know, Em,' he said without opening his eyes, so well did he know the sound of her footsteps, the movement of her, the feel that she was close to him. 'I could get quite used to this life of idleness.' He gave a great sigh of utter contentment. 'Yes, I could very well get to like it.' He opened one eye and squinted up at her against the light. 'What? No tea? I thought at least you were bringing me a cuppa.'

Emma chuckled. 'High time you waited on me a bit now.'

He made as if to get up until she put her hand on his shoulder, 'Sit down, sit down. I was only teasing.' When he sank back into the seat, she said, 'Mind you, I can see you don't need telling twice.' And they laughed together.

At the sound of whistling, her gaze went towards the mill where she could see Boydie leaning out of one of the small windows on the bin floor, waving a paint brush at a girl walking past the gate. Then she heard her grandson let out the longest wolf whistle she had ever heard in her life.

'Well, I never!' she said, but William only chuckled his deep, rumbling chuckle, closed his eyes and murmured, 'I don't think you have any need to worry about the Forrest blood continuing, Em.'

'Mm.' Emma was thoughtful now, listening to the young

voices calling to each other, flirting, laughing. A new beginning, she thought. Yes, it was time for a new beginning. Slowly she sat down beside her husband. 'William?'

'Mm,' he said sleepily.

'You know what we talked about? You are sure, aren't you? You really don't mind?'

His eyes opened and he reached out and took her hand. Gallantly, he raised it to his lips and kissed each wrinkled finger in turn. 'My dear, sweet Emma. The mill is yours, it always has been.' As she opened her mouth to protest, he silenced her gently, but firmly. 'No "buts". You do whatever you want with Forrest's Mill.' He paused and then said mischievously. 'But if it makes you feel any better, I agree with you anyway.'

'Oh you!' she said and flung her arms about him.

'There's a bus into town in half-an-hour,' he said airily.

'Right then,' she stood up, more purpose in her movements than for months. 'I'll do it! I'll go now.'

She was shown into the solicitor's office. A huge, leather-topped desk stood in the centre of the room, with two telephones, a large blotter and a tray for pens the only items on its surface. The window was flung open to the spring sunshine.

'Mr Revill will be with you in a minute, Mrs Metcalfe. Please, won't you sit down?' the briskly efficient secretary said.

But as the door closed leaving Emma alone, she moved towards the open window and stood beside it looking out. A bee flew in and buzzed around the room and Emma smiled. It seemed like an omen. She waited only a minute or two before the door opened once more and a young man entered, coming towards her with his hand outstretched.

'Mrs Metcalfe. I am Duncan Revill. My father, who I believe has always looked after your legal needs, retired a while ago now. I do hope you will allow me to be of whatever service I can to you?'

Emma felt a stab of disappointment but when she looked into his young face, she liked what she saw. She nodded and took his proffered hand. He guided her to a chair placed for clients but as she sat down, she saw him become aware of a noise in the room.

'Oh, there's a wasp. Let me . . .' He reached down into the waste paper basket at the side of his desk and picked out the discarded morning paper. Rolling it into a truncheon, he began to chase the insect. The bee swooped around his head and he lashed out wildly.

'It's a bee, young man,' Emma said firmly. 'You should never kill a honey bee.' She got up from her chair and went back to the window, pushing the open casement even wider. A fresh blast of air wafted into the room and the bee flew towards the window, encountered the glass and buzzed frantically for a moment. Emma leant forward and said softly, 'Away and tell your friends. Everything will be all right.'

The bee felt the draught and flew out. Emma watched it and then closed the window. 'Now, young man,' she said briskly. 'Where were we?'

'Well, not very far, actually.'

'Ah yes, well now,' she sat down. 'I want to leave Forrest's Mill to my grandson. But I don't want to wait until I'm dead and gone. I want him to have it now, or at least as soon as he's allowed to own it legally.'

It took an hour for them to agree all the terms but at last Duncan Revill looked up and said, 'Well, I think that's about everything, except I need the beneficiary's full name.'

'To Boydie—'

The young man was apologetic. 'I'm sorry, Mrs Metcalfe, but isn't that a nickname?' Emma's eyes, still their unusual brilliant colour, sparkled with mischief as Duncan Revill said gently, 'I shall need the boy's proper name on a legal document.'

Emma allowed her glance to roam out of the room, through the window towards the sky. She saw the clouds scudding across the sun, blown by a good milling wind, and fancied old Charlie could be up there looking down at her, smiling and nodding his approval.

So, she thought, you've got your way at last, Grandpa Charlie.

As she turned back to Mr Revill waiting patiently with his pen poised, a small playful smile twitched at the corner of her mouth. She could hardly keep the triumph from her voice as she said, 'To my grandson, *Charles Forrest Smith*.'

extracts reading groups
competitions books new
discounts extracts extracts discounts
competitions extracts
books new reading groups
new events extracts discounts events
events books reading groups
extracts new reading groups
interviews extracts events
events extracts books
discounts events
new books events interviews new books extracts
events new
discounts extracts discounts books
www.panmacmillan.com
extracts events reading groups books
competitions books extracts new

each floor to look about her. The machinery all stood silent, well oiled and kept in working order by her faithful William, but silent, oh so deathly still and silent. She shuddered and climbed again, bending to look out of the tiny windows, seeing below her the houses and beyond them, the flat fields of waving corn awaiting the combine harvester; a machine like those that had brought about the demise of her mill. She stood looking out of the topmost window down into the yard. It was a long way down. Far enough down to kill her beloved Grandpa Charlie.

She heard a bang and jumped, dragged back to the present, and saw William crossing the yard, glancing round him, calling her name. 'Em? Where are you?'

She blinked back the tears and a small, tremulous smile touched her lips. William, her dearest William, who, no matter what happened, loved her always.

Carefully she climbed down again and went out into the bright, mocking sunlight. She stood a moment, her gaze travelling slowly over the outline of her beloved mill, the sharp lines of the black shape became blurred as tears came into her eyes.

'There you are, love. All right?' Tender concern was in his voice.

Not trusting herself to speak, she nodded. Then, with an effort she said, in a voice that was not quite steady, 'I'll be in soon. There's just just something I must do.'

Slowly, she lowered her head, turned and began to walk towards the gap in the hedge. This was something only she and she alone could tell the bees. She walked into the orchard and as she approached the hives beneath the trees she could already hear an angry humming. They were all around her head, swooping and diving, their buzzing louder and louder in her ears. She flapped her hand in sudden fear but the droning went on and then she felt them on her hair, on her clothes, touching her face, her hands and arms. She felt a sharp jab in her arm like something sticking a pin in her and she realized that, for the first time in the whole of her life, she, Emma Forrest, had been stung by a bee. With a sob, she turned and fled from the orchard.